国际商务合同理论与实务

严 明 主编

黑龙江大学出版社

图书在版编目(CIP)数据

国际商务合同理论与实务/严明主编. —哈尔滨:黑龙江大学出版社,2009.7
ISBN 978-7-81129-112-4

Ⅰ.国… Ⅱ.严… Ⅲ.国际贸易-贸易合同-英语-高等学校-教材 Ⅳ.H31

中国版本图书馆 CIP 数据核字(2009)第 112581 号

书　　　名	国际商务合同理论与实务
著作责任者	严　明 主编
出　版　人	李小娟
责任编辑	张爱华
出版发行	黑龙江大学出版社(哈尔滨市学府路74号　150080)
网　　　址	http://www.hljupress.com
电子信箱	hljupress@163.com
电　　　话	(0451)86608666
经　　　销	新华书店
印　　　刷	哈尔滨市石桥印务有限公司
开　　　本	787×1092　1/16
印　　　张	25.75
字　　　数	432 千
版　　　次	2009 年 9 月第 1 版　2011 年 12 月第 2 次印刷
书　　　号	ISBN 978-7-81129-112-4
定　　　价	35.00 元

本书如有印装错误请与本社联系更换。
版权所有　侵权必究

目 录

第一部分 国际商务合同理论概述

第一章 合同与合同法概述 /3
第一节 多维视角下的契约理论 /4
第二节 合同的概念 /9
第三节 合同法的基本原则 /15
第四节 各国合同法及其体系 /20
第五节 国际商务合同法的产生、发展和前景 /24

第二章 合同的订立 /35
第一节 合同有效成立的要件 /36
第二节 要约 /47
第三节 承诺 /55
第四节 合同的主要条款 /64

第二部分 国际商务合同的法律关系确立

第三章 合同的解释原则 /77
第一节 一般原则 /78
第二节 大陆法系和英美法系比较研究 /84
第三节 国际公约与国际惯例 /88

第四章 国际合同的法律适用 /97
第一节 国际合同的概念和法律冲突的解决 /98
第二节 国际合同的法律适用一般原则 /101
第三节 国际条约与国际惯例的适用 /112

第四节 我国关于国际合同法律适用 /117

第三部分 国际商务合同的语言特征分析

第五章 国际商务合同的语体特征 /125
第一节 合同英语的语体风格 /126
第二节 合同英语的语言特征 /136

第六章 国际商务合同的条款与结构 /155
第一节 合同条款的语用性 /156
第二节 国际商务合同的结构 /163

第四部分 国际商务合同的起草与翻译

第七章 国际商务合同的起草原则与流程 /185
第一节 合同起草的技能 /186
第二节 合同起草的流程 /188
第三节 合同起草的具体实践 /195

第八章 国际商务合同的翻译原则与技巧 /203
第一节 商务合同翻译的原则 /204
第二节 商务合同的词汇翻译 /206
第三节 商务合同的句子翻译 /214

第五部分 国际商务合同范本

第九章 国际商务合同范本 /225
第一节 销售合同 /226
第二节 合资经营企业合同 /241
第三节 劳务合同 /262
第四节 租赁合同 /273
第五节 国际技术转让合同与国际许可合同 /276

附录一 CISG 联合国国际货物销售合同公约 /301
附录二 中华人民共和国合同法总则 /329
附录三 国际商事合同通则 /368
参考文献 /403

Table of Contents

PART I BASICS OF INTERNATIONAL BUSINESS CONTRACTS

Chapter 1 Introduction to Contracts and Contract Law/3
Section 1 Contract Theories from Different Perspectives/4
Section 2 Concepts of Contracts/9
Section 3 Basic Principles of Contract Law/15
Section 4 Municipal Contract Laws and Systems/20
Section 5 Establishment, Development, and Outlook of Internationa
l Business Contracts Law/24

Chapter 2 Formation of Contracts/35
Section 1 Requisites of a Valid Contract/36
Section 2 Offer/47
Section 3 Acceptance/55
Section 4 Major Clauses of Contracts/64

PART II LEGAL RELATIONSHIP IN INTERNATIONAL BUSINESS CONTRACTS

Chapter 3 Contract Interpretation/77
Section 1 General Principles/78
Section 2 Comparative Study on Legal Systems between the Civil Law
and the Common Law/84
Section 3 International Conventions and Usages/88

Chapter 4 Legal Application of the International Contracts/97
Section 1 Conflicts Resolution of International Contracts/98
Section 2 General Principles on Legal Application of International Contracts/101
Section 3 Application of International Conventions and International Custom/112
Section 4 Legal Application of the International Contracts in China/117

PART III LINGUISTIC ANALYSIS OF INTERNATIONAL BUSINESS CONTRACTS

Chapter 5 Variety Features of International Business Contracts/125
Section 1 Variety of Contracts in English Language/126
Section 2 Linguistic features of Contract English/136

Chapter 6 Clauses and Structures of International Business Contracts/155
Section 1 Pragmatics of Contract Clauses/156
Section 2 Structures of International Business Contracts/163

PART IV DRAFTING AND TRANSLATION OF INTERNATIONAL BUSINESS CONTRACTS

Chapter 7 Drafting Principles and Processes of International Business Contracts/185
Section 1 Contract Drafting Competence/186
Section 2 Contract Drafting Processes/188
Section 3 Contract Drafting Practice/195

Chapter 8 Translation Principles and Strategies on International Business Contracts/203
Section 1 Translation Principles on Business Contracts/204
Section 2 Translation Strategies on Vocabulary in Business Contracts/206
Section 3 Translation Strategies on Sentences in Business Contracts/214

PART V INTERNATIONAL BUSINESS CONTRACT SAMPLES

Chapter 9 International Business Contracts Samples/225
Section 1 Contracts for Sales of Goods/226
Section 2 Contracts for Joint Ventures/241
Section 3 Contracts for Labor Services/262
Section 4 Lease Contracts/273
Section 5 Contracts for International Technology Transfer and Contracts for International Licensing/276

Appendix I CISG/301
Appendix II General Provisions of Contract Law of PRC/329
Appendix III UNIDROIT Principles/368
Bibliography/403

第一部分
PART I

国际商务合同理论概述

BASICS OF INTERNATIONAL BUSINESS CONTRACTS

Chapter 1

第一章 合同与合同法概述
Introduction to Contracts and Contract Law

Henry Maine concluded that "the movement of the progressive societies has hitherto been a movement from status to contract". Roscoe Pound once said that "the social order rests upon the stability and predictability of conduct, of which keeping promises is a large item". So, what is the role of contracts in our society? What is the relation between the promise and the contract? What are basic principles underlying contract law? These questions and the other selected important issues are covered in this chapter.

 Learning Objectives

In this chapter, students will learn how to:
◎ learn contract theories from different perspectives;
◎ understand contracts, contract law, and basic principles thereof;
◎ comprehend contract law from both domestic and international levels;
◎ identify legal terms concerning contracts bilingually.

 Questions to Consider

1) What is the role of contracts in society?
2) How do we define a contract and an international business contract?
3) What are the basic principles of contract law?
4) What does contract law regulate?
5) What is the development of unified international business contracts law?

Part 1 Focusing on Legal Knowledge

第一节 多维视角下的契约理论
Section 1 Contract Theories from Different Perspectives

当我们谈到合同时,思维视角一般是局限在法律的角度上。我们首先从宽泛的角度来了解一下合同(contract),即契约。民法及其学说史上曾有合同与契约的区别。前者为当事人的目的相同、意思表示的方向也一致的共同行为。后者系当事人双方的目的对立、意思表示的方向相反的民事法律行为。也有人认为契约是个广义的学术术语,合同是个法律术语,多指民事合同。我国现行法已不再作这样的区分,而是把二者均称做合同。在本节中,我们对两者不作区分,共同使用。这一节中,我们从几个主要的视角作简要介绍,目的在于从包括法律角度在内的多维文化角度对契约(合同)有一个宏观的导引和认识,了解一下契约与历史、社会、经济、文化和法律的关系。

1.1 契约历史
History of Contract

文明的或者进步的历史体现为契约的历史。英国历史法学派的奠基人物和主要代表人物亨利·梅因(Henry Maine)在深入研究各国古代法律制度演变规律的历史过程后,在其19世纪伟大的著作《古代法》(Ancient Law)中提出:"迄今为止的进步社会活动,乃是一个从身份到契约的运动。(the movement of the progressive societies has hitherto been a movement from status to contract)"

在社会的现实关系中,身份是一个固定的状态,一个人在社会利益关系网络中的位置完全取决于他的身份,他的后天的性格、智慧、努力等一切禀赋都不能改变这样的特定状态。每个人的一切社会活动都严格地受到家庭网络和群体关系的束缚。随着人类文明进程的不断推进,这种状态逐渐让一种基于契约的社会制度取代,这种社会制度以个体性的自由(freedom)、权利(rights)、义务(obligations)和责任(liability)为主要特征。因此一个社会文明的标致之一则是无拘束的(unbinding)、自由的(free)和自发的(autonomous)个人作为社会的基本单元。

我们可以认为,"从身份到契约"(from Status to Contract)的历史最为鲜活和生动地展现于近代意义宪法产生的历史之中。契约的关系最早形成于英国早期的分封制:在封建社会(feudal society)时期的欧洲,深受古罗马法制定中保护关系和田庄制度的影响,普遍实行以赏赐和持有采邑为基础的封主和封臣制度,封建的国王为答谢其臣属在战时提供骑兵参战及日后能取得财政上的来源,在将土地赐给或封给其臣属的同时,往往颁发一种叫做"特许状"(Charter)的证明文书,赋予世俗贵族或教会贵族在其领地之内享有不受国王代理人的管辖之权。就这样,尽管封主和封臣的地位并不平等,仍然可以形成一种法律契约的关系。至少,权利和义务是双向的(mutual)。即使是最高统治者国王也不能以违背契约的方式命令封臣绝对服从。在《英国的法律与习惯》一书中,13世纪的王室法庭法官布莱克顿(Lord Brecton)指出:"国王必须服从上帝与法律,因为法律造就了国王。"就这样,一旦和国王发生冲突,英国贵族总是试图用法律高于国王的理论来限制王权。由此可见,契约作为一种代表了私性意志的社会制度使人类从基于身份而既定的社会利益网络关系 (network of social interests)中挣脱出来实现个人的自由。

1.2 契约社会
Contract Society

可以说,社会是契约的社会,它是由一个合同束(a bundle of contracts)构成的。美国学者熊彼特认为,契约论试图创立一种有关社会的综合性理论, 涉及社会的所有方面和所有问题。它实际上是一种政治哲学(political philosophy),蕴涵了深刻的哲学底蕴。

契约关系是社会关系(social relationship)的一种存在样式,是调整社会关系(governing social relationships)的一种必要手段,是社会、个人或市场主体建立在明确的目标指向、协调措施、行为规范基础上的一种根本的交往规范,它具有整合、规范和协调功能,以形成良好的社会环境和稳定的市场秩序。

契约方式是约定(agreement),是指契约双方依照一定的条件以独立人的身份所达成的协议关系,具有合意性(assent)、自愿性(voluntariness)和互利性(mutual beneficial)等特点。它以双方普遍接受和认同的规约为基础,把双方的平衡点和契合点作为彼此联结的纽带,以最大限度地体现双方的基本利益,实现理性意义上的契约精神,这实质上是对独立、自主、自由的理性精神的充分发扬。

契约关系在现实社会的政治和经济生活中呈现出高度的复杂性(complexity)和普遍性(universality)。在西方,社会关系的契约化使中世纪的人身依附关系(relations of personal dependence)得以解脱,出现了理论意义上的人的自由和现实意义上的独立个人。近百年来,它一直作为一种富有成效的理性方式,成为人们政治和经济生活的重要组成部分,用于建构各种政治和经济体制,协调各种社会关系,化解各种社会矛盾。

1.3 契约经济
Contract Economy

就当代社会的经济生活而言,契约是现代市场经济(modern market economy)的必然要求。在现代社会中,契约理念作为市场经济与市民社会交往主体之间意志自律(self-regulation of will)和自由公正(freedom and just)的产物,反映了市民社会(civil society)的基本精神,构成了市民社会的运作逻辑。

实际上,市场经济就是某种意义上的契约经济,市民社会就是某种意义上的契约社会,因为市民社会正是以各种契约的形式规范着交往主体的行为,实现着经济活动的理性与公平(rationality and fair)。随着社会的发展,市场经济的不断成熟,契约已经广泛进入社会经济生活的各个领域,成为现代经济秩序(modern economic order)的基础。大到国际经济的交流与合作、WTO与经济政策的制定与执行,小到市民社会的需求与满足、经济或经营主体的发展与运行,契约作为处理和协调国家与公民(state and citizens)、个人与社会(individuals and society)以及国与国之间(states and states)合作与发展的最有效的方式,逐渐为人们所公认。它不仅可以用法律的手段保障经济过程的公正,维护契约双方的基本利益,而且可以使人们自觉寻求和依赖契约规则,培养人们的合作和诚信意识。可见,当代契约精神从一个侧面反映了现代市场经济的自由、公平和效率的时代特点,也反映了经济或经营主体追求诚信、自主和公正的善良愿望,这是市场经济良性运转的重要标志。

1.4 契约文化
Contract Culture

就文化特质而论,传统社会以身份(status)为根本特征,现代社会以契约(contract)为根本特征,公民社会的建构是从身份走向契约的历史进程。就中国而言,从改革开放(reform and opening up)以来,随着市场经济的发展,公民社会建构(construction of civil society)已成为当前重大的理论和现实议题。公民社会是以市场经济为基础,以契约关系为中轴,以保障公民的基本权利为前提的高度理性化社会。

现代社会的契约内涵已被广义化：在经济层面，它是社会公认的让渡产权(transfer of property)的方式，是创设权利义务关系(creation of rights and obligations relationship)的途径；在政治层面，它是联结政府与公民的纽带，是公共权力合法性的根源；在伦理层面，它是个人或团体信守承诺的道德体现。契约正逐步成为调整社会关系的根本行为规范。

公民社会的契约文化体现着如下根本特征和价值追求：

(1)自由(freedom)。在私法自治的维度，契约的核心价值是自由。契约自由内含缔约自由、确定契约内容自由、选择契约相对人自由和缔约方式自由。在公民社会，契约取代身份成为人们设定权利义务关系的常规手段，当事人不是依仗特权而是凭借自身的努力，通过自由竞争，自己设定权利、履行义务和承担责任。每个人都可依法主张自己的意志，捍卫自己的权利。社会关系契约化从根本上解除了人对人的依附，造就了独立自主的个人。传统中国是一个国家与社会高度同质同构的总体性社会，国家几乎垄断着全部社会资源，并全面控制着社会生活，个体的生存和发展时刻处于国家的掌控之中。今天，社会资源的占有和支配已经多元化，相对独立的社会自主领域正在形成和扩展，社会生活的契约化进程随之推进，个人的独立性随之增强。个人对身份、组织的依附日益减弱，个人寻求自身生存和发展的社会空间逐渐扩大，新的角色群体、社会力量日渐活跃。

(2)平等(equality)。缔结契约是以主体地位平等为前提的，缔约双方地位平等，既不允许当事人把自己提升为他人的主人，也反对把自己贬低为他人的奴仆。公民社会反对专制、拒斥特权，把人们的平等要求普遍化，它既包含主体地位的平等、机会的平等、权益的平等，也包含主体及其权利受法律保护的平等(equality of legal protection)。在公民社会，契约是人们在社会分工基础上的基本交往方式，因而公民社会是一个互相协作的社会；契约是联结个人与个人及个人与社会的纽带，因而公民社会是一个有机团结的社会；契约使社会交往、变迁和整合机制理性化、制度化、规范化，因而公民社会是一个有序和谐的社会(orderly and harmonious society)。

(3)法治(rule of law)。契约文化与法治思想内在关联，法治所包含的人们对正义之法的渴望、对至理之法的认同、对至威之法的服从、对至信之法的信赖，正是源于契约当事人对公平利益的期待(expectation of fair interests)、对合理条款的认可(recognition of reasonable clauses)、对合同义务的履行(performance of contract obligations)、对有效合同的信守(good faith of valid contracts)的契约精神。社会关系契约化是步入法治社会的必由之路，法律的制定和实施必须以契约过程为中介。契约过程是人们表达自由意志(free will)的过程,是把自由意志注入并提升为法律的过程,也是国家意志与个人意志相结合的过程。公民社会与政治国家的分离、私人领域与公共领域的分离,必然要求法律从权力本位走向权利本位。保障权利、制约权力、使个人权利与国家权力和谐共处是法治思想和契约文化的共同追求,国家不再根据人的身份而是依据人的行为统一立法和公正执法,只有在契约面前人人平等才可能在法律面前人人平等。同时,契约也需要法治的支撑,公民社会对契约的法律保护是全方位的,它集中体现在两方面:其一,对契约法律效力的确认和保障;其二,对缔结契约活动的制约和规范,当事人自由意志的表达不能有悖于社会公理和社会道义,不能有悖于契约精神。

(4)契约文化的经济基础是市场经济(market economy)。"市场经济条件下,主体必须具有独立人格,享有基本人权,才能自主走向市场进行自由交换,商品是天生的平等派"①,市场交换中主体地位是平等的,主体的自由和平等(freedom and equality)是市场经济存在和有效运行的前提。市场经济是倡导自由竞争、优胜劣汰的开放型经济,商品交换打破了狭隘的时空限制,斩断了传统的宗法血缘纽带,人们从"熟人社会"进入"陌生人世界"。市场竞争使社会从按权力分配财富的零和博弈或负和博弈(权力是排他性的)走向按市场配置资源的正和博弈(市场是可以共享的)。

1.5 契约在法律上的地位
The Role of Contracts in Law

从传统私法(private law)的角度来说,契约以当事人私性的合意为基础和灵魂,保障交易秩序,促进商品生产,在促进民商事交往和市场经济正常、有序和理性的运作过程中扮演着异常重要且不可替代的角色。

从传统公法(public law)的角度而言,在西方法治文明的国家,在"任何人只能受到基于其自身同意而产生的义务的约束"或"公民的同意是国家权力的唯一正当来源"等观念盛行的自由主义社会中,作为国家根本法的宪法甚至一切法律制度——至少从理念的层面上——都是公民与国家经过博弈和妥协的理性谈判而订立的社会契约。

从国内法(domestic law)和世界法系(world legal systems/legal families)的角度上来说,在当今世界各国的法律中,无论其社会制度如何,合同法均有重要的地位。在中国及在大陆法系,合同法是民法的重要组成部分。在英美法系,合同法是与财产法、侵权行为法、信托法等并列的独立的法律。

---

① 《马克思恩格斯全集》第23卷,人民出版社1972年版,第103页。

从国际法(international law)角度上看,近一个世纪以来,国际统一合同法逐步产生和发展,《联合国国际货物销售合同公约》(UNCCISG)和《国际商事合同通则》(the UNIDROIT principles)是该统一法的重大成果。

第二节 合同的概念
Section 2 The Concepts of Contracts

当今世界,无论社会制度、法系、种族、语言、文化等如何不同,都几乎毫无例外地使用着合同(contract)。从生产至分配及流通领域的每个环节,是一个又一个紧密相连的合同,使社会生活处于相对稳定的状态。在现实生活中,合同的使用是相当普遍的,例如买卖货物(sale of goods)、出租房屋(lease of house)、购买财产或人寿保险(property or life insurance)、运输货物(transportation of goods)、聘用人员(employment)等等,都要签订合同。有位西方学者说,现代社会是"合同社会"(contract society),离开合同寸步难行。此话也许有点夸张,但是,合同确确实实在当代社会生活的各个层面发挥着重要作用。

到底合同的概念是什么?不同法系(legal systems or legal families)、不同国家下的定义各不相同。以下我们从比较法(comparative law)的角度,把中国合同法与大陆法系、英美法系发达国家的合同法或与国际统一合同法,进行对比研究。了解了合同的概念,国际商务合同也就自然不难理解了。

2.1 中国法
Chinese Law

1999年3月15日颁布的《中华人民共和国合同法》(The Contract Law of the P.R.C.)第2条规定:"本法所称合同是平等主体的自然人、法人、其他组织之间设立、变更、终止民事权利义务关系的协议。(A contract in this Law refers to an agreement establishing, modifying and terminating the civil rights and obligations between subjects of equal footing, that is, between natural persons, legal persons or other organizations)"此规定采用狭义式与排除式相结合的方法,将合同定位为市场交易的法律形式,从而排除了有其特性和规律的身份关系的协议。

根据以上合同的定义来分析,合同主要具有以下四方面的特征:

(1)合同是当事人意思表示一致的协议(agreement)。这是合同最本质的特征。不管双方(或多方)当事人在磋商协议的过程中有过什么意见分歧,但是到最后,在受要约人表示承诺时,他们就有关的主要问题已经达成了合意,这样才建立了合同关系(privity of contract),否则就谈不上合同以及赖之而存的权利义务关系。

(2) 合同是双方(或多方)当事人的民事法律行为(civil juristic act)。这是合同区别于单方法律行为的重要标志。单方法律行为成立的基础条件是当事人的单方意志,如被代理人的事后追认行为,而合同是基于双方(或多方)当事人的合意得以成立的。

(3) 订立合同的目的是为了产生某种民事权利义务 (civil rights and obligations)方面的效果,包括设立(establish)、变更(alter)、终止(terminate)民事权利义务关系的几种情况。

(4) 合同须具有合法性 (legality)、确定性 (definiteness) 和可履行性(feasibility)。合同的合法性是合同以实现法律效果为目的的协议的必然要求,我国立法者与合同法学对此予以强调。我国《合同法》第 8 条明文规定:"依法成立的合同,受法律保护。(The contract established according to law is protected by law.)"合同的确定性是指合同内容必须确定,即约定明确,一为履行合同提供依据,二为对当事人意思表示的解释确立标准。在中国,当事人对合同履行地、价格、期限等约定不明、内容难以确定时,可直接依据法律规定。中国《合同法》第 125 条还规定了合同解释(interpretation of contracts)的有关原则。可履行性与合法性有联系,是指合同标的(contract object)具有履行的可能,导致合同有效,否则,不能履行的合同会导致合同的解除或无效等。

2.2 大陆法系
Civil Law System

大陆法系对合同的基本观点是,合同是债(debt)的一个种类。债是一个总概念,在此之下,合同、侵权行为(tort)、代理权的授予(delegation of power of attorney)、无因管理 (spontaneous agency)、不当得利 (unjust enrichment) 均是产生债的原因,这些都是特定的民事主体之间的权利义务关系。

法国法学家(Jurist)波蒂埃在其 1761 年《合同之债》一书中对合同下了这样的定义:合同是"由双方当事人互相承诺或由双方之一的一方当事人自行允诺给予对方某物品(promise to accord/give something)或允诺做或不做某事(promise to do or not to do something)的一种契约(agreement)"。该定义强调的重点是,合同义务必须在当事方自由订立合同时才产生,就是说,合同不是由法律直接强加给当事人的,而是在受约束的当事人之间的协议中产生的,或更慎重地说,是法律上视为签订"协议"的行为产生的。

《法国民法典》(French Civil Code)第1101条基本上采用了波蒂埃的上述定义,它规定"契约是一种协议,依此协议,一人或数人对另一人或另数人负担给付、作为或不作为之债务。(A contract is an agreement by which one or several persons bind themselves, towards one or several others, to transfer, to do or not to do something)"此定义同样强调协议,即当事人们之间就有关义务达成了一致意见。同时,此定义将合同视为债的一个种类。

《德国民法典》(German Civil Code)未正面就合同下定义,它把合同纳入法律行为、债务关系的范畴内,其第305条规定:"以法律行为发生债的关系或改变债的关系的内容者,除法律另有规定外,必须有当事人双方之间的契约。(For the creation of an obligation by legal transaction, and for any modification of the substance of an obligation, a contract between the parties is necessary, unless otherwise provided by law)"

2.3 英美法系
Common Law System

英美法系国家对合同定义的理解,与大陆法系国家有所不同,特别是传统理论。

在英国合同法中,诺言(promise)具有非常重要的地位。英国《不列颠百科全书》对合同下了这样的定义:"合同是依法可以执行(enforceable in law)的诺言。这个诺言可以是作为(act),也可以是不作为(omission)。"

美国也有相似的定义。美国法学会(ALI)《第二次合同法重述》(Second Restatement of Contracts)第2条规定:"合同是一项或一组这样的诺言:它或它们一旦被违反,法律就会给予救济;或者是法律以某种方式确认的义务的履行。(A contract is a promise or a set of promises for the breach of which the gives a remedy, or the performance of which the law in some say recognizes as a duty)"

美国当代最负盛名的合同法学者之一、《第二次合同法重述》的起草人法恩斯沃思撰写的《合同法》一书,共包括五个部分。除了第一部分"引言"和第四部分"第三方当事人的权利(the rights of the third party)"外,其他三个部分都以诺言为讨论的对象。其中第二部分的标题为"诺言的可强制执行性(the enforceability of promises)",第三部分的标题为"诺言的范围和后果(the scope and consequence of promises)",第五部分的标题为"诺言的强制执行(the enforcement of promises)"。诺言在英美合同法中的重要意义,由此可见一斑。

英美法上述关于合同的传统定义,是由英国早期的"诺言之诉(suit of promise)"发展而来的。英美法强调判例法的作用,其合同法的理论主要是由法官创制和发展的 (made and developed by judges)。在审理案件的过程中,法官关心的主要是如何为当事人提供救济(remedy)。在特定的案例中,违反约定的通常只是一方,法官所直接观察到的是该方违反了自己许下的诺言,而不是双方之间发生的抽象的权利义务关系。

除上述关于合同的传统定义外,英美法还有关于合同的现代定义。

1979年版美国《布莱克法学辞典》对合同下了这样的定义:合同是"两个或两个以上的人创立为或不为某一特定事情的义务的协议(Agreement between two or more parties that creates for each party a duty to do something or refrain from doing something)"。这个定义与大陆法系的定义比较接近,意味着合同不再是一方当事人的行为,而必须是两个或两个以上的当事人达成了合意。

英国《牛津法律大辞典》对合同下的定义是:合同是二人或多人之间为在相互间设定合法义务而达成的具有法律强制力的协议(legally enforceable agreement)。此定义一是强调协议,二是强调法律强制力,比较全面。

作为美国重要的成文法组成部分的《统一商法典》(the Uniform Commercial Code/UCC),在第1-201条第11款对合同也下了一个类似的现代定义:"合同指当事方受本法以及任何其他适用的法律规则影响而产生的协议的全部法律义务。(Contract means the total legal obligation which results from the parties agreement as affected by this Act and any other applicable rules of law)"

从英美法以上三个现代定义来分析,它们比强调诺言的传统定义更准确、更全面,它们都不约而同地强调协议,与大陆法的定义比较接近。因为诺言仅仅是一方的意思表示,仅仅强调了单方当事人的义务,未能抓住合同最为本质的特征——双方当事人之间的合意。从另一角度来看,上述现代定义比较强调合法性,英国《牛津法律大辞典》的定义直接用了"合法"的字眼,而美国《统一商法典》的定义则用迂回手法——"受本法以及任何其他适用的法律规则影响而产生的",也隐含了合法的意思。

2.4 国际法
International Law

作为国际统一合同法的重大成果,国际统一私法协会(UNIDROIT)制定的《国际商事合同通则》(Principles of International Commercial Contracts/PICC),未就合同正面下定义,但其第3.2条"协议的效力"(the effectiveness of agreement)可以说是侧面下了定义:"合同仅由双方的协议订立、修改或终止,除此别无其他要求。"该条注释指出:"本条的目的在于明确:仅仅是当事人之间的协议就足以使合同有效订立、变更或终止,而不必考虑某些国内法所规定的进一步要求。"很清楚,《合同通则》主张,当事人之间的协议即构成合同。其制订者的意图是为了让合同尽可能方便地得以成立,促进国际商事关系的发展,扫除一切人为的障碍。

1980年《联合国国际货物销售合同公约》(United Nations Convention on Contracts for the International Sale of Goods/CISG)未就合同下任何定义,从其关于合同成立的规定来分析,主要是要求要约(offer)与承诺(acceptance)一致。该公约第23条规定:"合同于按照本公约规定对要约的承诺生效时订立。(A contract is concluded at the moment when an acceptance of an offer becomes effective in accordance with the provisions of this Convention)" 就是说,有效的要约加上有效的承诺,即等于合同,除此之外别无其他要求。

1998年欧洲合同法委员会(Commission of European Contract Law)修订的《欧洲合同法原则》(the Principles of European Contract Law/PECL),也未就合同下定义。

2.5 综合分析
Comprehensive Analysis

从以上阐述可以看出,不同法系、不同国家对合同下的定义各有不同。但是,我们同时也可以看到,中国法和法国法的合同定义以及英美法的现代定义有相通之处:它们都认为当事人之间存在协议,即当事人之间就有关问题达成了合意。而这一点,恰恰是合同的本质特征。由此我们可以得出如下结论:在合同定义问题上,中国法与发达国家的法律没有本质的区别。

至于与国际统一合同法相比较,由于《国际商事合同通则》和《联合国国际货物销售合同公约》对合同成立的要求比较宽松,中国法关于合同的定义与其也没有本质的区别。

2.6 国际商务合同的概念、分类和特征
Concepts, Types and Features of International Business Contracts

基于以上概念,从广义上讲,国际商务合同从字面上看就是增加了国际要素(international element)和商务要素(business element)。国际商务合同有时也称之为国际商事合同、国际经贸合同 (international economic and trade contracts)或国际经济合同(international economic contracts)。国际经济合同的范围要大一些,国际商事合同这一概念在西方国家经常使用。在这里,国际商务合同的使用不作严格区分,但通常在内容上多数涉及国际货物买卖。在龚柏华主编的《国际经济合同》一书中,国际经济合同指的是在不同国家当事人之间(between the parties from different states)为一定经济目的(for the economic purpose)而达成的、规定双方当事人权利与义务(rights and obligations)、具有法律约束力的(legally binding)法律文书。

与国内商务合同比较,国际商务合同具有以下基本法律特征:

第一,合同主体具有不同国籍或营业地出于不同国家。这是基本特征。其主体主要是自然人或法人,国家和国际组织在一定条件下也可以成为国际商务合同的主体。《联合国国际货物销售合同公约》第1条规定:"本公约适用于营业地在不同国家的当事人之间所订立的货物销售合同:(a)如果这些国家是缔约国;或(b)如果国际私法规则导致适用某一缔约国的法律。(This Convention applies to contracts of sale of goods between parties whose places of business are in different States: (a) when the States are Contracting States; or (b) when the rules of private international law lead to the application of the law of a Contracting State)"对于中国而言,合同主体一方或双方不具有中国国籍,如中国某公司与外国某公司订立买卖合同,进口外国货物。

第二,合同客体跨国界移动。标的可以是货物、技术、资金、权益或服务。对于中国而言,合同客体位于中国国境或者跨越中国国境,如中国某公司同外国某公司签订买卖合同,其标的物从中国出口。

第三,合同适用法律复杂。其法律涉及合同当事人各方的国内法、当事人选择的第三国法律、国际条约或国际惯例。《中华人民共和国合同法》第126条规定:"涉外合同的当事人可以选择处理合同争议所适用的法律,但法律另有规定的除外。涉外合同的当事人没有选择的,适用与合同有最密切联系的国家的法律。在中华人民共和国境内履行的中外合资经营企业合同、中外合作经营企业合同、中外合作勘探开发自然资源合同,适用中华人民共和国法律。(Parties to a foreign-related contract may select the applicable law for resolution of a contractual dispute, except as otherwise provided by law. Where parties to the foreign-related contract fail to select the applicable law, the contract shall be governed by the law of the country with the closest connection thereto. For a Chinese-foreign equity joint venture contract, Chinese-foreign contractual joint venture contract, or a contract for Chinese-foreign joint exploration and development of natural resources which is performed within the territory of the People's Republic of China, the law of the People's Republic of China shall be applied)"

国际商务合同种类繁多。在我国,其种类主要包括:(1)国际货物买卖合同(contracts for international sale of goods);(2)国际技术转让合同(contracts for international technology transfer);(3)中外合资经营企业合同(contracts for Sino-foreign joint ventures);(4)中外合作经营企业合同(contracts for Sino-foreign contractual joint ventures);(5)国际工程承包合同(contracts for international engineering projects);(6)补偿贸易合同 (contracts for compensation trade);(7)中外合作开发自然资源合同(contracts for Sino-foreign cooperative development of natural resources);(8)涉外劳务合同(contracts for foreign labor services);(9)国际租赁合同(contracts for international leasing affairs);(10)涉外信贷合同(contracts for Sino-foreign credits and loans);(11)国际 BOT 投资合同(contracts for international Build-Operate-Transfer)。

第三节　合同法的基本原则
Section 3　Basic Principles of Contract Law

所谓合同法的原则,是适用于合同法的特定领域乃至全部领域的准则。适用于合同法特定领域的准则,是合同法的具体原则。例如适用于合同履行的实际履行原则 (specific performance)、适当履行原则(appropriate performance),适用于损害赔偿范围的完全赔偿原则(full compensation)等,均属此类。适用于合同法全部领域的准则,是合同法的基本原则。例如合同自由原则、诚实信用原则等,即属基本原则。

本节试图探讨的问题是合同法的基本原则。在此问题上,各个国家有不同的观点,我国法学界也众说纷纭,不一而足。

《国际商事合同通则》规定了国际商事合同领域的三项基本原则:缔约自由原则 (freedom of contract)、合同必须信守原则 (binding character of contract)、诚实信用和公平交易原则(good faith and fair dealing)。

著名的国际贸易法权威施米托夫认为,两种不同社会制度的国家都普遍承认合同法上的两条基本原则:(1)"当事人意思自治原则"(autonomy of will of the parties),即除国家法律规定的限制外,当事人可以自由地就他们的合同条款作出约定;(2)"合约必须遵守"的原则,即除少数为法律所准许的合同落空的抗辩(counterplea)等例外情况,合同必须真诚地履行(perform sincerely)。

英国著名法学家盖斯特认为,合同法的原则主要有:合同自由原则、合同的神圣性(holiness)、信赖(reliance)、希望(expectation)和赔偿(compensation)。

崔建远教授主编的《合同法》认为,合同法的基本原则是合同自由原则、合同正义原则和鼓励交易原则。

陈小君教授主编的《合同法学》认为,合同法的基本原则是意思自治原则、平等原则、公平原则、诚实信用原则、公序良俗原则。

我们认为,合同法的基本原则主要是:合同自由原则、诚实信用原则、公平原则、公序良俗原则。

3.1 合同自由原则
Principle of Freedom of Contract

合同自由原则,现在已经成为不同法系、不同国家公认的合同法的一项重要原则,可以说是合同法的核心、精髓,不过各自的解释和偏重点有所不同。

从渊源来说,合同自由原则应该追溯到世界历史上资产阶级的第一部民法典——《法国民法典》。以亚当·斯密为代表的自由主义经济思想是其经济理论的根据,18 世纪至 19 世纪的理性哲学是其哲学基础,资本主义市场经济是其经济基础。学说认为,1804 年的《法国民法典》第 1134 条规定表达了合同自由原则。该条规定如下:

"依法成立的契约,对缔结该契约的人(parties of contract),有相当于法律之效力(validity in law)。此种契约,仅得依当事人的相互同意或法律允许的原因撤销之。前项契约应善意履行之(perform in good faith)。"

上述规定所确立的合同自由原则,历经两个世纪一直沿用至今。不仅大陆法系的国家确立了该原则,英美法系的国家也接受了,该原则还扩展到了社会主义国家。

该原则之所以能历久不衰,是因为它反映了商品经济的本质要求。我国现在实行社会主义市场经济,具有确立合同自由原则的经济基础,虽然《民法通则》(General Principles of Civil Law/GPCL)和《合同法》使用的术语是"自愿原则"(principle of voluntariness),但实际上反映了我国的合同自由原则。《中华人民共和国合同法》第 4 条规定:"当事人依法享有自愿订立合同的权利(the rights to be voluntary to enter into a contract),任何单位和个人不得非法干预。"该条确立的就是合同自由原则。该合同法还在第 8 条规定,依法成立的合同,对当事人具有法律约束力,受法律保护,充分提供了对合同自由原则的法律保障机制。

合同自由原则包括以下内容:(1) 缔约自由,即当事人可以自由决定是否与他人缔结合同。(2) 相对人自由,即当事人可以自由决定与何人缔结合同。(3) 内容自由,即双方或多方当事人可以自由决定合同的内容(content of contract)。(4) 变更或解除合同的自由,即当事人可协商变更(change)或解除(cancel)合同,或行使解除权将合同解除。(5)方式自由,即当事人选择合同形式的自由,包括书面形式 (written form)、口头形式(oral form)、行为形式(behavioral form)等等。

应当看到，当事人以上几个方面订立合同的自由，必须符合法律规范，才能产生法律上的约束力。如果当事人的合意违反了强行性规范(enforceable rules)或社会公共利益(public interests)，该合意则会被否定，归于无效(avoidance)。

事实上，综观世界各国合同法的历史和实践，从来没有任何一个国家实行过绝对的合同自由，只不过是限制范围和程度不同罢了。在某种意义上，一部合同自由的历史，就是合同如何受到限制，经由醇化，而促进实践合同正义的记录。

3.2 诚实信用原则
Principle of Good Faith

诚实和信用是人与人之间关系所要遵循的基本道德规范(moral rules)，古今中外，概莫能外。

在中国，两千多年前的孔子就强调"民以诚而立"，并把"信"(good faith 或作 confidence)作为与"仁、义、礼、智"(benevolence, righteousness, propriety, wisdom)并列的儒家道德的基本范畴。

诚实信用升华为法律原则 (legal principles)，始自古代罗马法(Roman law)，最初体现在一般恶意辩诉权(malicious prosecution)中。后来，它被吸纳为民法(civil law)的重要准则之一，最为明显的是德国。在《德国民法典》制定时期，经济危机与社会动乱使得经济关系混乱不堪，立法上更加注重道德规范的调节功能，《德国民法典》专为合同设立了比罗马法和法国民法伸缩性更大、适应性更强的诚实信用原则，其实质在于授予法院以较大的自由裁量权 (discretion)，与法国合同法中对法官裁判 (judge's verdict/judgment)的严格限制形成较鲜明的对比。

在国际合同法的最新成果——包括中国在内的 58 个成员国组成的"国际统一私法协会(UNIDROIT)"精心制定的《国际商事合同通则》(Principles of International Commercial Contracts)中，诚实信用是明文规定的当事人不得排除或限制的三项基本原则之一。《欧洲合同法原则》(Principles of European Contract Law)同样也把诚实信用原则作为一项重要原则加以规定。此处的诚实信用原则，并非按不同的国家法律体系中所采用的一般标准来适用。《国际商事合同通则》第 1.7 条用了"国际贸易中的诚实信用和公平交易(good faith and fair dealing in international trade)"的字句，强调必须按照国际贸易的特殊情况去解释，其要求有可能高于某一国的国内标准。

在我国《民法通则》和《合同法》中，也将诚实信用原则作为一项重要原则加以规定。由于该原则适用范围广，对其他法律原则具有统领、指导作用，故有人称之为"帝王规则"。

一般认为,诚实信用的原则涉及双重利益关系(double types of privities of interests),即当事人之间的利益关系和当事人与社会利益之间的关系。诚实信用原则的目标是要求在两重利益关系中实现平衡。所以,该原则的首要要求就是,在市场交易中在不损害其他竞争者和社会公共利益(public interests)的前提下,去追求自己的利益(individual interests)。

在经济全球化、科学技术日新月异的今天,诚实信用的原则愈显重要。我国入世后,与其他成员方的民商事交往日益频繁,市场经济对社会信用的依赖程度越来越高。在 WTO 这个"经济联合国"里,没有信用就没有地位,各种假冒、伪劣商品(fake and shoddy commodities)以及类似的行为是不能长久维持下去的。我国各类企业(enterprises)(包括私人企业),只有在国际经贸活动中恪守诚实信用原则,才能取信于天下,才能吸引更多的外资来华,才能使中国商品更多地进入外国市场。

3.3 公平原则
Principle of Fairness

公平原则要求民事主体本着公正的观念从事合同活动,正当地行使权利和履行义务,在民事活动中兼顾他人利益和社会公共利益。公平原则实际上是社会道德的观念,是正义(justice)的观念,反映了人与人之间应保持一种正当善良的利益关系。

在《布莱克法律辞典》中,对公平(fair)定义如下:"具有不偏不倚和诚实的品格;无损害,无偏袒,无私利;正义的;平等的;利益平衡的;在利益冲突中平等的。"由此看来,在西方人眼中,公平的含义是相当广泛的。

与合同法中的公平原则有关联的,是作为世界贸易组织的基本原则之一的公平贸易原则。该原则是指各世贸组织成员被要求在进行国际贸易交往中,应进行公平的贸易竞争(fair trade competition),不得采取不公平的贸易手段(unfair trading measures)进行国际贸易竞争或扭曲(distort)国际贸易竞争。该原则不允许成员方政府对出口商品(export commodities)实行补贴(subsidy),也不允许成员方企业对外倾销(dump)商品,同时要求加强对知识产权(intellectual property)的保护,从而创立和维护公平竞争的国际贸易环境。

3.4 公序良俗原则
Principle of Public Policy and Good Custom

公序良俗是公共秩序与善良风俗的简称,是现代民法一项重要的概念和法律原则。它的主要功能,是在市场经济中维护国家社会一般利益和一般道德观念,因而在现代民法中具有至高无上(supremacy)的地位。

在法国、德国、日本等大陆法国家,是否遵守公序良俗是直接影响合同效力的重要问题。

《法国民法典》第1131条规定"无原因之债(abstract debt),或者基于错误原因或不法原因之债,不发生任何效力(invalid at all)。"其第1133条又进一步规定:"如原因为法律所禁止,违反善良风俗或公共秩序,此种原因为不法原因。"就是说,如果一个合同违反法律规定,违反善良风俗或公共秩序,它就不发生任何效力。无论一个法律制度对合同自由原则多么遵从,它也要拒绝履行与法律或良好道德相冲突,违反"公共政策"或违反善良风俗或违反"公共秩序"的合同。

德国法学家梅因·克茨先生在其《欧洲合同法》第9章"违法与不道德(illegality and immorality)"中,列举了违反公共秩序与善良风俗的几种情况:(1)与家庭生活和性道德原则的冲突;(2)对个人和经济活动自由的不当限制,包括不竞争约定(non-competition agreement),等等。

在英美法系,对公序良俗问题,长期的判例法(case law)中也树立了有关原则:

(1)违反公共政策的协议(agreement in violation of public policy)无效。公共政策是英美法中富于弹性的概念,一般包括 联邦以及各州的法规政策或目标,以及公众利益、社会环保要求等等。具体说来,例如不合理地限制贸易、限制竞争的协议,不公平的协议,贿赂或扰乱政府官员的协议,均属此类。

(2)不道德合同(immoral contract)无效。这是指违反社会公认的道德标准,若法院予以承认会引起正常人愤慨的合同。

凡属类似以上列举的非法协议 (illegal agreements),均是无效的(invalid),不构成有效合同,其法律后果是既不产生权利,也不产生义务,当事人不能要求履行合同,也不能要求赔偿损失。法院原则上也不允许以无效合同提起诉讼。

中国法律未专门使用公序良俗的概念,但从其一些法律规定来看,实际上存在公序良俗原则的内容。《中华人民共和国民法通则》第7条规定:"民事活动应当尊重社会公德 (social ethics),不得损害社会公共利益(public interests),破坏国家经济计划(state economic plan),扰乱社会经济秩序。"《中华人民共和国合同法》第7条规定:"当事人订立、履行合同,应当遵守法律、行政法规,尊重社会公德,不得扰乱社会经济秩序,损害社会公共利益。"

第四节　各国合同法及其体系
Section 4　Municipal Contract Laws and Systems

所谓合同法，是有关合同的法律规范的总称 (body of rules governing contracts)，是调整平等主体之间的交易关系的法律(laws governing persons or entities with equal status)。在现代各国民事法律制度中，合同法是重要的组成部分。一般认为，合同法主要调整财产流转关系(transfer of property)，规制交易行为(transaction act)。

综观各国合同法，在内容方面繁简不一，取舍各有不同，但一般来说，合同法主要包括以下一些内容：合同的订立 (formation)、合同的履行(performance)，合同的效力(effectiveness/validity)，合同的担保(warranty)，合同的转让与变更(assignment and modification)，违反合同的救济方法(remedies for breach)，合同的消灭(termination)，合同的解释(interpretation)，等等。在不同法系、不同国家，合同法的体系不尽相同，以下分别阐述之。

4.1 中国合同法
Contract Law in China

与西方发达国家相比，中国的合同法形成得比较晚。在清朝末年之前，中国一直没有集中统一、系统的合同法(unified and systematic contract law)。后来清末政府和民国政府在民法立法中对合同作出专门规定，内容较为详尽。如1930年民国政府制定的民法典中的债编，除设有合同的一般通则(general provisions)外，还有买卖等4种具名合同(specific contracts)的具体规范。

新中国成立以后，国家宣布废除国民党的旧法统，逐步制定了一些关于合同的法规，主要是以红头文件形式发布的行政条例和规章。由于种种原因，那一时期中国实行集中统一的计划经济体制，作为商品交换法律形式的合同制度也就不可能充分发展。实际上，真正系统、完整地进行合同立法，是在1978年改革开放以后。1981年颁布实施了《中华人民共和国经济合同法》(the Economic Contract Law of the PRC)，这是新中国制定的第一部合同法，从此结束了解放后32年在合同领域无法可依的状况，同时也揭开了合同法大规模执法工作的序幕。此后，又颁布了包含合同法总则内容的《中华人民共和国民法通则》(1986年)，颁布了《中华人民共和国涉外经济合同法》(1985年)(the Foreign Contract Law of the PRC)、《中华人民共和国技术合同法》(the Technology Contract Law of the PRC)(1987年)。各地、各部门也订立了一些有关合同的法规，如1987年12月30日国务院批准、1988年1月20日对外经济贸易部发布的《中华人民共和国技术引进合同管理条例施行细则》。至此可以说,中国在合同法领域已经全面完成了立法工作。然而,随着改革开放的不断深入和扩大,经济、社会的不断发展,上述三部合同法并存的局面暴露出许多问题,不能完全适应新的形势,有必要制定统一的合同法。1993年10月,在全国人大法工委的主持下,统一合同法的立法方案经讨论正式出台。经过上上下下5年多艰苦、细致、慎重的工作,合同法草案(draft)六易其稿,终于在1999年3月15日第九届全国人大第二次会议通过了《中华人民共和国合同法》(the Contract Law of the PRC)。

中国合同法的体系充分借鉴吸收了成文法法典化的模式,分为总则(general provisions)、分则(specific provisions)、附则(supplementary provisions)三大部分,一共23章(chapters)428个条目(articles)。第一部分总则包含8章129条,其内容是适用于各种合同的一般性规则,包括一般规定、合同的订立、合同的效力、合同的履行、合同的变更与转让、合同的权利义务终止、违约责任和其他规定。第二部分分则包含15章298条,分别就买卖(sales)、供用电水气和热力 (supply and use of electricity, water, gas or heating)、赠与(donation)、借款(loans)、租赁(lease)、融资租赁(financial lease)、承揽(work)、建设工程(construction project)、运输(transportation)、技术(technology)、保管(storage)、仓储(warehousing)、委托(commission)、行纪(brokerage)、居间(intermediation)等15类有名合同作出专门的规定。第三部分附则仅有1条,规定了施行日期和原三部合同法的废止。

中国合同法从本国的实际出发,既注意总结本国以往立法、司法实践经验,又注意参考借鉴发达国家立法的成功经验和有关的国际公约(international conventions)、国际惯例(international customs),从而实现了科学性、先进性和可操作性的结合,达到了较高的水平。

4.2 大陆法系的合同法
Contract Law in Civil Law System

从全球范围来看,大陆法系的合同法在成文化、法典化(codification)等方面都走在前列,较早地建立了合同立法的体系。大陆法国家的民法理论把合同作为产生债(debt)的原因之一,把有关合同的法律规范与产生债的其他原因,如侵权行为(tort act)等法律规范并列在一起,作为民法的一编,称为债务关系法或债编。

在世界历史上第一部资产阶级民法典——《法国民法典》(the French Civil Code)中,立法者把有关合同的内容集中在第三卷"取得财产的各种方式"作出规定,该卷第三编的标题为"契约或约定之债的一般规定"。其内容包括合同有效成立的要件、债的效果、债的种类、债的消灭等,这些均属合同法的一般原则。此外,该卷在其后各编中再进一步对各种有名合同作出具体规定,包括买卖、互易、合伙、借贷、委任、保证、和解等合同。在《法国民法典》中,合同规范占了该法典全部条文总数的一半左右,地位十分显赫。从合同法体系的角度来分析,它并不十分完备,但仍不失为开历史先河的第一部民法典。

20世纪初,大陆法系又一民事立法的典范——《德国民法典》(the German Civil Code)诞生了。该法典设有"总则"一编,以法律行为的概念,对有关合同成立的共同性问题作出规定。而在其后的各种债务关系篇章,实际上是合同法各论,分别对买卖、互易、使用租赁、使用借贷、合伙、保证、和解等18种有名合同作出了具体规定。《德国民法典》比《法国民法典》又前进了一大步,前者对合同法的规范相当科学严谨、系统完整,而且专门为解决合同中的某些共同性问题设立了诚实信用的原则。德国民法中合同法的严谨概念、科学编制体系以及合乎社会发展规律的原则性规定,堪称其他大陆法系国家合同立法的楷模。

4.3 英美法系的合同法
Contract Law in Anglo-American Law System

在英美法系国家,合同领域的法律原则主要包含在普通法之中,这是几个世纪以来由法院以判例形式发展起来的判例法。除印度以外,英美法系各国均无系统的、成文的合同法。所以,英美法系的合同法主要是判例法、不成文法。虽然,英国、美国等英美法国家也制定了一些有关某种合同的成文法,如英国1893年的《货物买卖法》(Sale of Goods Act)、美国《统一商法典》(Uniform Commercial Code)等,但它们只是对货物买卖合同及其他一些有关的商事合同作出具体规定,至于合同法的许多基本原则,如合同成立的各项规则等,仍需依据判例法所确立的法律原则行事。

英国合同法的原则几乎完全是由英国法院制定的,迄今立法机关对这种原则的发展所起的作用仍然不大。这种原则多半是在最近200年中发展起来的:因为合同法是商业发展的产物,是随着英国从以农业为主向以商业和工业为主的国家过渡而发展起来的。19世纪的英国判例奠定了今天英国法律界所称的正统的合同理论。这个正统合同理论不分合同的标的,适用于各种类型的合同。19世纪英国合同法形成时代,其理论框架是学理,不像大陆法那样以成文法法典为依据。直至今天,没有一个为大家接受的合同法的框架。英国法不使用债法这个范畴,也没有法国法那样的民事合同(civil contract)、商事合同(commercial contract)和行政合同(administrative contract)三大基本分类,其合同法具有明显的自主性特征。

英国大学开设的普通法(Common Law)课程,其内容为合同法与侵权行为法(tort law),财产法(property law)不包括在内。把合同法与侵权行为法作为普通法的内容讲授是有充分理由的。因为普通法是判例法,合同法与侵权行为法主要是由判例发展起来的,成文法占次要地位。

美国合同法是由判例法(case law)和制定法(statutes)共同构成的,其中判例法是美国合同法的主要渊源。在美国判例法发展的过程中,学者(scholars)的著述发挥了非常重要的作用。学者的著述本身并不是法律,它对法院的审判没有任何约束力,而仅有参考作用(reference)。然而,学者著述将篇幅浩繁而杂乱无章的判例,归纳成以一定的原理为依据的有机整体,使判例中表现出来的顺应时代要求的新倾向得到及时的归纳总结,法官经常参考学者的一些观点,从而影响判例法的发展。

在美国合同法领域,美国法学会(American Law Institute/ALI)主持整理、发表的两次合同法重述,具有相当重要的影响。该学会于1933年发表了其第一项研究成果——《合同法重述》(Restatement of Contracts),后来被称为《第一次合同法重述》。该重述以条文的形式,归纳和总结了合同法领域的判例法中存在的原理、原则和具体规定。1981年又发表了《第二次合同法重述》,对前者补充了若干新的制度,对"契约自由"等问题重新作了解释。以上两部合同法重述尽管对法院的审判活动没有强制的约束力,但是在法官从以往的判决找不到明确的答案时,往往就会援引(cite)或参考(refer to)它们的规定。

美国统一州法全国委员会(National Conference of Commissioners for Uniform State Law/NCCUSL)和美国法学会共同主持制定的《统一商法典》(UCC),是美国合同法的一个重要组成部分。该商法典公布于1952年,以后又作过多次修订,现已为美国除路易斯安那州以外的所有各州所通过和采用。有人称之为"49个半州适用UCC",因为保留大陆法传统的路易斯安那州,是部分采纳UCC,对UCC某些内容持保留态度。

统一商法典的制订者最重要的宗旨之一,是缩减成文法的篇幅,将《统一买卖法》(Uniform Sales Act)中过去大部分留由普通法去解决的许多合同法原则包含进去,使重要的原则都条文化,避免过去由于同一类判例多如牛毛、判决又常常有人为造成的不确定性(indefiniteness),增加法律规则的透明度(transparency)。该法典的第一篇是"总则",第二篇是"买卖"(sale),这两篇中的许多规定是合同法的一般规则,其适用实际上不局限于货物买卖合同。对于美国绝大部分已通过立法采纳了该法典的州来说,该法典的规定是法院必须遵循的法律,故其法律效力高于前述《第一次合同法重述》和《第二次合同法重述》。

第五节　国际商务合同法的产生、发展和前景
Section 5　Establishment, Development & Outlook of International Business Contracts Law

事实上,国际商务合同构成了国际合同的主要组成部分。在本节行文中,我们使用国际合同(international contracts)这一概念,以涵盖国际商务合同(international business contracts)。

合同法是各个主权国家制定的调整本国国内各种合同法律关系的法律规范,一般说来,它们没有域外效力(extraterritoriality)。在国际商事交往中,由于各国合同法以及其他法律的差异和冲突(differences and conflicts),对包括国际贸易在内的国际商事活动带来许多法律障碍,严重影响国际经济贸易的发展。在此背景下,19世纪后半叶起,国际上兴起了各种各样的统一私法运动,包括统一国际合同法的工作。

所谓国际合同,是国际商事、经济交往中不可或缺的一种工具,一个合同一旦具有国际因素(international elements)便是国际合同[在我国法律中通常称为涉外合同(foreign contracts)],而规定国际合同的法律规范的总和便是国际合同法。此处的所谓国际因素,主要是指跨越国界,从某一当事人的角度来看,上述商事法律关系是一种涉外民事关系,即在法律关系的主体(the subject)、客体(the object)和法律事实(the juristic fact)三个要素中,至少有一个要素与外国有联系。

1994年3月17日美洲国家组织第五届美洲国家间关于国际私法特别会议第三次全体会议通过的《关于国际合同适用法律的美洲国家间公约》对国际合同下的定义是:"如果合同当事人在不同的缔约国有其惯常居所(habitual residence)或者营业地(place of business)或者合同与一个以上国家有实际联系,则合同便为国际合同。"此定义与前面所述的定义意思一致,同样强调国际合同须有国际因素。

《国际商事合同通则》前言的注释对国际合同作了如下表述:"一份合同的国际性可以用很多不同的标准来确定。《通则》并未明确规定这些标准,只是设想要对'国际'合同这一概念给予尽可能广义的解释,以便最终排除根本不含国际因素的情形,如合同中所有相关的因素只与一个国家有关。"此概念很清楚,除了纯粹的国内合同(domestic contract)之外,合同只要有一点国际因素,都视为国际合同。

从国际与国内渊源来看,国际合同法主要由国内调整国际合同的法

律规范以及国际统一私法规范(rules of private law)组成。就这些规范的法律性质而言,它们既有合同实体法规范(substantive rules),又有合同冲突法规范(rules of conflict)以及规定国际合同时效(time of limitation)的属于程序法(procedural rules)性质的规范。

我们认为,国际统一合同法是指国际组织(International Organizations)[包括政府间国际组织(IGO)和非政府间国际组织(NGO)]制订的、调整国际合同法律关系的法律规范的总和。其渊源是有关国际合同规范的国际公约(conventions)和国际惯例(customs)。

国际合同法领域可能是进行私法国际统一最为活跃的一个法律部门。100多年来,许多国际组织、许多法律界和贸易界人士为国际合同法的统一,作出了艰苦的努力,逐步取得了一项又一项的重大成果。迄今为止,在实体法方面,我们认为国际统一合同法的主要成果是:国际统一私法协会(UNIDROIT)制定的《国际货物买卖合同成立统一法公约》(Convention Relating to a Uniform Law on the Formation of Contracts for the International Sale of Goods,简称ULF),联合国国际贸易法委员会(UNCITRAL)制定的《联合国国际货物销售合同公约》(United Nations Convention on Contracts for the International Sale of Goods,简称CISG),国际统一私法协会制定的《国际商事合同通则》(Principles of International Commercial Contracts),欧洲合同法委员会(Commission of European Contract Law)制定的《欧洲合同法原则》(European Contract Principles)。以下分别阐述之。

5.1 国际统一合同法的萌芽
International Uniform Contract Law in Embryo

从1929年起,国际统一私法协会(UNIDROIT)即决定草拟一项有关际货物买卖的统一法(包括合同法方面的内容),并且做了一些准备工作,后因爆发第二次世界大战而被迫一度中断。20世纪50年代,该协会继续拟定此方面的统一法草案。应当看到,统一国际货物买卖合同的法律,既有必要,也完全可能。因为世界各国关于买卖合同的法律,特别是适用于国际货物买卖合同的法律,基本上是属于任意性(permissive)的规定而不是强制性(compulsory)的规定,除须服从公共秩序或社会公共利益的制约外,各国一般允许当事人按照"契约自由原则"和"意思自治原则",自行确定其合同的内容和条款,国家对这类合同干预较少。经过十多年的酝酿、讨论和修改,终于在1964年海牙会议(Hague Conference)正式通过了《国际货物买卖统一法公约》(The Uniform Law on International Sale of Goods/ULIS)和《国际货物买卖合同成立统一法公约》(The Uniform Law on the Formation of Contract for International Sale of Goods/ULF)。后者,我们认为是国际统一合同法最早的萌芽,对后来问世的《联合国国际货物销售合同公约》(CISG)以及《国际商事合同通则》(the UNIDROIT principles of international commercial contracts)均产生了积极影响。

5.2 国际统一合同法的第一个里程碑
The First Milestone of International Unified Contract Law

然而,前述两项海牙公约(Hague conventions)并未被各国广泛接受和采纳,批准加入的仅有大约10个国家,而且绝大部分都是欧洲国家。许多国家认为,这两项公约受欧洲大陆法的影响较多,内容烦琐,有的概念晦涩难懂,故对其持保留态度。应当说,两项海牙公约未能达到统一各国买卖法的预期目的。1969年,刚刚成立不久的联合国国际贸易法委员会(UNCITRAL)决定,由其继续完成统一国际货物买卖法的历史使命,成立了包括社会主义国家代表在内的专门工作小组拟定公约草案,以使公约能得到不同社会经济制度和不同法律制度的国家的广泛接受。经过约10年的酝酿准备,于1978年完成了起草工作,后又反复征求各国意见,终于在1980年维也纳联合国大会通过了《联合国国际货物销售合同公约》(CISG)。由于该公约吸纳了不同法律体系买卖法和合同法中的合理成分,较好地平衡了国际货物买卖中买方和卖方的利益 (interests of the buyer and the seller),具有科学性、合理性和实用性,得到各国贸易界、法律界的普遍认同。迄今为止,已有50多个国家加入了该公约,实践中适用该公约的合同越来越多。

在《联合国国际货物销售合同公约》的101条规定中,有许多条文是关于合同的成立 (formation of contracts)、合同的履行 (performance of contracts)、违约的救济方法(remedies for breach)的规定。从国际合同法的角度来看,该公约统一了不同法系、不同国家在上述重大问题上的合同法规范,其影响实际上远远超出了货物买卖合同领域,对国际统一合同法的发展作出了重大贡献。我们认为,在国际合同法统一化的进程中,《销售合同公约》是第一个重要的里程碑。

在《销售合同公约》通过后28年的今天,从各种不同角度来分析该公约,当然可以挑剔其各种局限性,例如,其适用范围(the scope of application)较窄,未就合同的有效性(the validity of contracts)等问题作出规范,等等。然而,必须指出,《销售合同公约》在统一国际合同法方面的巨大贡献,确实是功不可没,而且将永垂史册。它开历史之先河,在国际合同法领域统一了各法系、各国五花八门的规范,为后来统一国际合同法的进程开辟了道路,也是制定国际贸易统一法的一个典范。

5.3 国际统一合同法的第二个里程碑
The Second Milestone of International Unified Contract Law

随着国际贸易内涵的拓宽和各国合同法的革新发展,国际法学界、商业界要求进一步发展和完善国际合同法的一般原则和惯例。在此历史背景下,国际统一私法协会于1971年决定,成立一个指导委员会(Steering Committee)来探求阐述国际商事合同一般原则的可行性。该委员会由大陆法系的大卫(R. David)、英美法系的施米托夫(Schimitthoff)、社会主义法系的波普斯库(Tudor Popescu)等著名法学家组成。1980年又成立了特别工作小组,其成员扩大至十几个国家,包含世界各主要法系在合同法、国际贸易法领域的专家、学者、律师(中国专家亦在其内),起草有关实质性条文。经过14年反复讨论和修改,终于在1994年5月国际统一私法协会理事会第73届会议通过了《国际商事合同通则》(the UNIDROIT Principles of International Commercial Contracts,以下简称《合同通则》)。国际统一私法协会当时拥有58个会员国,这意味着这些会员国都接受了《合同通则》的各项规则。而且,由于《合同通则》不是国际性公约,不必经过各个国家批准加入的烦琐手续,其他非会员国的当事人也可以自由适用该通则。

《合同通则》在继承《销售合同公约》(CISG)有关国际合同法的合理成分的基础上,尽可能地兼容了不同文化背景和不同法律体系的一些通用的法律原则,同时还总结和吸收了国际商事活动中广为适用的惯例和规则,因而对于指导和规范国际商事活动具有重大的影响力。此外,《合同通则》是对国际商事合同法的综述,它比《销售合同公约》具有更广泛的适用性。《销售合同公约》仅适用于一般货物贸易(sale of goods),而《合同通则》可以适用于各种国际商事合同(international business contracts),如特许经营协议(franchise agreement)、技术许可协议(technology license agreement)、专业服务合同(professional service agreement)等。

《合同通则》的内容相当丰富和广泛,包括总则(general provisions)、合同的订立(formation)、合同的效力(validity)、合同的解释(interpretation)、合同的内容(content)、合同的履行(performance)、不履行的救济方法(remedies for non-performance)等等,对国际合同法的各方面问题作出了全面规范。它具有科学性、现代性、合理性、可操作性等特征,是迄今为止较为完善的合同法准则。如同《销售合同公约》在国际货物买卖领域所取得的重大成就一样,《合同通则》在国际商事合同法领域是一项划时代的重大成果。所以说,《销售合同公约》是国际合同法统一化进程中的第一个里程碑,而《合同通则》则是该进程中的第二个里程碑。而且,由于《合同通则》所适用的范围比前者广阔得多,适用的机会更多,推广和普及的速度将更快,它比前者具有更加重要的意义。

首先,《合同通则》为国际合同法的统一奠定了全面的法律原则,必将加速国际合同法统一化的进程。《合同通则》是由代表世界各主要法系的、众多国家的合同法和国际贸易法专家(experts)、学者(scholars)、律师(lawyers),以个人身份进行研究、起草工作的,不固化于各自国家的法律原则和观点,因而能够充分吸纳现代合同法的最新成果,提炼和确立了许多过去国际公约所没有的法律原则。例如关于合同效力问题的规定,关于标准条款(standard terms)和格式合同(standard contracts)的规定,关于艰难情形(hardship)的规定,关于缔约过失(culpa in contrabendo)责任的规定,等等。这些由当今国际商事实践中总结升华的最新法律原则,具有科学性、先进性、合理性和实用性,克服了《销售合同公约》的局限性,在更宽广的领域统一了国际合同法。可以预见,随着时间的推移如市场经济的深入发展,《合同通则》尚需不断修改和完善,但是就目前而言,它的各项法律原则和规定是比较全面的,在相当长的一段时期内仍将是适用的。

其次,《合同通则》将对各国合同法的立法工作产生积极的影响,促使各国合同法相互靠近,逐步趋于统一。

不可逆转的经济全球化进程,促使各国经济贸易交往在广度、深度等各方面不断扩展,同时也使各国民商事法律逐渐相互渗透,相互靠近,这是任何力量也无法阻挡的潮流。在国际贸易法领域相继问世的国际公约(convention)、条约(treaty),也促使缔约国在国内立法中作出相应的调整和修改。当今世界各国在制定新法、修订旧法时,都十分注重借鉴其他国家和国际公约的立法成果和经验,其内在动因是追求科学性、先进性,力求与国际通行规则保持一致。例如,中国在制定《中华人民共和国合同法》时,就充分借鉴了《销售合同公约》和《合同通则》的法律原则(legal principles)和具体规定(particular provisions),包括关于要约与承诺(offer and acceptance)的一系列规定,关于对违约的损害赔偿范围(scope of compensation)的规定,关于预期违反合同(anticipatory breach)和中止履行合同(termination of performance)的规定,等等,有些条文还直接沿用了这些国际统一合同法的语句。

5.4 区域性国际统一合同法的典范
Model of Regional International Unified Contract Law

20 世纪 80 年代以来,欧洲合同法委员会 (Commission on European Contract Law)一直坚持不懈地致力于制定一部统一的欧洲合同法。随着欧洲经济共同体在经济一体化道路上的快速发展,经过长期艰苦的努力,1996 年 6 月,欧洲合同法委员会在斯德哥尔摩第 8 次会议上通过了《欧洲合同法原则》(the Principles of European Contract Law)的第一、第二部分，1998年7月又作出了全面修订。

《欧洲合同法原则》在许多方面吸收了《联合国国际货物销售合同公约》的基本原则和合理成分，比较全面地体现了国际上普遍接受的规则。《欧洲合同法原则》涵盖了合同法总则部分的大部分重要内容，对于从合同订立直至履行、不履行在内的合同的整个生命历程，均作出规范，在一些问题上还有新的独特建树，堪称区域性国际统一合同法的典范。

《欧洲合同法原则》的内容相当丰富、全面，它包括以下规范：

第一章"一般规定(general provisions)"，对《欧洲合同法原则》的适用范围、一般义务、术语等问题作出规定。

第二章"合同的成立(formation)"合同成立的条件、要约与承诺、磋商责任(即我们通常所言缔约前的责任)等问题作出规定。

第三章"代理人的权限(authority of agents)"的适用范围、代理的类型、直接代理、间接代理等问题作出规定。

第四章"有效性(validity)"19个条文，对自始不能、错误、欺诈、胁迫等问题作出规定。特别值得一提的是，该章第4:104条、第4:106条分别就传达的信息不准确、不正确的信息作出规定，这是《联合国国际货物销售合同公约》以及《国际商事合同通则》所未涉及的。鉴于其合理性和科学性，应当视其为《欧洲合同法原则》的新建树。

第五章"解释(interpretation)"合同解释的一般原则、相关情况等问题作出规定。

第六章"内容与效果(contents and effects)"的内容(如产生合同债务的陈述、默示义务、价格的确定等)以及其效果作出规定。

第七章"履行(performance)"履行的地点和时间、履行的顺序、履行的方式等问题，作出规定。

第八章"不履行与救济的一般规定(non-performance and remedies in general)"对履行、不履行方的补救等问题，作出了具体规定。

第九章"对不履行的特殊救济(particular remedies for non-performance)"就履行请求权、中止履行权、合同的解除、减价、损害赔偿与利息等问题，作出规定。

5.5 国际统一合同法的前景
Outlook of International Unified Contract Law

在20世纪末产生了《合同通则》这一国际统一合同法的重大成果，绝对不是偶然的，有着深刻的社会根源。20世纪50年代以来，随着世界经济和科学技术的迅速发展，经济全球化的格局在20世纪八九十年代逐步形成,各国之间的经济、贸易往来日益密切。国际贸易的规模从1950年的607亿美元增长到1995年的43 700亿美元,45年期间增长了71倍,在此期间国际贸易的增长速度超过了全球生产的增长速度。在1987年至1994年举行的"关税与贸易总协定(GATT)"乌拉圭回合谈判中,国际贸易的内涵从单一的货物贸易扩展到知识产权的交易(transaction of intellectual property)、服务贸易(trade in service)、投资贸易(trade related to investment),各国代表就国际贸易前述各个领域的问题达成了20多项协定(treaty)和协议(understanding/agreement)。1995年1月1日成立了世界贸易组织(WTO),预示着国际贸易的发展进入了新时期。《合同通则》正是在这一背景下问世的,它顺应了经济全球化对作为上层建筑一个重要部门的法律的内在要求,为国际经济贸易的发展进一步铺平了道路。

在21世纪,国际统一合同法到底将如何发展?21世纪是崭新的世纪,以上一世纪末世界贸易组织的成立和运行为新起点,全球范围的国际贸易将在发展的深度、广度等方面产生新的突破。而国际统一合同法,也将伴随上述进程,不断地向前发展,具体体现在以下三个方面:

第一,各国际组织将在修订(amendment)和完善(improvement)现有国际统一合同法的基础上,继续致力于制定新的国际统一合同法,不断开拓新的领域。

随着国际经济贸易实践的深入发展,新问题总是层出不穷的。例如20世纪80年代逐渐发展起来的国际电子商业就是一个新领域,其中涉及电子合同(electronic contracts)的各种特殊法律问题,例如电子合同如何成立,电子合同的形式,电子合同的签名,电子合同的认定,等等。联合国国际贸易法委员会(UNCITRAL)近年来做了大量工作,终于在1996年6月通过了《贸易法委员会电子商业示范法》(the UNCITRAL Model Law on Electronic Commerce),为各国当事人提供了一套可以选择使用的规则,同时也为各个国家制订电子商业法提供了样板。在2001年7月5日,又通过了《联合国国际贸易法委员会电子签名示范法》(The UNCITRAL Model Law on Electronic Signatures),为建立统一的国际电子商业规则奠定了基础。但是,应当看到,这些已经制定的示范法和规则,仅仅对有关问题构筑了法律规则的基本框架,是初步的尝试,还有一些规则有待于在实践中进一步修改和完善。

可以预见,作为当今世界统一国际贸易法最有权威性、最重要的机构——联合国国际贸易法委员会(UNCITRAL),作为统一国际私法的主要倡导者之一的国际统一私法协会,在21世纪都将为国际统一合同法作出新的贡献。

第二,各国政府将更加踊跃地加入国际统一合同法中的一些公约、条约。

国际统一合同法是一种新生事物,各国政府对其认识各有不同,加入其中的公约的时间会有先后。例如《联合国国际货物销售合同公约》(CISG),迄今为止加入的国家是50多个,世界上还有大约四分之三的国家尚未加入。在21世纪,随着适用该公约的案例逐年增多,该公约的科学性、实用性将进一步凸现,未加入的国家将更新认识,越来越多地进入缔约国的行列。

第三,各国立法机构在修订本国合同法或其他相关法律时,将更多地借鉴和参考国际统一合同法,从而产生趋同化的效果,推进国际合同法统一化(tendency to unification)的进程。

总之,在21世纪,随着经济全球化进程的加速和深化,国际统一合同法在全球范围将进一步发展和普及,对世界贸易和经济的发展产生积极的影响。

Part 2 Focusing on Words and Phrases

1. Finding Meaning in Context

Words	Meaning in General English	Meaning in Legal English
agreement	一致,同意;[语法]一致,呼应	契约;协约,协定
act	行为;举动;动作	决议;条例,法令
civil	市民的;民用的;文明的;民间的	民事的;根据民法的
custom	习惯,风俗;惯例,常规	习惯法
remedy	医药;药品;补救;疗法	赔偿;补偿;救济

2. Useful Expressions in Legal English

1) A contract in this Law refers to an agreement establishing, modifying and terminating the civil rights and obligations between subjects of equal footing, that is, between natural persons, legal persons or other organizations. (See art. 2 of the Contract Law of the P.R.C.)

2) A contract is a promise or a set of promises for the breach of which the gives a remedy, or the performance of which the law in some say recognizes as a duty. (See art. 2 of the Second Restatement of Contracts)

3) A contract is concluded at the moment when an acceptance of an offer becomes effective in accordance with the provisions of this Convention. (See art. 23 of the CISG)

4) The parties to a contract shall have equal legal status. No party may impose its will on the other party. (See art. 3 of the Contract Law of the P.R.C.)

5) The parties shall have the rights to be voluntary to enter into a contract in accordance with the law. No unit or individual may illegally interfere. (See art. 4 of the Contract Law of the P.R.C.)

6) The parties shall abide by the principle of fairness in defining the rights and obligations of each party. (See art. 5 of the Contract Law of the P.R.C.)

7) The parties must act in accordance with the principle of good faith, no matter in exercising rights or in performing obligations. (See art. 6 of the Contract Law of the P.R.C.)

Part 3 Evaluating Your Achievements

词汇日志 Vocabulary Log

contract	合同；契约
contract law	合同法
Civil Law System/Romano – Germanic Law System/Continental Law System	民法法系/罗马日尔曼法系/大陆法系
Common Law System/Anglo – American Law System	普通法系/英美法系
offer	要约
acceptance	承诺
freedom of contract	契约自由
good faith	诚实信用
fairness	公平
formation	订立
validity	效力
performance	履行
breach	违约
CISG	联合国国际货物销售合同公约
UNIDROIT PICC	国际统一私法委员会国际商事合同通则

章节练习 Check Your Progress

1. Fill in the Blanks

1) According to Ancient Law written by Sir Henry Maine, the movement of the progressive societies has hitherto been _____.

2) A contract in Chinese Contract Law refers to an agreement _____ the civil rights and obligations between subjects of equal footing, that is, between natural persons, legal persons or other organizations.

3) The basic principles of Chinese contract law include _____.

4) The content of contract is different from country to country. In general, it involves _____.

5) The two milestones of International Unified Contract Law are _____.

2. Legal Terminology
1) Contract
2) Freedom of contract
3) Good faith
4) Equality
5) Fair

3. Sentence Translation
1) 契约关系是社会关系的一种存在样式，是调整社会关系的一种必要手段，是社会、个人或市场主体建立在明确的目标指向、协调措施、行为规范基础上的一种根本的交往规范，它具有整合、规范和协调功能，以形成良好的社会环境和稳定的市场秩序。
2) 现代社会的契约内涵已被广义化：在经济层面，它是社会公认的让渡产权的方式，是创设权利义务关系的途径；在政治层面，它是联结政府与公民的纽带，是公共权力合法性的根源；在伦理层面，它是个人或团体信守承诺的道德体现。在法律上，它是指平等主体间创设、变更和终止民事权利和义务关系的协议。契约正逐步成为调整社会关系的根本行为规范。

自我评价 Self-Assessment Log

In this Chapter, you worked through these activities. How did each of them help you become a better learner? Check A lot, A little, or Not at all.

	A lot	A little	Not at all
I understood some theories related to contract in a broad sense.	☐	☐	☐
I learned words and expressions on the basics of contract.	☐	☐	☐
I gathered information about contract basics from the Internet.	☐	☐	☐

(Add something) _____

_____

Chapter 2

第二章 合同的订立
Formation of Contracts

A necessary starting point of a transaction is the formation of contract. Without formation of a contract, there is no contract, and no deal done. Contract is a dynamic process, which starts from formation and terminates by appropriate performance, breach compensation, or cancellation. It may involve surety, changes, assignment, and other links. Anyhow, the formation of contracts is the most important part of contract. How to form a contract? What are the differences on the formation of contract in different legal systems?

 Learning Objectives

In this chapter, students will learn:
◎ the essential elements of a valid contract;
◎ offer;
◎ acceptance;
◎ major clauses of a contract.

 Questions to Consider

1) How to form a valid contract?
2) What is an offer?
3) What is an acceptance?
4) What are the major clauses of a contract?

Part 1 Focusing on Legal Knowledge

合同的订立(formation)是交易行为的前提,没有合同的订立就没有交易,就没有合同。合同是个动态全过程,始于订立,终结于适当履行、违约责任承担或合同解除。其间可能涉及担保、变更、转让等环节。只有合同订立才能启动上述环节。

合同的订立,是指缔约人为意思表示并达成合意的状态,是动态行为与静态协议的统一体。合同的订立与合同的成立(establishment)不尽相同:后者可以说是前者的组成部分,标志着合同的产生和存在,属于静态协议;前者的含义广泛,可以被看成是一个过程,既包括缔约各方相互协商(negotiation)、讨价还价(bargain)、相互妥协(compromise)的复杂的动态环节,也包括合同成立这个瞬间完成的静态环节,又可以说涵盖了交易行为的大部分。另外,合同订立也不同于合同的生效(coming into force/becoming effective)或有效(valid/effective)。前者是当事人意思自治(autonomy of will of the parties),是当事人的意志结果;后者是指合同产生法律上的约束力(legally binding effects),是国家通过法律评价合同的表现,是法律认可当事人的意思的结果。合同的订立是合同生效的前提,只有符合法律的规定才会生效。

所以,合同的订立,是合同法中最重要的组成部分,如果它被否定了,也就谈不上以之为基础的合同内容(content)、履行(performance)、转让(assignment)、违约责任(liability for breach)、救济(remedy)、终止(termination)等等。

第一节 合同有效成立的要件
Section 1 Requisites of a Valid Contract

1.1 西方国家生效合同的要件
Requisites of a Valid Contract in Western Countries

对于合同的成立,西方国家法律均要求具备一定的条件,即所谓合同有效成立的要件。

《法国民法典》(the French Civil Code)第三卷第三编第二章是"契约有

效成立的要件"(Of the Essential Requisites for the Validity of Agreements），包含四节共26条。其中第1108条是提纲挈领的规定："契约有效成立应具备四项根本条件：负担债务的当事人的同意(the consent of the party who binds himself)；其订立契约的能力(his capacity to contract)；构成权利义务客体的确定标的 (a definite object which forms the subject-matter of the undertaking)；债的合法原因(a lawful cause in the obligation)。"虽然各国对合同有效成立的具体要求不尽相同，但是它们有共同点。综合起来，西方国家对合同有效成立的要件主要有以下几项：

1.1.1 合意 Agreement

合意是合同成立的最基本的条件，一般而言，它包括要约和承诺(offer and acceptance)。

英美法强调，当事人之间必须达到"相互间的一致(mutual assent)"，有的称之为"意愿的汇合(meeting of the minds)"。其意思是，双方当事人均了解有关条件，对此达成了一致意见，而且已做好准备受有关条件的约束。"意愿的汇合"，强调必须是客观的，通过某种形式表现出来，一般是通过要约、承诺反映出其意愿。有时候，某些事件(例如错误、胁迫、不正当影响等) (mistake, duress, and undue influence)会破坏相互间的一致，此种合同就是"有缺陷的协议"。

一些国家的法律认为，要约和承诺是成立合同的基本步骤，当事人都是通过要约和承诺达成合意或协议的，这两个步骤缺一不可。例如，前述《法国民法典》第1108条规定契约有效成立的第一个要件，是"负担债务的当事人的同意(The consent of the party who binds himself)"，实际上指的就是合意，可见合意这一条件之重要。《德国民法典》(the German Civil Code)第145节第3条，《瑞士民法典》第5条，《荷兰民法典》第185条，都规定只有通过要约和承诺才能订立合同。

另外一些国家的法律，是将通过要约与承诺成立合同作为一种方式，同时也允许以其他方式(例如行为方式等)成立合同。例如美国《统一商法典》(the Uniform Commercial Code/UCC)，除在第2-206条对"订立合同的要约与承诺"作出规定外，同时在第2-204条"订立合同的一般要求"第1款规定："货物买卖合同可以通过任何足以表明当事方已达成协议的方式订立，包括通过承认合同存在的双方的行为而订立。(Article 2-204: A contract for sale of goods may be made in any manner sufficient to show agreement, including offer and acceptance, conduct by both parties which recognizes the existence of a contract)"就是说，关键在于达成了协议，至于是否通过要约和承诺，则在所不问。

此外，还有一些国家并不在意要约与承诺的问题。在《法国民法典》中就根本没有提及，其中第 1108 条规定契约有效成立的第一个要件，是"负担债务的当事人的同意"，实际上指的就是合意，强调了合意这一条件之重要。《葡萄牙民法典》和《奥地利民法典》也几乎没有提及。

还有观点认为："事实上，合同绝不是毫无例外地通过要约和承诺的方式订立的。当然，在要约被承诺时，双方当事人需表示必要的同意。但是，如果双方当事人的任何其他行为充分说明其愿受合同的约束，则这种行为就足够了。长期以来，实际上根本没有必要必须将同意写进要约和承诺中，因为双方当事人是面对面地订立合同。"

《欧洲合同法原则》(the Principles of European Contract Law)在第 2：211 条专门就"非经要约承诺形成的合同"规定："尽管合同的形成过程无法解析成要约与承诺，本节中的规则经适当修正仍得适用。(The rules in this section apply with appropriate adaptations even though the process of conclusion of a contract cannot be analyzed into offer and acceptance)"

正是因为存在以上一些分歧，《联合国国际货物销售合同公约》(CISG) 制定了关于要约和承诺的统一规则，《国际商事合同通则》(the UNIDROIT Principles of International Commercial Contracts)则基本上沿用这些规则。

1.1.2 缔约能力 Capacity to contract

所谓当事人的缔约能力，是指合同当事人据以独立订立合同并独立享有合同权利(rights)、履行合同义务(obligations)的主体资格。从事合同行为的当事人可以分为自然人 (natural persons)、法人 (juristic persons/legal persons)和非法人的其他组织。依据不同的当事人和不同的合同，法律对其资信状况、认知能力、独立承担责任的能力有不同的要求，当事人订立合同必须具有相应的缔约能力，当事人的缔约能力对合同的效力有着重大的影响。各国法律都完全肯定成年人(adults)和精神状态健康的人的完全缔约能力，也都不绝对否定未成年人(minors)和精神病人(mentally incompetent persons)的缔约能力。但在如何确定未成年人和精神病人的范围及其缔约能力的有无、大小等方面存在一些差异。

英美法较为简单地规定成年人与未成年人的年龄界线。

在英国，从 1970 年 1 月 1 日起，根据《1969 年家庭法律改革法》(The Family Law Reform Act 1969)的规定，成年人的法定年龄降低到 18 周岁，年龄不满 18 周岁的自然人称为未成年人。英国《1983 年精神健康法》(The Mental Health Act 1983)规定，精神病人由保护法院的法官们负责照管。这些法官对于他们照管的精神病人的财产享有广泛的权利，他们可以代表这些病人订立合同,并且强制实施精神病人已经订立的合同。

在美国,绝大多数州都制定法律,把成年人的标准定在年满18周岁。18周岁以下的人是未成年人,没有订立合同的能力。现代法律认为,由于精神上的缺陷所造成的能力丧失,可以是多种原因,其中包括思维和行为迟钝、精神病、大脑损坏、老年性大脑退化以及酗酒和吸毒等。

大陆法对缔约能力的规定较为复杂和系统。

在法国,《法国民法典》第1123条规定:"任何人,非经法律宣告无能力者,均得订立契约。(Any person may enter into a contract, unless he has been declared incapable of it by law)"法国民法中的行为能力,是法律赋予公民支配及行使全部主观实体权利的资格,它直接系于公民的人身,是其从事法律活动的根据。根据《法国民法典》第1108条的规定,合同当事人必须具有缔约能力,是合同有效成立的根本条件之一。在法国,确认合同当事人是否具有缔约能力的标准主要有两个:一是年龄标准,《法国民法典》第5488条第1款规定:"年满18周岁为成年,满18周岁的人,有能力实施民事生活之所有行为。"未成年人为无实施法律行为能力的人,未成年人只有通过解除亲权而依法获得行为能力。二是精神状态标准,《法国民法典》第489条第1款规定,"任何人,为使某项行为有效,应当精神正常、健康;但是,以精神原因提出行为无效之诉的人,应当证明在此行为之时刻存在精神紊乱。(In order to enter into a valid transaction, it is necessary to be of sound mind. But it is for those who seek annulment on that ground to prove the existence of a mental disorder at the time of the transaction)" 精神紊乱的成年人,在法国被称为受法律保护的成年人,或丧失行为能力的成年人。根据第1124条的规定,受法律保护的未成年人,在法律规定的限制范围内,无缔结契约之能力。(Non-emancipated minors are incapable of entering into a contract, to the extent defined by law)

德国的法律(中国的法律也类似)既规定了成年与未成人的年龄界线,又对未成年人作了不同层次的分类,较为合理地考虑到未成年人的年龄、智力、能力的差异性,将未成年人进一步分为无民事行为能力人(persons with full capacity for civil conduct)和限制民事行为能力人(persons with limited capacity for civil conduct),在此基础上再相应确认他们的缔约能力。在德国,《德国民法典》第2条规定,"满18周岁为成年(Majority is attained upon the completion of the eighteenth year of age)",成年人为完全行为能力人。第104条规定,未满7周岁者和因精神错乱不能自由决定其意志者,为无行为能力人。第106条规定,已满7周岁未满18周岁的未成年人,其行为能力为限制行为能力。

1.1.3 对价或约因 Consideration

关于合同有效成立的要件,英美法系国家要求存在对价,而大陆法系一些国家则要求存在约因。

(1) 英美法

对价(consideration,也有人译成约因)是英美法的一个独特概念。其定义是:"合同一方得到的某种权利、利益、利润或好处,或是他方当事人克服自己不行使某项权利或遭受某项损失或承担某项义务。(Some right, interest, profit or benefit accruing to the one party of a contract, or some forbearance, detriment, loss or responsibility given, suffered or undertaken by the other)""法官在解释对价时,主要强调双方当事人各有得失、相互给付(counterpart)",即"我给你某物,是为了你给我他物"。

英美普通法把合同分为签字蜡封合同(contract under seal)和简式合同(simple contract)两大类。前者以遵守特定的形式为合同生效的条件,这是英国早年沿用下来的一种合同形式,需要举行隆重庄严的仪式,主要是经双方当事人签字、盖章、蜡封、交付的环节,否则就不发生法律效力。在15世纪以前,对违反签字蜡封合同的情形,可提起违约之诉,履约方可获得违约补救。后者以存在对价关系为条件。对价是判断当事人双方之间有无法律上的权利和义务的主要依据。一方当事人作出许诺(promise),另一方当事人提供了对价,法院就有了强制执行这一合同的依据。

根据英美法判例所确立的法律原则,一项有效的对价必须具备以下条件:1) 对价必须是合法的(legal)。2) 对价必须是待履行(executory)的对价或已履行(executed)的对价,但不能是过去的对价(past consideration)。3) 对价必须具有某种价值,但不要求充足、相等。4) 已经存在的义务或法律上的义务不能作为对价。5) 对价必须来自受允诺人(promisee)。

英美法传统的对价理论,在一些问题上已经不适应当代社会生活的需要。有鉴于此,美国《统一商法典》在一些规定中,突破了对价理论,作出有利于商品经济发展需要的新规定。例如,第2-201条明确规定,关于改变现存合同的协议,即使没有对价也具有约束力。又如第2-205条规定,在货物买卖中,在一定条件下可以承认无对价的"确定的要约"(firm offer)。近年来,英国法院的少数判例也有改变对价原则中的不合理因素的趋势。

总而言之,英美法系对对价原则的态度正在逐渐演变之中,总的倾向是采取比较灵活的做法,以使传统法律原则适应现代商业的发展需要。

(2) 法国法的约因。约因(cause)是法国法合同有效成立的要素之一。债的约因是指订约当事人产生该项债务所追求的最接近和最直接的目的。在双务合同中,存在着两个约因,即双方当事人之间存在相对给付的关系。例如,在买卖合同中,卖方的交货义务,是以买方付款(payment)为约因;而买方的付款义务,则以卖方交货(delivery of goods)为约因。

1.1.4 形式 Form

合同形式(form)应该符合法律规定。合同可分为要式合同(formal contracts)与不要式合同(informal contracts)两类。前者是指必须按照法定的形式或手续订立的合同,后者是指法律不要求按特定的形式订立的合同。当代西方发达国家在合同形式问题上,都采取"不要式原则(principle of informality)",即当事人可采取任何方式订立合同,只是对某些特殊种类的合同,才要求以法律规定的特定形式订立。

西方国家要求某些合同需按法定形式成立,其目的和作用有二:一种是作为合同生效的要件;另一种是作为证明合同存在的证据(evidence)。德国法侧重于作为合同有效成立的要件,它只要求土地买卖合同必须具备法定形式。法国法侧重于作为证据要求,它规定赠予合同、设立抵押权合同、夫妻财产制合同须采用法定形式。

英国法要求下列合同以书面形式作为成立的条件,否则无效:汇票与本票(bill of exchange and promissory note)、海上保险合同、债务承认、卖方继续保持占有的动产权益转让合同。此外,还有一些合同要求须以书面文件作为证据,否则法院不予强制执行,此类包括保险合同、土地买卖合同和金钱借贷合同。这种书面形式要求来源于 1677 年英国《欺诈法》(Statute of Frauds),其目的是为了防止原告捏造事实,在根本不存在合同的情况下提起诉讼,进行欺诈。但该法律也有漏洞,有些被告也可借口无书面形式,逃避其依据口头合同所承担的义务,于是后来又修改该法律。继承英国法传统的美国,沿用了英国的《欺诈法》,几乎所有的州都制定了自己的《欺诈法》,内容大同小异。此法要求下列合同必须以书面形式作为证据:不动产买卖合同,从订约时起不能在一年之内履行的合同,为他人担保债务的合同,价金超过 500 美元的货物买卖合同。

在合同形式问题上,《国际商事合同通则》与《销售合同公约》一样,采取十分开放的态度,其第 1.2 条标题非常鲜明且无形式要求,内容是:"通则不要求合同必须以书面形式订立或由书面文件证明。合同可通过包括证人在内的任何形式证明。(Nothing in these Principles requires a contract to be concluded in or evidenced by writing. It may be proved by any means, including witnesses)"合同得益于各种现代的通讯方式,使许多国际商事交易能非常迅速地进行,并且无纸化。《合同通则》顺应了国际贸易发展的大趋势,其无形式要求的原则虽然不会被所有的国家采纳,但会得到许多法律体系的认可。上述第1.2条表明,采用无形式要求的原则,意味着口头证据在司法程序中的可接受性。

1.1.5 合法性 Legality

（1）英美法

就英美法来说,合法性是指合同的目的或目标必须是合法的,合同标的(subject matter)、合同的成立和履行也必须合法,而不能是非法的(illegal)。此要求强调合同不能是成文法所禁止的,不能违反普通法,不能与公共政策相抵触。

根据某些美国法学著作的分类,下列三类协议是非法的:

1)违反成文法的协议(agreement in violation of statutes)。这方面涵盖的范围广泛。例如,法律要求需要有执照(License)才能开业的专业人员,如医师、律师、药剂师等,无执照却擅自与他人订立协议从事专业服务,即属此类。又如,贷款人收取高于法定利率的高利贷协议,限制贸易的协议,均视为违法。2)违反公共政策的协议(agreement in violation of public policy)。公共政策是英美法中富于弹性的概念,一般包括联邦以及各州的法规政策或目标,以及公众利益、社会环保要求等等。具体说来,例如不合理地限制贸易、限制竞争的协议,显失公平的协议,贿赂或扰乱政府官员的协议,均属此类。3)不道德的合同(immoral contract)。这是指违反社会公认的道德标准,若法院予以承认会引起正常人愤慨的合同。

凡属类似以上列举的非法协议,均是无效的,不构成合同,其法律后果是既不产生权利,也不产生义务,当事人不能要求履行合同,也不能要求赔偿损失。法院原则上也不允许以无效合同提起诉讼。

（2）大陆法

在大陆法系,各国都在民法典中对合同违法、违反公共秩序和善良风俗等问题作出明确规定。

《法国民法典》在第三卷第三编第二章"契约有效成立的要件(essential requisites for the validity of agreements)"中,把违法、违反公共秩序等问题与约因、标的与客体联系在一起,加以规定。其中主要的规定有:"第1128条,得为契约标的者,以许可交易之物为限。(Only things which may be the subject matter of legal transactions between private individuals may be the object of agreements)""第1131条,无原因之债,或者基于错误原因或不法原因之债,不发生任何效力。(An obligation without cause or with a false cause, or with an unlawful cause, may not have any effect)""第1133条,如原因为法律所禁止,违反善良风俗或公共秩序,此种原因为不法原因。(A cause is unlawful where it is prohibited by legislation, where it is contrary to public morals or to public policy)"

从上述规定可见,按照法国法,构成合同非法的主要是两种情形:一是交易的标的物不合法,如贩卖毒品等违禁品的合同;二是合同的约因不合法,即合同所追求的目的不合法。

德国法注重于法律行为和整个合同的内容是否有违法情事。《德国民法典》在总则篇第二章"法律行为"中规定:"法律行为违反法律上的禁止者,无效。(A juristic act which violates a statutory prohibition is void)"并且还规定,违反善良风俗的法律行为亦无效。上述规定不仅适用于合同,也适用于合同以外的其他法律行为。

1.1.6 意思表达的真实性 Genuineness of the assent

此要件强调,双方当事人是在正常情形下达成合意的,此合意是他们意思的真实表示。此要件通常集中体现在影响合同效力的几个重要因素,诸如是否存在错误(mistake)、欺诈(fraud)、胁迫(duress)、显失公平(obvious unfairness)、不正确说明(misrepresentation)、不正当影响(undue influence)等等。如果确实存在上述情况,依据各国法律规定,受不利影响的一方当事人有权主张合同无效,或主张撤销合同。

1.2 国际统一合同法的有关规定
Relevant Regulations in the International Unified Contract Law

1.2.1 《联合国国际货物销售合同公约》CISG

该公约没有对合同有效成立的要件作出全面的规范,仅在第23条规定:"合同于按照本公约规定对要约的承诺生效时订立。(A contract is concluded at the moment when an acceptance of an offer becomes effective in accordance with the provisions of this Convention)"该公约主张,一般是通过要约与承诺成立合同。"但是,如果根据该项要约或依照当事人之间确定的习惯做法或惯例,受要约人可以做出某种行为,例如与发运货物或支付价款有关的行为,来表示同意,而无须向要约人发出通知,则承诺于该项行为作出时生效。(第18条第3款) (However, if, by virtue of the offer or as a result of practices which the parties have established between themselves or of usage, the offeree may indicate assent by performing an act, such as one relating to the dispatch of the goods or payment of the price, without notice to the offeror, the acceptance is effective at the moment the act is performed, provided that the act is performed within the period of time laid down in the preceding paragraph)"

在合同形式方面,该公约的第11条规定也是非常宽松的:"销售合同无须以书面订立或证明,在形式方面也不受任何其他条件的限制。销售合同可以用包括人证在内的任何方法证明。(A contract of sale need not be concluded in or evidenced by writing and is not subject to any other requirement as to form. It may be proved by any means, including witnesses)"

综上所述,在《销售合同公约》项下,合同成立的主要条件是当事人之间达成协议,别无其他。该公约第4条明确规定,本公约除非另有明文规定,与以下事项无关:(a)合同的效力,或其任何条款的效力,或任何惯例的效力;(b)合同对所售货物所有权可能产生的影响。就是说,上述问题需由适用的国内法来调整。[This Convention governs only the formation of the contract of sale and the rights and obligations of the seller and the buyer arising from such a contract. In particular, except as otherwise expressly provided in this Convention, it is not concerned with: (a) the validity of the contract or of any of its provisions or of any usage; (b) the effect which the contract may have on the property in the goods sold]

1.2.2 《国际商事合同通则》PICC

该通则未对合同成立的条件作出全面的规范。其第3.1条"未涉及的事项(Matters not covered)"明确规定:"通则不涉及由以下原因而导致的合同无效:(a)无行为能力;(b)无授权;(c)不道德或非法。[These Principles do not deal with invalidity arising from (a) lack of capacity; (b) lack of authority; (c) immorality or illegality.]"以上三项涉及合同成立条件的情事,通则作出排除,留由适用的国内法管辖。

《通则》第3.2条规定:"合同仅由双方的协议订立、修改或终止,除此别无其他要求。(A contract is concluded, modified or terminated by the mere agreement of the parties, without any further requirement)"在该条的注释中又明确指出,成立合同无须对价,无须约因,所有合同只须双方同意。

关于是否要通过要约与承诺成立合同的问题,《通则》第2.1条规定:"合同可通过对要约的承诺或通过当事人充分表明其合意的行为而成立。(A contract may be concluded either by the acceptance of an offer or by conduct of the parties that is sufficient to show agreement)"《通则》的基本观点是当事人的合意本身足以构成合同。它按传统采用了"要约"和"承诺"这两个概念,目的在于确认当事人间的协议是否已达成、何时达成。《通则》将这两个概念视为必要的分析手段。同时,《通则》也认为,商事合同,特别是涉及复杂交易的合同,通常是经过长期谈判达成的,往往无法明确区分要约和承诺。这种情况下,很难确定合同协议是否已达成以及何时达成。根据本条的规定,即便不能确定订立时间,合同也可因当事人足以表明其合意的行为而成立。

为说明上述问题,《通则》的注释还举例如下:

A 和 B 举行谈判,为开发一种新产品而建立一合资企业(joint venture enterprise)。经过长期谈判后,虽没有任何形式上的要约或承诺,并且尚有一些次要的问题待解决,但双方当事人业已开始履行。当后来双方当事人未能就那些次要问题达成一致意见时,法庭(court)或仲裁庭(arbitral tribunal)可以判定,自双方当事人开始履行时起合同已成立,因为这已显示了当事人愿受合同约束的意向。

1.2.3《欧洲合同法原则》PECL

与《联合国国际货物销售合同公约》和《国际商事合同通则》未正面规定合同成立的条件完全不同,《欧洲合同法原则》在第二章"合同的订立(Formation)"专门设立了第 2:101 条,标题为"合同成立的条件(Conditions for the Conclusion of a Contract)",其内容如下:

(1)合同符合下列条件即成立而无须其他的要件:

(a) 当事人意欲在法律上受拘束(The parties intend to be legally bound),以及(b)它们形成了充分的合意(They reach a sufficient agreement)。

(2)合同无须最终形成书面的形式,或以书面的形式证明,或是符合其他的形式要件。合同可采用任何方式加以证明,包括证人。(A contract need not be concluded or evidenced in writing nor is it subject to any other requirement as to form. The contract may be proved by any means, including witness)

从上述规定来看,《欧洲合同法原则》对合同成立的要求是非常宽松的,仅仅要求两项:一是法律上受约束的意图,二是形成了充分的合意。什么"对价"(英美法的要件之一)、"约因"(cause) (法国法的要件之一),什么书面形式、书面形式的证明,统统都不要。以上规定,充分反映了当今世界合同法立法的主流倾向——采取"不要式原则(principle of informality)",尽可能扫除人为的障碍,尽可能让合同得以成立,促进经济和其它社会活动的发展。

关于何为"充分的合意",《欧洲合同法原则》专门在第 2:103 条作出规定如下:

(1)如果条款:

(a) 已被当事人充分地界定进而使合同能够被强制执行,或者(b)能够依本原则加以确定, 即为存有充分的合意。[(a)have been sufficiently defined by the parties so that the contract can be enforced, or (b) can be determined under these Principles]

(2)但如果一方当事人拒绝达成合同,除非当事人在某种特定的事情上形成合意,则不存在任何合同,除非对上述事情的合意已经形成。(However, if one of the parties refuses to conclude a contract unless the parties have agreed on some specific matter, there is no contract unless agreement on that matter has been reached)

1.3 中国法关于合同成立的要件
Requisites to Form a Contract in Chinese Law

中国《合同法》关于合同成立的要件,主要有两个方面:

1.3.1 缔约人 Parties

第9条规定:"当事人订立合同,应当具有相应的民事权利能力和民事行为能力。(In entering into a contract, the parties shall have appropriate capacities for civil rights and civil acts)"此处的当事人,包括第2条所规定的自然人、法人和其他组织。根据《民法通则》的规定,18周岁以上的公民可独立缔约,16周岁至18周岁的公民,以自己的劳动收入为主要生活来源的,也可独立缔约。未成年人和精神病患者可独立订立纯获利益的合同,其他民事活动须由其法定代理人代理。法人应当在核准登记的经营范围内从事经营。

1.3.2 当事人意思表示一致 Agreement of assent

缔约人须就合同条款达成协议,合同才能成立。

此外,《民法通则》第55条规定:民事法律行为应当具备下列条件:(1)行为人具有相应的民事行为能力;(2)意思表示真实;(3)不违反法律或者社会公共利益。以上三项要件再加上标的须确定与可能,一共四项,作为合同的一般有效要件。

由上可见,与西方国家合同有效成立的要件相比较,除了中国法律不要求存在对价或约因(consideration)之外,基本要求是相似的,彼此之间有相通之处。

关于合同订立的方式,中国合同法规定采取要约、承诺方式。(第13条)

关于合同订立的形式,中国合同法规定,有书面形式、口头形式和其他形式。如第11条规定:"书面形式是指合同书、信件和数据电文(包括电报、电传、传真、电子数据交换和电子邮件)等可以有形地表现所载内容的形式。["Written form" refers to a form such as a written contractual agreement, letter, electronic data text (including a telegram, telex, fax, electronic data exchange and e-mail)that can tangibly express the contents contained therein]"

中国合同法原则上允许当事人选择合同形式,但同时要求以下合同必须采取书面形式:

（1）法律、行政法规规定采用书面形式的。这类合同包括《合同法》分则中所规定的 6 种合同：1）借款合同(Contracts for Loan of Money)（自然人之间借款另有约定的除外）；2）租赁期限 6 个月以上的租赁合同(Leasing Contracts)；3）融资租赁合同(Financial Leasing Contracts)；4）建设工程合同(Contracts for Construction Projects)；5）技术开发合同 (Technology Development Contract)；6）技术转让合同(Technology Transfer Contracts)。

此外，一般说来，需经政府审批或登记的合同也应采取书面形式，例如中外合资经营企业合同、中外合作经营企业合同、不动产转让合同等。

（2）当事人约定采用书面形式的。

上述两类应采用书面形式订立合同，当事人未采用书面形式但一方已经履行主要义务，对方接受的，该合同成立（第 36、37 条）。

第二节　要约
Section 2　Offer

合同是当事人意思表示一致的结果。各国合同法把合同的意思表示，分解为要约和承诺两个概念。如果一方当事人向另一方当事人提出一项要约，而后者对该项要约表示承诺，双方当事人就成立了一项具有法律约束力的合同。也有人称要约和承诺为成立合同的最基本的两个法律步骤。

2.1 要约的定义
Definition of an Offer

要约(Offer)是一种订立合同的意思表示，提出的一方称为要约人(Offeror)，其相对方为受要约人(Offeree)。要约可用书面形式，也可通过口头、行为表示。

《国际商事合同通则》第 2.2 条对要约的定义如下："一项订立合同的建议，如果十分确定，并表明要约人在得到承诺时受其约束的意旨，即构成要约。(A proposal for concluding a contract constitutes an offer if it is sufficiently definite and indicates the intention of the offeror to be bound in case of acceptance)"此定义有两个要点：

第一，要约的确定性(definiteness)，即该订立合同的建议必须十分明确地许诺，此建议一旦被承诺即为合同成立。一般说来，要约应当对将来协议的条款有十分明确的表述，越详细越被视为确定。但这也不是绝对的，即使某些重要条款在要约中可能尚未确定，也不能据此就判定该要约是不确定的，尚需参考其他有关情形。

第二,要约人受约束的意旨(intention to be bound),即该建议需明确地表示,要约人在得到对方对该要约承诺时愿受其约束。然而,这种意旨有时未必被明确地表述,通常要根据各例具体情况去推断。

一般而言,建议包含的交易条件和细节越详细、越明确,就越容易被推定为要约。此外需注意区分要约和邀请要约(invitation for offer)。虽然邀请要约的目的也是为了成立合同,但它本身不是要约,而只是邀请对方向自己发出要约。例如在商业活动中,有些公司向有关当事人寄送报价单(quotation)、价目表(price lists)和商品目录(catalogues)等,其内容可能包括品质、规格、价格、交货期等,但这些都不是要约。其目的是为了吸引对方向自己报出订货单,此种订货单才是真正的要约,经承诺后才能成立合同。

由此可见,要约与邀请要约的根本区别在于:作为一项要约,它一经对方承诺,要约人即需受其约束,合同即为成立;而作为邀请要约,即使对方完全同意有关交易条件,该发出方仍可不受其约束,除非他对此表示承诺。

关于要约是否需向特定人(specific persons)发出的问题,往往牵涉到广告(advertisement)是否构成要约,对此各国法律规定不一。关于普通的商业广告,原则上不认为是要约,而仅视为邀请要约。然而英美法院的一些判例主张,要约既可向某一人发出,也可向某一群人发出,甚至可向全世界发出。只要广告的文字明确、肯定,足以构成一项允诺(promise),亦可视为要约。

在此问题上,北欧各国法律的规定不同,其强调要约必须向一个或一个以上的特定人发出,广告原则上仅是邀请要约。

《销售合同公约》14条第二款规定:"除非提出建议的人明确地表示相反的意向,非向特定人提出的建议,仅应视为邀请要约。(A proposal other than one addressed to one or more specific persons is to be considered merely as an invitation to make offers, unless the contrary is clearly indicated by the person making the proposal)"

《国际商事合同通则》对此未作规定,不以"向特定人发出"作为构成要约的一项因素。

《欧洲合同法原则》第2:201条的标题为"要约",规定如下:

"(1)一项建议一旦符合下列要件即构成要约:(a)它意欲在对方承诺后即形成合同,并且(b)它含有相当确定的条款以形成合同。[A proposal amounts to an offer if: (a) it is intended to result in a contract if the other party accepts it, and (b) it contains sufficiently definite terms to form a contractz](2)要约可以向一个或者多个特定的人或者向公众作出。(An offer may be made to one or more specific persons or to the public) (3) 一项由职业性供应人以公开的广告或价目表或者以商品展示的方式作出的以特定价格供应商品或服务的建议，被推定为是按此价格出售商品或提供服务的要约，直至库存商品售罄或者供应人提供此项服务的能力告尽。(A proposal to supply goods or services at stated prices made by a professional supplier in a public advertisement or a catalogue, or by a display of goods, is presumed to be an offer to sell or supply at that price until the stock of goods, or the supplier's capacity to supply the service, is exhausted)"

由此可见，《欧洲合同法原则》不以"向特定的人发出"作为构成要约的一项因素，而且该规定独具匠心地对"职业性供应人"的订约建议明确规定为要约，还进一步规定了具体的解决问题的办法，直至库存商品售罄或其能力告尽，这是非常值得称道的。

2.2 要约的撤回与撤销
Withdrawal and Revocation of an Offer

一项要约，一旦被发出，并到达受要约人，就具有约束力。简言之，要约到达生效。这一法律原则，大陆法系与英美法系是一致的。《国际商事合同通则》第2.3条(1)款就此明确规定："要约于送达受要约人时生效。(An offer becomes effective when it reaches the offeree)"

要约的撤回，与要约的撤销，是两个完全不同的概念。要约的撤回(Withdrawal of offer)，是阻止要约生效的行为，即：在要约已被发出但尚未到达受要约人的这段时间里，要约人通知对方取消此项要约，使其不发生效力。

对此问题，《国际商事合同通则》第2.3条(2)款规定："一项要约即使是不可撤销的，也可以撤回，如果撤回通知在要约送达受要约人之前或与要约同时送达受要约人。(An offer, even if it is irrevocable, may be withdrawn if the withdrawal reaches the offeree before or at the same time as the offer)"

撤回要约的实用价值在于：要约人在发出要约之后，迅速地发现了要约有误的情形下，或是国际市场该种商品价格或外汇汇率突然发生了不利于己方而需要取消要约的情形下，要约人可用更快的通讯方式通知对方。若此撤回通知能赶在要约送达之前或同时送达，均可成功地撤回要约。

要约的撤销(revocation of an offer)，是针对已发生效力的要约而言，是消灭要约效力的行为。就是说，在要约已到达受要约人之后，要约人通知对方取消该项要约，从而使要约的效力归于消灭。撤销要约的实用价值类似撤回要约，主要起因于交易的重要条件发生了不利于要约人的剧变。《国际商事合同通则》第2.4条(1)款规定："在合同订立之前，要约得予撤销,如果撤销通知在受要约人发出承诺之前送达受要约人。(Until a contract is concluded an offer may be revoked if the revocation reaches the offeree before it has dispatches an acceptance)"

2.3 要约的约束力
Binding Effects of an Offer

要约的约束力是一个重要问题。此处的约束力,是就要约人而言;而对受要约人来说,是无所谓约束力的,他收到要约,只是取得承诺该要约的权利,并不因此而承担必须承诺的义务。

要约对要约人的约束力,是指要约人在发出要约之后至对方承诺之前的这段时间内,能否撤销要约或变更要约的内容。以下分别阐述英美法、大陆法以及国际统一合同法的规定。

2.3.1 英美法 Anglo-American Law

英美普通法(common law)认为,要约原则上对要约人无约束力,要约人在受要约人发出承诺之前,任何时候均可撤销要约或变更要约的内容。即使要约人在要约中规定了有效期限,他也有权在期限届满之前撤销要约。上述法律原则建立于对价原则之上,其理念是:

一个人所作的允诺之所以有约束力,是由于取得了对方的某种对价。例如,要约人在要约中申明,若受要约人支付 100 英镑,则该项要约在 10 天之内不予撤销,若受要约人支付了此金额,双方就成立了保证该项要约于 10 天内有效的担保合同,要约人就必须受此约束。但是如果受要约人没有付出任何对价,那么要约人也就没有义务保证不变更或不撤销要约。

显然,上述原则使受要约人缺乏应有的保障,受要约人有可能会蒙受因信赖该要约而与第三方订立合同所造成的损失。

美国在经历很长时间的司法审判实践之后,《第二次合同法重述》第 2 卷(1981 年)根据法院判决总结出一个新的规则。它在其第 87 条第 2 款否定了一项要约在要约人明知受要约人相信该项要约,并且根据该要约进行了财产上的处置,而且这种处置在事实上涉及受要约人很大的经济利益时,该项要约应被视为不可撤销的基本原则。但是在这种情况下,无论如何,"在避免产生不公正的必要范围内",该项要约应当是有约束力的。尤其是在商事交易中,建立要约有约束力的原则是非常必要的。

为适应当代商品经济发展的需要,美国《统一商法典》第 2-205 条规定:"在货物买卖中,在一定条件下可承认无对价的确定的要约,即要约人在其要约确定的期限内不得撤销要约。其条件是:要约人必须是商人;要约已规定期限,或者如果未规定期限,则在合理期限内不予撤销,但无论如何不得超过 3 个月;要约需以书面做成,并由要约人签字。(An offer by a merchant to buy or sell goods in a signed writing which by its terms gives assurance that it will be held open is not revocable, for lack of consideration, during the time stated or if no time is stated for a reasonable time, but in no event may such period of irrevocability exceed three months; but any such term of assurance on a form supplied by the offeree must be separately signed by the offeror)"

美国《统一商法典》的上述规定,彻底地改变了普通法关于没有对价、要约即无约束力的规则,在此问题上将历来神圣不可侵犯的"对价理论"抛至九霄云外,确实是适应商品经济发展的重大突破。

2.3.2 大陆法 Civil Law

德国法主张,要约原则上对要约人具有约束力。《德国民法典》规定,除非要约人在要约中注明不受约束的字句,均须受其要约的约束(Whoever offers to another to enter a contract is bound by the offer, unless he has excluded being so bound);若在要约中规定了有效期,则在该期限内不得撤销或更改;若未规定有效期,则依通常情形在得到答复以前,不得撤销或更改其要约。瑞士、希腊、巴西等国均采取此种原则。

法国法原则上主张,要约人在其要约被受要约人承诺以前可撤销要约。法国的法院判例认为,如果要约人在要约中指定了承诺期限,他亦可在期限届满以前撤销要约,但需承担损害赔偿的责任。即使在要约中未规定期限,但若根据具体情况或交易习惯,要约视为应在一定期限内等待承诺者,要约人如果不适当地撤销要约,亦需负损害赔偿之责。

2.3.3 国际统一合同法 International Unified Law

如前所述,两大法系对要约可否撤销问题的分歧较大,难于协调。《合同通则》在此问题上完全继承了《销售合同公约》的原则。

首先,《合同通则》和《销售合同公约》以英美法的规定作为原则,"在合同订立之前,要约得予撤销,如果撤销通知在受要约人发出承诺之前送达受要约人"[《合同通则》第 2.4 条(1)款,《公约》第 16 条(1)款]也就是说,要约人撤销要约的权利至受要约人发出承诺时即为终止。这种处理可能会给要约人带来不便,因为他并非始终知悉是否尚可撤销要约,但这是基于保护受要约人的合法利益,应当缩短可撤销要约的期限。

其次,《合同通则》和《销售合同公约》又以大陆法多数国家的规定作为例外,明确规定:

"但是,在下列情况下,要约不得撤销:(a)要约写明承诺的期限,或以其他方式表明要约是不可撤销的;或(b)受要约人有理由信赖该项要约是不可撤销的,而且受要约人已依赖该要约行事。[(a) if it indicates, whether by stating a fixed time for acceptance or otherwise, that it is irrevocable; or (b) if it was reasonable for the offeree to rely on the offer as being irrevocable and the offeree has acted in reliance on the offer]"[《通则》第2.4条(2)款,《公约》第16条(2)款]。

以上(a)款规定了要约包含不可撤销的表示的情形,如明确声明是"确定的要约"(firm offer),"此要约直至收到贵方的答复均有效"等等,此外尚可从要约人的其他表示或行为推断出来。(b)款所言受要约人的信赖,既可源于受要约人的行为(例如马上为生产做准备、购买或租用设备等等),也可源于要约本身的性质(例如对某项要约的承诺需要受要约人进行广泛且费用昂贵的调查,或某项要约的发出意在允许受要约人继续向第三方发出要约)。从法理来分析,受要约人基于对该要约的信赖已采取了行动,例如以承诺该要约为基础马上付款购买配套生产设施,而要约人却突然撤销该要约,这对受要约人是不公平的,有违诚实信用和公平交易的原则,因而是不可取的。

2.4 要约的消灭
Termination of an Offer

此用语又称为要约的终止,是指要约失去效力,要约人不再受该要约的约束。

根据各国法律以及国际统一合同法,在下述情况下要约失去效力:

2.4.1 要约的期限期满 Expiration of the time limit in the offer

(1)要约如果明确规定了有效期,则在此期限终了时,要约自行失效。

(2)要约如果没有规定承诺期限,分两种情形:1)口头要约若未得到当即承诺,要约当即失效。2)若当事人以函电方式发出要约,许多大陆法国家(包括德国、瑞士、日本等)的《民法典》都规定,在隔地人之间发出要约而又未规定承诺期限者,如不在相当期间内或"依通常情形可期待承诺达到的期间内"作出承诺,要约当即失效。至于此期间到底以多少天为适当,属于所谓"事实问题",应由法官根据两地距离的远近、要约与承诺所采取的方式来决定。英美普通法主张,若要约没有规定承诺的期间,应在"合理的时间(reasonable time)"内承诺,超过此时间,要约即告失效。何谓合理时间,也是"事实问题",应由法官根据具体案情来确定。

2.4.2 要约被要约人撤回或撤销 Withdrawal or revocation of the offer by the offeror

当事人如果根据适用法律的规范,成功地撤回或撤销了其原先发出的要约,该要约即被消灭。

2.4.3 要约被受要约人拒绝 Rejection of the offer by the offeree

《合同通则》第2.5条参照《销售合同公约》第17条作出规定如下："一项要约于拒绝通知送达要约人时终止。"

对此规则,两大法系是一致的。需注意的是,上述拒绝可以是明示的,也可以是默示的。后者指受要约人的答复似有承诺的意思,但对要约作了实质性的添加、限制或修改。这种默示的拒绝应视为反要约。

2.4.4 要约人或受要约人死亡、破产 Decease or bankruptcy of the offeror or the offeree

大部分国家的法律规定,要约人或受要约人任何一方死亡、破产,该要约即归于消灭。但是,也有一些国家的法律规定,尽管发生死亡或无行为能力的情况,要约仍然是可承诺的。例如德国、荷兰等国,在民法典中作出这样的规定。然而有人却认为,这些规则都是残缺不全的,而且其回答确实依赖于案件的具体情况,特别是依赖于当事人的个人品格和能力,这与有关合同有密切关系。例如,一位艺术家作出的一项要以特定的金额进行画像的要约,一旦该艺术家或其主题、肖像人死亡,便很难通过承诺而订立合同。

2.5 中国合同法关于要约的规定
Regulations on Offer in Contract Law of China

关于要约的定义、要约的生效、要约的撤回、要约的撤销、要约的失效,中国合同法的规定是参照《销售合同公约》、《合同通则》制定的,仅仅是个别词语有点差异,此处不赘述。以下仅阐述中国合同法关于要约的有特色的规定。

2.5.1 要约与要约邀请 An offer and invitation to an offer

鉴于实践中经常会发生要约与要约邀请混淆不清的情况,我国《合同法》第15条明确规定:"要约邀请是希望他人向自己发出要约的意思表示。寄送的价目表、拍卖公告、招股说明书、商业广告等为要约邀请。商业广告的内容符合要约规定的视为要约。(An invitation for offer is an expression of an intent to invite other parties to make offers thereto. Mailed price lists, public notices of auction and tender, prospectuses and commercial advertisements, etc. are invitations for offer. Where the contents of a commercial advertisement meet the requirements for an offer, it shall be regarded as an offer)"

商业广告到底是不是要约?这是一个颇为复杂的问题。

上述第15条规定可以这样表达:一般来说,商业广告是要约邀请,但如果该商业广告内容具体明确,表明经受要约人承诺,要约人即受该意思表示约束,即视为要约。

上述第 15 条规定,实际上是吸收了英美法在判例法中确立的有关法律原则。此方面英国最早的一个判例是卡利尔诉石碳烟球公司案(Carlill V. Carbolic Smoke Ball Co.)。在该案中,生产厂商在报纸上刊登广告称,对于任何一位服用其生产的预防药物"石碳烟球"后仍得流行性感冒的人,公司赔付 100 英镑。该广告还宣称,为表明其诚意,已经在一家银行存入了 1000 英镑。一位老妇 Carlill 购买并服用该药物,仍得了感冒,遂入禀法院告该生产厂商,厂商以广告不是要约为由进行抗辩(defend)。法官主张,该广告的文字明确、肯定,已足以构成一项允诺(promise),应当视为要约。此判例所形成的法律原则,一直沿用至今。至于应当如何判断商业广告内容是具体明确的,对此问题若发生争议应当如何处理,我国合同法关于要约的规定应当如何完善修改,还需拭目以待。

2.5.2 数据电文要约的生效 Effectiveness of offer by means of electronic data

根据当今世界使用电子合同的具体情况,中国合同法在第 16 条 2 款作出了与时俱进的饱含现代气息的规定如下:

"采用数据电文形式订立合同,收件人指定特定系统接收数据电文的,该数据电文进入该特定系统的时间,视为到达时间;未指定特定系统的,该数据电文进入收件人的任何系统的首次时间,视为到达时间。(An offer becomes effective when it reaches the offeree. If a contract is concluded through data-telex, and a recipient designates a specific system to receive the date-telex, the time when the data-telex enters such specific system shall be the time of arrival; if no specific system is appointed, the time when the data-telex first enters any of the recipient's systems shall be regarded as the time of arrival)"

上述规定确立了数据电文要约的合法性,并参照联合国国际贸易法委员会 (UNCITRAL)《电子签名示范法》(the Model Law of Electronic Signatures),就数据电文要约作出规定。即使对比当今一些发达国家的合同法,上述规定也是先进的。此举清楚地说明,我国立法在某些方面已经达到一个新的先进水平,对批驳那些妄自菲薄、"月亮也是外国的圆"的观点无疑是一个有力的论据。

第三节　承诺
Section 3　Acceptance

3.1 承诺的定义
Definition of an Acceptance

一般说来,承诺(acceptance)是指受要约人按照要约所指定的方式,对要约的内容表示同意的一种意思表示。

要约一经承诺,合同即告成立。当今世界大部分国家以及国际公约、惯例均采取此法律原则,有人称之为"二环节"。然而也有少数国家的法律规定,在经要约、承诺的基本法律步骤之后,尚需由双方当事人签订书面合同,只在此时合同才视为成立,有人称此类法律原则为"三环节"。

3.2 承诺应当具备的条件
Elements of an Acceptance

一般说来,根据各国法律以及国际统一合同法,一项有效的承诺应具备以下条件:

3.2.1 承诺必须由受要约人作出 Made by the offeror

受要约人包括其本人及其授权的代理人。换句话说,只有受要约人才有承诺的权利,其承诺才具有法律效力,任何第三方对要约表示同意,均不是有效的承诺,不能成立合同。

3.2.2 承诺必须在要约的有效期间内进行 Accepted within the valid period in the offer

在要约未规定有效期的情况下,承诺则必须在"依照常情可期待得到承诺的期间内"(大陆法),或是在"合理的时间内"(英美法)。超过上述时间的承诺,一般视为新的要约。《合同通则》第 2.7 条对"承诺的时间"明确规定:"要约必须在要约人规定的时间内承诺,或者如果未规定时间,应在考虑了交易的具体情况,包括要约人所使用的通讯方法的快捷程度的一段合理时间内作出承诺。对口头要约必须立即作出承诺,除非情况另查明。(An offer must be accepted within the time the offeror has fixed or, if no time is fixed, within a reasonable time having regard to the circumstances, including the rapidity of the means of communication employed by the offeror. An oral offer must be accepted immediately unless the circumstances indicate otherwise)"

3.2.3 承诺必须与要约的内容一致 Consent with the content of the offer

在此问题上,传统的英美普通法要求非常严格,实行所谓"镜像规则"(the mirror image rule),即:承诺必须像一面镜子一样,反照出要约的内容,不容许丝毫差异,否则即视为反要约。

大陆法的法律原则与上述规则相似。

在商事交易中,受要约人有时会在承诺中对要约作出一些微小的附加、修改或限制,如果因为这些无关宏旨的变更,就使得合同不能成立,势必有碍于贸易发展。此外,镜像规则与在商业活动中进行讨价还价的人的合理愿望相违背,它使那些想寻找借口来推翻实际上已达成交易的人有机可乘。于是,美国《统一商法典》对传统的"镜像规则"作出重要的革新,其第 2-207 条(1)、(2)款规定如下:

(1)一项明确且及时的承诺表示,或一项合理时间内寄送的书面确认书,即使对原要约或原先同意的条款规定了追加的或不同的事项,仍起承诺的作用,除非该承诺明示规定,以同意该追加的或不同的事项为条件。(A definite and seasonable expression of acceptance or a written confirmation which is sent within a reasonable time operates as an acceptance even though it states terms additional to or different from those offered or agreed upon, unless acceptance is expressly made conditional on assent to the additional or different terms)

(2)追加事项应被解释为对合同的追加的建议。在商人之间,这些追加事项构成合同的一部分,除非:(a)该要约明确表示,承诺限于该要约的条件;(b)追加事项实质上(materially)改变了要约;(c)对追加事项的异议通知已经发出,或者在收到追加事项的通知后的合理期间内发出。[The additional terms are to be construed as proposals for addition to the contract. Between merchants such terms become part of the contract unless: (a) the offer expressly limits acceptance to the terms of the offer; (b) they materially alter it; or (c) notification of objection to them has already been given or is given within a reasonable time after notice of them is received]

上述两款是相互独立的。(1)款规范承诺是否有效的问题:只要受要约人不以要约人同意其追加事项为条件,则承诺有效,该合同成立。(2)款规范在合同成立的情况下,在商人之间,追加事项是否构成合同的一部分的问题:只要属(a)、(b)、(c)三种情形中的任何一种,追加事项即不成为合同的一部分,应以要约所含的条件成立合同。

《合同通则》第 2.11 条继承了《销售合同公约》的原则,它在(1)款首先肯定了各国传统的法律原则,强调作为原则,承诺的内容应与要约一致,对要约意在表示承诺但载有添加、限制或其他变更的答复,即视为对该要约的拒绝,并构成反要约;然后在(2)款中规定,作为一种例外,承认一定条件下的带有变更的承诺。但是,对要约意在表示承诺但载有添加或不同条件的答复,如果所载的添加或不同条件没有实质性地(Materially)改变该项要约的条件,除非要约人毫不延迟地反对这些不符,则此答复仍构成承诺。如果要约人不反对,则合同的条款应以该项要约的条件以及承诺通知中所载的变更为准。

《合同通则》上述(2)款规定在一定程度上吸收了美国《统一商法典》第 2-207 条的合理成分,但并非照搬,两者之间有一点不可忽略的差异:

根据美国《统一商法典》的规定,即使要约人对承诺中所载的追加事项持反对态度,只要该承诺不以其追加事项为条件,就不影响该承诺的有效性,不妨碍合同的成立,而只能阻止这些追加事项成为合同的一部分。

而根据《合同通则》的规定,要约人对带有变更的承诺的反应具有决定性作用,只要他毫不延迟地反对那些不符之处,就可以否定带有变更的承诺的效力,从而否定合同的成立。此处将成交的主动权授予要约人,是合情理的,因为在原要约条件上追加事项的是受要约人,是他改变了交易条件,然后球便踢到了要约人这边,最后应由要约人定夺。

关于什么是"实质上变更要约的条件"(alter the terms of the offer materially),《销售合同公约》第 19 条(3)款作出了明确的界定:"有关货物价格、付款、货物的质量和数量、交货地点和时间、一方当事人对另一方当事人的赔偿责任范围或解决争端的添加或不同条件,均视为在实质上变更要约的条件。(Additional or different terms relating, among other things, to the price, payment, quality and quantity of the goods, place and time of delivery, extent of one party's liability to the other or the settlement of disputes are considered to alter the terms of the offer materially)"也就是说,含有对以上 6 个方面条款的添加或不同条件的承诺是无效的承诺,构成一个反要约。有人认为,对以上 6 个方面之外的条款作出变更,例如包装条款、单据条款、船舶名称等等,一般不视为实质上的变更。

然而,以上对非实质性变更的解释仅是一些学者的见解,这种看法能否成立,应根据《销售合同公约》制定 22 年来和今后的司法实践或仲裁实践对此所作的解释和判决,才能得出比较肯定的结论。因为按照某些国家的法律或判例,商品的包装在有些情况下也是很重要的,甚至会被认为是属于商品品质的内容之一。有鉴于此,如果在承诺中对要约所提出的包装条款作出了变更,不一定会被认为是非实质性变更。英国法院的判例曾经认为,商品包装是一项"要件(condition)"。所以,对这一问题应慎重对待,不宜一概而论。

3.2.4 承诺的传递方式必须符合要约所提出的要求 The means of communication of acceptance be in compliance with the requirement in the offer

有些要约要求受要约人以电报或传真等快速传递方式承诺,受要约人应依此行事,否则承诺无效。如果要约未对承诺的传递方式做出规定,承诺一般应按要约所采用的传递方式。但是,如果受要约人采用比要约所指定或所采用的方式更为快捷的通讯方式承诺,例如要约指定或采用航空邮寄,但受要约人在有效期内采用电报或传真方式,这个承诺法律上是有效的。

3.3 承诺生效的时间
Time of Effectiveness of an Acceptance

根据大多数国家的法律和国际公约(conventions)以及国际惯例(customs)的规定,承诺一旦生效,合同即为成立,故承诺生效的时间事关重大。在此问题上,两大法系的分歧比较大。

3.3.1 英美法的"邮箱规则" Mailbox rule or deposited acceptance rule

英美法关于承诺生效时间的一般规则是,一项承诺于发出时生效。(An acceptance becomes effective upon dispatch)

此项规则有利于受要约人,尽管承诺在发出后未被要约人收到(even if the acceptance is not received by the offeror),它也被视为有效(valid)。例如,以书信或电报作出承诺时,只要受要约人把书信投入邮局信箱,或把电报稿交给电讯局,承诺立即生效。即使表示承诺的信函在传递过程中丢失,只要受要约人能证明确实已向邮局、电讯局交足邮资,写妥地址,合同仍视为成立。其理由是:要约人曾默示地指定邮局作为他收受承诺的代理人,故一旦受要约人把承诺交到邮局,就等于交给了要约人,承诺即时发生效力。即使由于邮局的原因使含有承诺内容的信函遗失了,那也应由要约人负责,与受要约人无关,不得因此而影响合同的成立。然而实际上这些均是表面的理由,真正的理由是为缩短要约人可撤销要约的时间,均衡要约人与受要约人之间的利益。前已述及,英美法由于固守对价原则,要约人在其要约被承诺以前,随时得以撤销要约,导致受要约人的利益处于不稳定状态。承诺采取"投邮生效"规则,要约人可撤销要约的时间实际上所剩无几,在一定程度上调和了两方当事人之间的利益(comprise the interests of two parties)。

英美法院采纳"邮箱规则"的另一个理由是,这一规则固然有利于受要约人而不利于要约人,但要约人有权在要约中规定,承诺通知必须送达

才生效 (The offeror can stipulate in the offer that an acceptance will not be effective until it is received by the offeror)。因此,要约人只要这样规定,就可使自己处于有利地位。

3.3.2 大陆法关于承诺生效的规则 Rules on effectiveness of acceptance in the Civil Law

大陆法系各国关于承诺何时生效的法律原则各有差异,试图用一句话来概括会有失偏颇。以下分别介绍德国、法国和日本的有关原则。

德国法采取"到达生效"原则(receive of the letter of acceptance rule),即承诺在到达要约人时才生效,合同在此时成立。《德国民法典》第130条规定:"对于相对人以非对话方式所作的意思表示,于意思表示到达于相对人时发生效力。(A declaration of intention required to be made to another, if made in his absence, becomes effective at the moment when it reaches him)"根据这一法律原则,受要约人承担从发出承诺至到达要约人时止这段时间的风险,如果承诺函电在传递过程中遗失,承诺即不生效,合同不能成立。

《法国民法典》对承诺生效时间未作规定。法国最高法院认为,承诺生效时间取决于当事人的意思,故这是一个事实问题,应根据具体情况特别是当事人的意思来决定,但往往推定为适用"投邮生效",即承诺于发出时生效。

《日本民法典》在总则部分第97条规定,对隔地人间的意思表示,自通知到达相对人时生效,即采取到达生效原则。另外在契约一章第526条又规定,隔地人之间的契约,于发出承诺通知时成立,即对合同成立采取投邮生效原则。

3.3.3 国际统一合同法的规定 Rules in the international unified contract law

全盘继承《销售合同公约》关于承诺生效时间的原则,《合同通则》基本上采取到达生效原则。《合同通则》第2.6条(2)款规定如下:

"对一项要约的承诺于同意的表示送达要约人时生效。(An acceptance of an offer becomes effective when the indication of assent reaches the offeror)"

采纳到达生效原则优先于投邮生效原则的理由是:由受要约人承担传递风险,比由要约人承担更合理。因为是由前者选择通讯方式,他知道该方式是否容易出现特别的风险或延误,他应能采取最有效的措施,以确保承诺送达目的地。此处的送达,是指递送到被通知人的营业地或通讯地址。[《合同通则》第19条(3)款]

此外,作为一种例外,《合同通则》第2.6条(3)款规定:

"如果根据要约本身，或依照当事人之间建立的习惯做法或依照惯例，受要约人可以通过做出某行为来表示同意，而无需向要约人发出通知，则承诺于做出该行为时生效。(However, if, by virtue of the offer or as a result of practices which the parties have established between themselves or of usage, the offeree may indicate assent by performing an act without notice to the offeror, the acceptance is effective when the act is performed)"

3.3.4 比较分析 Comparative analysis

以上关于要约和承诺几个方面的阐述，初看起来，德意志法系(指大陆法系)和英美法系的做法似乎区别很大，然而在实践中并不是那样。因为，即使是根据德意志法系的做法，一项要约只要没有到达受要约人，它一直就是可以撤销的。但依英美法，在此种要约的情形，受要约人只有在将其承诺的意思表示提交给官方指定的部门如邮局后，也属于不可撤销。这一点的意思是，根据英美法系的做法，受要约人只是在其"考虑时间"、也就是从要约来临到承诺发出的这一段时间内承受要约撤销的风险。这一段时间在要约未定期限的情况下经常是很短的。

在要约是否可撤销的问题上，国际统一合同法(包括《销售合同公约》和《合同通则》)处理得非常巧妙，它将两大法系貌似水火不相容的两种不同的法律规则有机地结合在一起：

首先，以英美法的规则为原则。"在合同订立之前，要约得予撤销，如果撤销通知在受要约人发出承诺之前送达受要约人。(Until a contract is concluded an offer may be revoked if the revocation reaches the offeree before he has dispatched an acceptance)"[《通则》第 2.4 条(1)款，《公约》第 16 条(1)款]

其次，又以大陆法多数国家的规定作为例外。但是，在下列情况下，要约不得撤销："(a)要约写明承诺的期限，或以其他方式表明要约是不可撤销的；(b)受要约人有理由信赖该项要约是不可撤销的，而且受要约人已依赖该要约行事。(However, an offer cannot be revoked (a) if it indicates, whether by stating a fixed time for acceptance or otherwise, that it is irrevocable; or (b) if it was reasonable for the offeree to rely on the offer as being irrevocable and the offeree has acted in reliance on the offer)"[《通则》第 2.4 条(2)款，《公约》第 16 条(2)款]

《销售合同公约》1980 年通过，至今已有 28 年，1988 年实施至今也有 20 个年头了，尚未听说上述规定碰到什么麻烦，由此我们可以推断，其有机结合是成功的、可操作的。

关于承诺何时生效的问题，我们非常赞同一位德国著名法学家的下述见解:"现在我们必须认识到,关于承诺究竟应在发信的时刻还是只能在收信的时刻生效的探讨,在当代社会已经越来越没有什么意思了。因为在当代信息传播技术的条件下,比如在广泛使用传真技术(还应加上电子技术——引用者注)的情况下,即使发信人和收信人各自的住所相距遥远,发信和收信的行为也可以同时发生。"

3.4 逾期承诺
Late Acceptance

传统的法律原则主张,承诺逾期送达要约人则无效。在此问题上,《合同通则》第2.9条继承了《销售合同公约》第21条的灵活规定,旨在促成更多的国际商事交易,其具体规定如下:

(1)逾期承诺仍应具有承诺的效力,如果要约人毫不延迟地告知受要约人该承诺具有效力或就该承诺的效力发出通知。(A late acceptance is nevertheless effective as an acceptance if without undue delay the offeror so informs the offeree or gives notice to that effect)

(2)如果载有逾期承诺的信件或其他书面文件表明,它是在传递正常即能及时被送达要约人的情况下发出的,则该逾期承诺仍具有承诺的效力,除非要约人毫不延迟地通知受要约人:此要约已经失效。(If a letter or other writing containing a late acceptance shows that it has been sent in such circumstances that if its transmission had been normal it would have reached the offeror in due time, the late acceptance is effective as an acceptance unless, without undue delay, the offeror informs the offeree that it considers the offer as having lapsed)

第一款针对的是受要约人自己造成的逾期承诺,例如他发出承诺时,按正常传递速度计算,在到达要约人时已超过承诺的有效期限。在此情形下,如果要约人有意成立该合同,他毫不延迟地告知对方该承诺有效,则该逾期承诺即为有效,合同于逾期承诺送达要约人时成立。

第二款则针对不可预料的传递延迟导致的逾期承诺,在此情形下,受要约人对能及时送达承诺的信赖应得到保护,其结果是逾期承诺视为有效,除非要约人毫不延迟地拒绝。

综上所述,逾期承诺是否具有承诺的效力,取决于要约人的反应:在受要约人自己造成的逾期承诺的情形下,要约人马上表态认可承诺,该逾期承诺即为有效;在传递延迟导致逾期承诺的情形下,该逾期承诺本应有效,但如果要约人立即表态反对,合同即不成立。在碰到上述情形时,我国外经贸企业外销员应当依据我方成交意图、国际市场行情变化等因素,按部就班地及时作出反应,切不可凭据"想当然"行事,以致贻误商机。

3.5 承诺的撤回
Withdrawal of an Acceptance

撤回承诺,是受要约人阻止承诺发生效力的一种意思表示,发生在商品行情等因素起变化之时。

由于《合同通则》和《销售合同公约》基本上采取承诺到达生效的原则,故其承诺是可以撤回的。例如受要约人以信件、电报等方式发出承诺通知,从发出至到达对方有时间距离,当他意欲撤回承诺时,可用更快的通讯方式阻止承诺发生效力。

《合同通则》第 2.10 条和《销售合同公约》第 22 条同样规定如下:"承诺可以撤回,只要撤回通知在承诺本应生效之前或同时送达要约人。(An acceptance may be withdrawn if the withdrawal reaches the offeror before or at the same time as the acceptance would have become effective.)"德国等一些国家的法律也持此原则。

然而,在人类社会进入 21 世纪、电子合同的使用不断扩大的今天,适用于上述关于撤回承诺的规定的情形将日益减少。因为在成立电子合同的情形下,发出承诺与承诺的到达几乎是同一时刻,前后相差不过一二秒钟,故撤回承诺变为不可能。

英美法系对承诺采取"投邮生效"规则,故发出承诺后便不得再撤回。

3.6 中国合同法关于承诺的规定
Regulations on Acceptance in Chinese Contract Law

关于承诺的定义、承诺的生效、承诺的撤回、承诺对要约的变更等,中国合同法均采取了与《联合国国际货物销售合同公约》、《国际商事合同通则》相一致的规定,仅个别规定有细小的差异。比如,中国《合同法》第21条把承诺定义为:"承诺是受要约人同意要约的意思表示。(An acceptance is the expression of an intention of the offeree indicating assent to the offer.)"此处仅仅就中国合同法关于承诺的有特色的规定,作一些阐述和分析。

3.6.1 关于承诺对要约的实质性变更 Substantial modification of an offer

标题所述问题,《联合国国际货物销售合同公约》专门界定了有关货物价格等 6 个方面的事宜为实质性变更,而《国际商事合同通则》和《欧洲合同法原则》均无此方面的界定。大概是因为合同的种类比较多,难于作出统一规定。

中国《合同法》第 30 条就承诺对要约的变更等问题作出规定如下:"承诺的内容应当与要约的内容一致。受要约人对要约的内容作出实质性变更的,为新要约。有关合同标的、数量、质量、价款或者报酬、履行期限、履行地点和方式、违约责任和解决争议方法等的变更,是对要约内容的实质性变更。(The contents of an acceptance shall comply with those of the offer. If the offeree substantially modifies the contents of the offer, it shall constitute a new offer. The modification relating to the subject matter, quality, quantity, price or remuneration, time or place or method of performance, liabilities for breach of contract and method of dispute resolution, etc. shall constitute the substantial modification of an offer.)"

以上规定将8个方面的条款界定为实质性变更，而就除此之外其他条款作出的变更，一般视为非实质性变更。当然，此话也不能说得过于绝对，因为上述条文在列举了8个方面的条款之后，尚有一个"等"字，这就意味着8个方面的条款并未穷尽全部实质性变更条款。在各种各样的合同项下，有可能存在视8个方面的条款之外的某一方面条款为实质性变更条款的情形。假设一个电子计算机监控系统交钥匙工程，有关设备的安装条款涉及该工程非常重要的环节，但它不在上述8个方面实质性变更条款之列，有鉴于该条款的重要性，法院或仲裁庭在审理该工程合同是否成立的纠纷时，可认定设备的安装条款为实质性变更条款。

3.6.2 关于合同成立的地点 Place of the establishment of contracts

合同成立的地点，是一个非常重要的问题。它往往牵涉适用法律问题，因为在国际民商事合同项下，在合同未规定适用法律的某些情况下，有可能推定为适用合同缔结的法律。而适用不同国家的法律，其法律后果往往不同，有时甚至大相径庭，对当事人的利益有直接影响。故各国法律都几乎无例外地注重合同成立的地点事宜。

在中国《合同法》中，有两个条文专门就合同成立的地点作出规定如下："第34条承诺生效的地点为合同成立的地点。采用数据电文形式订立合同的，收件人的主营业地为合同成立的地点；没有主营业地的，其经常居住地为合同成立的地点。当事人另有约定的，按照其约定。(The place of effectiveness of an acceptance shall be the place of the establishment of the contract. If the contract is concluded in the form of data-telex, the main business place of the recipient shall be the place of establishment. If the recipient does not have a main business place, its habitual residence shall be considered to be the place of establishment. Where the parties agree otherwise, such agreement shall apply.)第35条当事人采用合同书形式订立合同的，双方当事人签字或者盖章的地点为合同成立的地点。(Where the parties conclude a contract in written form, the place where both parties sign or affix their seals on the contract shall be the place of establishment.)"

中国《合同法》在以上几个方面作出了明确、具体的规定，无疑有助于解决合同成立的地点问题。

3.6.3 数据电文承诺的生效 Effectiveness of the acceptance in the form of data-telex

中国《合同法》在第 26 条第 2 款就数据电文承诺的生效问题规定如下:"采用数据电文形式订立合同的,承诺到达的时间适用第 16 条第 2 款的规定。(Where a contract is concluded in the form of data-telex, the time of arrival of an acceptance shall be governed by the provisions of Paragraph 2, Article 16 of this Law.)"

以上所言第 16 条第 2 款的规定,在前面本章第二节"要约"的末尾已经引用并评论过,此处不重复。简单说来,这里承诺到达的时间,是该数据电文进入收件人指定特定系统的时间,未指定特定系统的,是该数据电文进入收件人的任何系统的首次时间。

随着时代的前进和科学技术的发展,电子合同将更大规模地进入各个领域,更加广泛地进入各类公司企业和千家万户,以上关于数据电文几个方面的规定,其实用性、可操作性将日益凸现。然而,以前瞻性的眼光来看,现有的条文还嫌过少和不细致。在修订中国合同法时,应考虑增补几条比较具体细致的条文,以全面规范电子合同的各种问题。

第四节 合同的主要条款
Section 4　Major Clauses of Contracts

所谓合同的条款(clauses of contract),又可称为合同的内容(content),是指双方(或多方)当事人依照程序,通过磋商达到意思表示一致,从而成立合同的具体内容。合同的条款固定了双方(或多方)当事人的权利义务关系,成为法律关系意义上的合同的内容。也有将合同的条款与合同的内容等同使用的,例如《国际商事合同通则》,其第 5 章标题即为"合同的内容(content)",对合同当事人的权利义务作出比较全面的规定,实际上讲的就是合同的条款。

根据西方国家"契约自由"和"当事人意思自治"原则,合同法属私法范畴,所以对合同的条款一般无强制性规范,可由合同双方(或多方)当事人自行协商订立。

中国学者对合同条款有各种看法。崔建远教授认为,合同的条款可分为三大种类:提示性的合同条款,合同的主要条款(指合同必须具备的条款,欠缺它,合同就不成立,例如当事人条款和标的条款),合同的普通条款(指合同主要条款之外的条款)。

以下按中国合同法的用语,先阐述合同的一般条款,然后再探讨合同的格式条款。

4.1 合同的一般条款
General Clauses of Contracts

中国《合同法》在第 12 条就合同的内容与条款规定如下:

"合同的内容由当事人约定,一般包括以下条款:(1)当事人的名称或者姓名和住所;(2)标的;(3)数量;(4)质量;(5)价款或者报酬;(6)履行期限、地点和方式;(7)违约责任;(8)解决争议的方法。当事人可以参照各类合同的示范文本订立合同。(The contents of a contract shall be agreed upon by the parties, and shall generally contain the following clauses: (1) titles or names and domiciles of the parties; (2) subject matter; (3) quantity; (4) quality; (5) price or remuneration; (6) time limit, place and method of performance; (7) liability for breach of contract; and (8) method to settle disputes. The parties may conclude a contract by reference to a model text of each kind of contract.)"

合同法的上述规定,我们权且把上述合同条款称为一般条款。西方国家的法律一般不专门就合同条款作出特别规范,但也有些国家对"默示条款"或"默示条件"作出规定。

英国《货物买卖法》(1979 年版)第 13—15 条对卖方的品质担保义务作出规定,要求卖方所出售的货物须符合下列默示条件:与说明和样品相符,具有商销品质(merchantability),须适合某种特定的用途,等等。根据英国法,只要买卖双方在合同中没有相反的规定,这些默示条件就依法适用于他们之间的买卖合同。卖方须严格遵守这些默示条件,违反这些默示条件会引起严重的后果,甚至导致买方拒收货物。

美国《统一商法典》第 2-313 至 2-317 条对卖方的品质担保义务作了规定,分为明示担保和默示担保:(1)明示担保(express warranty)。指卖方明白地、直接地对其货物所作出的担保,明示担保是合同的组成部分。(2)默示担保(implied warranty)。默示担保不是由双方当事人在合同中规定的条款,而是法律要求卖方应当达到的最低标准。如果买卖双方在合同中没有作出相反的规定,则这些法律上的规定将适用于他们之间的买卖合同。根据《统一商法典》,卖方有两项默示担保:适销性的默示担保和关于货物适合特定用途(fitness for particular purpose)的默示担保。

《国际商事合同通则》重申了被许多国家接受的原则,其第 5.1 条规定:"各方当事人的合同义务可以是明示的,也可以是默示的。(The contractual obligations of the parties may be express or implied.)"在国际商事交易中,合同各方当事人的义务不一定只限于合同条款所明确规定的义务,其他义务可以是默示的。默示义务(implied obligations)来源于合同的性质和目的,各方当事人之间确立的习惯做法和惯例,诚实信用和公平交易原则以及合理性(第5.2条)。例如,A出租一套电子计算机网络给B,合同未规定A对B所承担的可能的义务,诸如至少应提供关于计算机网络操作的基本信息。然而显而易见,高精尖产品的供应商必须向使用者提供最起码的信息,这是实现该合同目的所必需的,应视为是一种默示义务。

此外,《合同通则》还规定了获取特定结果的义务与尽最大努力的义务,当事人之间的合作义务,等等。

4.2 合同的格式条款
Standard Clauses of Contracts

此处所言格式条款(标准条款),可说是带点贬义,它由一方当事人单独制定,订立合同时未与对方协商。而另外有一种标准合同(model contract,也叫示范合同、格式合同),其条款是由某一国际组织或某一企业根据长期贸易实践制定的,由各国当事人自由采纳,可以协商更改。此种标准合同将合同的条款标准化、格式化,有利于节省谈判的时间和费用,同时又允许双方当事人协商修改,受到各国当事人的欢迎。例如国际商会1997年定稿的《国际货物销售示范合同》(the ICC Model International Sale Contract),尽管它仍有偏袒卖方利益之痕迹,但总体上还是比较全面的。

《国际商事合同通则》对第2.19条第(2)款标准条款(standard terms)定义如下:"标准条款是指一方为通常和重复使用的目的而预先准备的条款,并在实际使用时未与对方谈判。(Standard terms are provisions which are prepared in advance for general and repeated use by one party and which are actually used without negotiation with the other party.)"

我国《合同法》第39条第2款对格式条款下了类似的定义:"格式条款是当事人为了重复使用预先拟定,并在订立合同时未与对方协商的条款。(Standard terms are clauses that are prepared in advance for general and repeated use by one party, and which are not negotiated with the other party when the contract in concluded.)"

上述格式条款(标准条款)在各国现实生活中使用相当广泛,除国际贸易中使用外,消费零售业和服务业也采用,涉及面比较广。有鉴于此,许多国家立法以及国际合同法对此加以规范,大多数倾向于允许当事人双方(或多方)对条款进行协商,通过协商进行修改、补充,同时又对显失公平的条款和做法予以制裁或补正。

4.2.1 《国际商事合同通则》的规定 Regulations in the UNIDROIT principles

《合同通则》对标准条款问题非常重视,在第二章专门以4个条文作出规范。

(1)使用标准条款应适用订立合同的一般原则。《合同通则》第2.19条(1)款规定:"一方或双方当事人使用标准条款订立合同,适用订立合同的一般规则,但应受到本章第2.20条至2.22条的约束。(Where one party or both parties use standard terms in concluding a contract, the general rules on formation apply, subject to Articles 2.20 –2.22.)"此处所谓适用"一般规则",包括双方达成合意,一方当事人所建议的标准条款只有在对方接受的前提下才能有约束力。因此,合同本身所载有的标准条款,通常只有在签署整个合同后才能生效,至少是签约方必须在复制的条款下面而不是在其背面签字。例如:A 通常在其自己的标准条款基础上与用户订立合同,这些条款已印成一份单独的文件。当 A 向新用户 B 发出要约时,A 没有表示要遵照标准条款。B 承诺了该要约。这些标准条款不能在合同中采用,除非 A 能证明 B 知道或应该知道 A 只打算以其标准条款为基础订立合同,原因是例如这些条款在以前的交易中已被惯常地采用。

(2)标准条款中对方不能合理预见的意外条款(Surprising terms)无效。《合同通则》第2.20条规定,如果标准条款中某个条款是对方不能合理预见的,则该条款无效,除非对方明确地表示接受。在确定某条款是否属于这种性质时,应考虑到该条款的内容、语言和表达方式。(No term contained in standard terms which is of such a character that the other party could not reasonably have expected it, is effective unless it has been expressly accepted by that party. In determining whether a term is of such a character regard is to be had to its content, language and presentation.)

制定上述规定的主要理由在于,要防止使用标准条款的一方当事人过分利用其有利地位,以叵测的意图将某些条款强加于对方当事人。而对这些条款,如果对方当事人了解透彻的话,根本不可能接受。例如:A 是在汉堡经营商品的一位经销商。A 在其与用户的合同中使用了标准条款,其中有一条规定"汉堡友好仲裁"。在当地商业界,这一条款通常被理解为:可能发生的争议应提交一种特别仲裁,该仲裁按源于当地的特定程序规则进行。在与外国用户订立合同时,该条款没有效力。因为标准条款作为一个整体虽被接受,但不能理所当然地指望外国用户能够理解其中的准确含义,此时,不论该条款是否已翻译成该用户的本国语言。

(3)非标准条款优先。《合同通则》第2.21条规定:"若标准条款与非标准条款发生冲突，以非标准条款为准。(In case of conflict between a standard term and a term which is not a standard term the latter prevails.)"

标准条款是由一方当事人或第三人事先规定好的，并且是在未经双方当事人讨论其内容的情况下适用于某一合同。所以，一旦当事人双方就合同中的某些特别条款进行了专门协商并达成一致，则该非标准条款的效力优先于与之相冲突的标准条款，因为它更能反映双方当事人在具体交易中的意图。

(4)"最后指定(the last shot)"原则。《合同通则》第2.22条以"格式合同之争(battle of forms)"为题，规定如下："在双方当事人均使用各自的标准条款的情况下，如果双方对除标准条款以外的条款达成一致，则合同应根据已达成一致的条款以及在实质内容上相同的标准条款订立，除非一方当事人已事先明确表示，或者事后毫不延迟地通知另一方当事人，其不受此种合同的约束。"

上述规定是针对国际商事交易实践中的具体情况确立的。例如，双方当事人相互通过交换印制好的格式合同成交，各自的格式合同都有自己的标准条款，其内容有不一致的地方，应当如何处理？根据《合同通则》的上述规定，采取"最后指定"原则(又译为"最后一枪"原则)，即：双方当事人已就标准条款达成一致时，合同应根据已达成一致的条款以及两份标准条款中实质内容相同的条款订立。如果在事后，当事人才发现他们各自的标准条款之间存在冲突，没有理由允许当事人质疑合同的存在。在当事人已经开始履行合同的情况下，必须适用最后发出或引用的条款。

4.2.2《欧洲合同法原则》的规定 Regulations in the Principles of European Contract Law

《欧洲合同法原则》关于标准条款(此处称为"一般条款"、"未经个别商议的条款")的规定，与《国际商事合同通则》是一脉相承的，但其用语有些出入。

(1)第2:104条以"未经个别商议的条款(terms not individually negotiated)"为题，规定如下："1)未经个别商议的合同条款，只有当使用此类条款的一方当事人在合同达成之前或在达成合同之时，已采取了合理的步骤提醒了对方当事人的注意，始得被用来对抗不知存有此类条款的一方当事人。(Contract terms which have not been individually negotiated may be invoked against a party who did not know of them only if the party invoking them took reasonable steps to bring them to the other party's attention before or when the contract was concluded.)2)在一份合同文本中仅仅提及参照此类条款，该条款并非合理地提醒了对方的注意，即使对方签署了该文本。

(Terms are not brought appropriately to a party's attention by a mere reference to them in a contract document, even if that party signs the document.)"

（2）第 2:209 条以"相互冲突的一般条款（conflicting general conditions）"为题，规定如下："1)如果在要约与承诺中，除关于相互冲突的合同一般条款外，当事人已形成合意，合同仍然成立。只要一般条款实质上是一致的，它们便构成合同的组成部分。2)但如一方当事人有下列情形，合同不成立：事先已明确地且并非采用一般条款的形式表示其不欲基于第1款而受一份合同的拘束；或不曾不合理地迟延地通知对方当事人，它不欲受此种合同的拘束。3)合同的一般条款，是指为不定数量的特定类型的合同，事先已制作完毕的且在当事人之间未经个别商议的合同条款。"

值得指出的是：1)款强调双方合意即为合同成立，实质上一致的一般条款即构成合同的组成部分。2)款规定了合同不成立的两种情形。3)款就一般条款下定义，指其就是第 2:104 条所言"未经个别商议的条款"。

（3）第 2:210 条以"专业人士的确认书（professional's written confirmation）"为题，对国际商事交易中常用的确认书（confirmation）规定如下："如果专业人士已达成合同，但尚未形成最终的文件，而一方不曾迟延地向对方发出一份书面通知，意在作为合同的一份确认书，但它含有附加的或不同的条款，这些条款将成为合同的构成部分，除非这些条款实质性地变更了合同的条款，或受领方不曾迟延地对此表示反对。"

此条肯定了确认书中的附加条款或不同条款视为合同组成部分的基本原则，同时确定了两种例外情形，其精神与《联合国国际货物销售合同公约》、《国际商事合同通则》完全一致。

4.2.3 中国《合同法》的规定 Regulations in the Contract Law of China

在制定中国《合同法》时，参照国际通行做法是一项重要的原则。事实上，中国合同法关于格式条款（即标准条款）的规定，是参照《国际商事合同通则》制定的。

该法第 39 条确定了应遵循的公平原则和提请注意的义务，具体条文如下：

"采用格式条款订立合同的，提供格式条款的一方应当遵循公平原则确定当事人之间的权利和义务，并采取合理的方式提请对方注意免除或者限制其责任的条款，按照对方的要求，对该条款予以说明。（Where standard terms are adopted in concluding a contract, the party supplying the standard terms shall define the rights and obligations between the parties abiding by the principle of fairness, and shall inform the other party to note the exclusion or restriction of its liabilities in a reasonable way, and shall explain the standard terms upon request by the other party.)"

该法第 40 条规定了主张格式条款无效的几种情形:"格式条款具有本法第五十二条和第五十三条规定情形的,或者提供格式条款一方免除其责任、加重对方责任、排除对方主要权利的,该条款无效。(When standard terms are under the circumstances stipulated in Articles 52 and 53 of this Law,or the party which supplies the standard terms exempts itself from its liabilities, increases the liabilities of the other party, and deprives the material rights of the other party, the terms shall be invalid.)本条所言本法第 52 条规定的情形,包括下列五种:

(1)一方以欺诈、胁迫的手段订立合同,损害国家利益;(2)恶意串通,损害国家、集体或者第三人利益;(3)以合法形式掩盖非法目的;(4)损害社会公共利益;(5)违反法律、行政法规的强制性规定。[(1) a contract is concluded through the use of fraud or coercion by one party to damage the interests of the State; (2) malicious collusion is conducted to damage the interests of the State, a collective or a third party; (3) an illegitimate purpose is concealed under the guise of legitimate acts; (4) damaging the public interests; (5) violating the compulsory provisions of laws and administrative regulations]"而第 53 条所包括的,是无效的免责条款的两种情形,即造成对方人身伤害的,以及因故意或者重大过失造成对方财产损失的。

该法第 41 条规定了解释格式条款的三项原则:(1)对格式条款的理解发生争议的,应当按照通常理解予以解释。(2)对格式条款有两种以上解释的,应当作出不利于提供格式条款一方的解释。(3)格式条款和非格式条款不一致的,应当采用非格式条款。

Part 2 Focusing on Words and Phrases

1. Finding Meaning in Context

Words	Meaning in General English	Meaning in Legal English
offer	提议;提供;提出	要约;出价
consideration	考虑;商量;关心;照顾;理由	对价;约因
terms	学期	术语

2. Useful Expressions in Legal English

1) A contract for sale of goods may be made in any manner sufficient to show agreement, including offer and acceptance, and conduct by both parties which recognizes the existence of a contract. (Article 2-204 of UCC)

2) A contract is concluded at the moment when an acceptance of an offer becomes effective in accordance with the provisions of this Convention. (art 23 of the CISG)

3) A civil juristic act shall meet the following requirements: (1) the actor has relevant capacity for civil conduct; (2) the intention expressed is genuine; and (3) the act does not violate the law or the public interest. (Article 55 of the General Principles of Civil Law of the PRC)

Part 3 Evaluating Your Achievements

 Vocabulary Log

a valid contract	有效合同
offeror	要约人
offeree	受要约人
counteroffer	反要约
acceptance	承诺
legality	合法性
capacity to contract	缔约能力
genuineness of assent	同意的真实性
form	形式
withdrawal	撤销
revocation	撤回
parties	当事人
subject matter	标的
price and remuneration	价格和报酬
methods to settle dispute	争端解决方法
standard clauses	格式条款

 Check Your Progress

1. Fill in the Blanks

1) The CISG governs only _____ of the contract of sale and _____ of the seller and the buyer arising from such a contract.

2) The article 2.2 of Principles of International Commercial Contracts stipulates: A proposal for concluding a contract constitutes _____ if it is sufficiently definite and indicates the intention of the offeror to be bound in case of acceptance.

3) _____ is an expression of an intent to invite other parties to make offers thereto.

4) An acceptance is the expression of an intention of the offeree indicating _____ to the offer.

5) The contents of an acceptance shall comply with those of the offer. If

the offeree substantially modifies the contents of the offer, it shall constitute _____.

2. Legal Terminology

1) Offer and acceptance
2) The mirror image rule
3) capacity to contract
4) legality
5) genuineness of assent

3. Sentence Translation

1) Where standard terms are adopted in concluding a contract, the party supplying the standard terms shall define the rights and obligations between the parties abiding by the principle of fairness, and shall inform the other party to note the exclusion or restriction of its liabilities in a reasonable way, and shall explain the standard terms upon request by the other party.
2) The modification relating to the subject matter, quality, quantity, price or remuneration, time or place or method of performance, liabilities for breach of contract and method of dispute resolution, etc. shall constitute the substantial modification of an offer.
3) Standard terms are clauses that are prepared in advance for general and repeated use by one party, and which are not negotiated with the other party when the contract in concluded.
4) A contract concluded through the use of fraud or coercion by one party to damage the interests of the State shall be invalid.
5) In case of conflict between a standard term and a term which is not a standard term the latter prevails.

自我评价 Self-Assessment Log

In this Chapter, you worked through these activities. How did each of them help you become a better learner? Check A lot, A little, or Not at all.

	A lot	A little	Not at all
I learned the essential requisites of a valid contract.	❏	❏	❏
I knew what offer and acceptance are.	❏	❏	❏
I comprehend the major clauses of a contract.	❏	❏	❏
I searched and read relevant materials online or/and in library.	❏	❏	❏

(Add something) _____

第二部分
PART II

国际商务合同的法律关系确立

LEGAL RELATIONSHIP IN INTERNATIONAL BUSINESS CONTRACTS

Chapter 3

第三章 合同的解释原则
Contract Interpretation

In determining whether a valid international business contract has been made, in interpreting its terms, in implying the omitted terms and clarifying the ambiguous contract terms, and in ascertaining whether the contract has been performed as agreed, courts throughout the world look at the contract clauses, usages and practice of the parties, as well as the rules and principles of the contract for interpretation.

 Learning Objectives

In this chapter, students will learn how to:
◎ define general principles of international business contracts interpretation;
◎ classify means of contract interpretation;
◎ understand the significance of contract interpretation;
◎ compare different interpretation principles and practices in civil law and common law system.

 Questions to Consider

1) What are the main features of international business contracts interpretation?
2) What are the distinctive interpretation principles in international business contracts?
3) How do you perceive the significance of contract interpretation?

Part 1 Focusing on Legal Knowledge

第一节 一般原则
Section 1 General Principles

1.1 合同解释的必要性
Necessity of Contract Interpretation

合同解释(contracts interpretation),特指因合同有关条款(terms/clauses)不明确,或虽然明确但却因其他种种原因而使双方当事人在对条款的理解上发生争议,而由法院通过审查,对这些条款的确切含义所进行的认定。合同的解释源于合同纠纷(conflict)。如果合同当事人对合同理解无歧义,自不用解释;当事人对合同内容理解不一致时,为明确合同内容,分清彼此的权利(rights)和义务(obligations),才会有合同解释。狭义上,合同解释只涉及相关条款的内容;广义上,合同解释还包括法院对合同条款缺漏的填补(imply)和对合同性质的确定。

合同之所以需要解释,是因为语言文字有多义性。另外,当事人法律知识欠缺,也往往造成合同中的用词不当。还有当事人出于不正当目的(undue purposes),故意使用不适当的文字词句,掩盖其真实意思。因此,法院在审理案件时,往往需要先对合同的内容进行解释。在诉讼(litigation)中,当事人双方往往提出各自不同的解释意见,但最终作为判决的事实依据的,是法院对合同的解释。合同解释在很多情况是不可避免的,其必要性主要在于以下几个方面:

1.1.1 合同当事人自身的局限性 Limitation of contracting parties

首先,当事人不是先知,既不可能掌握订立合同(contract formation)的完全信息,也不能预见合同订立后的一切情况,遗漏是难免的;其次,合同当事人不是语言法律专家(expertise),对合同的措辞用语不可能处理得天衣无缝,语词错误是很正常的。

1.1.2 语言本身的局限性和复杂性 Complexity and limitation of language

语言只是一种符号(sign)或象征(symbol),和社会物质生活并没有完全的一一对应关系,很多东西是语言无法涵盖的。语意的表示和特定的语境有关,同一词语,结合不同的环境(context),语意就可能大不一样。另外,很多语词的含义本来就是不确定的。用来订立合同的语词也不例外。因此,合同中的语词歧义或误解也就难以完全避免。

1.1.3 社会生活充满变数 Variability of social life

往往在合同订立后出现很多当事人订立合同时所无法预见(unforeseen)的新情况,这也需要对合同的内容重新理解。

1.2 国际商务合同解释的含义与类型
Definition and Categories of International Business Contracts Interpretation

1.2.1 国际商务合同解释的含义 Definition of international business contracts interpretation

"合同解释,是确定当事人双方的共同意思(mutual minds),是指对合同及其相关资料的含义所作的分析和说明。"就解释主体(subject)而言,合同解释有广义和狭义之分,前者中的主体不仅包括法院(court)、仲裁机关(arbitrator),还包括当事人本身以及相关的其他人,比如诉讼代理人(litigation representative)、证人(witness)、鉴定人员(expert witness)和公证人员(notary public)等等,后者仅指法院和仲裁机关。就解释客体(object),即合同解释工作指向的对象而言,亦有广义和狭义之分,广义解释(broad interpretation)包括确定合同是否成立、确定合同的性质和明确合同条款的含义等等,狭义解释(restricted interpretation)仅指明确合同条款的含义和内容。只有法院和仲裁机关对合同条款含义和内容进行确定,才是有权解释,是国际商务合同在进入司法和仲裁程序后所直面的最基本和最重要的过程。因此,国际商务合同解释就是在国际贸易语境下,受理合同纠纷的各法院及仲裁机关对合同及其相关资料的含义作出的具有法律拘束力的分析和说明。

1.2.2 国际商务合同解释的类型 Categories of international business contracts interpretation

国际商务合同解释与其上位概念合同解释在基本类型(basic category)的划分上是相同的,即都可划分为两大类,阐明的合同解释(clarified interpretation)与补充的合同解释(complementary interpretation)。

在大陆法(civil law system)上,阐明的合同解释亦称确定解释、意义发现解释,主要是对模糊或有争议的文义(literal meaning)的阐明,被学者们认为是本来意义上的合同解释。但是由于各种主观或客观原因,特别是在国际贸易的复杂环境中,缔约人(contracting parties)在订立合同时经常会给合同留下许多漏洞,这时就需要有权解释者在国际贸易中由法官和仲裁员对漏洞予以填补(imply)。在这个区分前提下，我们可以把上述两类合同解释作如下定义：阐明的合同解释是指在国际商务合同当事人的意思不够明确时，借解释方法(interpretation approaches)使合同文义趋于明确，从而确认合同类型之所在或确定合同当事人所意定的合同内容。

在国际商务合同解释中，阐明的合同解释是法院或仲裁机关通过解释相关的合同文字来解决有关争议的。然而，争议有时候是因为合同对之后出现的某些情况没有作出决定而产生的。当事人没有实现"对所有的可能情形有充分(sufficient)约定的合同"这个不现实的目标。这个概念指的是一个假想的范例合同(sample contract)，其当事人被假定为有能力基于合理的成本而明确地分配未来发生各种可能清醒的风险。在国际贸易交往中，造成国际商务合同漏洞的原因很多，包括当事人自身的缔约素质不高、认为争议发生的可能性不大、当事人不愿提及某个问题、匆忙或者粗心、争议的发生无法预见等。事实上，合同漏洞的补充常被法官或仲裁员适用任意性规范予以解决。特别是国际商务合同，其类型特征十分明显，很容易就被归入特定的合同类型中，然后再引用合同准据法(governing law)上的一般任意性规范和有名合同中的特别任意性规范加以补充。比如，《联合国国际货物销售合同公约》(CISG)第五十六条规定的"如果价格是按货物的重量规定的，如有疑问，应按净重确定"和《国际商事合同规则》(PICC)规定的"如果一项金钱债务未明确规定某一具体货币，则付款应以付款地的货币进行支付"，都是任意性规范(arbitrary rules)对合同漏洞的补充。不可否认的是，任意性法律规范在判案过程中确实起着补充合同漏洞的作用，这一点与补充的合同解释极为类似。在瑞士法上，任意性法律规范或称补充性法律规范是与依抽象规则补充合同、法官自己制定规则补充合同相并列的合同补充解释方式。

补充的合同解释是指国际商务合同当事人于缔约时，由于预见不足、表达能力有限或欠缺法律知识等原因，致使其意思表示留有漏洞，而由法官或仲裁员借解释方法对该漏洞予以填补。补充的合同解释应该主要受到合同自体的约束。所谓的合同自体，不是仅指合同本身的条文，还涉及合同的外在环境，包括具体的商业环境和抽象的价值环境等，它们共同形成了以合同为中心的内外在体系。而在国际贸易争议中，法官和仲裁员正是基于合同文本(contract terms)和环境等诸多因素而进行补充合同解释的。他们所解释的是当事人所创设的合同规范整体，所补充的是个别的合同条款。所以，补充的合同解释仍然具有合同解释的性质。

《国际商事合同通则》规定了国际商务合同中补充的合同解释的适用(application)和规则。"如果合同当事人各方未能就一项确定其权利和义务的重要条款达成一致(agreement),应补充一项适合于该情况的条款。在决定何为适当条款时,除其他因素外,应考虑以下情况:各方当事人的意图伪合同的性质与目的诚实信用(good faith)和公平交易(fair dealing)原则合理性。"在适用原则上,补充的合同解释与阐明的合同解释相比,显然更倾向于客观主义(objectivism),因此应该采用"最少介入原则(principle of minimum intervention)",以防止过大地变更合同内容而侵害当事人的意思自治。在适用规则上,主要应该依靠整体解释(integration interpretation)规则、习惯(custom)和惯例(practice)解释规则对合同进行补充解释,并辅之以目的解释规则和诚信解释规则。

1.3 合同解释的一般原则
General Principles of Contract Interpretation

1.3.1 当事人意愿优先原则 Priority of the intention of contracting parties

当事人意愿优先,是指合同解释应探求当事人真意(true will),当事人的意愿只要不违反强行法(statute)及公序良俗(public order)即具有法律拘束力(legally binding effects),且这种拘束力不仅针对当事人而言,对法官解释权也确定了边界。因为,合同解释本质上是个性的,这种个性体现为当事人意愿(intention),合同自由原则要求当事人在自由意志下订立的合同受法律保护。

(1)合同目的应依当事人意愿确定。

合同目的(contract purpose)是当事人通过合同所要实现的期望,在当事人意愿中居于核心地位,合同内容的设定均表现了合同目的。因此,合同目的确定有助于对具体合同条款中当事人真意的探求。

(2)合同条款和合同陈述应作不同解释要求。

合同条款是当事人合意(meeting of minds)的结果,所以应依双方共同意图进行解释。确定共同意图并不容易,如果情况表明某种意图存在,法官应肯定其效力。合同陈述(contract presentation)以及在合同中一方的行为由于只是该方意思的表达(expression of intention),因此原则上应依该方当事人意图进行解释,但应以对方知道或不可能不知道其理解为条件(condition)。

(3)合同是双方意思表示一致的决定。

一个合同中如果既有标准条款(standard terms)又有协商条款(negotiable terms),协商条款的效力应优于标准条款,这是尊重当事人自由意志的必然要求。

(4)对合同漏洞的补充应依当事人推定意图(implied intention)优先填补。

1.3.2 文义解释原则 Literal interpretation

文义解释是指依合同所用语言的字面含义进行解释。当事人在合同中的真意或目的要通过一定语言文字予以表达,并使合同内容固定化,所以依文义解释合同是最为常用的解释方法。但由于语言文字的多义性,以及当事人借助语言文字进行表达的能力参差不齐,使语言的表达可能与当事人真意不一致,因此在适用该原则时应注意:

(1) 合同正式文本优先于辅助资料。

在合同订立至履行(performance)完毕过程中,当事人之间可能存在多种与合同有关的交流文件,如电报(telegraph)、信函(letter)、合同草案(memorandum)、通知书(notice)等,所以解释合同原则上应以正式文本为基础,辅助资料只起证明正式文本内容的作用,一般不得以辅助资料否定正式文本的内容。当然,如果有证据表明当事人依共同意愿改变了正式文本的内容,则另当别论。

(2) 对列举事项的解释,非当事人明示排除其他可能时,不得作限制概括规定的理解。

(3) 文义解释必须合乎当事人的缔约目的,否则,不予适用。

各国法律均规定了合同解释不得拘泥于所用语句而有害于当事人真意的探求。

1.3.3 公平合理的原则 Principles of fairness and justice

该原则要求合同解释既要合乎公平,又要合乎事理。具体方法要求表现在:

(1) 解释合同时应综合所有资料予以判断,以尽可能准确地确定当事人真意。

这些情况包括:当事人之间最初接触情况、已确定的习惯性做法、订约后当事人的行为、合同性质(nature of contract)和目的、通常所赋予合同条款或陈述的含义、交易惯例等。

(2) 解释合同时应符合社会经验(social experience)。

社会经验(social experience)是为大多数人所肯定或视为当然的事项,解释合同也必须符合社会经验,凡与社会经验不相符合的判断不能成立。

(3) 解释合同时应依公平合理的要求。

合同条款有两种或两种以上含义时,应取对双方均有利的解释;可作有效(valid)解释,也可作无效(void)解释时,应取有效解释;条款含义不明时,应作不利于条款提出者或合同起草者的解释;有歧义时,应作不利于债权人的解释,但无偿合同例外。

1.3.4 整体解释原则 Principle of integrated interpretation

整体解释是指对合同各个条款应作相互解释,以确定各个条款在整个合同中所具有的正确含义。因为当事人在合同中所运用的条款或表述并非孤立地存在,而是构成整个合同内容的不可分割的组成部分,各个合同条款之间原则上无优劣之分,不论在合同中处于何种位置,对合同都有同样的重要性。因而,不仅单个条款应从整个合同来理解,而且合同条款间应作相互解释。这要求,在两个条款有矛盾时,应尽可能调和它们之间的冲突,使其均为有效,而不是排除其中一个的效力。但该原则的使用也有例外情况:其一,合同中有关缔约目的的表述具有指导作用,与其他合同条款可能具有相关性(connection),也可能不具有相关性。其二,合同条款的冲突不可能调和时,应依专门条款(specific terms)优于一般条款(general terms)、主要条款(primary terms)优于次要条款(secondary term)、使合同有效的条款优于使合同无效的条款原则进行取舍。其三,当事人明确规定的条款的优先性(priority)应予尊重。

1.3.5 依交易惯例及诚实信用原则 Principles of transaction practice and good faith

交易惯例是指某地区或某行业从事交易的惯常做法,这种惯常做法在一个地方,一种行业或一类贸易中已得到经常的遵循,从而使人有理由期望它在该有争议的交易中也将得到遵守。交易惯例与一般习惯不同,交易惯例只在商业交往中才能适用。依交易惯例解释合同应当注意,某惯例是否存在及其内容如果是一个事实问题,应由主张方举证证明,同时还须证明交易对方已经知道或不可能不知道此种惯例。不过根据当事人意思优先的规则,如当事人已排除某惯例的适用,则不能作为解释的依据。

诚实信用原则是指当事人应以善良的、诚实的心理去行使权力和履行义务。诚信原则在合同中,一方面产生当事人的附随义务(collateral obligation),另一方面又是明确和补充合同内容的依据,所以各国法律均将其规定为合同解释的原则。由于诚信原则具有强行法(statute)特征,故法官可依职权适用,而不受当事人特约的影响。

第二节 大陆法系和英美法系比较研究
Section 2 Comparative Study on Legal Systems between the Civil Law and the Common Law

2.1 大陆法系与英美法系合同解释原则
Contract Interpretation Principle in the Civil Law and Common Law Systems

关于合同解释理论，如从风格、类属的区分而言，传统上认为，有大陆法系(civil law system)和英美法系(common law system)之分，且这两大法系在立法(legislation)和学理(jurisprudence)认识上均有分歧，在司法判断上也表现出独特的处理风格。但就其理论的历史演进和发展趋势而讲，则呈现出两个显著的特征：其一，18 世纪至 19 世纪中后期"意思说"(intention)和"表示说"(expression)两军对垒而平分秋色；其二，19 世纪末，20 世纪以后"意思说"和"表示说"则呈相互吸收、相互借鉴和相互融合的互动趋势。

一般而言，大陆法系多采用意思说，其理论认为，合同行为的实质在于当事人的内心意思，合同本身不过是实现当事人意思自治的手段。合同解释的目的仅在于发现或者探求当事人的"真意"。而发现或探求当事人"真意"则应从当事人订立合同时的主观去认定。因此解释契约时，应探究缔约当事人的共同意思，而不拘泥于文字。

同一时期，英美法系国家则采用"表示说"。按英美法学者的观点，合同解释应以维护法律秩序为出发点，当事人的内心意思非他人所能得知的，只有表示出来的意思才能作为他们合同的依据。合同价值的实现，必须依靠社会的承认。因此，确定合同的效力只能以当事人表现于外部的意志为准，进而确保交易的安全。正如英国法学家切希尔和菲富特指出："合意不是一种心理状态，而是一种行为(act)，并且作为一种行为是从行动中演推出来的，因此，判断当事人的合意，不是看他们说什么，而是看他们做什么。"

美国《合同法重述》第 20 条的注释亦认为："法律所要求的不是相互间的同意，而是这种同意的外部表示。"并以此认识为基础确立了合同解释的两大规则：即证言规则（parole evidence rule）和平意规则（plain meaning rule）。美国《统一商法典》第 2-202 条规定："书面文件构成最终意思表示，当事方在确立性备忘录中所同意的条款或当事方所商定的最终协议条款，不得以任何前顾协议（pre-existing agreements）或同时达成的口头协议（oral agreements）加以反驳。"平意规则则规定:对合同文字的解释必须按它通常具有的,普通说话者所理解的平白朴实的意思去理解。如果文字简单明了,就要按文字本身具有的意义去解释,而不得求助于任何外部证据。因此,解释合同不是去探求当事人难以捉摸的内心意思,而应以其所使用的语言文字和行为的一个"合理标准(reasonable standard)"确定合同内容。

"意思说"和"表示说"两军对垒、平分秋色的态势到19世纪后期,特别是20世纪初以后,便发生了较大的变化,"意思说"和"表示说"相互吸收借鉴的趋势已现端倪。当然,英美法系的表示说也受到挑战。突出表现在合同解释的客观标准在得到进一步发展的同时,对当事人意图的探求也日益受到重视。具体体现在两个方面:一是默示条款(implied terms)理论的确立;二是"假定意图(assumption of intention)"理论的勃兴。默示条款理论认为:即使合同中未明确规定的条款,解释者亦可依法加入,以实现情况和正义的要求。"假定意图"理论则主张:解释者应根据变化了的情况去试图发现当事人如果当初设想到这种情况以及大概会具有的意图,然后再假定双方会同意一种公平合理的解决办法,并宣布这种解决办法是什么,进而解决当事人之间的纷争。

"二战"以后,西方发达国家相继进入现代市场经济时期,特别是进入80年代以来,"意思说"和"表示说"在发展过程中呈相互借鉴和吸收的互动融合趋势,以"意思说"为原则,以"表示说"为补充,或以"表示说"为原则,以"意思说"为补充的"折中说"倾向已在1980年《联合国国际货物销售合同公约》得以较充分体现。

2.2 大陆法系的合同解释方法
Contract Interpretation Approaches in Civil Law System

以法国为代表的大陆法系国家,合同解释的最终目的是探求当事人的真实意思,即遵循意思主义原则。因此,合同解释的依据,是指应根据何种资料确定合同事实上的或者应该具有的内容,以避免法官漫无标准地解释,保证当事人真正意图的实现。要求法官在对合同的解释过程中,应当以当事人在签订合同时的真实意思为准,而不能拘泥于合同条款文据的字面含义。合同条款文据的字面含义,如果不能反映当事人的真实意思,就应当通过其他途径,来探究其真实意思。

按照大陆法系各国的立法与司法实践,这些依据一般包括当事人表示之意思、事实上的习惯、任意性规范和诚信原则。从理论上说,合同解释首先是一个事实判断(factual judgment)问题,其主旨在于明确个性的表意行为之法律含义。因此,在合同解释中应强调从事实出发,从实际表意内容出发。我国台湾学者,多认为法律行为解释须依先事实、后推定的顺序进行,即以最富于具体的事实性者为优先。据此,当事人表示之意思,最富事实性,因此为第一次序;事实上的习惯,可推定当事人有依此意思者,为第二次序;任意性规范,为法律上之推定,应为第三次序。

2.2.1 当事人表示之意思 Intention of the contracting parties

史尚宽说:"法律行为之内容,依构成法律行为之意思表示内容而定。明确法律行为(legal acts)之意义,结局为明确所构成法律行为之意思表示之意义。"因此,合同当事人所表示之意思(合同文本),不仅是合同解释的对象(object),同时也是合同解释最基本的依据。然而,合同为双方法律行为(bilateral legal acts),表意人有关意思之表示,在传达于相对人后,相对人之了解常与表意人所预期的效果不完全一致。因此,合同解释上之当事人真意,究竟应以表意人所理解的意思表示为依据,还是以相对人所理解的意思表示为依据,抑或以双方当事人之外的一般人所客观理解的意思表示为依据? 一般而言,在大陆法上,关于这一方面的理论,一直是与意思主义或表示主义的影响分不开的。

2.2.2 事实上的交易习惯 Transaction usage in fact

具体的表意行为往往与当事人的语言环境和推定环境相联系,因而在解释合同时,有时也必须依据习惯来确定其内容。事实上,意思表示所使用之表示方法,如果在当事人间并无反对之合意,则一般依交易习惯上的通行符号。此外,表示方法所使用之符号,虽不依交易习惯而定,但其表示内容在当事人间除有反对之合意外,仍得依交易习惯而定之。习惯在合同解释制度上,既可作为解释依据,亦可作为补充依据。

有的学者还认为,事实上的习惯因解释当事人之意思而成为合同内容,有优于任意性规范的效力,此种意义上的习惯有改废(alteration or termination)任意性规范的效能。习惯之性质既属事实,则可能存在习惯违反强行法规者,不违反强行法规而违反任意法规者,不违反(violate)强行法规及任意法规者,这样三种情形:

(1) 如果习惯违反强行性规范(compulsory rules),则该习惯是否对于表示内容无决定力,或者虽有决定力,却因其赋予合同内容以违法性,故使其无效?

有学者认为,依此种习惯使法律行为无效(void),毕竟不是当事人所欲,从当事人成立合同以追求经济利益之通常目的来看,应解释为当事人并无依据该习惯的意思。

(2) 如果事实上的习惯不违反强行性规范而违反任意性规范,并且该习惯为当事人所知悉,则一般认为习惯应优先于任意性规范,具有解释合同内容之决定力。既然习惯具有事实之性质,生活于一定交易圈内的当事人应当有遵循圈内习惯之信念。可见,与任意性规范相比较,习惯更利于维护私法自治原则,因此其效力当然优先。

2.2.3 任意性规范 Arbitrary rules

近代合同法的意思自治原则意味着,只要合同不违反公序良俗及强行法的规定,当事人得自己决定合同的内容。当事人得想象各种法律未予规定的合同及其内容,并对法律已规定的合同引进各种不同于法律规定的条款。但法律尚需引导当事人的意思,使其走向最符合公平原则、习惯以及经济、社会效益的目标。因此,在坚持私法(civil law)自治的基础上,现代民法中的法律行为制度需要解决两方面的问题:一是须确定法律行为不得逾越的合法范围和有效成立的条件;二是建立详尽的法律推定规范体系,以弥补当事人具体意思表示不明确或不完整的漏洞,尽量使社会生活中每一次具体表意行为均具有确定而完整的法律意义。

任意性规范具有两方面的具体功能。首先,如果当事人知悉任意性规范的存在,却既未订立异于该规范的条款,也未订立同一内容的条款,则可认为当事人将合同内容的决定委托于任意性规范。在此意义上,任意性规范有省却当事人劳力之功效,并有助于私法自治原则的推行。其次,如果当事人并不知有任意性规范的存在,在订立合同时,根本未涉及该规定事项,则任意性规范借法律之力加诸合同内容,则有防止当事人间纠纷之发生,甚至挽救合同无效的功能。此时,任意性规范有助于私法自治之达成。

2.3 英美法系的合同解释方法
Contract Interpretation Approaches in Common Law System

与大陆法系不同,英美法系在合同解释上奉行表示主义(或称为客观标准主义)。对合同解释,认为应当以合同当事人通过合同本身所客观表现出来的意思为准,应严格按照合同条款文据所表达的字面含义为标准,而无必要去探究当事人订立合同时的真实意图。他们的解释方法和规则有:

(1) 文义解释(literal interpretation)

文义解释为英美法系最主要的合同解释方法。因此,法官解释合同时,虽然也以合同的文本为依据,但他们都是按照普通词义规则得出文词之意义。至于此种意义是否反映当事人真意,在所不问。

(2) 整体解释(integrated interpretation)

整体解释原则的基本规定与大陆法系差异不大。

(3) 有效含义有限规则(restricted rules for effective meanings)

这是英美法系特有的。如合同某一条款包含两种含义,依其中一种应当认定为有效(valid),依另一种含义认定无效(void),则应当依据使合同有效的含义进行解释。

（4）版本优先规则（priority of versions）

同一份合同，铅印本（type version）与打印本（printed version）内容发生冲突时，以打印本为准；打印本与手写本内容发生冲突时，以手写本（manuscript version）为准。如果同一合同，部分内容是打印，部分内容是手写，两者冲突，则以手写记载为准。

（5）数字文字优先规则（priority of figures）

同一份合同中，数字兼用英文数字与阿拉伯数字（Arabic numerals）书写的，二者相冲突时，以英文数字为准。

（6）有利于无过错一方当事人的规则（in favor of innocent party）

如一方当事人应当对合同条款不明确而负责，在解释合同时，则不应使无过错（innocent party）的对方当事人因条款不明确而受损害，只能作出有利于无过错方的解释。

（7）专门条款限制规则（restricted rules for special terms）

如果在合同一般条款后还有专门条款（按某一特定合同的一方或双方当事人一切写入其中），那么，在解释合同时，应使一般条款的含义受到专门条款的限制。随着社会、经济的发展，英美法系传统上奉行的严格文义解释原则，已经受到怀疑或者说挑战。

美国《合同法重述》第201条在"Whose Meaning Prevails"题下规定：1）如果各当事人赋予允诺、协议或其条款以相同意义，则按照该种意义进行阐释。2）如果各当事人赋予允诺、协议或其条款以不同意义，则按照其中一方所理解的意义进行阐释。只要在缔约当时，该当事人不知他方当事人有不同理解之意义，并且他方当事人知悉该当事人所理解的意义；或者该当事人没有理由知悉他方当事人所理解的意义，而他方当事人有理由知悉该当事人所理解的意义。3）除本条规定外，当事人任何一方并不受他方当事人所理解之意义的约束，即使可能导致合意不成立之结果。这种规定，就明显地受了客观主义理论的影响。

第三节　国际公约与国际惯例

Section 3　International Conventions and Usages

3.1 国际商务合同解释的特点
Features of International Business Contracts Interpretation

把合同解释放到国际贸易的语境下去考察，并不是简单的概念位移。

与一般合同解释相比,国际商务合同解释具备着比较显著的特点。这些特点是以国际商务合同的两大特点为基础的,即"跨国性"和"商业性"。

3.1.1 当事人择法的优先适用 Priority of contracting parties' choice of governing law

对国际商务合同关系的调整是国际私法的一个重要组成部分,法院或仲裁机关在进行国际商务合同解释的时候,其最终要调整的对象是国际的(international)或跨国的(cross-national)合同关系。与国内民商法中的合同关系相比较,国际商务合同关系就一个国家而言可称之为"涉外合同关系",其最重要的特点在于它的跨国性,即合同与两个或两个以上国家存在着某种联系。国际商务合同的跨国性,就决定了它适用法律的原则必然与一般合同解释存在较大的差异。这种差异突出地表现在合同当事人可以自己选择适用的法律。尽管国际私法中所涉及的一些与人身有关的法律关系也具有鲜明的跨国性特点,如婚姻(marriage)、收养(adoption)和继承(heritage)等,但是当事人并不能完全自主地选择所适用的法律。而在国内贸易合同中,由于不涉及跨国因素,其适用只受国内(domestic)商事法律规范的调整,因此它所适用的法律是统一并且确定的,合同当事人也无法选择适用的法律。但是,在国际商务合同中,合同当事人却可以自己选择适用的法律。这在很多法律文件中都有体现,《关于合同义务法律适用的公约》中就承认合同当事人明示或默示选择适用于其合同关系的法律,是一项基本原则。《国际商事合同通则》在"前言通则的目的"中规定:"在当事人一致同意其合同受通则管辖时,适用通则。"《国际贸易术语解释通则》的"引言"中明确指出:"今后商人们愿意使用本通则应在他们的合同中明确规定受《1990 年通则》的管辖。"关于国际商事仲裁的国际公约和示范规则也均确认,当事人可以自由为自己选择适用于合同的法律。例如《华盛顿公约》第 42 条规定:"仲裁庭应当依据当事人可能约定的法律规则决定争议。"《国际商会仲裁规则》第 17.1 条规定:"当事人得自由约定仲裁庭处理案件实体问题所应适用的法律规则。"

从中可以看出,当事人的合意在国际商务合同解释上,可以说是具有分水岭的意义。具体说来,在国际商务合同解释的法律适用上,当事人可以合意选择所适用的法律,合同解释根据当事人选择的法律进行解释,当事人没有选择或选择不明确的时候,法院或仲裁机构依据合同准据法为其选择适用的法律。

由国际商务合同的"跨国性"特点可以得出国际商务合同解释不同于一般合同解释的最鲜明的特点,就是在法律适用上,当事人的选择优于解释者的选择。

3.1.2 以国际"商人法"及商事环境为依据 Based on Merchant Law and business environment

国际商务合同的另一个特点是它的"商业性",这说明了国际商务合同的当事人是"商人(merchant)",那么国际商务合同解释另一个有异于一般合同解释的特点就是它注重以国际"商人法(merchant law)"为依据,并且以国际商事情境为综合借鉴。

"尽管合同当事方试着通过选择法律的条款来减少对外国法的了解,他仍然必须知道外国法的强制性规则和免责条款。同样地,仲裁员也经常通过选择法律的条款而用国际间的法律或'商人法'来取代内国法的适用。"丹麦的教授曾列出了可用于合同解释的多项"商人法"的来源。

国际公法《关于条约法的维也纳公约》中就有关于适用于国际私法合同的规定。

国际统一私法《海牙规则》曾被美国转化为内国法——《美国海上货物运输法》和《联合国国际货物销售合同公约》都是统一国际私法的成功范例。

合同法的普遍原则能在大多数国家的法律体系中找到的关于合同法普遍原则的最好例子就是"有约必遵守(pacta sunt sevanda),它在普通法系中称为"sanctity of contract"。

国际组织制定的规则合同还可以参照一些国际组织制定出版的规则,这些组织包括联合国、欧洲经济合作与发展组织和国际统一私法协会。

商业惯例最明确的惯例就是国际商会(ICC),制定的《国际贸易术语解释通则》(INCOTERMS)和《跟单信用证统一惯例》(UCC)标准形式合同,国际商会就制定了许多标准形式合同的范本,例如,它制定出版的关于代理经销协议的标准格式和应用于起草"不可抗力(force majeure)"和艰难情事(hardship)条款的参考指南。

仲裁裁决汇编:尽管并不被广泛报道,仲裁书也为合同解释规则的适用提供了重要的来源。

可以看出,国际"商人法"涵盖了从国际公法到私法、商业惯例等许多方面,而国际商事环境作为国际商务合同解释的重要考察方面,也包含着地域商业特点和国际通行标准等一系列综合要素。

3.1.3 对仲裁机关解释合同的青睐 Favors in contract interpretation by arbitration

由于国际商务合同"跨国性"和"商业性"的共同作用,产生了国际商务合同解释的另一个特色,就是解释主体更频繁地表现为国际仲裁机关。

首先，正如英国著名学者施米托夫所说，"商事仲裁的首要原则是当事人意思自治"，这显然与国际商务合同解释中当事人"优先找法"的现象产生了契合。国际商务合同当事人几乎总是来自不同的国家，一方当事人的"本国法院（domestic court）"是另一方当事人的外国法院。因此，合同当事人都倾向选择中立（neutral）审理地的中立机关来解释合同，而不是在某一方当事人的本土。

其次，国际商务合同的当事人作为"商人"，往往出于经济目的的考虑，更喜欢通过仲裁解释合同。这是因为，国际商务合同解释的结果直接决定了当事人的权利义务，仲裁庭将以裁决的形式作出决定。这种裁决是终局的（final），并非像某些法院判决那样可以进行上诉（appeal），而且它在国内和国际上都可以通过法院诉讼直接予以执行。就国际商务合同当事人所关注的国际上的可执行性而言，仲裁裁决与法院判决不同，因为比较互相执行判决的条约而言，适用于仲裁裁决执行的国际条约诸如《纽约公约》在国际上得到的接受程度要大得多。

3.2 国际商务合同解释的原则
Principles of International Business Contracts Interpretation

3.2.1 当事人意思自治的原则 Principles of autonomy of intentions of the contracting parties

在当今飞速发展的国际贸易往来中，贸易自由化（freedom of transaction）原则是国际贸易法的基本原则之一，而国际贸易法的目标就是："调整在国际贸易这个竞技场上国家、法人（legal person）、个人的行为准则，在不违反一国强制法律规定和公共秩序的情况下，广泛承认合同双方的自主权利，即自由确定合同内容，自由选择管辖合同的法律，自由决定将其争议提交仲裁或司法解决的权利。"因此，当事人意思自治作为一项重大原则，突出体现了国际商务合同自由的精神，而国际商务合同语境下的当事人意思自治的原则与合同法的基本原则也是不谋而合。在国际商务合同的订立过程中，除了少数立法和公共政策（public policy）的限制，"当事人基本上可以完全按自己的意愿去拟定合约条文，包括改变法律已有的规定等"。

因此，作为合同法的一项基本精神，当事人意思自治原则在解释合同时必须得到遵循。国际商务合同解释应该依照先事实、后推定的顺序进行，而合同当事人的意思表示是最富事实性的，因此理应作为解释工作的首要顺序。之所以要探求当事人的真意，就是因为当事人意思自治是合同法的基本原则，更是私法自治的重要体现。当事人意思自治的原则不但是合同的基础，还是合同的目标，它贯穿于国际商务合同解释的始终。要实现这一原则,不仅需要解释者的承认和尊重,还需要合同当事人的共同努力。"如果一个人欲把意思自治作为合同目标而不是通常认为的合同基础来实现,那他就必须要确定其意思的表达能够反映真实的信息和真正的平等。"

3.2.2 以客观主义为主、以主观主义为辅的原则 Principle of objective interpretation prevailing over subjective interpretation

在如今国际贸易盛行的大环境下,合同订立人存在着地域、语言、文化背景等各方面的差异。那么,收信人在收到表意人的一定意思表示之后,对该意思表示信息的理解往往与表意人所预期的效果并没有完全吻合。那么,国际商务合同解释中对当事人真意的探求就产生了如此的疑问:最终是要以表意人所理解的意思表示为准,还是以收信人所理解的意思表示为准,抑或是以双方当事人之外的"理性第三人(a reasonable third person)"所能客观理解的意思表示为最终标准?

关于这一方面的争论,在大陆法系中一直存在着形式主义和表示主义的理论分歧。"古日耳曼法和最初的罗马法均采取严格的形式主义,自然在法律解释上必然是表示主义。到了罗马优帝时代,才完全采取意思主义,即把当事人的真正意思作为债的基础。"根据这一渊源发展而来的意思主义,基于意思自治的立场,把表意人所理解的"表示意思"当做合同解释的依据,促使主观主义解释原则在世纪晚期时占据了法律文化的主导地位,并在《法国民法典》、《德国民法典》及《瑞士债务法》等很多国家的民法典里得到了实证的体现。诚然,以意思主义为核心的主观解释原则高举着契约自由(freedom of contract)及私法自治(autonomy of civil law)的族旗,但当合同当事人对合同条款的理解存有争议的时候,它却很难探求当事人内心的真意。基于合同社会化的立场,新近的合同解释学说对客观主义解释原则进行了修正以后,得出了主流的观点是:"以客观主义为主,而辅助以主观主义方式,即主要以客观解释为主,主观主义作为参照。"

Part 2 Focusing on Words and Phrases

1. Finding Meaning in Context

Words	Meaning in General English	Meaning in Legal English
intention	目的;意图	意思表示
civil (law)	市民的;公民的	大陆法
common (law)	共同的;普通的	英美法
implied (term)	暗示的	(合同)推定的(条款);默示的
good faith	真诚;善意	诚实信用

2. Useful Expressions in Legal English

1) Contract provisions are typically given a strict interpretation in favor of the party who drafted the terms, since that party had the opportunity to draft a clear and definite contract.

2) The contract terms are usually supplemented and restricted by laws that serve to protect the parties and to define specific relationships between them in the event that provisions are indefinite, ambiguous, or even missing.

Part 3 Evaluating Your Achievements

词汇日志 Vocabulary Log

contract interpretation	合同解释
clarified interpretation	阐明的合同解释
complementary interpretation	补充的合同解释
civil law system	大陆法系
common law system	英美法系
arbitration	仲裁
international convention	国际公约
international usage	国际惯例
intention	意思表示

章节练习 Check Your Progress

1. Fill in the Blanks

1) This Agreement is the entire understanding between the parties. The Seller is not bound by any statements representations, promises, or inducements, regardless of whether made by the Seller, an agent, or employee, unless it is set forth in this Agreement. The Buyer specifically agrees that no reliance has been placed on any representations other than the provision contained in this Agreement." This is called _____provision.

2) For contracts made internationally, missing or indefinite terms may be filled in by _____ and_____.

3) The distinctive principles of international business contract include_____ and _____.

4) The characteristics of international business contract interpretation are _____ and _____.

2. Legal Terminology

1) clarified interpretation

2) priority of the contracting party's intention

3) complementary interpretation

3. Sentence Translation

1) Where the parties attach the same meaning to the terms used in their agreement, the interpretation of the agreement should be in accord with that meaning even if a third party might interpret the language differently.

2) Words Used Given Their Ordinary Meaning. The words of a contract generally are to be understood in their ordinary and popular sense unless the parties use them in a technical sense or a special meaning is given to them by usage.

3) Whatever an objective observer might think, if the contracting parties attach different meanings to the same term, then neither is bound by the understanding of the other unless one of them knew or had reason to know what the other understood the disputed term to mean.

4) Rest.2d § 204 provides that when the parties omit a term from their contract which is essential to the determination of their rights the court will supply a term which is reasonable.

自我评价 Self-Assessment Log

In this Chapter, you worked through these activities. How did each of them help you become a better learner? Check A lot, A little, or Not at all.

	A lot	A little	Not at all
I discussed the features of international business contracts interpretation with my classmates.	❏	❏	❏
I learned words and expressions in contract interpretation.	❏	❏	❏
I gathered information about contract interpretation principles from the Internet.	❏	❏	❏
I evaluated the differences between civil law and common law in contract interpretation in theory and practice.	❏	❏	❏

(Add something) _____

_____

Chapter 4

第四章 国际合同的法律适用
Legal Application of the International Contracts

The international contract is the most important form of international business. With the liberalization of international trade to meet the requirement of the economic globalization, the scope of the main body of the international contract should be enlarged. The law chosen by the two parties together, the law which has the closest relation with contract and the rules of uniform substantive law are the most important foundations for the settlement of the international contract disputes. With the existence of the preliminary problems, the application of various laws will be involved.

 Learning Objectives

In this chapter, students will learn how to:
◎ define the international contracts;
◎ settle the disputes of international contracts;
◎ choose the applicable law of contracts;
◎ understand the relative legal terms concerning contracts.

 Questions to Consider

1) What characters does the international contract have?
2) How do you understand the applicable law of contracts?
3) Can you list the types of selection of laws in an international contract?

Part 1 Focusing on Legal Knowledge

第一节 国际合同的概念和法律冲突的解决
Section 1　Conflicts Resolution of International Contracts

1.1 国际合同的概念及法律特征
Definition and Legal Characteristics of International Contracts

1.1.1 概念 Definitions

根据国际私法原理，所谓"国际合同"，是指由于某种跨国因素的存在而涉及不同国家的立法管辖权或不同国家之间法律的选择的合同。"跨国因素（transnational factor）"和"法律选择（choice of laws）"两种情况并存是我们确定国际合同的依据，两者缺一不可。但前者是前提，后者是关键。跨国因素把一项合同与两个或两个以上的国家联系起来，因而使得该合同具有了国际性，可能产生法律选择问题。但是，有了跨国因素，却未必当然涉及有关国家的立法管辖权（jurisdiction），未必当然发生法律选择问题，因而该合同也并非当然属于国际合同。然而，对于跨国因素的界定单凭当事人的国籍是不够的。

1980年《联合国国际货物销售合同公约》（United Nations Convention on the Contract for International Sale of Goods）第一条就规定该公约"只是用于营业所在地在不同国家的当事人之间所订立的货物销售合同"。这里说明只有营业所在地（place of business）或住所（domicile）在不同国家的当事人之间所订立的合同才是国际货物销售合同。而不管当事人的国籍如何。下面的例子可以进一步说明这一点。

Case: 世界银行给中国政府一笔贷款，用以修筑一条高速公路。为顺利完成工程，有关方面还成立一个法人组织——高速公路指挥部负责建设工作。工程项目采用国际招标方式。中标者中有几家中国公司。后来一中国公司与公路指挥部之间发生纠纷，根据合同规定，纠纷应提交中国某涉外仲裁机构仲裁。

Issue: 本案中涉及的合同是否具有国际性？

Analysis: 本案主体虽然是两个中国法人，合同的签订和履行等相关因素均在中国,但是合同文本必须是以《世界银行贷款项目招标采购文件范本》为基础订立,承包人的承包资格必须报世界银行审查认定,合同履行情况亦应报世界银行,特别是本工程如发生设计变更或协议补充以及分包、转让都必须报世界银行批准才能生效,工程交工、验收最终要经世界银行确认等,这些都说明本案具有了国际因素。

因此,所谓国际合同就是涉及两个或两个以上国家法律利益的合同。这一方面说明某个合同是否具有国际因素主要取决于是否同时有两个国家存在法律利益,而不仅仅局限于主体、客体及法律事实三个方面,因而扩大了国际合同的情况;另一方面又说明由于有两个或更多的国家存在法律利益,因而才具有法律冲突的问题。

1.1.2 法律特性 Legal characteristics

国际合同具有如下法律特征:

(1) 国际性(internationality),这是国际合同与国内合同的最主要区别。确定国际性的通常标准有:

* 当事人具有不同的国籍;
* 合同当事人的营业场所位于不同国家的领域之内;
* 合同的履行涉及了两个或两个以上的国家。

(2) 复杂性(complexity),国际合同的复杂性体现在两个方面:一是国际合同不仅涉及当事人的国内法,还涉及外国法,以及国际公约和国际惯例;二是由于国际合同跨越了国界,因此它总是和国际货物运输、保险、结算和支付及国家的对外贸易管理联系在一起。因此国际合同所涉及的法律问题比国内合同更为复杂。

(3) 法律冲突性(conflictive),国际合同争端的法律适用即准据法的选择,涉及不同国家的法律,这些国家的法律往往又是相互冲突的。

1.2 国际合同法律冲突解决的一般原理
General Principles of Legal Conflict Resolutions

法律冲突是指涉及两个或两个以上不同法领域的民事法律对该民法关系的规定各不相同,却又竞相要求使用于该民事关系,从而造成的该民事关系在法律适用上的冲突现象。简言之,法律冲突就是因所涉各民事法律对同一民事关系规定不同而发生法律适用上的冲突。从国际私法理论和各国实践来看,在解决国际合同法律冲突方面历来存在两种不同的方法。

1.2.1 分割论和单一论 Unitary theory and scission theory

所谓分割论就是指将合同分割为几个不同方面,分别适用不同地方的法律。比如将合同分割为合同的形式、合同的履行、当事人的缔约能力、合同的解释与撤销等。一般而言,这一方法可以追溯到法则区别时代。早在巴托鲁斯创立法则区别说时就认为,合同形式及合同的实质有效性问题适用合同缔结地法;合同的效力适用合同履行地法;当事人的缔约能力则应适用当事人住所地法。之后,这一理论为许多国家立法和实践所沿用。[1]此外,除了这种将合同诸要素加以分割的做法以外,还有一种做法是把合同的权利义务加以分割,分别适用不同法律。例如,萨维尼就认为,合同义务是以履行地为本座的,因此在双务合同中,每一方当事人的履行义务应分别适用各自的住所地法。

这种分割的方法虽然在一定程度上解决了复杂的合同法律适用问题,但在实践中也存在一定问题。1952年瑞士法庭就曾认为,把合同的形式和合同的效力区分开来分别适用不同的法律,常常是十分困难的,有时直到判决作出之前,准据法仍然不明确,不肯定。因此反对者认为,从法律的观点来看,合同是一个整体,无论是形式,还是合同的解释和履行都应受到一个法律支配。这就是所谓的单一论。

单一论就是指将合同看做一个整体,统一适用一个地方的法律。采取这一观点的国家或学者认为,将合同分割为若干方面受不同国家的法律支配,往往给法院带来很大麻烦。同时也不符合当事人的正当期望,虽然从保护当事人期望出发,应当适用各自的居住地法,因为每个当事人都希望使用自己的法律。但当事人的期望应该针对整个合同而言,并非仅仅针对自己的义务。因此合同只能作为一个整体受一个法律支配。目前,欧洲国家大多采用这一做法。1980年欧共体(European Community)签订的《罗马条约》(Rome Convention)以及1986年海牙《国际货物买卖合同法律适用公约》(Convention on the Law Applicable to Contracts for the International Sale of Goods)都采用单一论做法。

1.2.2 主观论和客观论 Subjective theory and objective theory

在确定国际合同准据法中,国际私法历来存在两种不同方法,即主观论和客观论。前者是指合同准据法应当由当事人自由选择;后者则是指定应当根据合同与某个场所(或地域)之间的客观联系来确定准据法。

主观论最早由杜摩兰提出,根据契约自由原则,当事人既然有权根据自己的意志来创设自己的权利义务,他们当然有权决定适用于他们合同的法律。由于这一方法符合资本主义商品经济的发展需要,因此一经提出就为许多国家与学者赞同和接受。自20世纪40年代以来诞生一系列有

---

[1] 1875年美国最高法院亨特法官在斯科德诉芝加哥联众银行(Scudder v. Union National Bank of Chicago)中认为,有关合同的解释及其合法性问题适用合同缔结地法,有关合同的履行规则适用合同履行地法。

关国际民商事交往的公约,如 1955 年《国际有体动产买卖合同法律适用公约》、1980 年欧共体《关于合同义务法律适用公约》、1986 年海牙《国际货物买卖合同法律适用公约》等,都无一例外接受这一理论。可以认为主观论已经成为国际私法确定合同准据法的一个重要方法。

客观论是国际私法确定合同准据法的一种传统方法,认为合同的成立与效力总是与一定的场所相联系,因而最适合于合同的法律就是合同关系在那里"场所化(localization)"了的地方法律。凡是将合同的法律适用与场所相联系的观点均被归类于确定合同准据法的客观论。其衡量"场所化"的标准,就是看反映与合同有关的一系列因素与某国发生的联系。比如,合同的缔结地(place of contract conclusion)、合同的履行地(place of contract performance)、当事人的住所地(domicile of parties)或居所地(residence of parties)、物之所在地(lex situs[①])以及法院(court)或仲裁地(seat of arbitration)等实践中都曾被用来作为场所化的衡量标准。实践中,由于这种单一的标准存在一些固有缺陷,因此现代社会开始采用"关系的集中地"、"重心所在地"、"最强或最密切联系地"等对这种传统方法加以改良。

从当今的普遍理论及实践来看,主观论的意思自治原则和客观论的最密切联系原则业已成为国际司法中确定合同准据法的两个相辅相成的重要方法。

第二节 国际合同的法律适用一般原则
Section 2 General Principles on Legal Application of International Contracts

国际合同的法律适用的一般原则就是指确定国际合同准据法的规则。合同准据法(applicable law of contract)指适用于合同成立和效力问题的法律,其功能在于确定合同当事人的权利和义务。合同准据法的确定,是国际合同法律适用的核心问题。国际私法发展至今,确定合同准据法的基本原则有意思自治原则(the theory of the autonomy of the parties)和最密切联系原则(the theory of the most significant relationship)。

[①] The term lex situs (Latin) refers to the law of the place in which property is situated for the purposes of the Conflict of laws.

2.1 意思自治原则
The Theory of the Autonomy of the Parties

2.1.1 意思自治原则的含义 Meaning of autonomy of the parties

意思自治原则,亦称"意思自主论"、"主观论"等,是指根据合同当事人双方共同的意思表示来确定合同准据法的一项法律适用原则。其实质在于赋予合同当事人一种选择法律的特殊权利。根据这一原则,在合同法律适用中,当事人可以自由地选择某一国法律,并按照该国法律在合同中设立自己的权利与义务。

目前意思自治原则是各国处理合同纠纷的首要原则。意思自治原则具有以下特点:

* 意思自治原则符合签约自由原则(freedom of contract);
* 有利于当事人预知行为的后果及维护合同关系的确定性以及稳定性;
* 有利于合同争议(dispute)的迅速解决。

意思自治原则最早是由杜摩林在16世纪提出,其主张合同应当适用合同当事人意思所指向的法律。在今天,"当事人意思自治"早已从一种思想理论演变为一项法律原则。按照这项法律原则,合同当事人有权选择支配他们所订立的国际合同的法律。在每个具体的国际合同中,这种权利必须由各方合同当事人共同一致地行使——其表现形式是合同当事人之间就支配他们合同的法律达成的协议。该协议常常载于合同当事人所订立的国际合同中,称做"法律选择条款(choice of law clause)"。该原则已经成为各国普遍接受用以解决合同法律适用问题的基本原则。

在普通法系(Common Law System)各国,自从英国法院于1865年在"佩尼舒勒及东方航运公司诉香德案"和"劳埃德诉吉伯特案"确立了"当事人意思自治"原则以来,该原则已经在其他英联邦国家的法律实践中得到承认。美国在20世纪中叶以前,一直遵循的是合同订立地法规则,即以合同订立(contract conclusion)地法来支配合同,直到20世纪50年代后,美国判例法才大规模地转向"当事人意思自治"原则。在大陆法系(Civil Law System)各国,也以各自不同的方式接受了当事人意思自治原则。

各国学者普遍认为,采用这一原则至少有以下几方面的好处:

* 有利于当事人预见法律行为的后果和维护法律关系的稳定性;
* 由于当事人在缔结合同时就约定了一旦发生争议应该适用的法律,有利于争议的迅速解决。

2.1.2 当事人选择法律的方式 Approaches of choice of laws

选择法律的方式通常涉及明示选择(express choice of law)和默示选择

(implied or inferred choice of law)的问题。明示选择是指当事人在缔约之前或争议发生之后,以文字(in writing)或口头(orally)明确做出选择法律的意图。最通行的就是在合同中列入"法律选择条款(choice of law clause or proper law clause)"或通过标准合同作出统一约定。这种方式明确、具体、易于确定,因而各国普遍接受。

默示选择是指当事人实际上也选择了法律,但是由于某种原因没有明确表达出选择法律的意图。对于默示选择,各国态度并不完全一致。有些国家如中国、土耳其、秘鲁等不承认任何形式的默示选择;有些国家如美国、荷兰等则有限度地接受默示选择;而像英国、法国、德国、瑞士等国家则完全承认默示选择,由法官通过当事人的缔约行为或其他一些因素来推定当事人的选法意图。

根据这些完全承认默示选择国家的司法实践,推定当事人意图必须以另外的某种明示出来的因素作为参照,用来推定的因素多种多样,经常被使用的是合同中订立的"管辖权条款(jurisdiction clause)"或"仲裁条款(arbitration clause)"。在他们看来,"选择了法官就选择了法律"。

但在实践中,法院用来推定的因素并不都合理。如有的国家将合同中采用票据形式、合同的起草格式、支付的货币种类与以前交易的联系等作为推定依据。这些依据实际上带有很大的偶然性,并不都反映当事人的真实意图。在英国的某些判例中法官甚至因合同是用英文书写而推定当事人有选择英国法律的意图,这显然是荒唐的。由此可见,默示选择是法官用来达到某些特定目的的手段,它并不能真正代表当事人的意思,但却100%代表了法官的意图,实际上是法官在选择法律。

2.1.3 选择法律的范围 Range of choice of laws

当事人选择法律的范围问题主要涉及:

* 当事人选择的法律是否包括冲突法;
* 当事人选择的法律是否应当与合同有客观联系。

就第一个问题而言,绝大多数国家和公约都认为当事人所选择的法律仅仅是实体法(substantive law),而不包含冲突法。如1980年欧共体《关于合同义务法律适用公约》第15条就明确规定,凡适用依本公约确定的任何国家的法律,意即适用该国现行的法律规则而非其国际私法规则。对于第二个问题,目前尚存一定争议。欧洲大陆学者大都主张当事人选择法律,必须与合同有客观联系,而不得任意选择与合同毫无联系的国家法律。例如,波兰1936年原《国际私法》规定,当事人对合同准据法的选择只限于当事人的国籍国法、住所地法、合同缔结地法、履行地法、标的物所在地法。

2.1.4 对意思自治的限制 Restriction on autonomy of the parties

目前当事人意思自治原则已为世界各国所普遍接受,但同时各国也都在立法上设置种种条件加以限制。对意思自治的限制主要体现在限制当事人选择法律(choice of law)的范围。

(1) 当事人的选择仅限于特定国家的任意法,不能排除有关国家强制性法规(national mandatory statutes)的适用。

私法学者们历来认为当事人只能选择某国法律中的任意法,而不能以自己的选择违背本应适用于合同的强行法。早在提出意思自治学说的时候,杜摩兰就已经指出,那些具有强制性的习惯是不能依当事人的意思而排除其适用的。这就注定当事人意思自治只能适用于任意法的范围。1804年《法国民法典》第三条规定:"有关警察与公共治安的法律,对于居住在法国境内的居民具有强制性;关于人的身份与权利能力的法律适用于全体法国人,即便其在国外居住时亦同。"这就意味着,在这些方面当事人不得进行法律选择。强制性规则的限制,近年来还较多地被运用在保护弱势当事人(weaker party)的情形。如在消费合同、雇佣合同中对当事人选择法律的自由进行适当限制。

(2) 当事人的选择必须是善意的,并不得违背公共秩序。

所谓"善意(good faith)"即指当事人通过法律选择有意采取法律规避的手段,规避(avoid)有关国家法律中的强制性规定,这是从选择法律的动机和目的上对当事人作的道德限制。各国民法一般将诚实信用作为基本原则,该原则运用于涉外合同的法律选择上就表现为当事人无论选择什么法律都必须出于善意并且合法。实践中,英国率先采用善意标准对当事人的法律选择加以限制。1939年,英国枢密院司法委员会在维他食品公司诉尤纳斯船运有限公司(Vita Food Products Inc. v. Unus Shipping Co. Ltd)[①]中,怀特法官就指出,毫无疑问,英国法是当事人意图适用的准据法,如果当事人在合同中作出了明确意思表示,这种表示就是决定性的,只要这种意图是善意的、合法的,是不能以违反公共政策为由加以排除的。这一主张看似合理,但就善意这点看来实则非常模糊。善意是一个十分主观的范

---

① 英国法官和学者从此案中总结出了许多英国国际私法中确定合同准据法的原则和规则,特别有关意思自治。这些原则和规则都源于审理此案的赖特勋爵(Lord Wright)的意见。这一案件虽然不是英国法院首次引进意思自治原则的例子,但在此案中,赖特勋爵重申了意思自治的观点,使这一原则在英国牢固确立。在该案中,根据提单上"合同受英国法支配"的条款,英国法被确定为合同准据法,据此,赖特勋爵认为,英国法现已完全确定,合同准据法是当事人想要适用的法律。在此案中,赖特勋爵还说道,合同中关于在英国仲裁的规定将引进英国法作为支配该交易的法律,那些通晓国际商业的人都知道这种规定是多么常见,即使当事人不是英国人,交易也完全在英国外进行。

畴,到底什么是善意,不同的国家、不同的法律体系、不同的法官都可能有不同的标准,当事人选择是否出于善意,完全由法庭自由裁量。

"公共秩序(public order)"是私法上很有弹性的范畴,它是私法制度中一国统治者维护本国利益的有力武器。这里没有必要讨论什么是公共秩序,只要认识到是意思自治的限制最普遍的手段就足够了。私法学者、各国判例、立法及国际公约在其他对意思自治的限制上,可能存在分歧,但在公共秩序上都是十分一致的。公共秩序的积极作用是在法律冲突中保护有关国家利益不受损害,其消极作用是影响法律适用的确定性及结果的可预见性。在意思自治状况下,公共秩序除了有一般消极作用外,还直接违反当事人意愿,影响契约自由,因此必须十分的慎重。公共秩序和意思自治原则都是国际私法中十分重要的法律制度,任何一个的不慎运用都会使对方领域产生不利因素。然而,当事人的意志似乎总是处于比较弱势的地位,其实现与否受制于法院所代表的国家意志,因此,在意思自治背景下讨论公共秩序时,慎用和宽容是必然的了[①]。

(3)当事人选择法律必须有合理的依据。

在1971年的第二部《冲突法重述》[The Restatement of Conflicts of Law (Second)]中,美国学者就强调指出,允许当事人在通常情况下选择准据法,并不等于给他们完全按照自己的意愿去缔结契约的自由。当事人选择法律时,必须有一种"合理的依据(reasonable basis)",而这种合理的依据,该书认为主要表现为当事人或合同与所选法律之间有着重要的联系,否则选择应被法院认为无效[②]。如果当事人选择与合同毫无联系的国家的法律,那么就必须有合理的根据,也就是说当事人选择的法律与合同虽然没有实质联系,但当事人选择的法律并不是为了规避与合同有实际联系的国家的强制性法律规则,而是因为当事人选择的法律十分先进并且为双方共同熟悉。此时,就应当认为当事人的选择具有合理的根据,就应当允许他们选择该国法律。

2.1.5 某些特殊类型的合同排除当事人的意思自治 Eliminating autonomy of the parties in particular types of contracts

(1)与国家、民族利益有重大关系的合同

因为此种合同关系重大,国家一般将其置于本国法律支配之下,而排除当事人选择其他法律,以免对国家、民族利益造成危害,而由国家立法规定适用于该类合同的法律,一般被称为"直接适用的法律"。该类法律的

[①] 沈娟:《合同当事人意思自治的确定和限制》,http://www.iolaw.org.cn1.
[②] American Law Institute, Restatement of the Law of Conflict of Laws, Second,1971, Volume 1,556-557.

适用不依赖于联结点的指引,而是根据其体现的政策与案件的联系程度决定适用范围。就合同领域而言,直接适用的法律除主要来源于法院地的法律之外,亦有来自于与案件有重大利益和联系的国家的法律。

(2) 保护弱方当事人特殊利益的合同

随着国际经济交流日益频繁,国际劳务输出(international export of labor services)和国际消费(international consumption)逐渐增多,双方当事人处于不平等的交易地位,失去了意思自治的社会基础。一般而言,提供劳务方和消费者一般处于不利的弱者地位,他们的合法权益容易受到侵犯,在法律选择上,他们也往往处于被动地位。为改变这种处境,以保护弱方利益,许多国家的法律和国际公约,都对此类合同作了特殊规定,当事人不得进行法律选择,或者规定合同当事人只能选择特定地域的法律。

(3) 保险合同

从某种意义上讲,保险合同(insurance contract)是提供服务的合同,因此也可以认为是一种消费合同。为保护投保人利益,在保险合同中一般也不采用意思自治原则,而是适用投保人或被保险人习惯居所地国法。

(4) 不动产合同

关于土地及其附着物、建筑等不动产合同(contact of real estate),几乎任何国家都是规定受不动产所在地法律支配。不过,1980年罗马公约在这方面的规定相对宽松,它允许当事人选择适用于处置和使用土地的合同的法律,在没有选择时,推定合同与土地所在地有密切联系。瑞士国际私法规定,有关不动产或其使用的合同,由不动产所在地的法律支配,但也允许当事人选择法律。

在特殊合同领域中排除意思自治原则的适用,强调法律的保护和政策定向。纵观各国法律,绝对的赋予当事人以法律选择权的国家是不存在的,各国至少不会将其强行法让位于当事人自己选择的法律。各国将其国家意志和政策定向不同程度地体现在其涉外合同法律适用规则中,从而削弱当事人意思的自治能力和合同与某项法律之间的联系。而且无论涉外法律适用原则怎样发展,这种现象是必然存在的,而且还有不断增强的趋势。正如莫里斯所言,确定一些特殊理性的合同的自体法,习惯上已经有了一些固定的规则,没有必要再运用别的规则。不过,由于各国取消或减少这种限制的呼声日渐高涨,各国在将来肯定会不断减少对当事人选择法律的限制。

2.2 最密切联系原则
Theory of the Most Significant Relationship

2.2.1 最密切联系原则的含义 Meaning of the most significant relationship

最密切联系原则又称"最真实联系原则"、"最强联系原则",是指合同当事人没有选择法律或选择无效的情况下,由法院综合分析与合同或当事人有关的各种因素,推断出与案件有最密切联系的地方的法律,予以适用的一项原则。

作为一种理论,最密切联系原则在方法论上可以追溯到法律关系本座说。如前所述,法律关系本座说的核心理论就是,任何一个法律关系在逻辑上和性质上都与一个特定的法域有固定联系,这种联系就是法律关系本座,而本座所在地的法律便是法律关系所应适用的法律。正是在这种思想的启发下,德国学者吉尔克创立了"重力中心说(theory of the center of gravity)"或称"关系聚集地说(grouping of relations)",根据这一学说,合同受有关连接点最为集中的地方法律支配。1954年美国纽约上诉法院审理的奥汀诉奥汀案(Auten v. Auten)就运用了这一理论。一般认为,重力中心说或关系聚集地说就是现代意义上的最密切联系原则的雏形。

与法律关系本座说不同的是,根据最密切联系原则,法律关系没有固定的联系地,法院就具体案件灵活选择与案件有最密切联系的法律;而法律本座说强调每一个法律关系只有一个本座,且只能机械适用这个本座所在地法律。人们普遍认为,最密切联系原则既强调法律选择的灵活性,又兼顾其确定性或稳定性,因此可以说是"20世纪最富有创意、最有价值和实用的国际私法理论"[①]。其独特之处就在于,它完全抛弃了传统的机械做法,代之以一种灵活的分析方法。

2.2.2 最密切联系原则的适用 Application of the most significant relationship

由于最密切联系原则没有确切的、限定的内容,因此如何确定最密切联系地成为学者们以及各国关注的焦点。

(1)质与量的分析

在美国,确定最密切联系地时,它不仅要求考虑所有客观联系因素,且应考察那些"质"或称之为"软性"的标准。美国1971年《第二次冲突法重述》开宗明义地指出,世界是由各自独立的、具有不同法律制度的国家组成,因而,任何事件、交流和争议的发生总是与一个以上的国家有密切

---

① 赖来琨:《当代国际私法学之构造理论》,神州图书出版有限公司2001年版,第591页。

联系。因此法院应当:①在宪法的限制范围内,遵循本州有关法律选择的规定;②没有规定时,则根据下列因素进行选择:
* 州际和国际制度的需要;
* 法院地的有关政策;
* 在决定问题时,其他有利益州的政策和利益;
* 当事人正当期望的保护;
* 特别法律所含基本政策;
* 结果的确定性、可预测性和统一性;
* 法律易于确定和适用。

按照莫里斯教授的解释,这些因素没有主次顺序之分,其重要性因因案件性质不同而异,法院应予以综合考虑。

然而根据《第二次冲突法重述》的规定,上述7个要素并不能使法院当然作出恰当的法律选择,为鉴别哪一地方(国家)与争议问题有最密切联系而适用上述因素时仍需运用一些客观联系因素。《第二次冲突法重述》第188条规定,法院仍应考虑下列因素:合同缔结地;合同谈判地;合同履行地;合同标的物所在地;当事人住所地、居所、国籍、合同成立地及营业地。

Case:本案当事人奥汀(Auten)夫妇1917年在英国结婚,他们在英国共同生活到1931年,当时双方都具有英国国籍。奥汀夫妇婚后生育了两个子女且一起住在英国。1931年,奥汀先生抛妻别子,只身前往美国。奥汀先生1932年在墨西哥经法院判决获准离婚,然后与另一女子卡丽娜结婚。1933年,奥汀在英国的原配夫人来到美国纽约与奥汀先生达成分居协议,双方约定,由奥汀先生每月付给奥汀夫人50英镑作为其与子女的抚养费,双方维持分居现状,任何一方都不得向对方提起与分居有关的诉讼。在签订协议后,奥汀夫人即返回英国,与子女共同生活。奥汀先生仅支付了几次生活费,就没有再支付,致使奥汀夫人维持与子女的生活出现困难,于是,奥汀夫人按律师建议在英国法院对奥汀先生起诉,以被告通奸为由提出分居要求。该诉讼在英国法院提起时是在分居协议签订一年以后,即1934年,到判决作出时已是1938年,判决结果是被告必须向原告支付生活抚养费。据说,在英国这一诉讼并未进入审理程序,它只是经律师建议而使用的一种向被告要钱的手段。原告也明确表示其起诉的目的不是要解除协议,而是要该协议能够强制执行。在英国法院的判决作出之后的几年里,奥汀先生仍未向奥汀夫人支付生活抚养费。后来原告认识到在英国诉讼并未奏效,就于1947年在美国纽约州法院对奥汀先生提起诉讼,要求其按双方签订的分居协议支付生活费共计26 564美元。被告辩称,原告在英国法院提起诉讼已使1933年协议失效,从而结束原告依该协议获得抚养费的权利。纽约地方法院认为该案应适用纽约州法律。根据纽约州法律,原告在英国法院提起诉讼,获得临时给付的裁决,因而纽约地方法院接受被告辩护,而驳回原告诉讼。原告不服,提起上诉。二审维持原判。原告不服,又在纽约州最高法院提起上诉。

Issue: 本案美国法院应该适用纽约州法律还是英国法律?

Analysis: 纽约州最高法院富德(Fuld)法官认为,上述两个法庭之所以主张适用纽约州法律,是由于美国《第一次冲突法重述》中有这样的规定:有关合同履行、解释以及效力等问题应当由合同缔结地法来调整,而有关合同实际履行问题则应当由合同履行地法来调整,而且"许多案例似乎把这些规范是为具有结论性的规范"。但是富德法官却又指出,该案中,更应采用另一种方法,即被称之为"重力中心地(center of gravity)"或"关系聚集地(grouping of contracts)"的法律选择方法。根据这种方法,法院并不把当事人意志或合同缔结地或者合同履行地视为至高无上的因素来考虑,而是把与具体案件有最密切联系的国家法律视为决定性因素,并适用该国法律。

因此,法官富德指出,"通过对与纽约和英国有关联系因素的考察,我们不得不得出结论,必须适用英国法律来解决"该案件。而不是适用纽约州法律,因为在该案中,纽约与该案的唯一联系是,它是分居协议的缔结地,但就是这种联系亦具有偶然性质。然而该分居协议的双方当事人都是英国公民,他们的协议导致了他们分居,更何况他们在英国结婚、在英国生孩子,并作为一个家庭在英国生活了 14 年之久,而且奥汀先生也是在英国遗弃其妻子和孩子的。可见英国在处理该案件和适用其法律方面具有最重大关系。

最终,纽约州最高法院否定了原判,主张适用英国法律来判决此案。

综上,我们可以看出,美国在运用最密切原则时,要考虑质和量两个方面的因素。质的分析即法官在选择法律时,应当根据各种因素相对重要的程度,确定在特定问题上与案件有最密切联系的国家的法律来加以运用。量的分析,就是要求法官将与有合同关系的全部联结因素列举出来,然后将联结因素在数量上最集中的那个国家或地区确定为最强联系地。美国纽约州最高法院 1954 年审理的奥汀诉奥汀案(Auten v. Auten)案,正是这一分析方法的最好例证。

(2)合同自体法

合同自体法(proper law of contract)理论最先由英国法学家创立。它可以

---

① The "lex loci contractus" is the Latin term for "law of the place where the contract is made" in the Conflict of Laws.

说是从 17 世纪荷兰法学家胡伯的学说中受到了很大启发。胡伯曾认为,合同的形式及实质要件受合同缔结地法(lex loci contractus①)支配,但如果当事人意欲适用另一个地方的法律,合同缔结地法就不应优先使用。受胡伯影响的第一个案件就是 1760 年罗宾逊诉布兰德(Robinson V. Bland)案。在该案中,曼斯菲尔德勋爵说,国际礼让和国际法所确立的一般规则是,在合同解释和履行方面应考虑合同缔结地而不是法院地。但是如果当事人订约时想到的是另一个国家,则该规则允许有例外①。然而,在以后的 100 多年中,英国学者对什么是合同自体法的理解并不完全一致。

韦斯特勒克教授在其所著的《国际私法》一书中认为,合同自体法就是支配合同内在生效和效力的法律。而戴西则认为合同自体法应该由当事人意思自治来决定。莫里斯认为两种观点都有偏颇,他将上述观点结合起来指出,合同自体法是当事人意图适用于合同的法律,或者当事人意思没有表示,也不能根据情况作出推断时,则指与交易有最密切和最真实联系的法律②。莫里斯这一定义被多数学者接受。

根据莫里斯的理论,合同自体法一般通过三种方式进行确定:

* 当事人明确选择了法律,则该法是自体法;

* 当事人没有明确选择法律,但根据合同条款、性质及其他情况可以推断出他们选择的法律,该法仍可以成为自体法;

* 当事人既未明确选择法律,又不能从有关情况中作出推断,那么与交易有最密切、最真实联系的法律为自体法。

(3) 特征履行地方法

特征履行地方法(approach of characteristic performance)最早由哈堡格(Harburger)于 1902 年提出,到 1955 年海牙国际私法会议在《关于有体动产的冲突法公约》中正式被采纳。特征履行地方法主要是大陆法国家运用最密切联系原则的一种方法。它要求法院根据合同的特殊性质,以何方履行的义务最能体现合同特殊性来决定合同的准据法。1987 年《瑞士联邦国际私法》第 117 条第 2 款规定,最密切联系地视为存在于应当履行特征性义务的一方当事人的惯常居所地国家,或如果合同是在从事职业或商业活动的过程中订立的,则视为存在于其营业地所在国家。这里所谓的"特征性履行"系指合同关系中最能代表合同特征的履行行为。可见,该说一方面允许考虑每一合同的特殊性,另一方面又不使合同不加区别地

---

① [英]莫里斯著:《法律冲突法》,李来尔等译,中国对外翻译出版公司 1990 年版,第 267 页。
② [英]莫里斯著:《戴西和莫里斯论冲突法》,李双元译,中国大百科全书出版社 1998 年版,第 1114 页。

受制于事先确定好的系属，无须为了灵活性而失去可预见性①。1964年《希腊民法》第25条就规定，合同债务适用于当事人自愿受制的法律，如果没有这种法律，适用按照全部具体情况对该合同适用的法律。1979年《匈牙利国际私法》第29条也规定，不能确定准据法，应适用履行地最有特征性义务的义务人住所地、惯常居所地或主事务所所在地法。采用这种方法仍不能决定准据法的，以与合同关系的主要因素最有密切联系的法律做准据法。此外，还有德国、瑞士、土耳其等国家都采用这一方法。

特征履行在立法和实践中需要解决两个关键性问题：确定合同特征履行的标准，即依据什么标准来判定哪一方的义务履行为特征性履行；确定合同特征履行的场所，即在确定特征履行方式之后，又要在空间上寻找一个连接点，以最终确定合同的准据法。

对于确定合同履行的标准，理论上一直存在分歧，归纳起来主要有两种观点：第一种观点认为，既然在双务合同中一方当事人要支付货币来履行义务（如价款、佣金）。即所谓的金钱履行，而另一方面则为非金钱履行（如交货、提供劳务）。在一般情况下，为金钱履行的那一方履行的义务较为简单，也就是所有合同的共性；而非金钱履行的履行义务较为复杂，不同类型的合同也各不相同，这种复杂性正是我们对合同的种类和特征加以区别的依据。以买卖合同为例，买方的义务是支付货款，领受货物，卖方的义务是交货。这里，卖方的交货义务就体现了这个合同的特征，所以卖方义务的履行就构成合同的"特征履行"。将合同中非支付金钱的一方所履行的义务确定为特征性履行正是这一观点的主要内容。采用这一标准在大多数情况下的确能合理地找到与合同有最密切联系的法律，且简单明了，易于掌握和操作。但在无货币介入的合同关系中，就显得无能为力了。

第二种观点认为，客观上并不存在确定合同特征履行的标准。确定合同特征履行，并不是专指合同本身固有的不可改变的性质，而是要通过考察合同的功能，尤其是合同企图实现的具体社会目的，考察合同各方面的相互间的关系，从而将最能体现社会功能的一方当事人的义务确定为特征性履行。这种观点采用弹性分析方法，即认为确定合同特征性履行应该是具体合同具体分析，在分析中不仅要考虑各方面当事人的具体利益，更要考虑合同所起的社会作用。

通过考察各国的立法和司法实践，我们不难发现，确定合同特征履行地方法，大致有以下做法：

* 首先根据最密切联系原则来确定合同准据法，以特征履行方法确

---

① 陈卫佐：《瑞士国际司法法典研究》，法律出版社1998年版，第155页。

定最密切联系地。如,1987年《瑞士联邦国际私法》第117条规定,对于合同所适用的法律,当事人没有作出选择的,则合同适用依可知情况中与其最有密切联系的国家法律。与合同有最密切联系的国家,是指特征义务履行人的惯常居所地国家,如果合同涉及业务活动或商务活动,则指营业机构所在地国家。

* 按照合同的不同性质和种类,运用特征履行方法分别确定各种合同所适用的法律。如1966年《波兰国际私法》第27条列举了34类合同,而1982年《南斯拉夫法律冲突法》则将合同划分为20种,在当事人没有选择法律情况下,规定了各种合同的不同联结点(connecting factors)。

综上,特征履行说与其说是一种理论,还不如说是一种分析、确定最密切联系地的方法。根据这种方法,一般以特征义务履行人的住所或惯常居所地或者其营业地国家作为最密切联系地。不过,这也不是固定不变的标志。换言之,如果情况证明合同与另一个地方的法律有更加密切的联系,则可以不适用特征义务履行方的住所地法或惯常居所地法或其营业所在地法,而应该适用具有更加密切联系的国家法律。

第三节 国际条约与国际惯例的适用
Section 3 Application of International Conventions and International Custom

3.1 国际条约的适用
Application of International Conventions

3.1.1 理论依据 Theoretical basis

一国法院在国际合同案件的审判中适用国际条约这一问题归根结底涉及国际法上的一个基本理论和实践问题:国际法和国内法的关系。长期以来,国际法理论界对于国际法与国内法关系问题,形成了相互对立的两派:一元论和二元论。一元论认为国际法与国内法同属一个法律体系,内国法院可以直接适用国际条约。尤其是一元论中的"国内法优先说"将国际条约视为本国国内法的一部分,即"对外公法",可以供内国法院直接援引;二元论却认为国际法并不能为国内个人创设任何权利和义务,内国法院如要适用国际条约,则需经国内权威机关将国际条约整体或部分地纳入或转化为国内法。

国际法对内国法院以何种方式适用国际条约并没有统一的规定,这主要取决于各国国内法的规定。目前在国际法理论上国家对国际条约的适用方式主要有以下几种:

（1）纳入方式(adoption)，即国际条约无论是整体还是部分都不能被内国法院直接适用，而内国法院要适用国际条约，必须经内国权威机关的"纳入"。具体而言，由内国宪法作出原则性规定或通过立法机关的行为（如批准条约，公布条约等等），从总体上承认国际条约为内国法的组成部分并可以在内国直接适用。凡是本国签署的已生效的条约，经本国法律程序即自动成为该国国内法的一部分，对该国产生直接适用的效力。

（2）转化方式(transformation)，是指条约须经国内立法转化为内国法才能在国内适用。即通过国内最高立法机关的立法活动制定出一个相关内容的国内法规，使条约转化为内国法规则，以便内国法院适用国际条约。而这种适用国际条约的方式与"纳入"不同，前者是一种间接适用方式，后者则是一种直接适用方式。

（4）综合方式(integration)，即一个国家同时采用纳入和转化两种方式适用国际条约。根据条约的性质或内容的不同，要求有些条约以纳入的方式在内国直接适用，而另一些条约须经过立法机关的立法转化为内国法后才能在内国直接适用。

3.1.2 各国的司法实践 Judicial practice in different countries

对于适用国际条约，国际法理论中有以上三种方式，但是各国的具体实践却十分复杂：

（1）英国的实践。由于英国没有成文宪法，英国缔结条约的程序取决于宪法性原则。一般来说，英王有权缔结或批准国际条约，但是对于一些包含影响英国国民私人权利的条约，必须经过英国议会的同意后，才能成为英国国内法的一部分，可以由英国法院在国内适用。但是，为了防止国际条约在国内法院的滥用，英国国会可以利用未来颁布的国内法法令来废除先前承认国际条约的法令。这样，在国际条约与英国国内法发生冲突时，英国国内法院有义务优先适用国内法。

（2）美国的实践。美国适用国际条约采用综合方式。联邦最高法院将美国所缔结或参加的国际条约划分为"自执行(self-executing)条约"和"非自执行(non self-executing)条约"。《美国联邦宪法》第6条中规定，自执行条约是全国最高法律，即使与任何州的宪法或法律有抵触，各州法官均应遵守。而对于非自执行条约，则要经过必要的国内立法才能约束美国国内法院。但是，这些条约都不得违背美国联邦宪法，否则便归于无效。在美国批准或缔结的国际条约与除了美国联邦宪法以外的国内法相抵触时，美国以它们在美国生效的时间来决定何者优先适用，实行后法优于前法的原则。

（3）法国的实践。法国对于国际条约的适用，由宪法加以规定。1958

年《法国宪法》第 55 条规定:"经合法批准的条约或协定,在颁布后,具有法律权威,但以缔约他方实施该条约或协定为条件。"法国缔结或参加的国际条约经合法批准并公布后便具有高于法国国内法的法律权威,但是法国的宪法也规定国际条约不得违宪,否则不予批准或认可。这表明,在法国实行的是国际条约优先于国内法的原则,但以互惠为条件。

(4)比利时的实践。比利时规定国际条约的效力高于国内法,即使国内法规定在后,也不能否认国家先期承认的国际条约的规定。

3.1.3 国际条约的选择 Choice of international conventions

当事人能否合意选择适用国际条约,尤其是普遍性的国际条约,最终是由各国国际私法规范决定的。然而,国际条约的制定,尤其是缔约国数量较多的国际性公约,其规定往往吸收各国法律制度的优点,代表了相关法律制度的发展趋势,容易为双方当事人所接受。

如果缔约国法院根据公约的规定适用国际条约,那是缔约国的义务,与当事人的意思自治无关。但是,如果当事人所属国是条约缔约国,一国法院能否认可当事人自己通过合意排除该条约的适用?抑或,如果一国法院没有义务适用某一国际条约,那么能否认可当事人自己通过合意选择适用该条约?

一般来说,关于当事人选择适用国际条约的问题,有关的国际条约均持比较慎重的态度。这是由于全面允许当事人协议选择适用条约,将有可能导致条约适用的扩大化,在缺少"强制条款"的情况下,有可能减损本应适用的内国法对特定利益的特殊保护。从某些条约的立法过程中可以看出,一方面,它们并不禁止当事人协议选择适用条约;另一方面,它们也不希望当事人的意思自治减损本应适用的内国法的强制规则。因此,很多国际条约对于当事人意思自治选择的效力不作明确的规定。

然而,由于国际私法公约尤其是统一国际实体私法条约具有典型的私法性,而私法又是以"私法自治"为基本精神,所以,大多数统一国际私法条约都规定,可以通过当事人的意思自治来全部或部分地排除条约的适用。

1980 年《联合国国际货物销售合同公约》中第 6 条明确规定,公约不具有强制性,国际货物买卖当事人可以通过意思自治全部拒绝受公约支配,或部分减损公约的效力。因此,合同各方可以通过意思自治全部或部分排除《联合国国际货物销售合同公约》,即使合同各方所属国均为缔约国。当然,该公约要求排除公约适用的一致意思表示必须是真实的。

1980 年《国际合同义务法律适用公约》第 3 条第 2 款规定,当事人得在任何时候以协议变更其合同所适用的法律,无论以前适用的法律系根据本条选择结果或依本公约其他规定的结果。但是,上述国家立法和国际公约对当事人在订立合同之后选择或变更合同准据法的权利作出限制:其一,不应损害合同形式效力;其二,不应对第三者的权利造成不利影响。

3.2 国际惯例的适用
Application of International Customs and Practices

国际私法中指称的国际惯例主要是在国际民商交往过程中逐步形成的为国家(地区)、当事人所普遍承认并遵守和采纳的习惯做法、规则、先例和原则的总和。国际惯例涉及国际民商交往中的货物贸易、银行保险、海商海事、知识产权等领域。

3.2.1 国际惯例的法律效力和适用 Legal effects and application of international customs and practices

严格来说,国际惯例不是国家立法,也不是国际条约,不具有当然的法律效力,要取得法律效力必须经过国家认可。国家认可国际惯例的法律效力一般有间接和直接两种途径。前者是国际惯例通过当事人的协议选择而间接取得法律约束力,它是国际惯例取得法律效力的最主要途径;后者则不以当事人协议为条件而是直接通过国内立法或国际条约赋予国际惯例以法律约束力。

一般而言,从国际惯例适用方式上而言,存在三种方法:明示认定方法;默示推定方法;强制适用方法。在国际条约中也有关于国际惯例适用的规定。以《联合国国际货物销售合同公约》为例,关于明示认定方法,该公约第9条规定:"双方当事人业已同意的任何惯例和他们之间确立的任何习惯做法,对双方当事人均有约束力。"这一条款简明概括了明示认定方法,即判断国际惯例是否有效,关键在于判断国际惯例是否经当事人"业已同意",这种同意趋于明示,包括口头、书面和其他形式。当事人同意的国际惯例,包含传统惯例和变型惯例。在国际交往中,双方当事人根据彼此的具体需要,在平等互利基础上对传统惯例共同进行必要修改和补充,这就是对传统惯例的变型,修改和补充的内容只要不破坏惯例实质,就具有约束力,否则无效。

关于默示推定方法,《联合国国际货物销售合同公约》第9条规定:"除非另有协议,双方当事人应视为已默示地同意对他们的合同或合同的订立适用双方当事人已知道或理应知道的惯例,而这种惯例,在国际贸易上,已为有关贸易所涉同类合同的当事人所广泛知道并为他们所经常遵守。"这一条款概括规定了默示推定方法。它说明此方法多用于当事人有共同选择某一国际惯例的意向,但没有明确的意思表示的情况,它以推定的形式适用惯例,排除了当事人争执。

关于强制适用方法，《联合国国际货物销售合同公约》未作规定。这种方法适用于以下两种情形：

* 依当事人意思自治原则或冲突规范，其纠纷应适用某国法律（准据法），而所援引的准据法未作规定，当事人又没有选择国际惯例的。

* 当事人所选择的国际惯例并不能全面地解决争议或违反本国（即纠纷处理机构所在国）有关公共秩序的规定，当事人又没有重新选择国际惯例的。

强制适用方法是内国通过颁布法律或司法解释等立法形式为纠纷处理机构提供的适用方法。

3.2.2 国内强行法的限制 Restrictions on domestic compulsory law

当事人的选择只能在特定国家的任意法范围内进行，因此，国际惯例不能与有关国家的强行法相抵触。尽管国际商业交易的当事人可以在最大程度上协议其合同的内容并使之受国际商事惯例的支配，但是，他们不能完全排除内国法的基本原则对其合同关系的控制作用，因为不同国家的法律为确保标准合同和一般交易条件对贸易限制的公正与合理，而对它们的适用和效力有不同的严格要求。所以，国际贸易当事人应使他们的合同关系受内国法的控制，以使这种合同合法有效。比如，以毒品、武器为标的的合同在许多国家的国内法上是无效的。1980年《联合国国际货物销售合同公约》第4条规定，本公约除非另有明文规定，与任何惯例的合法性无关。据此，如果一个包含特定国际惯例的合同依可适用的国内法无效，则该惯例也是无效的。

3.2.3 公共秩序的限制 Restrictions on public order

公共秩序制度是国际私法上一个极为重要的制度。一国的法院依某一冲突规则将适用某一外国的法律为准据法，如果发现适用该法律的结果与本国的社会重大利益相悖，则可排除该外国法的适用。公共秩序制度在当今各国都是存在的，但是只有我国在立法中明确认为可用公共秩序排除国际惯例的适用。有的学者认为，这种限制主要表现在下列两种情况中：①如果当事人的合同关系受制于一外国法律，则这种国际惯例不得与该国法律的强制规定及其所规定的公共秩序相抵触。②如果当事人的合同关系受一般法律原则的支配，则该国际惯例的效力以不违反这种一般法律原则中的强制性原则和公共秩序为前提条件。

第四节 我国关于国际合同法律适用
Section 4 Legal Application of the International Contracts in China

我国关于合同法律适用的法律规定主要见之于《民法通则》第145条的规定和《合同法》第126条的规定以及最高人民法院于1988年发布的《民通意见》等立法和法律文件之中。

4.1 意思自治原则
The Doctrine of the Autonomy of the Parties

我国《民法通则》第145条规定："涉外合同的当事人可以选择处理合同争议所适用的法律,法律另有规定的除外。"《合同法》第126条也作出了同样的规定。这一规定表明,我国与世界大多数国家一样,在立法上确立了意思自治原则。根据最高人民法院过去《关于适用〈涉外经济合同法〉若干问题的解答》(以下简称《解答》)的规定,我们在运用意思自治原则的时候,应注意以下几个问题:

(1)关于选择法律的方式

根据《解答》第2条第2款的规定,合同当事人的法律选择必须采取明示的形式,因此默示选择法律在我国是无效的。

(2)关于法律选择的时间

在我国,当事人可以从订立合同时起直到人民法院开庭审理之前,随时通过协议选择所适用的法律。

(3)关于法律选择的范围

按照《解答》的规定,当事人协议选择的法律或者人民法院依最密切联系原则确定的处理合同争议所适用的法律,指的是实体法,而不包括冲突法,从而在合同的法律适用上排除反致的可能性。在选择法律的空间范围上,《解答》并未要求必须选择与合同有实际联系的国家的法律。因此在中国,合同当事人可以选择中国内地法、港澳地区法律或外国法。

(4)关于强制性规则

按照《合同法》第126条第2款的规定,在我国境内履行的中外合资经营企业合同、中外合作经营企业合同以及中外合作勘探开发自然资源合同,只适用中国法律。这就意味着,对于上述三种合同当事人不得通过法律选择以期适用外国法。

(5)关于公共秩序

《民法通则》及《解答》明确规定,应适用的法律为外国法律的,不得违反我国法律的基本原则和社会公共利益,否则将不予适用。

4.2 最密切联系原则
Theory of the Most Significant Relationship

《民法通则》和《合同法》都规定，当事人未作法律选择的，或选择无效的情况下，则应适用与合同有最密切联系的国家的法律。这就表明，最密切联系原则作为对意思自治原则的一个补充，在立法上得到确立。在决定最密切联系地的问题上，我国采取了在欧洲大陆颇为流行的"特征履行"的方法。最高人民法院的《解答》规定，如果当事人没有选择合同所适用的法律，对于下列合同，人民法院按照最密切联系原则确定所应适用的法律，通常是：

（1）国际货物买卖合同，适用合同订立时卖方营业所所在地法律。但是如果合同是在买方营业所所在地谈判并订立的，或者合同主要是依买方确定的条件并应买方发出的招标订立的，或者合同明确规定卖方须在买方营业所所在地履行交货义务的，则适用合同订立时买方营业所所在地法律。

（2）银行贷款或者担保合同，适用贷款银行或担保银行所在地法律。

（3）保险合同，适用保险人营业所所在地法律。

（4）加工承揽合同，适用加工承揽人营业所所在地法律。

（5）技术转让合同，适用受让人营业所所在地法律。

（6）工程承包合同，适用工程所在地法律。

（7）科技咨询或设计合同，适用委托人营业所所在地法律。

（8）劳务合同，适用劳务实施地法律。

（9）成套设备供应合同，适用设备安装运转地法律。

（10）代理合同，适用代理人营业所所在地法律。

（11）关于不动产租赁、买卖或抵押合同，适用不动产所在地法律。

（12）动产租赁合同，适用出租人营业所所在地法律。

（13）仓储保管合同，适用仓储保管人营业所所在地法律。

依据《解答》的规定，在适用当事人营业所所在地法律时，如果当事人有一个以上营业所的，应以与合同有最密切联系的营业所为准；当事人没有营业所的，以其住所或居所为准。《解答》同时规定，如果合同明显地表明另一个国家或地区的法律比上述规定的法律有更加密切的联系，人民法院应以该另一国家或地区的法律作为处理合同争议的依据。

4.3 我国有关适用国际条约和国际惯例的规定
Application of International Conventions and International Customs and Practices

4.3.1 国际条约的适用 Application of international conventions

"条约必须信守"是国际法上公认的原则，我国在规定合同法律适用的同时，亦确立了这一原则。1986年《民法通则》第142条第2款的规定：

"中华人民共和国缔结或者参加的国际条约同中华人民共和国的民事法律有不同规定的,适用国际条约的规定,但中华人民共和国声明保留的条款除外。"该条款规定了所谓的"国际条约优先原则"。根据规定,可以得出如下结论:

(1)中国参加的统一实体法条约可以在中国直接适用。在司法实践中,当事人可以在法律关系中直接适用有关的国际公约。

(2)在有统一实体私法条约的情况下,法官不适用冲突规范确定准据法,而是直接适用公约中的相关规定。如果公约中没有包含案件中的某些问题,对这些未尽事宜则适用冲突规范确定某个相关国家的法律作为准据法。

(3)中国法律与国际私法条约的内容不一致时,适用公约的规定,即中国参加的民商事条约在适用效力上对于中国的国内法有一定的优先性,但并没有排他性。

(4)中国参加条约时作出的保留不适用于中国。对于保留的部分,法官依据中国的冲突规范确定准据法解决。

4.3.2 国际惯例的适用 Application of international customs and practices

我国《民法通则》第 142 条第 2 款明确规定:"中华人民共和国法律和中华人民共和国缔结或者参加的国际条约没有规定的,可以适用国际惯例。"从该条款可以看出:

(1)某一涉外民商事关系或案件如果属于我国缔结或参加的某一国际统一实体法条约的适用范围,应按照该国际条约的实体规范来处理。

(2)如果该国际条约对于处理该涉外民商事关系或案件没有相应的实体规范,应该适用法院地国家(即中国)的冲突规范,而首先应考虑适用国际条约中的统一冲突规范;没有统一冲突规范时,适用国内冲突规范;既没有统一冲突规范又没有国内冲突规范时,则适用有关冲突规范的国际惯例。

(3)如果根据冲突规范所指引的中国法律对该涉外民商事关系或案件无相应的实体规范,就可以适用有关实体规范的国际惯例来处理。

(4)该涉外民商事关系的当事人可以根据有关意思自治的冲突规范在争议发生前后选择适用国际惯例。

Part 2 Focusing on Words and Phrases

1. Finding Meaning in Context

Words	Meaning in General English	Meaning in Legal English
jurisdiction	权限	立法管辖权
domicile	住处	住所（指一个人永久居住的地方）
proper law	适合的法律	自体法
place of business	营业所	营业所在地
custom	风俗	惯例,惯例法
conflict	争执	（法律）冲突
autonomy	自治,自主	自主权
reasonable	讲道理的,合情合理的	合理的,公平的,正当的,适当的
conclusion	结论	（合同）缔结

2. Useful Expressions in Legal English

1）The proper law of the contract is the main system of law applied to decide the validity of most aspects to the contract including its formation, validity, interpretation, and performance.

2）The term conflict of laws is usually used by common law countries, while for civil law countries the term private international law is more appropriate.

3）The parties are free to enter into a contract and to determine its content.

4）The parties may exclude the application of these Principles or derogate from or vary the effect of any of their provisions.

Part 3 Evaluating Your Achievements

词汇日志 Vocabulary Log

party	当事人
jurisdiction	立法管辖权
domicile	住所
proper law	自体法
business place	营业所在地
custom	惯例
conflict	法律冲突
autonomy	自主权
reasonable	合理的
conclusion	缔结

章节练习 Check Your Progress

1. Fill in the Blanks

1) The CISG applies to contracts of sale of goods between parties whose _____ are in different States when these States are Contracting States.

2) The proper law of the contract is the main system of law applied to decide the validity of most aspects to the contract including its _____, validity, interpretation, and _____.

3) When the parties have not used express words, their intention may be inferred from the _____ and nature of the contract, and from the general circumstances of the case.

2. Legal Terminology

1) autonomy of the parties
2) the most significant relationship
3) proper law of contract

3. Sentence Translation

1) The parties are bound by any usage to which they have agreed and by any practices which they have established between themselves.

2) When the parties express a clear intention in a formal clause, there is a rebuttable presumption that this is the proper law because it reflects the parties' freedom of contract and it produces certainty of outcome.

自我评价 Self-Assessment Log

In this Chapter, you worked through these activities. How did each of them help you become a better learner? Check A lot, A little, or Not at all.

	A lot	A little	Not at all
I knew the definition and characteristics of international contracts.	❏	❏	❏
I learned words and expressions concerning conflicts of law.	❏	❏	❏
I understood general principles of legal conflict resolutions.	❏	❏	❏
I grasped with legal application of the international contracts.	❏	❏	❏

(Add something) _____

_____

第三部分
PART III

国际商务合同的语言特征分析

LINGUISTIC ANALYSIS OF INTERNATIONAL BUSINESS CONTRACTS

Chapter 5

第五章 国际商务合同的语体特征
Variety Features of International Business Contracts

The application of English language in various fields and industries has its own specific characteristics with certain diversities and varieties. International business contracts English is assigned to English for Professional Purposes and English for Academic Legal Purposes. Similar with other contracts, the international business contract is an agreement on the relations of rights and obligations shaped through goods trading and economic cooperation between the parties and it is also a code of conduct for the parties to settle economic disputes, to make the litigation and arbitration. The uniqueness of this contract is the specific language style of writing, because it has to achieve a special kind of verbal communication purpose. Therefore it has high standard of language using.

 Learning Objectives

In this chapter, students will learn how to:
◎ understand the definition of register;
◎ define variety;
◎ briefly grasp the lexicon features of contract English;
◎ understand syntactic features of contract English.

 Questions to Consider

1) Can you explain what variety is?
2) What are the linguistic features of contract English?
3) What are the syntactic features of contract English?

Part 1 Focusing on Legal Knowledge

第一节　合同英语的语体风格
Section 1　Variety of Contracts in English Language

1.1 语体风格概述
An Introduction to Variety

1.1.1 语域 Register

运用某种语言进行交际时,不仅要懂得使用它的语法规则去构成句子,而且要根据不同的语境选择相应的文体,才能运用得体,收到良好的交际效果。我们在学习英语的过程中,往往因缺乏"文体意识(stylistic awareness)"或者说缺乏"文体洞察力"(stylistic insight)而造成语域(register)误用。所谓"语域",指的是语言运用的场合。场合主要是社会场合。然而,社会之大,场合之多,不可胜数。如若缺乏文体分析的能力(stylistic competence),语域误用也就在所难免。韩礼德说"选择错误的语域,混淆不同的语域,是外国人学习另一种语言时最常犯的错误",就是这个道理。

文体学(stylistics)是一门运用现代语言学理论和方法研究文体的科学,是一门研究语言的表达效果的学问。人们一般认为它渊源于古希腊的修辞学(rhetoric),20世纪初,形成了文体学。随着现代语言学理论的发展,特别是20世纪60年代社会语言学的兴起,促进了文体学的发展。它依据现代语言学的原理,对语言的各类文体进行调查和描述,首先将注意力放在口语,后来进而研究各类书面语,如科技文章、法律文书和商业广告用语等。20世纪70年代,韩礼德在他的系统功能文体学模式里,主张把语言连同社会和人一起加以考察和研究,提出了"语域"理论。可以说,韩氏的功能主义理论为现代文体学的研究奠定了理论基础,语言对场合的适合性(appropriateness)成了现代文体学讨论的中心问题。其实,韩礼德的"语域"是指使用特有的一种语言(如科技英语、商务英语)的社会文化群体。由于使用目的和场合的不同而产生了语域的变异。韩礼德还认为语域变异的标记是语言材料,这标记可以表现在词汇方面,也可以表现在语法方面,它们随着语域的变化而变化。

由此可以推及商务合同英语是法律文化群体中所特有的一种英语，是现代英语的一种功能变体，其与普通英语（English for general purpose）的差异，不仅表现在目的和意义方面，而且表现在词语用法、句子组成和篇章的构建方面。由于商务活动涉及对外贸易、技术引进、招商引资、对外劳务承包、商务谈判、经贸合同、银行托收、国际支付与结算、涉外保险、国际旅游、海外投资、国际运输等范围，所以商务合同群体是一个庞大的社会群体。这个庞大的社会群体及英语在这个社会群体的交际过程中产生的语域变异应当引起语言研究工作者的注意，应从现代文体学的观点出发，针对这种变异的规律和结果，作一些有益于人们迅速掌握、正确使用商务合同英语的研究。

1.1.2 语体 Variety

在不同的社会活动领域内进行交际时，由于不同的交际环境，就形成了一系列运用语言材料的特点，这就是言语的功能变体，简称语体。简单说语言因其使用目的、场合、交际对象等的不同而形成不同的语体。

按照黎运汉对文体的分类，合同属于应用语体当中的公文事物语体，（事物语体是适合于公众事物领域有特定公文程式的话语）。语言的风格，就是人们为了适应特定的交际场合和达到某种交际目的时，使自己的语言产生的特殊语言气氛和语言格调。在不同的领域中，由于环境不同、对象不同、作用不同，就有着不同的交际用语，形成不同的语言风格。语言风格与语体色彩密切相关，不同语体的语言有着不同的特色。

国际商务合同的社会职能决定了它的文体和语言的特殊性，促使它形成了自己的文体风格。其语言特征表现为话语表达有既定的格式，行文具有逻辑性，措辞严谨，运用大量的专业词语，力求精准、明晰，杜绝表达中可能出现的歧义现象，排斥感情色彩的词语，句法严密完整，句子复杂，文辞严密，形成客观、正式、严谨的语言风格。

1.2 合同英语的语体风格——格式
Variety of contracts in english language——Structure

国际商务合同是缔约双方对享有的权利、必须履行的职责和义务的契约性书面文件，具有严格的法律效力。根据不同的标的，国际经贸合同可以分为多种，但格式基本上是一致的。正式书面合同文本的结构是它同其他实用功能文体相区别的外在标志。国际商务合同一般都由约首/序言、正文、约尾/结尾三个部分构成，具体内容在下一章将详细讲述。

1.3 合同英语的语体风格——语言
Variety of contracts in english language——Linguistic Features

1.3.1 严谨准确性(Faithfulness and Accuracy)

(1)合同写作必须严谨,用词造句必须十分准确。因为一旦落实成文字,就成了法律上的重要依据。合同起草者应竭力避免当事人在合同文字的理解上产生异议,导致纠纷,不能履行合同,甚至终止合同。准确就是要求把词语用在刀刃上,恰到好处,而不是模棱两可,令人费解或产生误会。合同起草者要特别注意英语中的一词多义或多种解释。

[例1]

The penalty shall be divided between Party A and Party B in New York City and Party C in Newark, New Jersey.

句中的罚款应由甲方乙方承担一半,另一半由丙方承担,而不是三方均摊,这是由于用了 between… and,如果三方均摊(equally)就应该用 among。

[例2]

The contracted merchandise shall be supplied by A and B and C in equal portions.

这句可解释为每方各供二分之一的货。但是由于第一个 and 把供货方分为两组——甲方和乙、丙方,也就是说,每组各供一半。一个 and 使得整句不知所云。

(2)合同的文字有别于文学作品,不追求文采、韵味、悬念、诙谐、想象等等,而是要求严密的句子和精确的词语。特别是一些主要的词句都有着严格的法律意义,一定要做到字斟句酌。如国际技术贸易中经常出现"排他性许可证(sole license)"和"独占性许可证(exclusive license)",两者各有明确的含义,决不可信手拈来。"排他性许可证"表示:在许可证交易中,技术受让方在协议有效期间,在协定的地区内,对许可证项下的技术具有独占权,不许授予第三方,只许在规定地区内使用该技术和出售该产品的许可证;而"独占性许可证"则表示:许可方不得再把同样内容的使用许可证协议授予该地域内的任何第三方,就连许可人自己也不得在该地区使用该项技术。

(3)合同起草者在使用确切的词语上应注意下列各点:

(1)应使用熟悉的(familiar)和惯用的(commonly accepted)术语(terms)和词语。

如果有两个词语可供选择,其中一个比较短并且比较熟悉,另一个比较长且不常用,那么应当使用前者。例如,销售洗衣机的协议如果使用了

"出售人"和"购买人"这样的称呼就会显得华而不实,"卖方"和"买方"这样的字眼会更合适。应当尽可能地避免使用拉丁词语。例如,mutatis mutandis 或者 inter alia 可以用"已作必要的修正……(the necessary changes being made)"和"与其他的事物……(amongst other things)"来代替。同时对于情态动词 shall,各种正式的法律用语和专业词汇,复合古体词以及大写字母的使用都要给予注意。

(2)要注意词语的搭配(collocation)和正确分辨同义词(synonyms)或近义词(near-synonyms)。

为了保证确切,通常要求重复同样的词语或术语来表达同样的意思(Exactness often demands repeating the same term to express the same idea)。不要忌讳重复,重复是为了避免误解。

(3)保持句子的完整(Completeness)

[例3]

从5月1日起到10月31日止这一期间内交货,但以买方信用证在3月15日前到达卖方不限。

译文:Shipment during the period beginning on May 1 and ending on Oct. 31 subject to Buyer's Letter of Credit reaching Seller before Mar. 15.

以上条款交货期间包括5月1日和10月31日这两天,译文应加上 both date inclusive;买方信用证到达日也包括3月15日这一天,因此介词 on 不能少。译成 Shipment during the period beginning on May 1 ending on Oct. 31, both date inclusive, subject to Buyer's Letter of Credit reaching Seller on and before Mar. 15. 才算完整。

1.3.2 一致性(Consistency)

(1)一致性是法律起草的"黄金法则",即"除非你要更改你的意思,否则不要更改你的用语(don't change your language unless you wish to change your meaning)"和"永远不要更改你的用语,除非你要更改你的意思,以及一旦你打算更改你的意思,就始终要相应地更改你的用语(Never change your language unless you wish to change your meaning and always change your language when you wish to change your meaning)"。一致性并不仅限于单个的词语,譬如说,分段也应保持一致性。

(2)各种不一致的情况:

1)使用两个或者两个以上的未明确定义的词语提及同样的事物。

例如,如果合同指的是"买方",就不应当在文件的后面部分改成"采购人"或"史密斯先生"。不同的指示可能会被视为代表的意思发生转变。同样的,不能留下任何余地而使福勒的《现代英语用法》(Modem English

Usage)中所述的"优雅的变体"得以发生。所谓"优雅的变体",是指表达的时候尽量地优雅,而不是为了表达清楚。法律文件的目的是精确地规定权利、权力或特权和义务或责任,而不是娱乐读者。

优雅的变体可能也会导致在不知情的情况下接受比本意更宽广或更狭窄的权利和义务。例如,如果租赁房子的协议称其为"房子",那就不应当改变成"房产"、"财产"、"建筑物"或者"不动产",因为会觉得对"房子"的称呼太多。所作的更改在合适的上下文中可以解释为指的是某些比房子更大或更小的物体。因此,如果房客与房东达成口头协议保持对"房子"的维修,那么租赁合同中规定他应当负责保持对"该财产"的维修的条款就可能包含广泛得多的含义,即房客同意该条款可以包括花园和外屋。

2)用未定义的方式使用已定义的词语或者术语。

如果词语或术语在法律文件中的意思已经经过定义,在文件中每个使用该词语的地方都必须采用能表示出是按照定义的含义来使用的方式。例如,如果在文件中使用的"公司"或"配偶"的意思已经经过定义,就必须按照能表现出所定义的意思的方式来使用它们。如果不这样做,读者可能会认为的意思将不是所要表达的意思。例如,根据股票销售协议的规定,A公司同意将其子公司X公司出售给B公司,那么X公司可能在文件中定义为"该公司(the Company)",而A公司和B公司分别称为"卖主"和"买主"。如果该协议写得很糟糕,以至于在应该用大写的"该公司(the Company)"的时候却用小写的"该公司(the company)"来指代,那么读者很可能会认为这个词汇在这个地方所指的是A公司或B公司或者某些其他公司。

1.3.3 简洁性(Simplicity)

(1)语言学家认为,词与文体紧密相关。商务合同属于实用文体,其内容和读者有很强的针对性,为了使读者一目了然,不存疑问,必须做到语言简洁、直截了当、条理清楚简练。也就是要求起草者用尽可能少的文字来清楚地阐明意思。要做到言简意赅,起草者必须避免使用或删除不必要的词语(unnecessary words)。但这并不是要不顾细节(particulars),或者可把细节删除。恰恰相反,重要的是要中肯(to the point)。而合同内容的完整(completeness)和词语的准确(preciseness)是简练的前提条件。比如:

In the event of a single arbitrator being unable to be agreed upon by the two parties……一旦一个仲裁员不能被双方同意……这种迂回曲折(circumlocution)、模棱两可的(roundabout)语句非常容易造成困扰。上句若改为:"If the two parties fail to agree on a single arbitrator……"效果会更好。

(2)要做到简洁性,应该做到以下几点:

1) 删去不必要的词和短语(remove unnecessary words)。

应当指出的是,合同内容的完整并不意味着文字的多余。在合同的遣词造句中,应惜字如金。一个词能概括的,不用两个词;一句话能讲清的,勿用两句话。力戒滥用和堆砌词句,而且多余的词句在合同的履行过程中,不可避免地会导致理解上的纷争。

[例 4]

This Contract is signed in Shenzhen, China, by the legal representatives (or authorized representatives) of the contract parties on September 15, 2004 in duplicate in English and Chinese languages, both texts being equally authentic.

此例行文啰唆(wordy),"This Contract","the legal representatives (or, authorized representatives) of the contract parties"都应删去。"本合同"和"合同当事人法定代表(或授权人)"在前言和签字部分都会出现,这里就不必重复了。为求简练,可改写如下:

Signed in Shenzhen, China on 15th day of September, 2004 in duplicate in English and Chinese languages, both texts being equally authentic.

[例 5]

The goods should be in good if not perfect condition on arrival at the destination. In this case an insurance certificate does not help any.

上述两例中"if not perfect"和"any"都应删去。合同起草者在遣词造句时应惜字如金,切忌行文中出现多余的词语。

2) 改写(rewrite),即词语的锤炼,这对合同起草者来说是一个选择和淘汰词语的过程。

[例 6]

There is well-grounded evidence to support the claim.

可改写为:

Well-grounded evidence supports the claim.

[例 7]

It is necessary for the Seller to advise the Buyer of the dispatch the goods.

可改写为:

The Seller must advise the Buyer of the dispatch of the goods.

上述两例中被改写的词语并非其本身有错。词无优劣,使用得当,必尽其能。

3) 用单词(single word)来替代词组或短语(group of words or phrases)。

有时候,在法律文件中会用转弯抹角的方式来表达意思,而该意思只需用一个词就可以表达。如果文件中大量存在这种婉转曲折的陈述,就会

变得毫无必要且冗长。例如:

in the nature of —like
for the reason that—for
because during the time that—while
for the period of—for
be of help to—help
for the purpose of — for

4）使用分词（participles）短语来替代从句（clauses）。

[例 8]

The "blue prints" refer to the copies of general drawings and production drawings which are used at present for manufacturing the contracted products or for improving design in future.

可用过去分词"used"来替代 which clause。可改写为:

The "blue prints" refer to the copies of general drawings and production drawings used at present for manufacturing the contracted products or for improving design in future.

[例 9]

Rules and regulations which govern the flow of commodities…

可用现在分词"governing"来替代 which clause。可改写为:

Rules and regulations governing the flow of commodities…

5）避免使用空洞而乏味（avoid using empty words）的并列同义词。

[例 10]

Again and again, time and time again, first and foremost, over and above, each and every one and the same, really and truly. 起草者应竭力使用单词来表达。但有些并列同义词组成的短语在法律文件中常出现。例如:null and void, part and parcel, approve and accept, mutually understood and agreed.

6）将两个相关的句子合并（combination）成一个句子。

[例 11]

The importer may lodge a claim for short weight.

The claim must be lodged within 10 days after arrival of the goods.

现将上述两句组成一个句子:

The importer may lodge a claim within 10 days after arrival of goods.

（3）综合改写后的句子要显得简明扼要，清楚具体。

[例 12]

本合同由甲方和乙方于 1998 年 3 月 29 日在中国上海市签订。本合同以英文和中文同时书写。一式两份，两种文本均为正本且具有同等效力。第19章中列出的附件1至附件9为本合同不可分割的组成部分，与本合同具有同等法律效力。

以上条款的行文就显得有些 wordy。其中第一句中，不需再重复地出现合同的当事人，因为合同的当事人在合同的前言部分和签字部分都要出现，这一句应改写为"本合同于1998年3月29日在中国上海签订"；第二句主要讲明的是：两种文字写成的合同，内容完全相同，因此直接写成"本合同一式两份，每份用英文和中文写成，两种文本具有同等效力"；最后一句中的"附件1至附件9"应删去。既然合同的附件已全部包括在第19章中，就没有必要再说明有多少附件。另外，合同已经规定了附件均列在合同的第19章中，并宣布为"本合同不可分割的组成部分"，所以再规定"附件与本合同具有同等法律效力"是多余的，应删掉，改写为"第19章中列出的附件为本合同不可分割的组成部分"。

经过分析，将上例条款改写如下：

本合同于1998年3月29日在中国上海签订，一式两份，每份用英文和中文写成，两种文字具有同等效力。

本合同第19章列出的附件为本合同不可分割的组成部分。

Signed in Shanghai, China this 29th day of Mar., 1998 in duplicate in English and Chinese languages, both texts being equally authentic.

The annexes as listed in Article 19 to this contract shall form an integral part of this contract.

1.4 合同英语的语体风格——语篇
Variety of contracts in english language——Discourse

1.4.1 什么是语篇 What is discourse

语篇泛指一个完整的语言材料，含所有形式的语言交流和所有文体的语言材料，如广告、谈话、演说、报告、小说等。各种类型的语篇，都有独特的模式，具有区别其他语篇的特征。不同的文体，章节安排、段落关系有所不同；不同的文体，其联系句子的手段，句群的排列和关系，段落的形式和联系区别很大。

批评语言学家Robert Hodge & Gunther Kress等认为，语言表述结构是以意识形态为根据的。一定的社会、文化群体，以及从事的相关活动，具有较为固定的语言表述方式。商务合同英语也有其固定的语言表达方式，它的语篇结构逻辑合理、意义连贯。所谓逻辑合理，包括句子结构合理，段落安排合理，语篇思维合理。所谓意义连贯，即句与句之间语义连贯，段与段之间内容连贯，上下文之间思路连贯。英语商贸合同形成了特定的语篇模式和组织结构。

一般而言,合同都采用从总则到条款的先宏观后微观的语篇结构,这有助于为当事人创造理解文本内容的语篇语境。另外,就整体结构形式而言,商务合同英语采用了分条列款的形式,平行性条款结构使用极为频繁。这种平行结构呈现于各种层次,有单词或词组之间的平行性结构,也有从句甚或段落之间的平行性结构,具有层次清晰、前后衔接、相互照应、结构对称、脉络分明、节奏明快等特征。

1.4.2 语篇分析的重要部分 Major contents of discourse analysis

(1) 语法手法 Grammar

语法手法在语篇衔接上起着重要作用。为了使语篇清晰明了,平衡句式大量使用,构成了语法手法的重要方面。平衡句式的重要功能之一是建立不同语法条款的平等关系。这种手法通常由三个或更多的相似句式组成,使合同的文字更为严密。

[例13]

This Contract shall be governed by and construed in accordance with the laws of China.

本合同应受到中国法律管辖,并按中国法律解释。

(2) 词汇衔接 Connection

词汇衔接在语篇层面的贡献有以下两个方面:词汇重复和词组搭配。词汇重复的使用使得内容更为有序、清晰,这种手段如同路标给读者指向。

[例14]

Party A hereby transfers and grants to Party B the exclusive and perpetual right to manufacture and sell the licensed products in Chinese Territories in accordance with the technology. Such transfer and grant shall cover all elements of the technology to the licensed products.

(3) 从属连词 Subordinate Conjunction

在英语商贸合同中,从属连词广泛应用,以显示不同从句之间的关系,所以 if, should, unless, after, in case, until 等广泛应用。

[例15]

After delivery is made, the Sellers shall send the shipping documents specified in Clause 11.

In case the Buyers fail to arrange insurance in time due to the Sellers failing to cable advice in time.

1.5 合同英语的语体风格——语境
Variety of contracts in english language——Context

1.5.1 什么是语境 What is the context

由于社会交际的需要,人们常在类似的语境中完成某一特定的交际任务。例如在国际商务活动中,有成交意向的买卖双方为了说明交易各方的责任和利益而签订合同,这类交际形式多次重复,就会形成一种语境类型。就商贸合同而言,语境因素非常重要,它不仅涉及商贸合同的风格,而且承接语境因素和语言特点之间的联系。由于商贸合同已成为经济的重要组成部分,涉及社会生活的方方面面,在这种语境下商贸合同并不寻求语言的美观,而是强调逻辑清晰和论理准确,以避免模糊和不清晰。合同本身的交际是通过书面文体表达其意。

1.5.2. 角色关系——正式程度、非人格性和可读性 Formal/informal, impersonality and readability

(1)正式程度取决于角色关系和它的语境因素。比如,私人谈话、公共演讲、游行示威、宗教祷词、政府会议和生日宴会。正规英语常见在官方文件、科技写作和法律文件中。非正式英语主要用在日常会话和私人信件中。在非正式英语中,我们可以看见典型的句式,包括省略句、简单句、问句、感叹句、俚语和俗语,所有这些特点极少在正式文体中被发现。在商贸合同中,正式词、科技术语、外来词、系指词、词组搭配、句号、长句、复杂句、状语从句、名词、动词、介词随处可见。所有这一切显示它的正式程度。

(2)非人格性主要用在正式写作中,不包括任何情感色彩,个人观点和对事物的评判。人称代词极少用在正式文体中。非人格性显示客观和公正。非人格性适用于商贸合同。随着经济的发展,对外贸易主要涉及商品的出口和进口。商业合同在国与国之间起着桥梁的作用,它的条款受约于法律。所有这一切导致了商贸合同的非人格性。商贸合同以书面形式体现,合同语言的庄重性使得其在措辞上避免模糊和不清晰。在合同的起草上,文字措辞公正而无偏见。如"你"、"我"、"他们"都被 Party A, Party B, Buyer, Seller 代替。正规词如 inwttness whereof, whereas, by and between 随处可见。Shall 多频率地使用暗含着法律责任和义务而不是一般将来时或表示意愿的情态动词。感情色彩的形容词绝迹、代词罕见,词语重复,所有这一切导致了商贸合同的非人格性特点。

(3)可读性。可读性主要涉及读者的理解能力。正式文件的文书由于其难词、古词、长句很难让读者理解,商贸合同也如此。

1.5.3 商贸合同的题材 Theme of business contracts

商贸合同的题材涉及社会生活的各个方面:劳务出口合同、合资企业合同、销售合同、出口合同等等。在合同语言里,外来词、指示词、科技词、古词、正规词、陈述词、长句、主动语态、一般现在时等是商贸合同的特点。

1.6 合同英语的语体风格——版式
Variety of contracts in english language——Format

国际经贸合同的公文性使其文本在版式上有特殊的要求,具体体现在排版和大小写字母等方面,力求使合同显得内容完整、重点突出、结构严谨、条理清楚。在排版方面,采用大小标题、分章节、分条款、分项目的编排方式。在合同前文之后使用定义条款,避免意义分歧而产生纠纷。使用附录、一览表等形式详细列出必要的细节作为合同的组成部分。标题在国际经贸合同中习惯全部用大写,若是中文合同则采用黑体或粗体的形式来表达,以示醒目。

第二节 合同英语的语言特征
Section 2 Linguistic Features of Contract English

2.1 词语的特点
Lexical Features

2.1.1 正式词语的使用 Adoption of formal words

合同既是经济文书,又是法律文书,在词汇方面有其特有的特征,是各种英语文体中规范程度最高的一种,即"庄重文体"。为了防止误解和歧义,起草合同时措辞要准确、具体、严密,且符合标准,使合同显得正式、严肃。其用语通常正式保守,而弹性较大的小词、口语词、俚语、俗语、方言、戏谑语不能出现在国际商务合同中。这些词就是常说的书卷用词(literary words 或 learned words),即所谓的"大词(big words)"。一般的常用词和正式用语:begin—commence 开始;change—revise 修正;buy—purchase 购买;go—proceed 进行;consent—agreement 同意;think—deem 认为;give—render 给予;cancel—rescind 撤销等。

[例 16]

At the request of Party B, Party A agrees to send technicians to assist Party B to install the equipment.

应乙方要求,甲方同意派遣技术人员帮助乙方安装设备。assist 较 help 正式;

This Contract shall be governed by and construed in accordance with the laws of China.

本合同受中国法律管辖,并按中国法律解释。construe 较 explain, interpret 正式；

The personnel shall not to partake in any political activities in Iraq.

所有人员不得参加伊拉克国内的任何政治活动。partake in 较 take part in 正式；

The Employer shall render correct technical guidance to the personnel.

雇主应该对有关人员给予正确技术指导。render 较 give 正式；

Party A shall repatriate the patient to China and bear the cost of his passage to Guangzhou.

甲方应将病人遣返中国并负责其返回广州的旅费。repatriate 较 send back 正式；

The Employer may object to and require the Contractor to replace forthwith any of its authorized representatives who is incompetent.

雇主认为承包人委派的授权代表不合格时，可以反对并要求立即撤换。require 较 ask 正式；公文体 forthwith 较 at once 正式；

The Chairperson may convene an interim meeting based on a proposal made by one-third of the total number of directors.

董事长可以根据董事会过1/3董事的提议而召集临时董事会议。convene, interim 都是正式用词。

In case one party desires to sell or assign all or part of its investment subscribed, the other party shall have the preemptive right.

如一方想出售或转让其投资之全部或部分,另一方有优先购买权。法律用词 assign 较 transfer 正式；

In processing transactions, the manufacturers shall never have title either to the materials or the finished products.

加工贸易中,厂方无论是对原料还是成品都无所有权。法律用词 title 较 ownership 正式；

The term "Effective date" means the date on which this Agreement is duly executed by the parties hereto.

"生效期"指双方合同签字的日子。法律用词 execute 较 sign 正式。

2.1.2 古体词语的使用 Use the old style words/archaism

（1）作为一种非常规范的书面语,国际商务合同中还大量使用古体词语。这里所说的古体词语是指在国际商务合同中经常使用一些已在其他类别的英文文体中很少或不再使用的词汇。如 hereof, thereafter, whereby 等是非常正式和庄重的用语,在现代英语中,甚至是英语书面语中已经极为少用,但它们在英语合同文本里面依旧是频频被使用。这些旧体词主要是副词,在合同中使用他们,主要是为了避免重复累赘之感,做到准确、简洁、严密,反映出契约性行文正式、严肃、庄重的文体特征,也同时体现了法律文体的晦涩。一些主要用词 here 代表 this,there 代表 that,where 代表 what/which。常见的有:

1) here + 介词组成的复合词。

hereinafter (later in this contract 在本合同下文)

herein (in this 在……之中)

hereby (by means of 特此)

hereof (of this 在本件中)

hereafter (after this time 今后;此后)

2) there+ 介词构成的复合词。

thereafter (afterwards 此后;以后)

thereof (of that 由此;因此)

thereinafter (later in the same contract 在下文)

therein (in that ; in that particular 在那里;在那点上)

thereby (by that means ; in that connection 由此;在那方面)

3) where+ 介词构成的复合词。

whereas (considering that ; but 鉴于;而)

whereby (by what ; by which 由是;凭那个)

wherein (in what , in which 在哪点上)

whereof (of what ; of which 关于哪事)

所举的这些词在日常应用中相当有限,但在合同中的反复出现率却相当高。

[例 17]

This Sales Contract is made by and between the Sellers and the Buyers whereby the Sellers agree to sell and the Buyers agree to buy the under-mentioned goods according to the terms and conditions stipulated below.

兹经买卖双方同意,由卖方售出买方购进下列货物,并按下列条款签订本合同。

If either of the Parties fails to fulfill its obligations under this Contract, it shall compensate the other party for all its economic losses resulting therefore.

合同一方如不履行本合同或公司章程的义务,违约一方得赔偿另一方因此而遭受的经济损失。

All disputes in connection with this Contract or arising in the execution thereof shall first be settled amicably by negotiation.

凡有关合同或因执行本合同所发生的一切争执,双方应以友好方式协商解决。

(2)其中 WHEREAS 常大写,位于约首引出签约背景和目的。IN WITNESS WHEREOF 作为所协议事项的证据,该短语常用于合同的结尾条款。Hereinafter、whereby 也用在文本开头,用来加强语气。

[例 18]

WHEREAS the Employer is desirous that manpower can be rendered available for the construction of High-Rise Residential Complex in Baghdad, Iraq.

鉴于雇主欲请劳动力建造伊拉克巴格达的高层住宅综合大楼。

WHEREAS the Contractor is desirous to provide the manpower for the Works.

鉴于承包人想为此工程提供劳动力。

IN WITNESS WHEREOF, the parties have executed this Contract in duplicate by their duly authorized representatives on the date first above written.

作为所协议事项的证据,双方授权代表于上面首次写明的日期正式签订本协议一式两份。

This Agreement is made and entered into by and between AA Corporation (hereinafter called Supplier) and BB Company (hereinafter called Distributor) whereby Supplier agrees to grant to Distributor the exclusive right to sell the Products in the Territory on the terms and conditions stipulated as follows:

本协议由 AA 公司(以下简称供货人)与 BB 公司(以下简称经销人)签订。凭此协议供货人同意授予经销人按下列条款在指定地区销售指定产品的独家权利。

The Seller hereby is to warrant that the goods is up to the quality and is free from all defects.

卖方兹保证货物达到质量标准,没有瑕疵。

2.1.3 法律词汇的使用/专业术语的使用 Use the legal language/technical terms

(1)法律用语和合同专业术语

合同是具有法律效力的经济文书,其语言属于法律范畴。其中大量使用了正式的法律用语及国际商务方面的专业词汇。这些用词体现合同的庄重和严肃,从而体现了法律文体的威严。但大量的法律用语和合同专业术语又使得合同晦涩难懂,所以通常需要专业人士的解释。

1)法律词汇(legal words)

作为具有法律效力的契约性文件,合同中使用了较多的法律专业的术语。法律术语有狭义与广义之分。狭义的法律术语如 action(诉讼),final(终局裁决)等,不以大众是否理解或接受为转移,是商务合同语言准确表达的保障,是其独有的现象。而广义的法律术语则包括在法律文体中被赋予特定法律意义的常用词语,这类词语把握不准确的话很容易导致翻译和理解当中的模糊性,因此要格外留意。如,"The contract is concluded in case of acceptance of the offer"很容易译为"提议一旦接受,合同随即订立"。而实际上,"acceptance"与"offer"是合同法中两个重要的法律术语,其规范的译文分别为"承诺"、"要约",前者是指受要约人对要约内容表示同意,而后者则指一方希望与另一方订立合同。

2)专业术语(technical terms)

专业术语是指在某一学科或特定领域中使用的专门用语。这些专门用语有特定的含义,为该领域中的人们所熟悉。他们受到国际认可,并且有通用性,意义准确,无歧义。为准确地描述和表达商务活动中的各种单据、条款、交易的环节和双方所要承担的权利和义务,专业术语在商务合同中的频繁使用就显得极为普遍。例如,policy(保险单),negotiable(可转让的),liability(责任、义务),right of recourse(追索权),factoring(保理)等。无疑,这些专业术语可避免冗长的解释,简化交易过程,提高工作效率。

由于国际商务合同的种类很多,涉及面广泛。合同涉及的内容不同,使用的专业术语也数量巨多。根据国际商会制定的《2000年国际贸易术语解释通则》(INCOTERMS 2000),国际通用的十三种贸易术语分为 E、F、C、D 四个组。常见的术语有:

价格术语缩写:EXW 工厂交货(……指定地),FCA 货交承运人(……指定地),FAS 船边交货(……指定装运港),FOB 装运港船边交货(……指定装运港),CFR 成本加运费(……指定目的港),CIF 成本、保险费加运费(……指定目的港),DAF 边境交货(……指定地)等。

付款术语:Payment in Advance(预付货款),Payment after Arrival of the Goods(货到付款),Cash against Documents CAD(凭单付现),Remittance Against Documents(凭单付汇)等。

[例 19]

A meeting of partners is held at the end of every year. At the meeting, the manager should report the state of business and, having made out an inventory, a balance sheet and a profit and loss account, submit them to be verified by the partners.

每年年底召开股东会,由经理报告营业情况,并开具财产清单、资产负债表及损益表,呈交股东审核。

这段文字句式结构不复杂,但有几个财经术语:partner 合伙人、合股人,business 商业、企业、营业,inventory 财产清单、商品目录,balance sheet 资产负债表、资金平衡表,account 账户,verify 查证、核实。

For each transaction, Party A shall allow Party B ……% discount on the basis of C & F London.

每笔交易甲方均应按成本加运费到伦敦的价格给予乙方百分之……的折扣。C & F（Cost and Freight）,意为成本加运费。

By means of an irrevocable, confirmed L/C payable by draft at 30 days sight.

凭不可撤销的、保兑的信用证见票 30 天付款。L/C（Letter of Credit）,是一个术语缩写,意为信用证

（2）普通词有特定意义或特定用法（Common words with uncommon meanings）

合同中会涉及许多专业术语,这些词在合同中都有单一、明确的含义,不能理解为普通、常用的意思,如 collection , confirm , acceptance , tolerance , more or less , 这些词通常分别理解为"收集"、"确认"、"接受"、"承受"、"大约";而在合同中这些词可用作术语,其含义则分别为"托收"、"保兑"（confirmed L/C）、"承兑"（Documents against Acceptance）、"公差"及"溢短装"等。又例如,dirty of Bill of Lading（不洁提单）和 flat price（统一价格）很容易误解为"不洁提单"和"平价"。

[例 20]

The Seller shall present the following documents required for negotiation/collection to the banks.

这是支付条件中经常出现的句子,句中 negotiation 和 collection 是专业术语,如果理解为"谈判"和"收取"等常用意思,译文则会含糊不清,令人费解。而此处的意思应为"议付"和"托收"。

句子可译为:卖方必须将下列单据提交银行议付或托收。

[例 21]

Partial shipment is allowed.

这是合同中有关货物装运的规定,如果把 partial shipment 译为"部分装运",此条款则会出现明显的漏洞,合同一方可理解为只需部分发货,其余不装运亦可。而准确的译文则为"允许分批装运",即卖方可以几次发货。

其他如 telegraphic transfer（电汇）, usance L/C（远期信用证）, force

majeure（不可抗力）及 sales by sample（凭样品销售）等也是常见专业术语。此外,合同中有许多表示机构、名称的用语,英译时必须正确理解该词构词变化及在合同中的特定含义,不能张冠李戴,如:consignor,consignee,shipper,carrier 这四个表示名称的词经常在装运条款及提单上出现,意思容易混淆,如把 shipper 理解为"承运人"或"船公司",与 carrier 等同,实际上它们是完全不同的两家单位,shipper 正确的译文应为"发货人",与 consignor 意思相同。

(3)其他的特殊用语

IN CONSIDERATION OF 以……为约因/报酬

约因是英美法系的合同有效成立要件之一,没有则合同不能依法强制履行。但是,大陆法系的合同则无此规定。

Now therefore, in consideration of the premises and the covenants herein, contained, the parties hereto agree as follows:

兹以上述各点和契约所载条款为约因,订约双方协议如下:

In consideration of the payment to be made by Party A to Party B, Party B hereby covenants with Party A to complete the building in conformity with the provisions of the Contract.

乙方特此立约向甲方保证按合同规定完成工程建设,以取得甲方所付的报酬。

NOW, THEREFORE 兹特

此短语用于 WHEREAS 条款之后引出具体协议事项的常用开头语,并与其后 hereby 的结合。如果无 HEREAS 条款,则本短语可省略:

NOW, THEREFORE, it's hereby agreed and understood as follows;

兹特协议和谅解如下:

NOW THESE PRESENTS WITNESS（兹特立约为据）

本句话也是用于 WHEREAS 条款之后引出具体协议事项。

PRESENTS = the present writings 是主语,WITNESS 是谓语:

NOW THESE PRESENTS WITNESS that it is hereby agreed between the parties hereto as follows:

兹特立约为据,并由订约双方协议如下:

IN THE PRESENCE OF 见证人

本短语只在有见证人时使用——在订约双方当事人签名的下方由见证人签名作证,一般是相关的律师(attorney)或公证处(notary public):

IN THE PRESENCE OF the parties hereto have hereunder set their respective hands and seals:

作为协议事项的证据,订约双方各自签名盖章如下:
For and on behalf the First Party(甲方代表):
The EMPLOYER（雇主）…
Capacity（职位）…
In the Presence of（见证人）…
Capacity（职位）…
Address（地址）…
For and on behalf of the Second Party(乙方代表):
The CONTRACTOR（承包人）…
Capacity（职位）…
In the Presence of（见证人）…
Capacity（职位）…
Address（地址）…

2.1.4 同义词/近义词的使用 Reduplication of the synonyms and near-synonyms

（1）为了避免歧义或误解,国际商务合同中极少使用代词,对一些关键性的词/词组较多使用重复同义词或同义词词组来确保合同双方的权利和义务。因为并列成分之间通常意义交叉,可以在内容上互相补充,从而使表述更全面,更缜密严谨,也更具有弹性。既可以保证内容上准确,又维护了法律文件的独解性尊严。而且表面上看同义词表达相同的意义,但是它们在合同中除了体现共同的一面外,还强调起个性的一面。所以,在使用同义词时,对其具体所指的意义加以分析是很有必要的。

例如合同中经常使用的 perform、fulfill 都表示执行、履行的意思,都可以用在 contract 之前,表达"履行合同"。但是,在具体选用时却要有区别:perform 在法律上表述的含义是 to do what one party is obliged to do by a contract, fulfill 的含义是 to do everything which is promised in a contract, 所以使用该词,可以辨别合同方的义务和权责。In accordance with the Agreement, both Party A and Party B promise to perform the contract.(甲乙双方同意按约定履行合同)The contractor shall fulfill all of its duties and obligations in carrying out its work and services hereunder.(承租人必须忠实守信和履行下列各项规则)常见的同义、近义词有:"terms, conditions"（条款）, furnish and provide （提供）, "clause, covenant ,agreements"（协议）, "negligence, fault, failure"（失误）, rights or obligations（权利或义务）等。

[例 22]
This Agreement and any rights or obligations hereunder are not transferable

or assignable by one party to this Agreement without the consent of the other party hereto.

本协议以及本协议所规定的权利或义务，没有另一方的同意就不得擅自转让。

该例中的形容词 transferable 和 assignable 属同义形容词。

[例 23]

This contract shall be submitted to the Approving Department of the People's Republic of China for approval.

The effective term of this Contract shall begin on the effective date hereof and end on the date the term of the lVC (Joint Venture Contract) expires ...

Any termination of this Contract for any reason shall be reported to the original approving authorities.

本合同呈中华人民共和国主管部门批准。

本合同有效期限是自合资合同生效之日起至期满之日止……

若因任何原因或任何一方造成终止合同，均需报原合同批准之机构批准。

（2）同义词并用的现象（juxtaposition）。例如, by and between, terms and conditions, fulfill and perform, losses and damages, make and enter into 等同时出现在合同用语中，比单独使用某一词表述的意思更为完善，但必须要根据合同的具体内容和权利与义务关系，小心谨慎选择合适的词汇用语，切忌滥用同义词。

[例 24]

This agreement is made and entered into by and between Party A and Party B.

本合同由 A、B 双方制定并且签署。

在句中 made and entered into 是一组同义词，表示签订协议。By and between 是另一对同义词，表示由甲方和乙方签署。

（3）与数量、金钱、价格、期限等相关的数字在合同中非常重要，这也是合同当事人最为关心的。为杜绝漏洞，保证数字的唯一和准确，合同中重复数字的表达，选择先采用"单位 + 阿拉伯数字"，后用英文重复表述的方式。

[例 25]

US 4,800 (Say U. S. Dollar Four Thousand Eight Hundred only).

Total value: US .5, 200, 000. 00 (Say US Dollars Five Million Two Hundred Thousand only)

2.1.5 常规词"shall"的专业用法 Use the legal term "shall"

(1)权利义务的约定部分构成了商务合同的主体,情态动词的准确使用旨在明确约定当事人的权利(可以做什么),当事人的一般义务(应当做什么),强制性义务(必须做什么)和禁止性义务(不得做什么)。

"shall"是国际商务合同中经常会出现的一个词,把握该词的确切含义,必须理解其用法上的特殊性。合同等法律文书中,shall 并非单纯表示将来时,而且不受主语人称的影响,它是一个法律词汇,相当于汉语中"应当"、"应该"或"须",表示法律责任或法律上可强制执行的义务,具有约束力,而不是一般的道义责任。同样,其否定式表达则相当于汉语中的"不得",不能理解为"不应该"或"不能"。

[例 26]

This Contract shall be written in English in four copies. Each party shall keep two copies.

本合同应以英文写成,一式四份,双方各持两份。

This Contract shall become effective upon and from the date on which it is signed.

本合同签字生效。

The seller shall not be responsible for failure or delay in delivery of the entire lot or a proportion of the goods under this contract in consequences of any accident of Force Majeure.

卖方因不可抗力事故,对未能或延期交付本合同的部分或全部货物,不承担责任。

The Employer shall make a prepayment of 20% of the contract value to the Contractor within 10 days after signing the Contract.

雇主应于签约后十天内向承包人支付相当于承包合同价值 20%的预付款。

No assignment shall be effective should there be any violation of the above stipulations.

违反上述规定的,其转让无效。

The Contract shall thereafter be automatically extended for a period of one year.

本合同今后应自动延长一段时间,为期一年。

Party A shall pay the interest.

甲方须/应负担利息。

Party A shall not be liable for any losses or damages to the machinery caused by a fire, flood, strike, natural calamities or any other causes which is beyond the control of Party A and thus unavoidable.

甲方对因火灾、水灾、罢工、自然灾害或其他甲方不能控制或不可避免的原因给机器造成的损失或损害不负责任。

(2)在法律英语中用 shall 来替换 will、should 和 may。"Will"无论语气还是强制力要比"shall"弱,宜译为"将"、"原"。它只表示对合同一方的某种建议或合同双方之外第三方的行为的说明,不构成法律约束。"Should"意为"应该",带有主观意思,用来表示语气较强的假设、比如"万一",表示"这样做最好"。若用于条件句中,则表示较低的可能性。"May"表示"可以"、"可能"。这两个意思在日常用语中都可用"can"来表达,但是在合同中几乎只用"may"而不用"can",因为前者比后者语气更正式。

[例 27]

The parties hereto shall, first of all, settle any dispute arising from or in connection with the contract by friendly negotiations. Should such negotiations fail, such dispute may be referred to the People's Court having jurisdiction on such dispute for settlement in the absence of any arbitration clause in the disputed contract or in default of agreement reached after such dispute occurs.

本句中的 shall 和 may 表达准确。出现争议后应当先行协商,所以采用了义务性"约定",如果协商解决不了,作为当事人的权利,用选择性约定 may 也很妥当。如果 may 和 shall 调换位置会怎么样?前半句的 shall 换用 may 后,意思变成了当事人可以通过协商解决,意思上说得过去,但后半句的 may 换用 shall 后,变成了应当诉讼解决,好像一出事,就要诉之法庭,这就有些极端了。

本句可译:双方首先应通过友好协商,解决因合同而发生的或与合同有关的争议。如果协商未果,合同中又无仲裁条款约定或争议发生后未就仲裁达成协议的,可将争议提交有管辖权的人民法院解决。

2.1.6 外来词的使用 Use foreign words

(1) 商务合同英语中使用的商务类专业术语有不少源于拉丁语或法语,有些则是由其词根派生或合成,许多术语都有相同的前缀或后缀。它们的意义比较稳定,利于精确地表达概念。例如,商务合同中常用的 ad-valorem duty(拉丁语:从价关税),bona fide holder(拉丁语:汇票的善意持票人),vis-à-vis(法语:与……相比较),pro rata tax rate(拉丁语:比例税率,即 proportional tax rate),force majeure(法语:不可抗力),pro forma(拉丁语:估算表)。

(2) 商务合同英语中同时也使用了为数不少的主要来源于拉丁语或法语的法律类专业术语。随着基督教传入英国(公元 597 年),一些拉丁语词汇就开始直接或间接地进入英语。拉丁语词汇进入英语主要采取两种方式:间接方式(即有些拉丁语词汇直接进入法语,然后由法语再转入英语并被英语接受)以及直接方式(即有些拉丁语词汇直接进入英语,并取得合法地位)。例如: crimen falsi(伪证罪), de facto fort(事实上侵权行为), de facto agreement(未经合法手续或正式承认的事实上的协议), action in persinam(债权诉讼), proviso(限制性条款), void ab initio(由最初开始即属无效)等。同样,由于历史的原因(公元1066年"诺曼征服"后,法语成为当时英国的官方语言),英语中许多法律术语由法语借用或转化而来,例如:complaint , statute , verdict ,warrant ,bail 等。

2.1.7 使用大写字母 Use capitalized letters

在英语商务合同中,有些词或条款必须大写,包括合同当事人;一些特定的组织,比如说仲裁机构;关键字;特定条款和附录;相关法律法规;价格条款等。字母大写的目的是强调重要条款,如:Contract(合同), Agreement(协议), Party A(甲方), Party B(乙方), the Seller(买方), the Buyer(买方), the Agent (代理人)等。要达到的效果是一旦打开合同书就能够注意到这些条款和项目。

[例28]

The Sellers shall mark on each package with fadeless paint the package number, gross weight, net weight, measurement and warning such as: "KEEP AWARY FROM MOISTURE""HANDLE WITH CARE""THIS SIDE UP".

一旦合同履行者看到该合同,无论是在装货、运输还是卸货过程中,根据该说明,货物都会得到妥善的处理。

2.2 句式特点
Syntactic Features

2.2.1 条件句 Conditional sentences

英语句子类型的表意功能各不相同,商务合同英语对句子类型的选择存在着明显的倾向性和侧重性。

合同要求准确严密的规约当事人的权利、义务和责任,因而合同英语思维缜密,逻辑性强,既要考虑到各种不同情况,又要排除各种例外情形。合同条文在规定双方应该履行的义务之外,还考虑到各种可能发生的情况和处理办法。所以合同条款中有较多的条件句,尤其是在有关付款、违约责任、不可抗力、财产处理和仲裁等中更是屡见不鲜。常常由 in case(万一), unless(除非), provided that(假设), should +S +V 结构引出条件状语。

[例29]

In case equipment and technical information , which are requested in the contract, are found missing, SINO shall be able to request INVESTOR for replacement.

合同规定设备和技术资料如有遗失,中方得要求投资人补交。

If either party considers it necessary to extend the agreement, the proposing party shall notify the other party two months prior to its expiration.

如有任何一方认为有必要延期,则建议的一方应于期满前两个月通知另一方。

… and shall automatically become null and void at the expiration of the said period if not extended by mutual agreement.

如果期满时双方不协商延期,它即自动失效。

In the event the Company purchases such items outside China, the Company shall entrust Party B to procure such items provided that the price of such items shall not be higher than that of similar items in the international market.

如果合作经营公司在中国境外购买这些原料、设备时,可委托乙方购买,但价格不应超过国际市场同类产品的价格。

2.2.2 非人称句式 Impersonal sentences

因为合同是法律文书,而法律是客观、公正的,所以合同一般采用第三人称的语气以表明合同是建立在平等、公平的基础之上。因此,合同中一般没有人称代词I、we、you、they、it等出现,一是为避免误解,二是为了公平。同时为了使句子保持结构平衡,特别是为了使合同内容的叙述全面、严谨,减少主观色彩,对合同中的双方一视同仁,合同中常常使用非人称句,即"it +be + 形容词或分词 +that"的结构。因为非人称句式可表示一种严肃、正式、庄重的感觉。

[例 30]

It is mutually agreed that the Certificate of Quality and Weight issued by the Chinese Import and Export Commodity Inspection Bureau at the port of shipment shall be taken as the basis of delivery.

买卖双方约定以装运口岸、中国进出口商品检验局签发的品质和重量检验证书作为品质和数量的交货依据。

2.2.3 复杂长句及完整句 Complex or complete sentences

长句在国际商务合同中频繁使用,是因为合同语言要求表意全面、严谨,每一句话都要表达一个内容完整而又没有丝毫模糊的意义。若要将各方的权利和义务在有限的条款中完整、明确地体现出来,就必须运用各种附加语、修饰语及说明语,把各种可能性都考虑在内,同时把所有可能产生的误解及歧义都排除在外。虽然句子结构复杂,常常是句中有句,层层修饰,但表达的内容相对更为准确、严密、逻辑性强,一般超过英文语体的句子平均长度(17词),有时,一个句子就构成一个段落。

[例如 31]

All profits paid by the company to Party C, all salaries and allowances paid by the company to foreign personnel, all direct expenses incurred as a result of the technology transfer and which must be paid by the company to Party C in foreign currency and all other payments that must be made by the company in foreign currency that be made in United Slates Dollars or some other freely convertible currency that is mutually agreed upon.

该公司支付给C方的利润、外来人员的工资、津贴和因技术转让而发生的应以外币支付的直接费用,以及所有其他应以外币支付的款项,应以美元或相互同意的可自由兑换的货币支付。

The prices stated are based on current freight rates, any increase or decrease in freight rates at time of shipment is to be the benefit of the buyer, with the seller assuming the payment of all transportation charges to the point or place of delivery.

合同价格是以现行运费计算,装运时运费的增减均属买方。卖方则承担至交货地的全部运费。

2.2.4 陈述句 Assertive sentences

合同大多采用陈述句的形式来表达,因为合同是具有法律约束力的正式文件,在签约前双方经过多回合的磋商、谈判才可能就合同中的各项条款达成共识和确认,因而不会出现疑问句,否则还会就有疑问的地方进行新一轮的谈判,直到双方都认可为止。又因合同是客观反映事实的公文体书面文件,因而也不会出现表达个人情感的感叹句和祈使句。祈使句一般只出现在来自上级部门或领导的指示、通知、批复等文书。

[例 32]

The Buyer agrees to buy and the Seller agrees to sell the under – mentioned goods on terms and conditions stipulated below.

2.3 时态和语态
Tense and Voice

2.3.1 多用被动语态 Use more passive voice

在许多情况下,商务合同英语要求突出动作的对象,而不重视动作的完成者,也就是说,商务合同英语的文体因素和语言环境要求强调客观事实,而尽量减少个人感情、意愿的影响,从而使论述更客观、平实。因而动词的被动语态形式有很高的出现率。但是,在涉及双方的义务、责任和权利时,则需慎用被动语态,因为被动语态可弱化语气强度,使意义含糊,甚至造成责权不明。因此,需视实际情况,适当地使用被动和主动语态,或者在被动语态中用 by 短语结构引出施事者,进一步明确责任和义务的来源。

[例 33]

Party B is hereby appointed by Party A as its exclusive sales agent in Singapore.

乙方被甲方委托为在新加坡的独家销售代理商。

Insurance shall be covered by the Buyer against all risks, including war and strike risks, for 110% of the invoice value.

买方应按发票金额的 110% 投保一切险,包括战争险和罢工险。

The territory covered by this agreement is confined to the United Kingdom only.

本协议下所含的地区只限于联合王国。

This agreement is made and entered into by and between the China National Cereals, Oils & Foodstuffs Import & Export Corporation.

本协议由中国粮油进出口公司与……公司签订。

2.3.2 多用现在时 Use more simple present tense

因为合同是具有法律效力的文书,合同条款中规定的是双方的权利和义务,这些权利和义务具有一定的通用性,大多成为相关方面的国际惯例。因此,合同语句经常采用现在时,尽管很多条款规定的是合同签订以后的事项。

[例 34]

Licensee may terminate this Contract 90 days after a written notice thereof is sent to Licensor upon the happening of one of the following events:

当有下列事件之一发生,被许可人提前 90 天向许可人发送书面通知后,可以终止合同:

Licensor becomes insolvent or a liquidator of Licensor is appointed;

许可人无力偿付债务或其破产清算人已被指定;

The patent described in Article 2 is not issued within 30 days from signing this Contract; and

第二条规定的专利未在签约后 30 天之内发布;

Licensor fails to perform its obligations under this Contract.

许可人未能履行其合同义务。

2.3.3 直接表达方式用得多，间接表达方式用得较少 Use more direct style and less indirect style

[例 35]

This Article applies only to bondholders who have been paid in full.

本条款只适用于已全部偿付的债券持有者。

2.3.4 尽量使用一个动词，避免使用"动词 + 名词 + 介词"的同义短语 Use simple verbs

[例 36]

Party A shall make an appointment of its representative within 30 days after signing the Contract.

甲方应于签约后 30 天内指派其授权代表。宜用 appoint 代替 make an appointment of.

[例 37]

Party A will give consideration to Party B's proposal of exclusive agency.

甲方愿意考虑乙方独家代理的建议。宜用 consider 代替 give consideration to.

Part 2 Focusing on Words and Phrases

1. Finding Meaning in Context

Words	Meaning in General English	Meaning in Legal English
discourse	演讲,论述	语篇
variety	多样性	语体,语体风格
register	注册,登记	语域
context	上下文	语境
final	最终的,最后的	终局裁决
offer	提供,贡献	要约
acceptance	接受	承诺
collection	收集	托收
confirm	确认	保兑
flat price	平价	统一价格
action	行动	诉讼
policy	政策	保险单

2. Useful Expressions in Legal English

1) The annexes as listed in Article 19 to this contract shall form an integral part of this contract.

2) This Contract shall be governed by and construed in accordance with the laws of China.

3) The Buyer agrees to buy and the Seller agrees to sell the under-mentioned goods on terms and conditions stipulated below.

Part 3 Evaluating Your Achievements

词汇日志 Vocabulary Log

register	语域
terms	术语
roundabout	模棱两可的
stylistic competence	文体分析的能力
stylistic awareness	文体意识
lexical features	词语的特点
archaism	古体词语
syntactic features	句式特点
Force Majeure	不可抗力
literary words/learned words	书卷用词
right of recourse circumlocution	追索权
balance sheet	资产负债表

章节练习 Check Your Progress

1. Fill in the Blanks

1) The origin of modern stylistics is _____.

2) The linguistic features of contract English are many, among all of them, generally we will mention _____, _____ and _____.

3) In the sentence "The obligations contained in Articles 10.5 and 10.6 shall neither be affected by the liquidation of the contract nor by a premature termination of the same", we should use the word _____ to take the place of "cancel" and _____ to "end", because we'd better use formal words.

2. Legal Terminology

1) register

2) variety

3) discourse

3. Sentence Translation

1）在英语学习过程中，造成语域误用的原因主要是缺乏"文体意识"或者说缺乏"文体洞察力"。

2）为了保证合同文字确切，通常要求重复同样的词语或术语来表达同样的意思。

3）雇主认为承包人委派的授权代表不合格时，可以反对并要求立即撤换。

4）本合同应受到中国法律管辖，并按中国法律解释。

5）Partial shipment is allowed.

6）A meeting of partners is held at the end of every year. At the meeting, the manager should report the state of business and, having made out an inventory, a balance sheet and a profit and loss account, submit them to be verified by the partners.

自我评价 Self-Assessment Log

In this Chapter, you worked through these activities. How did each of them help you become a better learner? Check A lot, A little, or Not at all.

	A lot	A little	Not at all
I discussed the linguistic features of contract English.	❑	❑	❑
I learned words and expressions in register, variety and context.	❑	❑	❑
I gathered information about schools of discourse.	❑	❑	❑
I learned lexical features of contract English.	❑	❑	❑
I grasped syntactic features of contract English.	❑	❑	❑
I could make a list of the features of contract language.	❑	❑	❑
I could modify some wordy contracts.	❑	❑	❑

（Add something）_____

_____

Chapter 6

第六章 国际商务合同的条款与结构
Clauses and Structures of International Business Contracts

The commonly seen English contract formats are from Britain and the United States, Japan, Hong Kong and Singapore respectively. With a few exceptions, the entire contract, from the paragraphs, sentences to terms is more or less the same. The structure always includes three main sections of the preamble, main body and final clauses.

Although the language of business contracts requires accuracy and clarity, the use of vague words is not uncommon. In fact, if we use ambiguous language for assistance in drafting parties' rights and obligations, the terms will be more accurate and complete. The drafters of the contract should be proficient in the structure and variety, so that on the basis of equality, both sides could make the deal.

 Learning Objectives

In this chapter, students will learn how to:
◎ give the definition of vague words;
◎ understand the usage of vague words;
◎ divide the structure of a contract;
◎ understand the content of body.

 Questions to Consider

1) What are the functions of vague words?
2) How many parts are there in a contract?
3) What is the general content of body in the contract?

Part 1 Focusing on Legal Knowledge

第一节　合同条款的语用性
Section 1　Pragmatics of Contract Clauses

1.1 模糊性
Vagueness

1.1.1 定义和来源 Definition and source

模糊是语言的一个重要属性,指语言所指称的概念外延不明确,也就是某种语言形式表达意义范围界限的不明确性或不确定性。简单说来模糊语(vague words)指一些把事物弄得模模糊糊的词。这些词语就话语的正式程度或涉及范围,对话语的精确性进行修整或限定,使话语介于肯定和否定之间,体现了说话人的主观认识和评价(subjective understanding and evaluation)。

精确的语言在法律语体中的使用普遍得到人们的认知和注重,但模糊性的语言在法律实践中的应用却相当谨慎。其实,从主体,客体和语言本身的特点来看,模糊是法律语言的固有属性。模糊语言的产生是由于使用那些没有明确界限的词语,以至于在其程度或范围上仍存在选择的问题。例如,如果顾客从机动车销售商那儿订购了一辆红色小汽车,那么很显然蓝色的汽车不符合合同的要求。但是,一份蓝色汽车的订单并不能确定顾客心中所想的蓝色的深浅程度。藏青色的汽车也可以是在订单范围之内的,但是可能会被拒收。销售商可以要求顾客详细说明所要求的蓝色的深度,从而避免顾客拒收汽车。模糊的词语进入法律文件的途径之一,是因为觉得含义明确的词语可能会有刺激性或不愉快的含义而需要使用委婉语。

在法律中使用模糊表达方式的一个著名的例子是1890年的谢尔曼反垄断法(Sherman Antitrust Law)。这一法律禁止"对贸易的不合理的限制"(unreasonable restraints of trade)。什么叫做"不合理的"?这项法律并没有对此进行明确的定义,而是把给出定义的任务交给了法庭。这是立法机关不愿带头预先作出什么是被禁止行为的详细说明的例子。

1.1.2 分类 Classification

模糊主要包括静态模糊和动态模糊。

(1)静态模糊,又称语义模糊,是指客观存在于自然语言中的模糊特征。由于自然界中从一个概念到另一个概念存在着中间连续状态或不明晰的过渡,相关的概念只能表示一个大致的范围。总之,客观事物的繁复性与人类认知的特点造成了概念的模糊性。Ruth Kempson 将模糊分为四类:所指概念模糊、意义不确定、词义不具体、词项意义的确定存在分裂现象。他指出几类模糊概念:一些表示不定量限定概念的词、所有格结构、缺乏专指性、具体性的词类、英语中一些亲属词意义不明,如 uncle 与 aunt 可以指五种以上的亲属关系。

(2)动态模糊,又称语用模糊,是指语言在使用过程中所呈现出的模糊性,即说话人在特定语境或上下文中使用不确定的、模糊的或间接的向听话人表达数种言外之意的现象。如:Would you like to come in and sit down? 这句话能够表达邀请、请求、命令等三种不同的言外之意。

1.1.3 模糊和歧义 Vagueness and ambiguity

首先,模糊(vagueness)并不等同于"歧义(ambiguity)"。"模糊"所指的是一个特定的词语在范围和应用上的不确定性,即词语的所指范围边界的不确定性。这种不确定性通常是不能或无须通过上下文加以排除的,它缘于本体的模糊性(ontological fuzziness)和认识的模糊性(epistemological fuzziness)。这种模糊性语言融词汇内涵的可塑性、有限性与外延的模糊性、无限性于一体。

"歧义"指的是模棱两可,以及同一个词语可具有两个不同的独立含义。例如,合同中如果这样约定:I will pay back in a year,那么双方当事人对"in"就可能有异议,因为单从字面上看,"in"可以认为是"within"的意思(在……之内),但也可以理解为"after"之意(在……之后)。

如一借款纠纷,被告向原告借 2000 元钱,数月后,被告欲先还 500 元给原告,但被告到原告家时,只有原告之父在,原告的父亲应被告的要求,写一收条"还欠款 500 元整"。后原告要求被告偿还剩余 1500 元欠款时,被告坚持收条含义为"还"(hái)欠款 500 元整,即已还 1500 元,仅 500元未还,双方争执不下,诉诸法院。此案的问题,其实正是由于"还欠款"一词的歧义而产生的。依原告解释,"还欠款"应读作"还"(huán)欠款,"还"为动词;而依被告解释,"还欠款"应读作"还"(hái)欠款,"还"为副词。双方的分歧,不是产生于"还欠款"一词的外延界定,无论依何方解释,这一词的外延是明确的,双方争执的原因其实在于"还欠款"一词可有两种不同的含义,而这两种含义之间并无相通之处,这就是因词语的歧义性造成纠纷的显著案例。

模糊词反映了人的思维方式,在一定条件下,它的高度概括性可以起到更准确、更全面的作用,如果说模糊词语在法律语言中的正确运用是有其必要性的话,那么在法律语言中,对这种因语义模棱两可而引起的歧义性是要绝对避免的。这是因为模糊词语是语言学的一种现象,它反映了自然语言的一种本质特点,而语义上的模棱两可只能是不严谨、不周密的表现。从语法上讲,这是一种病句类型,在以严谨、准确为特点的法律语言当中出现这种情况,极有可能改变当事人权利义务的归属和各方利益的划分,进而影响法律本身的准确和庄重。

1.1.4 功能 Functions

(1)正面功能(advantages):在某些情况下使用模糊的表达方式是有好处的,它常被用来以一种渐进的方式说明一个问题,即用概括的语言认定一个问题,然后允许法庭或者行政机关加以详细说明。在合同中,尤其是在双方或多方当事人之间可以对文件的条款进行谈判的情况下,含糊的词语可以使当事人达到一定的妥协(compromise),以便交易能继续进行。

1)准确性功能(precision)

模糊和精确似乎是两个相悖的概念,而事实上,由于人的思维有模糊的特征,客观事物和现象虽然有时是清晰明确的,但人们却利用模糊判断和推理来准确把握事物的本质。当客观事实不符合某种典型现象时,最好的表达方式就是采取最接近的相关术语加上适当的模糊限制语来进行描写。模糊限制语其实是使话语更加符合客观事实(enhancing objectivity),而且所使用的限定成分越多,说话者对话语的真值承诺程度越高,所传达的话语信息的精确度也就越高。

[例1]

Party A agrees to help Joint Venture to invite and recruit Chinese experts, technicians, workers and other personnel and Party B agrees to help Joint Venture to invite and recruit foreign experts.

这里所使用的 other personnel 就是一个模糊词语。条款在列举了要招聘的各种人员(专家、技术人员、工人)之后,再加上 other personnel 这样的模糊词语,就使这一条款的规定有了一定的概括性,使表意更加严密,从而更大限度地包含了甲方需招聘的人员。若将 other personnel 省略或改用确切词语,则会使条款的订立失去表达的严谨性和内容的包容性。

[例2]

①The goods you ordered are out of order.

②Strictly speaking, the goods are partly out of order.

例①是肯定地下结论,而例②用了 strictly speaking 与 partly 这两个模糊限制语使句子的表述更加精确,不是全部缺货,而是部分地不能满足供应,这样既客观地描述了当时的情况,又为进一步合作提供了可能。比起例句①,②显得准确又得体。

2) 灵活功能(flexibility)

模糊性语言的运用可以提高法律语言的灵活性,使法律具备了较强的适应性。由于主体认知客观事物受到环境、时代、能力大小和价值评判的制约,在一定条件下,人们不可能对所有形形色色的社会现象、法律现象作出全面的认知并将其一一列举出来,也不可能对所有的法律行为逐条做出界定和定性,而法律语言又要维护法律的完整性(completeness),有效惩治各种犯罪,这就需要模糊性语言对这些缺漏和不足加以补充和充实,以便法律概念的外延扩大到法律所规定的范围。

比如在诸多关于数量、性质、时间的条款中,运用模糊语言可以避免把话说得过死或太绝而拴住自己的手脚或使自己处于被动地位。因此,模糊词语的恰当运用可以给自己在日后产生纠纷时留有回旋的余地,有效地保护自己。如果房地产开发商在商品房销售合同中约定:The greenery coverage will be between 25%~35%. 那么,房地产开发商就有较大的余地来确定绿地覆盖面积。

[例 3]

If the Supplier fails to commence the work necessary to remedy such defect or any damage to the Equipment caused by such defect within a reasonable time, the Buyer may carry out such work in a reasonable manner, and the reasonable direct costs incurred by the Buyer in connection therewith shall be paid to the Buyer by the Supplier, providing that the labor costs included in such costs shall be calculated based on the local costs incurred in the country in which the Contract Plant is to be constructed.

这里有三处出现模糊措辞。究竟多长时间算是 within a reasonable time (在合理的期限之内),什么方式可称为 in a reasonable manner(以合理的方式),多少直接成本才算是 the reasonable direct costs(合理的直接成本),这些均无明确或统一规定,但却运用得恰到好处,比用精确的数字表达得更准确,也更有说服力,体现了合同条款的预见性及适用性。

[例 4]

《香港合约法纲要》(Digest of Hong Kong Contract Law)中规定:要约在要约人规定的期限内有效。如果要约人没有规定期限的,要约在合理的期限内有效。合理的期限(a reasonable time)在此就是一个事实问题,其没有精确而受要约规定的条件影响,该立法目的在于体现法律条文的预见性、灵活性及适用性。英国上诉法院曾裁定:在能够合理地推定受要约人已经拒绝要约之际,合理期限即告结束。

3)礼貌功能(politeness)

在商业活动中,话语的礼貌对于交际活动的双方显得尤为重要,交际的态度会直接影响合作的成果与合作的前景。交际双方若需进行有效的交际必然是双方抱着互相理解和配合的态度,在觉得对方可能会因误解而使用导致交际不畅的言语时,交流需要维护和保全双方的"面子"。为了保存双方的面子,说话人会采取迂回的方式,这就需要求助于模糊限制语的帮助。出于礼貌的模糊语常采用的方法有:采用条件句提出一种可能性,表明只是对一种情况所作的判断,以及采用情态动词等。

[例5]

① Parts of your requirement are quite reasonable.

② To the best of his knowledge, the horse has no unsoundness of health on the date of sale that will cause the horse unfit for his training.

在例①中讲话人用了一系列模糊限制语 "一部分"、"相当"、"合理"等,只表示出会对这些要求进行考虑,绝没有任何实质性的承诺,比起直接回答"你的这些要求不是根本没道理,也有一些可能有道理,那些我们可能会给你解决"要灵活得多。这样对方容易接受,也给自己留下了较大的余地。例②中 to the best of his knowledge 的使用考虑到了交际双方对此事的认可程度,比起省略这样的限制所导致的表达上的断然,显得礼貌而周全。

4)严谨逻辑功能(insuring strictness and completeness)

在商务合同中,为了使语言能更准确地描述客观现象或更准确地表达思想内容,往往在语句中加入适量的模糊限制语,对于原有意义进行修饰和限制,使其稍微偏离原来所指而更接近所要描述的现象或所要传达的思想。利用模糊限制语在描述程度、数量、范围、形状等方面的伸缩性可以使表述与实际情况更接近,从而使命题更加严谨、周全。同时,借助模糊限制语无定量、无定界或无定指的特性可用尽量少的语言来传达最大限度的信息量,满足交际的需要,避免为力求精确而导致的累赘。

[例6]

① Under the typical pay, the individual earns the commitment on the contributions that he and his employers make, of about 2 percent per year.

② The sum of the expected guarantee payments and the 6 percent saving rate is almost always less than the tax.

例①句中的 about 与②中的"almost"都是减弱语,起模糊限制的作用。减弱了断言的程度,使句子意义与实际情况更加接近,表明实际情况虽然与句子所陈述的现象大体相符,但仍难免会有出入,模糊语的使用使论述更确切(concise)。

5)自我保护功能(Interests protecting)

合同行为是负有法律责任的行为,必须考虑到可能出现的问题,可能有一天阅读你的合同的人不仅仅是合同的双方,还可能是法官和陪审团。所以在合同写作时必须考虑可能出现的偏差,利用模糊限制语,以达到保护自己,减轻责任的目的。用于这一语用功能最常见的模糊限制语是情态动词、"may"、"might",表示判断的动词"appear"和"seem",以及限定词"about"、"mostly"、"almost"等。

[例7]

The net weight of the contents is about 250 kg, with 1kg as the margin.

这样的表达为商家留有余地。即便是全自动生产线的产品,也不能保证没有误差,所以,商业写作时要使用"大约""可能"等模糊语。

因此,虽然商务合同英语语体强调准确,但是为了实现特定的语用功能和意图,并不是完全排斥模糊语言的有意识的使用。模糊语言的使用(除言语过失以外)都是带有动机的。这种动机在合同语境中一般并非为了增强语言的感染力或是出于礼貌的考虑,而是为了使自己处于进退自如的主动地位,使对方承担语用模糊所可能造成后果的部分责任。模糊语言看似模糊、与精确语言相矛盾,但二者相结合却能使表达更完整,防止漏洞的产生,对双方的交易、劳务与技术服务以及索赔等的范围都起着限定作用,从而使合同条款合乎双方的意愿,并增加了可操作性。

(2)负面效应(disadvantages):作为一般规则,在法律文件起草中应当避免含糊的词语,因为它们可能会导致争议并且在极端的情况下可能会导致某种程度的不确定性,以至于写有这些词语的规定被认为是无效的。因此,在允许一方当事人接受额外的付款作为"杂费"或者"杂支费"的合同中,因为双方可能对该术语包括的内容理解不同,就存在着可能产生争议的风险。如果双方坚持使用这种含糊的词语,那么至少应当按照文件的目的对它们下定义,这样可以明确哪些属于、哪些不属于词语所在的上下文中的意思。例如,如果劳务合同授权雇员因为承担"急救工作"或者在"正常时间"之外所做的工作而获得额外的报酬,那么对这些含糊的词语都应当下定义。模糊有其特有的作用,但是我们必须小心谨慎,并且只有当利大于弊时,我们才应使用模糊的表达方式。

1)表达不清晰可能造成实践中的误解(misunderstanding)

民事和经济案件中不恰当地使用模糊词语,会导致无法明确当事人的权利义务,容易产生诉讼纷争。法律是调整人类社会关系的一种工具,因此必须明确每一法律关系各方具体的权利义务,才能起到"定分止争"的作用,达到社会稳定的目的。人们能通过法律找出自己行为的指向,按照法律的要求享有权利,履行义务,以此来划定个人与个人,个人与社会之间的界限,在这种情况下,法律语言的表达必须是明确,肯定的,如果这时的表述仍然模糊不清,人们就无法确知其真正含义,或对其含义争执不清,从而引起法律纠纷。如甲厂与乙厂签订一项沙石买卖合同,合同约定:甲厂向乙厂购买沙石15车,款到发货。而"车"是一典型模糊词语,其外延包括很广,界定困难,它不仅可以指代汽车、火车、自行车,甚至连板车也可以包括进去,各方根据自己的意思去解释时,只要仍包含在这个模糊范围内,就都是正确的。与此相类似的一个例子是一房屋装修合同纠纷。合同约定,装修方须用优质板材为房主装修,但什么是"优质","优质"与"非优质"的界限在哪里,难有定论。因此"优质"一词确为一模糊词语,对其不同理解成为纠纷的原因。

[例8]

Shipment: To be shipped before Feb. 28, 1998.(装船:1998年2月28日前)在这句话里,"before Feb. 28"存在两种解释,是否包含28日这一天?这可能带来当事人不同的理解问题。所以为避免概念上的模糊,合同最好改为:Shipment: To be shipped on or before Feb. 28, 1998.

2) 模糊语导致法律上的争端,经济上的意外损失(disputes and accidentally economic loss)

对于诸如"do our best","high quality","first class"之类难以准确定界的模糊语要避免使用。

[例9]

一家旅行社组织游客去张家界旅游,他们向一家票务公司通过传真订票,该票务公司用传真这样回复:"We've got your purchase order and we promised that we will give your company our best service."但是后来他们只能订到部分的车票,于是,他们给旅行社用传真回复:"There're not enough tickets of train. You had better cut your team down."旅行社认为票务公司没有履行合同,把他们告上法庭。法庭支持了原告。

同样是这家票务公司,他们在接到一家公司的订票请求时这样回复:"We have got your fax, and we will try our best to help you with your tickets."这次同上一次一样,当这家公司没能订到全部的票时把票务公司告上了法庭,但法庭没有支持原告。原因在于第二份传真中使用了"try to"这样的模糊表达。可见模糊语在准确表达意愿与能力,作出承诺时,保护了承诺方的利益。

总之,无论在立法还是司法实践中,模糊法律语言容量很大,表现的形式也较为复杂,它的使用有条件地受特定的语言环境的制约,使用不当会造成严重后果。英国法学家哈特说:"任何语言,包括法律语言,都是不精确的表意工具,都具有一种'空缺结构(open texture)',每一个字,词组和命题在其'核心范围'内具有明确无疑的意思,但是随着核心向边缘的扩展,语言会变得越来越不明确。在一些'边缘地带',语言则是根本不确定的,对法律的解释和适用不存在绝对或唯一的正确答案。解释者或者法官拥有自由裁量权,需要在多种可能的解释和推理结论中作出选择,甚至可以扮演创建新规范的角色。"这里,哈特揭示了模糊性是法律语言的本质特征之一。在针对模糊性问题上,要尽量克服模糊法律语言的消极因素的出现。同时,也要有意识地发挥模糊语言在法律语言中的积极功能,这样对弥补法律本身的不足,保护法律文本的体系完整,克服法律局限性以及维护法律的尊严具有重要作用。

第二节 国际商务合同的结构
Section 2 Structures of International Business Contracts

2.1 合同的前言
Preamble

2.1.1 合同的结构 Structures of contracts

正式书面合同文本的结构是指合同写作的规格、样式,是它同其他实用功能文体相区别的外在标志。合同一般由约首或序言、前言(preamble)、正文(body)和约尾或结尾(final clauses)三部分构成。

2.1.2 前言的内容 Content of the preamble

前言即合同总则,在合同上被称为"合同的效力条款(validity clauses of contracts)",是合同生效的基本条件。其主要内容有:具有法人资格的当事人的名称(字号)或姓名、国籍、业务范围、法定住址、合同签订日期和地点。前言主要明确合同的主体是谁;合同各方是否具有合法主体资格;合同及合同争议应适用的法律;合同履行地点;合同生效、终止、履行日期及争议时的司法管辖权等。

(1)合同名称:名称是合同的性质、内容、种类的具体体现,根据合同内容的不同而不同,如销售合同(sales contract)、购买合同(purchase contract)、赔偿合同(compensation contract)、托运合同(consignment contract)、代理合同(agency contract)等。合同的名称/标题一定要与合同内容相一致。

(2)合同当事人:可以超过两人,人数没有法律限定。当事人的名称第一次在合同中出现时应使用全称,以表示法律身份。只有在后来反复出现时才可以用简称,简称甲方和乙方,卖方和买方,许可方和被许可方等。(hereinafter referred to as /hereinafter called Party A and Party B, the Seller and the Buyer, the Licensor and the Licensee)

(3)法定地址:主要指营业地、住所地或者居所所在地。(principle places of business or residential addresses, etc.)住所应是固定的,而不是临时的,亦不是下属分公司的。

(4)签订日期/地点:他们是合同纠纷时适用于法律的问题。(the date and place of signing the contract)

(5)合同双方法律关系:在明确了当事人全称后,指明谁是买方、卖方,或者是出让方、受让方等。(legal relationship between the parties)

(6)同意订约的词句:例如"双方同意按照以下条款及条件买卖下列货物"。(Both parties agree to buy and sell the following commodities according to the terms and conditions stipulated below)

[例10]
标准的详细前言部分
GENERAL AGENCY AGREEMENT
General Principles
THE AGREEMENT dated the _____ of _____ is made BETWEEN:
_____, a company incorporated under the laws of _____, and having its registered address at _____ (hereinafter called the "Principal") and_____, a company incorporated under the laws of _____, and having its registered office at _____ (hereinafter called the "General Agent").

WHEREAS:—

The Principal is desirous of acquiring from _____ Co., Ltd., (hereinafter called the "Seller") the SGI Technology (hereinafter called the "SGI Technology").

The Principal and the General Agent have agreed that the General Agent shall be appointed as the Principal's sole exclusive Agent to negotiate, on behalf of the Principal, with the seller the price and other terms and conditions for, and all other matters connected with, the acquisition of the Technology by the Principal, subject to the terms and upon the conditions hereinafter set forth?

NOW IT IS HEREBY AGREED as follows:

总代理协议书

总则

本协议书于20____年_____月_____日由下列双方共同签订：

根据_____法律登记注册的_____公司，其地址_____（以下称"委托人"），与根据_____法律登记注册的_____有限公司，其地址_____（以下称"总代理人"）。

鉴于：

委托人欲从_____有限公司（以下称"卖方"）引进SGI技术（以下称"SGI"技术）。

委托人和总代理人双方同意，由委托人指定的总代理人系独家全权代表，委托人授权其代表可根据本协议所列的条款和条件，与卖方洽谈引进技术的价格及其他有关事项。

兹同意下列条款：

[例11]

简化/删除陈述事实部分（Recitals）的前言

COMMERCIAL CONTRACT

No.: _____

Date: _____

The Buyer: _____

Cable Address: _____ Telex: _____

The Seller: _____

Cable Address: _____ Telex: _____

This Contract is made by and between the Buyer and the Seller, whereby the Buyer agrees to buy and the Seller agrees to sell the under-mentioned commodity according to the terms and conditions stated below:

商业合同

合同号：_____

日期：_____

买方：_____

电报：_____ 电传：_____

卖方：_____

电报：_____ 电传：_____
按本合同条款,买方同意购入、卖方同意出售下述货品,谨此签约。

[例12]

一则补偿贸易合同的前言部分

This contract is made and entered into in Beijing this 18th day of March, 2001, by and between ABC corporation, a corporation duly organized and existing under the laws of the People's Republic of China with its domicile at Shanghai (hereinafter referred to as "Party A") and XYZ company, a company incorporated and existing under the laws of the United States with its domicile at Atlanta (hereinafter referred to as "Party B").

WITNESSETH THAT:

WHEREAS Party B has machines and equipment for Party B's manufacturing of auto safety belt and is willing to sell to Party A the machines and equipment…

WHEREAS Party A agrees to purchase from Party B machines and equipment…

NOW, THEREFORE, in consideration of the promises and covenants described hereinafter, the parties hereto agree as follows:

本合同于2001年3月18日在北京由按中华人民共和国法律组建成立的、营业地点在上海的 ABC 公司(以下简称甲方)和按美国法律注册成立的、营业地在亚特兰大的 XYZ 公司(以下简称乙方)共同签订。

兹证明：

鉴于乙方现拥有用于制造汽车安全带的机器设备,并愿将机器设备卖给甲方……

鉴于甲方同意从乙方购买该机器设备……

因此,考虑到本协议所述的前提和约定,甲乙双方特此立约。

2.2 合同的正文
Body of contvact

2.2.1 什么是正文 What is body

正文部分是合同或协议的主体,是合同的实质性条款。正文由法律条款组成,明确规定当事人各方的权利、义务、责任和风险等。每一条款的内容都必须明确、具体、完整,以避免意义含糊而发生纠纷。

2.2.2 正文的内容 Content of body

合同正文部分千差万别,但一般要包括以下几方面的条款：

(1) 合同的类型和合同标的种类、范围 type of contract and Scope of

the Object in the Contract

不同的合同类型有不同的范围和相应的条款。合同的种类：(1)国际货物销售合同；(2) 国际技术转让合同；(3) 中外合资／合作经营企业合同；(4)国际工程承包合同；(5)补偿贸易合同；(6)中外合作开采自然资源合同；(7)涉外劳务合同；(8)国际租赁合同；(9)涉外信贷合同；(10)国际 BOT(Build-Operate-Transfer)投资合同,等等。

合同标的是指合同当事人各方权利、义务所指向的对象，没有标的或标的不明确的合同是无法履行的。起草合同时，应明确标的种类是物、行为、劳务还是无形财产以及标的物的范围。合同标的不明确，这就意味着当事人各方的权利和义务不分明，合同就无法履行。各类合同都有自己的合同范围条款，包括公司的建立、业务范围、生产经营目的、范围和规模，合同标的的技术条件(technical conditions)、质量(quality)、标准、规格(specifications)、数量(quantity)，以及合同履行的期限、地点和方式。

[例 13]

Pursuant to the Buyer's Purchase Order, the Seller agrees to supply the Buyer with the goods, and the names, types, serial numbers, quantity and unit price of the goods as stipulated in the annex to this contract. The annex shall form an integral part of the contract.

根据买方购货单，卖方同意按合同附件所列货物的名称、型号、数量、单价的规定，向买方予以提供。该附件是本合同不可分割的组成部分。

[例 14]

Unit Price（per carton of 48 cans each）

Quantity FOB shanghai net CFR London net

Items（M/T）in US dollars

Tips & Cuts 10 13.00 15.00

Center Cuts 15 12.00 14.00

End Cuts 20 10.00 12.50

Remarks:

Packing: Standard export cardboard cartons

Shipment: Total quantity to be shipped during May, 20…

Payment: By irrevocable letter of credit opened in our favor two weeks before shipment and drawn at sight.

单价（每箱内装 48 罐）

数量 FOB 上海净价 CFR 伦敦净价

品名（公吨）美元 _____
带尖段装 10 13.00 15.00
无尖段装 15 12.00 14.00
段装 20 10.00 12.50
备注：
包装：标准出口纸板箱装
交货期：20ⅩⅩ年5月全部交运
付款方式：交货前两周开出以我方为抬头的即期的不可撤销的信用证

（2）合同的价格条件、支付金额、支付方式和各种附加的费用 The contract price, amount, method of payment, other various incidental charges

这部分内容涉及价格条款和支付条款两部分内容，是合同中极其重要的一部分内容，在草拟和审核这部分内容时，一定要用词准确，表达确切，要考虑语言和其他各方面因素，以减少日后的争议。

1）价格条款 terms of price：

价格是贸易中的关键所在（Price is the crux matter in business）。在国际贸易中，当事人应注意价格术语的选用。现今使用最广泛的是 FOB，CIF 和 CFR 三种术语。此外，当事人应确定商品计量单位的价格、货币、运费（海/空运费、内陆运费）、装卸费、仓储费、关税、手续费及培训费等由谁承担和风险划分。技术转让补偿贸易中，当事人还应订明设计费、试验费、专门技能费等。

[例 15]

Total Value Carrier air condition equipment（names, specifications, quantities, unit prices & origins as per attachment No. 1 to the Contract）totaling US $2,500,000.00（Say US Two Million Five Hundred Thousand Dollars only）CIF Shanghai or place designated by the Buyer.

总值250万美元整的"开利"空调设备（名称、规格、数量、单价、产地详见本合同附件一）CIF 上海或买方指定地点。

2）支付条款 terms of payment：

国际贸易中的支付，为了安全起见，往往必须有银行介入。支付金额即合同规定的总金额。但在履行合同过程中，按照合同支付条款规定，可采用汇付、托收、信用证、银行保证书、分期付款、延期付款、国际保理方式等。在起草这部分条款时，应详细规定支付金额（amount of payment）、支付工费（instrument of payment）、支付时间（time of payment）、支付地点（place of payment）和支付方式（method of payment）。

[例 16]

Terms of Payment

L/C shall be opened within 30 days by the buyer before shipment, the seller will remit the real value differences of buying and selling to the buyer after shipment.

If the buyer makes out the bill and settles accounts of foreign currency, the buyer shall remit the total value to the seller according to the invoice/receipt value opened.

付款条件

由买方或买方客户于装运期前 30 天内将有关信用证开给卖方,装运后由卖方将购销实际差价汇给买方。若由买方办理制单结汇,由买方凭卖方开具的发票/收据将货款汇给卖方。

[例 17]

Payment by collection

Any delivery, the seller shall send through the Seller's Bank a draft on the Buyer together with the shipping documents to the Buyer through the Buyer's Bank for collection.

托收付款

货物装运后,卖方应将以买方为付款人的汇票连同本合同的各种装运单据,通过卖方银行寄给买方银行转交买方,并托收货款。

(3)合同能否转让和合同转让的条件 The conditions for the assignment of contract

合同转让是一种特殊的合同变更,即合同条款一方将合同中的权利或义务的全部或者部分转让给合同另一方或合同以外的第三方,是主体的变更。有一类合同如中外合资企业、合作企业及外资企业合同,还有如"交钥匙合同"等都必须有转让条款。在起草这部分内容时,可以明确约定合同可以转让以及转让合同的条件和程序,但这些约定必须依法进行。

[例 18]

If one party to the Joint Venture intends to assign all or part of its investment subscribed to a third party, consent shall be obtained from the other party to the Joint Venture and approval from the examining and approving authorities is required. When one party assigns all or part of its investment subscribed to a third party, the other party has pre-emptive right. When one party assigns its investment subscribed to a third party, the terms of assignment shall not be more favorable than those to the other party to the Joint Venture. No assignment shall be effective should there be any violation of the above stipulations.

中外合资企业合同规定:"合营一方如向第三方转让其全部或部分出资额,须经合营他方同意,并经审批机构批准。合营一方转让其全部或部分出资额时,合营他方有优先购买权。合营一方向第三方转让出资额的条件,不得比向合营他方转让的条件优惠。违反上述规定的,其转让无效。"

(4)违反合同的赔偿和其他责任 Liability to pay compensation and other liabilities for breach of contract

违反涉外合同的责任是指涉外合同的当事人不履行合同、不完全履行合同、不符合双方在合同中约定的条件时,依有关法律的规定或合同的约定应当承担的赔偿责任或其他经济责任。

当事人应全面履行合同是责无旁贷的。起草者应在合同中明确规定违反合同当事人所承担的责任和承担责任的方式。关于违约责任条款,一般遵循过失原则和损害赔偿原则,即违约要承担责任,要赔偿。在涉外合同中明确约定违反涉外合同承担的经济责任,对于保证合同的履行,促使合同当事人全面履行合同中约定的义务有着重要的意义。

至于当事人,若一方违反涉外合同应承担的责任和承担责任的方式,当事人可以在合同中约定违约金(penalty),也可以约定赔偿损失(compensation for losses),也可以约定支付利息(payment of interest)、中止履行合同(suspension of the contract performance)或解除合同(cancellation of the contract)。

[例 19]

The Purchaser agrees to pay Corporation the Total Purchase Price, as follow:

买方同意向公司支付买价,总金额为:

The Purchaser shall, upon receipt of Corporation's respective invoices therefore, pay to Corporation all amounts which become due by the Purchaser to Corporation hereunder, including without limitation an amount equal to the taxes and duties.

收到公司的各种发票后,买方必须即刻付给公司业已到期应付的所有款项,包括各种税收费用在内,不得有例外。

If by reason of delay on the part of the Purchaser or Purchaser's agent or representative, any payments due to Corporation are not made in accordance with the agreed payment schedule, Corporation reserves the right to apply a late payment charge of one and one-half (1.5%) percent per month (19.569 per annum) on all overdue amounts and Purchaser agrees to promptly pay any such late payment charges which are properly due hereunder. In the event that one or more payments are delayed for sixty (60) days or more, Corporation shall have the right to stop all work under this Agreement and shall also have the right to claim such period of work stoppage and the effects thereof as excusable delay pursuant to Article 7 hereof (Excusable Delay). Purchaser agrees to reimburse Corporation for those additional reasonable costs incurred by Corporation resulting from such work stoppage (s) and restart (s). Should one or more payments be delayed for one hundred and twenty (120) days or more, this Agreement may, at Corporation's option, be deemed to be cancelled under the provisions of paragraphs (b) through (e) of Article 23 hereof (Termination for Insolvency & Cancellation).

如果由于买方或买方代理商或代理人的延迟，不能按议定的付款时间支付公司业已到期的款项,公司保留收取延付款的权利,延付款月率为到期未付款的1.5%(年率为19.569毛),买方也同意即刻交付本协议所规定的此种费用。如一次或数次延迟付款达60天或以上,公司有权停止本协议所规定的工作,并有权根据本协议第7条(可谅解的延迟)称此段工作停顿及其产生的后果为可谅解的。买方同意对公司因停工和重新开工的额外费用作合理补偿。如一次或数次延迟付款达120天或以上,根据本合同第23条(因无力清偿债务而终止和撤销)第2-5款规定,按公司的意愿,本协议可视为被撤销。

If, under the Contract, the Purchaser requests to cancel the Contract, ABC Company shall, upon written request by the Purchaser, advise Purchaser of the estimated cancellation costs for which Purchaser would be liable.

如果买方根据合同要求撤销合同时,ABC公司应根据买方书面要求,通知买方应承担的撤销费用。

(5)合同发生争议时的解决方法 The ways for settling disputes

在合同的执行过程中，经常会发生一些争议性问题。涉外合同的争议解决方法一般有和解(conciliation)、调解(mediation)、仲裁(arbitration)和诉讼(litigation)等。在合同的起草阶段就应该明确争议的解决办法。为了解决重大争议,国际商务合同中一般都有仲裁条款,包括仲裁地点、机构、程序和仲裁员的组成,费用负担和仲裁裁决的权威性等问题。在国际贸易中,一旦发现货物受损,当事人应根据受损的实际情况及在合同规定的范围,按照国际惯例提出索赔。当事人通过友好协商不能解决的索赔,应提交仲裁机构解决。

[例 20]

Should any dispute arise between the contraction parties, it shall be settled through friendly negotiations. But if there is no agreement to be reached, the disputes arising out of the execution or performance of this contract shall be submitted by the parties for arbitration. Arbitration shall be conducted by China International Economic and Trade Arbitration Commission in Beijing in accordance with its procedure rule. The award given by the Arbitration Commission shall be final and binding upon both parties. The fees for arbitration shall be borne by the losing party.

合同各方发生争议的，应通过友好协商解决。达不成协议的，应由合同方将执行合同当中发生的争议提交仲裁解决。仲裁应由中国国际经济贸易仲裁委员会在北京依照其仲裁规则进行。仲裁委员会的裁决为终局性的，对双方生效。仲裁费用应由败诉方承担。

Any disputes arising out of this Contract shall first be settled by the Parties hereto through consultation with their higher authorities in accordance with the spirit of mutual trust. Should such consultation fail to settle the dispute within thirty (30) days of notification to such higher authorities, mediation may be conducted by a third party selected by the Parties hereto.

合同双方对本合同发生的任何争议应首先通过各方主管部门本着相互信赖的精神予以解决。如在 30 天内本合同双方不能解决时，双方可推荐第三方予以调解。

（6）检验、试航、验收 Inspection, trial and acceptance

在国际货物买卖中，买方收到货物不等于买方接受货物。"收到（receive）"和"接受（accept）"是两个不同的概念。商检应包括对商品的质量、数量等的检验。但在大型成套设备、船舶等谈判和签约中往往把商检、试航、验收、保证质量和保证期联系在一起，明确所有权转移的条件、时间、地点及风险等。

[例 21]

Inspection: It is mutually agreed that the Inspection Certificate of Quality/Quantity/Weight issued by the China Commodity Inspection Bureau shall be taken as final basis of delivery and binding upon both parties.

商品检验：双方同意以中国商品检验局所签发的品质／数量／重量检验证作为交货的最后依据并对双方具有约束力。

（7）明确风险责任、约定保险范围 Responsibility for risks and insurance clauses

国际商务合同的履行,大多数时限长,路途远,可能受到多种因素的干扰,产生各种不测的事件(如遇不可抗力),如洪水、火灾、盗窃、海难、经营不善等。这类风险一旦发生,可能造成损失,从而产生承担风险损失的责任问题。因此,明确风险责任,避免引致不必要的争议,对于国际商务合同的各方都是十分重要的。风险往往和保险是联系在一起的,为了使风险造成的损失及时得到经济上的补偿,就需要办理保险。办理保险的实质是一旦发生风险责任,当事人可以将其转移给保险公司。

1) 不可抗力条款 Force Majeure:

也称意外条款,是国际经济合同中普遍采用的一项除外条款,或称免责条款。

不可抗力条款通常包括:确定不可抗力事故的范围,对此合同双方应取得共识,在条款写作时,应明确具体,防止含糊其辞,以免日后发生分歧。不可抗力所造成的后果,通常有两种情况:合同无法继续执行,终止合同;合同仍可继续执行,但需要延长履行合同期限。对于两种情况,即终止合同和延长履行合同期限,都需要在合同中明确规定。

[例 22]

Any event or circumstance beyond the control of the Parties to the Contract shall be deemed an event of Force Majeure and shall include, but not restricted to, fire, storm, flood, earthquake, explosion, war, rebellion, insurrection, epidemic and quarantine restriction. If, due to an event of Force Majeure, either Party is prevented from performing any of its obligations under this Contract, the time for performance under this Contract shall be extended by a period equal to the period of delay caused by such Force Majeure.

双方如遭遇无法控制的事件或情况应视为不可抗力事件,但不限于火灾、风灾、水灾、地震、爆炸、战争、叛乱、暴乱、传染病及瘟疫。如遭遇不可抗力事件的一方导致另一方不能履行合同规定的义务时,应将履行合同的时间延长,所延长时间应与不可抗力事件所延误的时间相等。

2) 保险条款:Clauses of Insurance:

由于国际商务合同的履行中可能遭受的变数较多,例如各种不可抗力事件,或者经营不善等,它们会导致损失的产生,所以由谁来承担风险损失的责任是一个重要问题。而办理保险则会使风险造成的损失及时得到经济上的补偿。所以在合同中明确风险责任和风险范围就可以避免日后发生保险责任纠纷。

《国际货物销售合同公约》规定:"卖方交付的货物必须与合同规定的数量、质量和规格相符。"《产品责任法》规定卖方不仅要对违约所造成的直接性经济损失负责,而且要对可能由此而引起的人身伤害和财产损失负责。

[例 23]

In case defects in the ship body or equipment are found by Party A within twelve months after delivery, and the defects are caused by bad materials, bad technology, or bad machinery used by Party B, and when the inspection report by the Ship Inspection Bureau of the P.R.C. is obtained, Party B shall send engineers to inspect the defects after receiving the Party A's notice. Party B shall be obliged to make all repairs without charge in case of Party B's negligence.

本船从移交之日起 12 个月内如果甲方发现由于乙方使用材料、工艺不良、机械不良原因而产生船体或设备上的缺陷,并取得中华人民共和国船舶检验局的证明,应通知乙方。乙方可派人检验,如果属乙方责任,乙方负责免费修复所有缺陷。

[例 24]

Under the term of CIF, the insurance shall be affected by the Sellers for 110% of the invoice value. Under the term of FOB, the insurance shall be covered by the buyers after shipment.

在 CIF 条件下,保险应由卖方办理,投保比率为发票金额的110%。在 FOB 条件下,保险应在装船后由买方办理。

(8)合同的有效期限,以及可以延长合同期限和提前终止合同的条件 Validity, Extension and Termination

对于需要较长时间连续履行的合同(a contract which needs to be performed continuously over a long period),如合资经营企业合同、合作经营企业合同、成套设备技术引进合同以及国际承包工程合同等,当事人可以约定合同的有效期限,并在合同中规定一旦有效期届满时,延长合同的条件或提前终止合同有效期的条件(the conditions for contractual extension and contractual termination before its expiration)。

[例 25]

This Contract shall come into force after it has been approved by the examination and approval authority of China.

本合同经中国审批机关批准后即生效。

This Contract shall be valid for two years after its effective date, and shall be renewable for further two years thereafter.

本合同从生效之日起有效 2 年,期满后可延长 2 年。

This Contract comes into effect on the first day of the engaged party's arrival at the AA University and ceases to be effective at its expiration. IT either party wishes to renew the Contract, the other party shall be notified in writing one month before it expires. Upon agreement by both parties through consultation, a new contract may be signed between two parties.

本合同自受聘方到校第一天之日起生效,到聘期届满时失效。如一方要求延长聘期,必须在合同期满前1个月以书面形式向对方提出,经双方协商同意后另签延聘合同。

2.2.3 总结—合同的内容 Content of contracts

名称(Title):合同应有名称,表明合同的性质和贸易方式,如国际贸易中的销售合同、补偿贸易合同等。

总则(General Principle):合同签订日期、地点、当事人和约因。

商品品名(Name of Commodity):商品的品名应采用国际上的通称,以便于计算关税和运价。

质量(Quality):合同中应列明商品的规格及其质量。

数量(Quantity):合同中应注明数量的计算单位(cartons, case, set, piece, etc.)和交货总量。

价格(Price):价格是至关重要的,应注明单价,计价的硬通货和总值。

包装(Packing):包装应注明内包装和外包装的容量、尺码、重量和唛头。

交货(Shipment & Delivery):要按《国际贸易术语解释通则》注明交货和提货的港口或地点,如 FOB shanghai, CIF New York, CFR Vancouver 等。

付款(Terms of Payment):合同中应明确规定付款方式,如 T/T, L/C, D/P, D/A 等,及付款的货币和日期。

保险(Insurance):保险条款中应订明投保人(insurer)、险别(coverage)、保险金额等。

检验(Inspection):合同中应规定检验标准、方法及费用。

索赔(Claim):合同中应订明索赔的原则、期限和双方认可的索赔报告或证明文件。

违约(Breach):合同中应规定违法、毁约(rescission)的因由、赔偿及债务债权的责任。

仲裁(Arbitration):合同中应规定仲裁范围、地点、仲裁委员会、仲裁人的选定、仲裁费等。

不可抗力(Force Majeure):指人类无法控制的以外事件,包括天灾和人祸,如闪电、风暴、水灾、战争、罢工等。

专利(Patent):若产品已有专利,要明确规定专利范围及责任。

保密(Confidential):若合同属于保密,应规定保密项目、范围和措施。

培训(Training):若有培训计划,应订明培训项目、期限、人次、费用等等。

适用法律（Applicable Laws）：若应遵循有关法规和条令，应在合同中订明，以便解决纠纷和争议。

其他（Miscellaneous）：凡合同中尚未订明的条款或事项，如合同的修改和展延、拒绝行贿受贿、产品的特殊关税等等条款都应列明。

结尾（Witness）：合同应经法人签字，根据需要加盖公章，方能生效。

[例 26]

一则技术转让合同的正文部分主要包括以下主要条款：

第一章　合同的内容与范围

SECTION1　CONTENT AND SCOPE OF THE CONTRACT

第二章　价格

SECTION2　PRICE

第三章　支付

SECTION3　PAYMENT

第四章　资料的提交

SECTION4　DELIVERY OF DOCUMENTATION

第五章　资料的修改和改进

SECTION5　MODIFICATIONS AND IMPROVEMENTS OF THE DOCUMENTATIONS

第六章　考核和验收

SECTION6　VERIFICATION AND ACCEPTANCE

第七章　保证

SECTION7　GUARANTEE

第八章　侵权和保密

SECTION8　INFRINGEMENT AND CONFIDENTIALITY

第九章　仲裁

SECTION9　ARBITRATION

第十章　不可抗力

SECTION10　FORCE MAJEURE

第十一章　合同生效、终止及其他

SECTION11　EFECTIVENESS, TERMINATION AND MISCELLANEOUS

2.3 合同的结尾
Final Clauses

合同的结尾也称合同的最后条款。一般包括合同使用的文字及其效力，有时还订立对合同进行修改或补充的内容及额外协议等。如果合同订有附件,应在合同中另立一章列出附件的具体内容,并在合同的结尾部分明确规定附件为本合同不可分割的组成部分。合同书的结尾部分有盖章证书形式和单纯书面形式两种。自然人没必要盖本人姓名的图章,美国人在前置的后面写上"Seal"或"L.S."等字样。结尾部分没有"Attest"的合同也照样生效,合同当事人签字时在场的任何人都可以签Attest。

[例27]

一则合同的结尾部分:

(1) This Contract is made out in English in quadruplicate and each Party shall hold two copies.

(2) Appendixes 1 to 9 to the Contract shall form an integral part of the Contract and have the same effectiveness as the Contract.

(3) This Contract shall come into force after the signatures by the authorized representatives of both parties.

(1) 本合同用英文写成,一式四份,各执两份。

(2) 本合同附录1-9,为本合同不可分割的组成部分,与合同正文具有同等效力。

(3) 本合同将在双方授权代表签字后正式生效。

[例28]

This Contract is made out in two original, each copy written in Chinese and English languages, both text being valid. In case of any divergence of interpretation, the Chinese text shall prevail.

本合同正文一式两份,分别以中文和英文书写,两种文本具有同等效力。若对其解释产生异议,则以中文文本为准。

[例29]

Any additional agreements and/or amendments to this Contract shall be valid only after the authorized representatives of both parties have signed written document (s), forming integral part (s) of this Contract.

本合同的任何额外协议和/或修改,只有在双方授权代表在书面文件上签字后才能生效,并成为本合同不可分割的组成部分。

2.4 英文合同格式图
Samples of English Contracts

LICENSE AGREEMENT　　标　题
On the of July 1,2007, ABC Corporation, a NEW York corporation, (hereinafter ABC), having a principal place of business at 2 Water St, New York, New York 12345, USA and DEF Company Limited, a Chinese corporation, (hereinafter DEF), having a principal place of business at 236Baishi St, Haidian District, Beijing 10088, China, agree in Beijing as follows:
Article 1 Background 1.00 The Licensor has developed certain processes, methods and techniques applied in manufacturing the Licensed Products hereinafter defined. 1.01…… Article 2 Definitions Articles 3 License
ABC Corporation By: 　(President) DEF Corporation (President)

Part 2 Focusing on Words and Phrases

1. Finding Meaning in Context

Words	Meaning in General English	Meaning in Legal English
assignment	任务,作业	转让
penalty	刑罚,处罚	违约金
interest	趣味,兴趣	利息
conciliation	抚慰,说服	和解
validity	确实性	合同的有效期限
suspension	暂停,悬浮	中止履行
rescission	撤回,撤销	毁约
coverage	项目,范围	保险范围

2. Useful Expressions in Legal English

1) This Contract shall come into force after the signatures by the authorized representatives of both parties.
2) Strictly speaking, the goods are partly out of order.
3) To the best of his knowledge, the horse has no unsoundness of health on the date of sale that will cause the horse unfit for his training.

Part 3 Evaluating Your Achievements

词汇日志 Vocabulary Log

ambiguity detriment	歧义
vagueness	模糊
preamble	前言
final clauses	结尾
terms of price	价格条款
flexibility	灵活
mediation	调解
arbitration	仲裁
litigation	诉讼
validity	有效期限
extension	延长合同期限
termination	终止合同的条件
pragmatics	语用
ontological fuzziness	本体的模糊性
epistemological fuzziness	认识的模糊性
objectivity	客观事实

章节练习 Check Your Progress

1. Fill in the Blanks

1) Within a specific contract, some key elements shall be comprised such as the name and domicile of the parties, the contract _____, quantity, _____, price or remuneration, _____ for breach of contract and methods of _____ settlement.

2) In the legal context, the phrase "_____" shall be translated similarly as its equivalent phrase "in order to".

3) Any event or circumstance beyond the control of the Parties to the Contract shall be deemed an event of Force Majeure and shall include, but not restricted to, fire, storm, _____, _____, war, _____, insurrection, _____.

2. Legal Terminology

1) validity clauses of contracts

2) Force Majeure

3) terms of price

4) insurance clauses

3. Sentence Translation

1) Both parties agree to buy and sell the following commodities according to the terms and conditions stipulated below.

2) Under the term of CIF, the insurance shall be affected by the Sellers for 110% of the invoice value. Under the term of FOB, the insurance shall be covered by the buyers after shipment.

3) This Contract is made out in English in quadruplicate and each Party shall hold two copies.

4) 本合同经中国审批机关批准后即生效。

5) 本合同从生效之日起有效 2 年,期满后可延长 2 年。

自我评价 Self-Assessment Log

In this Chapter, you worked through these activities. How did each of them help you become a better learner? Check A lot, A little, or Not at all.

	A lot	A little	Not at all
I discussed the meaning of vague words.	❏	❏	❏
I learned words and expressions in vagueness.	❏	❏	❏
I gathered information about pragmatics of contract clauses.	❏	❏	❏
I knew the structure of contracts.	❏	❏	❏
I learned words and expressions in body parts.	❏	❏	❏
I grasped information about content of the body.	❏	❏	❏
I could draw the framework of business contracts.	❏	❏	❏

(Add something) _____
_____

第四部分
PART IV

国际商务合同的起草与翻译

DRAFTING AND TRANSLATION OF
INTERNATIONAL BUSINESS CONTRACTS

Chapter 7

第七章 国际商务合同的起草原则与流程
Drafting Principles and Processes of International Business Contracts

After two weeks of negotiation, you have a document in front of you, with the title: CONTRACT. But is it really a contract? There is a famous English sentence that says: "This contract is not worth the paper it is written on." To avoid such a problem, lawyers and business professionals must know what a contract must contain and what it cannot contain. Contract drafting is an art and not a science. This Chapter allows students not only to be able to draft with absolute clarity and precision, but also use drafting skills effectively for persuasive and tactical purposes. It also ensures that a student following its progressive structure gains a thorough understanding of best practice when drafting contracts in a variety of situations.

 Learning Objectives

In this chapter, students will learn how to:
◎ understand fundamental contract drafting principles;
◎ go through the contract drafting process;
◎ undertake various contract drafting practice.

 Questions to Consider

1) Why do clients have lawyers draft contracts?
2) How do you evaluate a good contract drafting?
3) What are the boilerplate clauses in drafting a contract?

Part 1 Focusing on Legal Knowledge

第一节 合同起草的技能
Section 1 Contract Drafting Competence

1.1 专业知识与执业经验
Professional Knowledge and Experience

广义的法律文书起草(legal drafting)分为两个主要部分,即法律文件(legal documents)起草和诉讼文书(litigation texts)起草,前者包括合同(contracts)、遗嘱(wills)、产权转让证书(certificates of ownership transfer)和法律备忘录(legal memorandum)等,后者包括申诉说明(plea)或者诉状(complaint)等。从法律专业知识的角度,合同起草是法律文书起草的重要组成部分,充分体现了法律语言的典型特征;从法律操作实践的角度,"契约的总和即为市场"的法谚充分证明了市场经济社会中,合同无处不在的事实;从法律从业人员的角度,可以说律师是一个用文件来解决问题的职业。一份起草良好的合同能够减少不确定性(uncertainty),降低当事人的风险(risk),最大限度地维护当事人的权益(rights and interests)。

起草合同不仅仅是对标准文本或先例文本(precedents)的简单填入或替换,更重要的是要结合当事人的需求和相关事实作出专业判断;起草合同也不是对既有法律法规条款的照搬照抄,而是需要准确而且不断更新的法律知识(legal knowledge),凭借丰富的执业经验(practicing experience),进行严密的逻辑推理(logical reasoning),还需要具有高度的责任感(responsibility),对合同文本进行创作和不断完善,切实帮助当事人依法实现其预期利益。

因此,合同的起草需要原则的指引,但更需要实践的学习。从结果上最终体现在对合同法律语言与合同法律文本的驾驭能力上。

1.2 驾驭文本的语言运用能力
Language Application Competence to Contractual Texts

(1) 文本理解 Reading through text

合同语言(contract language)属于法律语言(legal language)的一种,

自身具有法律语言典型的正式性和严谨性的特征,同时在日益复杂的国际商事交往中,由于国际商事合同所具有的法律约束力(binding effect),更突显了合同的正式(formal)、准确(accurate)、规范(normative)以及权威(authoritative)的语言特征。因此,对于合同文本首先要有透彻的理解。

对于词语的理解既要考虑其字面含义(denotation),又要结合词语所在的上下文(context)考虑其引申含义(connotation)。如果遗嘱人在遗嘱(will)中将"我所有的钱"留给一位指定继承人,就可能产生若干问题。其一"所有"指代所拥有的部分还是全部;其二,"钱"仅仅是指现金,还是按照更广泛的理解指代所有的财产,上述问题并不明确。[1]

又如,由于汉语的语法结构导致的理解歧义,对于"起诉乙方的客户"一语可以产生不同的理解,既可以将整句理解为动宾关系,"起诉"理解为谓语,将"乙方的客户"理解为宾语,从而表示对乙方的客户提起诉讼;也可以将"起诉乙方"理解为修饰语,将"客户"理解为修饰对象,从而将整句理解为偏正关系、表示客户已向乙方提起了诉讼。

由此可见,对合同的准确理解是起草合同的首要环节,也是避免当事人产生纠纷甚或索赔的重要途径。

(2) 文本翻译 Translating across text

国际间的频繁商事交往和跨国贸易的繁荣发展决定了国际商事合同所具有的双语(bilingual)或多语(multilingual)沟通特征。因此合同起草者必须具备良好的语际转换能力,实现源语(source language)和译语(target language)之间自如转换。首先,合同起草者要站在读者的角度,充分理解源语的准确内涵;继而成为优秀的作者,运用恰当得体的目的语对文本进行再创作。

从合同起草的角度,对于文本的翻译过程是对文本理解的进一步细化和深入,同时又是创作目的文本的前提。在掌握必要的翻译原则(translation principles)和实用的翻译技巧(translation strategies)基础上,还要关注的是与客户的及时沟通,准确了解客户需求(the client's need)和真实意图(real intention),从而有利于对源语进行更为客观的把握。

例如常见的"草签文本"和"草签合同"这两个词语,在翻译时必须根据不同的语境来确定"草签"的意思。前者"草签文本"中的"草签"意味着负责人签写自己名字的首字母缩写,如 P.S. 表示 Peter Smith。因此,"草签

---

[1] Perrin V. Morgan [1943] AC 399
[2] 参见李克兴、张新红,《法律文本与法律翻译》,中国对外翻译出版公司(2006),第 51 页。

文本"应译为 an initialed text。而在"草签合同"中,"草签"意味着对尚未发生法律效力的合同条款进行确认。因此,"草签合同"应译为 sign a referendum contract。②

通过以上分析,译者娴熟的语言翻译技能和对于法律知识的准确理解对于合同文本的起草至关重要。

(3) 文本审校 Review on text

审查修改是合同正式签订前的最后工序,所谓"失之毫厘,谬以千里",合同起草后必须进行细致透彻的检查和审校。除却勘校(proofreading)文字错误和法律错误之外,起草者还必须为此在理想与现实之间进行选择和平衡,将专业性与交易的需要有机结合,仅强调合同的法律专业性而无视合同交易内容的现实需求,往往会使合同无法执行。而那些仅仅是为了满足交易的需求而设立的合同,又可能在法律上漏洞百出。

同时在合同的严密性和可操作性之间也要适当平衡,既要保证己方利益的安全实现,也要避免过于烦琐、严密所带来的负效应(side effect)。

简言之,合同起草者在对合同文本作最终的校验(final check)时,固然应以实现客户利益的最大化为己任,但也要在己方和对方利益之间适当平衡(appropriate balance),力求在双赢(win-win)中达到为客户服务的最佳效果。

第二节 合同起草的流程
Section 2 Contract Drafting Processes

2.1 清楚了解当事人需求
Obtain Clear Instructions from Clients

起草合同之前,首先要通过面谈询问(inquiry)的方式明确当事人通过合同执行欲达到的商业目的(business purposes),确定合同类型(contract types)和交易背景(transaction background)。在初步了解客户需求的基础上,通过书面法律咨询函(written inquiry)的形式进一步明确客户指示,并提出相应的法律建议,包括合同的交易结构建议(proposed structure)、交易要点(transaction terms),以及备忘录(MOU)等事项。

具体而言,起草者要了解参与交易的当事人的数量以及相互之间的关系;并且要了解各当事人的法律地位(legal status),包括法律行为能力和相应授权。例如,在一个涉及第三方当事人的交易中,甲是买方,乙是卖方,而丙是代表乙方向甲方提供服务或部件的分包商(subcontractor)。

甲方是一家中外合营企业(joint venture enterprise),乙方是一家香港公司,而丙方是一个非法人的美国财团(financial consortium)。乙方是甲方控股的外方投资者在香港成立的全资子公司(subsidiary)。因此甲方和乙方实际上是关联公司(affiliated companies),它们之间的交易是关联交易(affiliated transactions)。

其次,起草者还要考虑合同双方之前是否有过业务关系(business relation),该业务关系同现在的交易是否有关联。除此,还应该考虑在一个具体的交易中双方所处的地位。处于优势地位的一方有可能拒绝接受对方某些条款,从而影响合同的签订。

2.2 确认先例文本的应用
Consider the Use of Precedents

在了解当事人的需求基础上,在起草合同前还应该确认是否存在类似交易的范本或先例文本(precedents)。适用先例文本的优点是:第一是节省时间(time saving);第二是先例文本中的一些条款对起草者有很好的借鉴和提醒作用(reference and reminder)。但是应该避免照搬照抄类似先例文本,即仅仅更换当事人姓名和交易所涉及的具体金额。

是否采用合同先例文本以及如何加以利用需要考虑以下因素。

首先,要确定是否存在类似交易(similar transaction)的文本。如果存在先例文本,则要确定该文本的形式和内容对当前的交易是否适用,可以考虑以下四个标准(four criteria):

(1)该文本是否为特殊的交易或基于一系列特别的事实(particular facts)而制作。

(2)该文本是否因各方多次多轮谈判(rounds of negotiation)而存在诸多修改,如果经过多次修订(modification),则该合同通常包含若干不常见的、在一般情形不适用的条款,起草者就应放弃该先例。

(3)先例文本来源国(state of origin)的国情(national conditions in context)是否同本交易所在国的国情有较大差异。

(4)该文本适用的行业与该交易的行业(trade)是否相关。

即使确定了采用先例文本,起草者仍然需要对先例文本进行逐条审阅,仔细分析该文本的条款是否对当前交易适用,是否对当事人有利,并将其中条款所反映的问题列成清单作为注意事项(matters requiring attention),以提醒自己在相关问题中给予关注。

在对先例文本进行逐条审阅后要做两项相关的工作:(1)删除或修改仅仅针对先例文本所涉及的交易而起草的条款;(2)根据当前交易的具体情况加入新的条款。

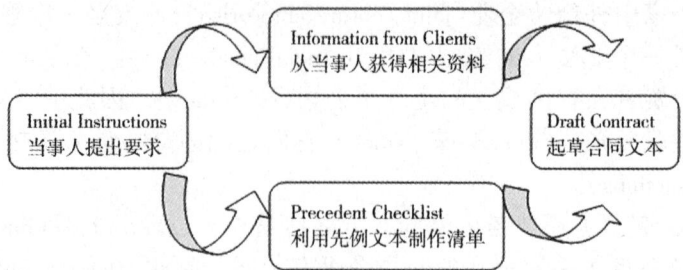

2.3 熟悉典型的商务合同结构
Get Familiar with the Structure of Typical Commercial Contracts

下图所列的是典型的商务合同结构,但这并非一成不变的固定模式,结合不同的交易内容(transaction content)和交易习惯(transaction custom),在具体起草合同的过程中,对合同结构的各个部分及其次序也会有所调整。

Preamble 合同首部
Preliminary Statements 前言(鉴于条款)
Definition 定义
Rights and Obligations (Operative Clauses) 具体操作条款
Warranties and Confidential Clauses 担保与保密条款
Breach and Disputes Settlement 违约救济与争端解决约定
Signature Page 签字页
Schedules and Annexes 附录与附件

(1)合同的起始部分是合同的首部(Preamble)。合同的首部列明合同的性质以及合同的各方,具体包括合同名称、合同日期、合同当事人(parties to the contract)名称以及签约地点。

(2)前言又称鉴于条款(preliminary statements),其主要目的是介绍合同的背景情况,但不涉及双方权利义务的实质性条款(substantive clause)。根据国际惯例,鉴于条款对合同双方没有约束力(no binding effect)。中文合同常见的鉴于条款如下:

[例1]

Upon friendly consultations conducted in accordance with the principles of equality and mutual benefit, the Parties have agreed to (describe subject matter of contract) in accordance with applicable laws and the provisions of this Contract.

双方本着平等互利的原则,经友好协商,同意按照相关法律以及本合同的条款(描述合同标的)。

(3)定义(definition)部分是整个合同至关重要的部分,因为其界定了整个合同的核心术语(terms)。定义在合同中的位置并非一定在前言之后,也可以将定义部分作为附录附在合同后面,但这种做法并不普遍。在定义条款的起草时,应注意以下问题:

a)对术语定义不要把具体权利义务(specific rights and obligations)作为定义加以规定,因为定义条款的目的是解释术语的含义,而不是操作条款的规定。

b)要避免循环定义,即在两个术语的定义中相互援引。例如:"原因就是引起结果的现象,结果就是被原因引起的现象。"此例句中,先用"结果"定义"原因",又用"原因"定义"结果",犯了循环定义的错误。①

c)除此,如果一个词语的通常含义就足以表达其意思,就没有必要在合同中进行定义。

[例2]

"Calendar Day" means any day on the Gregorian calendar. "日历日"指公历年度的任何一日。

因为"日历日"在整个合同中均没有特殊的含义,所以使用其普遍意义即可,没有必要在整个合同中专门加以定义。

(4)具体操作条款(operative clauses)又称为当事人合同权利义务(rights and obligations)条款,是合同的核心部分。每一个合同的具体操作条款根据交易的不同而有所不同。在起草有关当事人权利义务的条款时,不能局限于文字上的准确表述,而应考虑到该条款在实践中的可行性(feasibility)以及是否能够实际保护当事人的利益。总体而言,在起草具体操作条款时要遵循如下原则:

a)取保合同操作条款的可行性,即保证在交易过程中,双方能够根据合同条款实现其权利及履行其义务;

b)确保为当事人设立的救济措施(remedies)在出现纠纷时的可行性;

c)确保为各个环节的运作协调一致,避免出现前后矛盾或前后脱节的条款。

(5)陈述和担保(warranties and confidential clauses),该条款的目的是在合同中由一方对其所掌握的,而对方无法掌握或很难掌握的相关信息作出陈述,同时向对方担保陈述属实。例如,如果顾客欲买一座房子,买

---

① 吴坚、傅殿英,《实用逻辑学》,首都经济贸易大学出版社2005年版。

主就会假定卖主有适当的所有权(ownership);如果买主支付了购买价款,之后却发现卖主的所有权有缺陷(defect),买方会要求卖方退回购买价款并解除合同,或者卖主自己付钱修正有缺陷的所有权。

因此,起草者在审阅对方提供的合同时,如果看到陈述和担保条款,必须仔细审阅,因为一旦己方当事人违反了这些条款,就有可能造成非常严重的不利后果。

(6)违约救济与争端解决(breach and disputes settlement),该约定要求起草者在对合同利益的实现进行合理预期的同时,还要理性地预见到合同履行的潜在风险(potential risk)。因此,起草者应确保在为其当事人设定的违约责任条款中,避免含有苛刻的惩罚性条款,例如承担无限责任(unlimited liability)条款。虽然违约要承担违约责任,但起草者应尽量将其当事人所应承担的违约责任限定在合理范围内。责任上限条款对上市公司(listed corporations)非常重要,因为这些公司的管理层对公众股东负有义务,绝对不能使自己管理的公司因为某项交易有破产(bankruptcy)的风险。

(7)合同的尾部包括签字页(signature page)、附录(schedules)及附件(annexes),遵循不同的惯例,签字页和附录及附件的位置可以互换。确认签字的效力在中国签署合同的至关重要。对于比较重要的合同,通常是由法定代表人签署合同,也可以由持有法定代表人出具的授权委托书的其他人签署,或者在合同上加盖公司合同章或公章。

附录(schedules)和附件(annexes)通常没有实质区别,附录一般列出与合同某一条款相关的事项,这些事项附于合同之后而不是直接放入合同正文中,如设备销售合同中的设备清单(list of equipment)。另一类文件是双方在拟定合同时已经达成一致的相关协议,这些协议可以作为附件附在合同后面,例如在起草合营合同时,通常会规定,合营企业在成立以后应与合营各方签订一些相关的合同,如技术转让合同(technology transfer agreement)、商标许可合同(trademark licensing)等。

2.4 运用规范的商务合同语言
Apply Normative Contract Language

合法签订的国际商务合同是具有法律约束力的文件,这便决定了合同的起草者要使用法律词汇和书面用语,体现合同语言的正式性、准确性和规范性。

(1)选词准确 Pitching upon the words

一方面英语的一词多义现象在合同英语中普遍存在,决定了要透彻理解词义,必须结合上下文仔细推敲;另一方面合同表述的问题具有较强的逻辑性,词与词之间、段与段之间、条款与条款之间相互关联和制约,也决定了合同的选词应强调全面性和客观性。以"税"的选词为例,普通英语中通用的英文释义是"tax",但是例句中的合同条款在表述"税"的概念时,作出了较强的区分比较,体现了合同用语的准确性和正式性。

[例3]

The prices quoted above do not include any taxes, duties, impost and any other charges of any kind which may be levied in (countries).

以上所报的价格并不包括(在某国)所征收的各种税款、关税、进口税以及其他各种费用。

该句"税款"采用了 taxes,而关税和进口税则分别使用了 duty 和 impost,因为 duty 主要强调 the tax imposed by the government on merchandise imported from another country,可以理解为"关税",而 impost 指代纯粹的"进口税"。

(2)组句规范 Reconstructing the sentence

合同文件的严肃性要求合同语言必须明白通畅、清楚顺达。因此合同的行文要注重句式间的逻辑性和前后呼应,尤其要注意指称明确,不能随意用代词"其"、"各方"、"另一方"代替其他合同主体。

[例4]

The agreed text of a Trademark License Agreement is attached to this Contract as Appendix "C", parties agree to initial each page of Appendix "C" that he shall enter into the Trademark License Agreement as per the agreed text as soon as it is established as a joint venture limited liability company under the laws of the PRC and the other party has registered the trademark in the PRC and has the exclusive right to use the trademark.

以上条款中的"parties","he"以及"the other party"指称不明确,令人不知所云。应改写为:

The agreed text of a Trademark License Agreement is attached to this Contract as Appendix "C", Parties A, B, C and D agree to initial each page of Appendix "C" to confirm their agreement that the company shall enter into the Trademark License Agreement as per the agreed text as soon as it is established as a joint venture limited liability company under the laws of the PRC and Party C should register the trademark in the PRC and has the exclusive right to use the trademark.

合同的甲方、乙方、丙方和丁方同意将《商标使用许可协议》的内容作为本合同的附件 C。四方同意一旦按中国有关法律设立有限责任公司,公司应逐页确认按议定内容签订的《商标许可协议》,丙方应在中国注册其商标,并享有商标的独家使用权。

(3)符合合同文体规范 Adhering to norms of contractual style

国际商务合同具有结构性特征,合同所采用的基本文体格式是纲目、条款及细则,强调格式上的清晰规范,而不追求修饰韵味。尤其是古语词和特定词汇的频繁使用,成为体现合同文体特征的典型标志。

诸如 herein, hereto, thereafter, whereby 等英语中的古语词汇,在现代英语中已经很少应用,但在合同和其他法律文书中却频繁出现。这些词汇多半具有副词性质,在句中主要是为了避免重复,同时能够起到承接条款的作用。

[例5]

The Seller hereby warrants that the goods meet the quality standard and are free from all defects. 卖方在此保证:货物符合质量标准无瑕疵。

句中的 hereby 表示 by means of or by reason of this,"特此"、"在此"之意。除了古语词的频繁使用之外,国际商务合同用语中,情态动词 shall 使用频率非常高。作为一个严谨的法律专用词汇,shall 主要表示应当履行的义务(obligation)、债务(debt)或应承担的法律责任(liabilities),体现法律文件的命令性规范特征。

[例6]

Any amendments to Contract, or to any of the appendices annexed hereto, shall come into force only after a written agreement providing for such amendments…

对合同及合同所有附件的修正,应在修正案的书面协议……方可生效。

由此可见,shall 在表示合同义务时,更强调法律的强制履行性,但是如果脱离了表示权利、义务的语境,shall 的文体性特征就失去了体现的空间,应避免使用。

2.5 合同的审校与修改
Contract Proofreading

合同正式签订前的审查修改是不可或缺的必经程序,合同语言的严密性和专业性要求必须确保每个条款及相关文字均准确无误,因为对于合同内容的局部改变可能导致对先前内容的同步相关修改,同样对于文本或条款的修改、删减或添加甚至可能使整个合同条款的标点发生变动,即产生了波动效应(the Ripple Effect)。

为了防范波动效应,最大限度地减弱局部修订对于整篇合同行文的负面影响,在合同的审校过程中,应坚持统一性原则,即努力做到术语(terminology)、体例(format)和文体(style)的统一。

对于合同中反复出现的术语或关键词要做到行文统一,以第一次出现的术语为准,遇到较长的术语表达,可以采用"hereinafter referred to as + 简写"形式。例如,"By irrevocable letter of credit (hereinafter referred to as the L/C)",在后续出现的相同术语中,均可使用"the L/C"来表示信用证。这样在合同审校时,无论是查找还是替换,都相对容易,避免疏漏。

由于合同主要采取纲目、条款及细则的书面形式,统一的体例规范不仅是内容体系上的统一,也是逻辑上的统一。合同的逻辑排列顺序一般采用 Part(部分)、Chapter(章)、Section(节)、Article(条)、Paragraph(款)、Sub-paragraph(项)的表述形式。统一的格式编排将极大地节省合同的审校时间,提高审校效率。

合同的文体统一主要指合同整个文本都应贯穿条理性、客观性和规范性特征。尤其是经过审校修订后的合同部分仍要与合同的整体风格保持一致。

第三节 合同起草的具体实践
Section 3 Contract Drafting Practice

3.1 如何起草合资企业合营合同
How to Draft the Joint Venture Contract

根据1979年发展国家合资企业讨论会的决定,国际合资企业(International Joint Venture Enterprise)是指一个独立组成的公司实体(entity),由2个或2个以上国家或地区投资者提供资本资产,在一定水平上分享一定程度的经营管理责任,共同分担企业全部风险,除分享纯收益外,合资者均不得再从合资企业取得其他收益。

(1) 合资合营合同的功能和整体框架 Function and general structure of the joint venture contract

合资企业合营合同是国际商事合同中常见的合同类型,合资企业合营合同的结构比较规范,符合一般合同的基本框架要求,但在具体操作条款部分增加了与合资企业合营合同有关的相关条款,这主要取决于合资企业合营合同的功能:即合资企业合营合同是为了成立一个新的法律实体(legal entity)——合资企业,以期从事产品制造或提供服务而制定的法律文件。

合资合营合同首先要解决合资企业的设立问题,为合作经营提供一个平台;然后投资各方借助这个平台,进一步规划商务运作展开的模式,确定各方的权利和义务而不是具体规定商业业务。同时遵循法律文件制定的逻辑结构，合营合同还要预见到合同终止的情形，对可能产生的违约和合同终止后的后续事宜作出详细的规定和妥善的处理。

(2) 合资合营合同的主要内容条款 Major clauses of the joint venture contract

明确了合营合同的整体设计框架后，在合同双方进行初步意向性磋商之后，可以围绕合营合同的主要条款进一步确定双方的权利义务。总体而言，合营合同的主要条款应包含以下内容：

DATED 200[ ]年[ ]月[ ]日

JOINT VENTURE CONTRACT 合资经营合同
– by and between – 由
[PARTY A NAME]（甲方名称）
PARTY A 甲方
– And 与
[PARTY B NAME]（乙方名称）
PARTY B 乙方
IN RESPECT OF 签订
TABLE OF CONTENTS 目录
1. DEFINITIONS AND INTERPRETATION 定义和解释
2. PARTIES TO THE CONTRACT 合同双方
3. ESTABLISHMENT OF THE COMPANY 成立合营公司
4. PURPOSE, SCOPE AND SCALE OF OPERATION
   宗旨、经营范围及运营规模
5. TOTAL INVESTMENT AND REGISTERED CAPITAL
   投资总额和注册资本
6. BUSINESS PLANNING AND APPROVALS 业务计划和批准
7. RESPONSIBILITIES OF THE PARTIES 双方负责的事宜
8. BOARD OF DIRECTORS 董事会
9. OPERATION AND MANAGEMENT 经营管理
10. MARKETING AND SALES 市场营销
11. EQUIPMENT AND SERVICE PROCUREMENT 设备及服务的采购
12. INTELLECTUAL PROPERTY 知识产权
13. NON-COMPETITION 竞业禁止
14. SITE 经营场所

> 15. LABOUR MANAGEMENT 劳动管理
> 16. FINANCIAL AFFAIRS AND ACCOUNTING 财务与会计
> 17. TAXATION AND INSURANCE 税收和保险
> 18. REPRESENTATIONS AND WARRANTIES 陈述及担保
> 19. THE JOINT VENTURE TERM 合营期限
> 20. TERMINATION, DISSOLUTION, BUYOUT AND LIQUIDATION 终止、解散、相互收购股份及清算
> 21. BREACH OF CONTRACT 违约
> 22. CONFIDENTIALITY 保密义务
> 23. FORCE MAJEURE 不可抗力
> 24. SETTLEMENT OF DISPUTES 争议的解决
> 25. MISCELLANEOUS PROVISIONS 其他规定
> SCHEDULE A – DEFINITIONS AND INTERPRETATION 附录一
> SCHEDULE B – ANCILLARY CONTRACTS 附录二
> SCHEDULE C – CAPITAL CONTRIBUTION SCHEDULE 附录三
> SCHEDULE D – ADDITIONAL PERMITS 附录四
> SCHEDULE E – TAX CONCESSIONS 附录五
> CAVEATS AND DRAFTING NOTES 注意事项与说明

（3）合资合营合同的特别关注事项 Particular concern of the joint venture contract

在磋商并确定以上的合同主要内容的过程中，尤其值得关注的几个方面是：

1. 在合同项目初期，双方面临的最大风险是出资后合营项目无法保证切实启动，而导致当事人所投入的资金处于闲置状态。因此，要根据合营项目的具体情况确定己方当事人无法控制、但对合营企业能否成功启动有关键作用的事项，并考虑将这些事项成功完成作为己方当事人出资的先决条件，例如可以将诸如技术许可合同、零部件供应合同、厂房租赁合同作为附属协议（ancillary contracts），并规定此类附属协议的签署和生效作为一方或双方履行出资义务的先决条件（precedent conditions）。这样，各方可在投资之前就确保与合营企业启动和运营有关的事项均已确定，从而降低出现意外的风险，这一点对于缺乏控制权的少数股东（minority shareholders）尤为重要。

2．另外涉及董事会、经营管理等公司治理层面的管理模式以及相关部门的职权范围规定也同样应谨慎对待。少数股东为了确保自己的正当利益而与多数股东（majority shareholders）进行抗衡的主要途径是利用

合营合同中有关董事会职权的条款对多数股东（majority shareholders）的权力进行制衡。因此合同起草者必须明确自己所代表的利益主体，进而确定考虑问题的角度。

3．在设计合同的终止事项时，要明确违约的处理条款以及由此引发的争议解决（dispute settlement）方式，例如，明确是否可以采取仲裁方式（arbitration）以及具体的操作环节。同时还需要明确的是，合同的终止并不简单等同于合资企业的自动解散（dissolution），因为合资企业的解散还要涉及破产清算（bankruptcy and liquidation）等组织结构和资本结构的变动，因此应当将两个问题分而视之，分阶段分层次地逐步规定，作出细致安排。

Part 2 Focusing on Words and Phrases

1. Finding Meaning in Context

Words	Meaning in General English	Meaning in Legal English
will	意愿	遗嘱
article	文章	条款
remedy	补救方法	救济途径
dissolution	溶解	解散
duty	责任	关税

2. Useful Expressions in Legal English

1) Upon friendly consultations conducted in accordance with the principles of equality and mutual benefit, the Parties have agreed to (describe subject matter of contract) in accordance with applicable laws and the provisions of this Contract.

2) The Seller hereby warrants that the goods meet the quality standard and are free from all defects.

3) Any amendments to Contract, or to any of the appendices annexed hereto, shall come into force only after a written agreement providing for such amendments.

Part 3 Evaluating Your Achievements

词汇日志 Vocabulary Log

precedent	先例
drafting	起草
subsidiary	子公司
preamble	合同首部
schedules	附录
annexes	附件
preliminary statements	鉴于条款
warranties	担保
minority shareholders	少数股东
majority shareholders	多数股东
arbitration	仲裁
liquidation	清算

章节练习 Check Your Progress

1. Fill in the Blanks

1) The language application competence to contractual text refers to the ability of _____ through text; _____ _____ text; and _____ _____ text.

2) The beginning part of a contract is _____, which includes the nature of contract, the name of the contract, the _____ to the contract, the signing date, the signing _____ etc.

3) The general logic order of contract is arranged as Part, Chapter, _____, Article, _____, Sub-paragraph.

2. Legal Terminology

1) contract drafting
2) precedent text
3) substantive clause

3. Sentence Translation

1) 根据本协议规定,当事人任何一方不履行或延期履行其所承担的义务,应以违约论处。

2）考虑到包含于此的相互协议,缔约双方特此同意如下。

3）本合同规定的货物付款不意味着买方已完全接受货物的质量,所有货物要经过买方仔细检验后方可接受。

4）The property rights and interests of each member in the Association shall be always equal.

5）The joint venture enterprise shall have the Agreement executed and become bound thereby on the date.

6）In the event of any discrepancy between the two versions, the English version shall prevail.

自我评价 Self-Assessment Log

In this Chapter, you worked through these activities. How did each of them help you become a better learner? Check A lot, A little, or Not at all.

	A lot	A little	Not at all
I discussed the drafting competence for a contractor.	☐	☐	☐
I learned words and expressions in contract drafting.	☐	☐	☐
I gathered information about formal contract from the Internet.	☐	☐	☐
I evaluated my contract drafting skills.	☐	☐	☐

（Add something）_____

_____

Chapter 8

第八章 国际商务合同的翻译原则与技巧
Translation Principles and Strategies on International Business Contracts

Translation Principles and Strategies on International Business Contracts

With the development of international business, it is necessary for us to prepare bilingual contracts. Usually, we draft the contract in one language and then translate it into another language. Any mistranslation may lead to disputes between the parties to the contract. Therefore, we have to be very prudential and be aware of some translation strategies.

 Learning Objectives

In this chapter, students will learn how to:
◎ understand the legal translation principles;
◎ know the translation strategies on vocabulary;
◎ know the translation strategies on sentences;
◎ avoid mistranslation in translating international business contracts.

 Questions to Consider

1) What are the principles of legal translation?
2) What strategies can you apply to translating long sentences?
3) How to translate the special adverbs used in the international business contracts?

Part 1 Focusing on Legal Knowledge

第一节 商务合同翻译的原则
Section 1　Translation Principles on Business Contracts

1.1 准确性
Accuracy

准确性也就是要忠实于原文,在传递原文所包含的基本信息方面较少地失真,保持原文与译文之间的等值关系。这主要是由于国际商务合同(international business contracts)翻译不准确,往往会造成严重的法律后果,给当事人带来不必要的诉讼纠纷(disputes)。因此,在翻译商务合同时要尽最大可能再现原文本的所有信息,并保证译文所传递的信息没有遗漏(omission)、添加、篡改和歧义(ambiguity),客观上不令读者产生误解和困惑。

[例1]

投资商从开发区企业分得的利润汇出境外时,免征所得税。

译文:Profits gained by the investors from the Development Zone enterprises will be exempted from tax when remitted out of this country.

分析:译文有三处没做到"忠实"于原文,也就是说误传了原文的信息。第一,原文"投资商从开发区企业分得的利润"译为"Profits gained by the investors from the Development Zone enterprises(投资商在开发区企业的赢利)",意思已被改变。"分得的利润"应译为"dividend",而"profits gained by the investors from the Development Zone enterprises"则意为"由投资商在开发区经营企业所产生的利润",这是个很大的概念。这样翻译必然给外商造成错觉,以为他们经营企业所获的利润都可免税了。原文中"分得的利润"是指从利润中拿出的一部分按投资商或经营股份分配的红利(dividend),这个概念要比"profits gained"小得多。

第二,原文"免征所得税"译成"be exempted from tax",也未能做到"忠实"于原文。原文是指"免征个人所得税",应译为"be exempted from personal income tax",否则会造成概念模糊,信息传递扭曲。

第三,"汇出境外时"译成"when remitted out of China",暗含"征税是在汇款时进行"之意,这不是原文"汇出境外时"的内涵,此处"时"相当于英语的 if 条件从句。译为"if remitted out of this country"才能"忠实"地表达原文信息。①

1.2 统一性
Consistency

这一原则要求在翻译商务合同时,要尽量避免在译文中交替使用不同的词汇表达同一法律概念(legal concepts),同时也要做到译文中的商务术语(business terms)要和国际统一的汉英术语名称保持一致。在文学作品的翻译中,交替使用同义词和近义词来表达相同的概念或思想是可取的,并通常被认为只有那些对语言文字有较深造诣的译者才能得心应手地使用这种翻译技巧。然而,在翻译法律合同文本时,即便是使用从同义词词典中精挑细选出来的同义词来表达同一法律概念,也是不足取的,因为这极有可能使译文出现歧义,使试图曲解文意、别有用心的人士有机可乘。例如,在翻译合同文本时,我们不能把"offer"一会儿翻译成"报盘",一会儿又翻译成"报价",而应在译文中自始至终保持统一性。如果某一术语已经有国际通用的译名,那么在翻译时,就要采用该通用译名。例如,股东特别大会不应译为"special assembly",而应译为"Special General Meeting"。

1.3 专业性
Professionalism

专业性原则要求译者在翻译法律合同文本时要使用专业的法律概念和规范的法律术语(legal terms),从而避免将 Part A/Part B(甲方/乙方)翻译成"甲党/乙党"这样的外行话,也可避免因未使用规范的法律术语而产生的法律漏洞(legal loophole)。

[例 2]

Without prejudice to any rights which exist under the applicable laws or under the Subcontract, the Contractor shall be entitled to withhold or defer payment of all or part of any sums otherwise due by the Contractor to the Subcontractor.

误译:承包商依据适当的法律或分包合同在对拥有的任何权利不带成见的条件下,应该有权扣留或暂缓支付在不同情况下应由承包商支付给分包商的任何全部或部分金额。

---

① 肖辉:《财经、商贸汉英互译误译举隅——兼谈其翻译原则》,*US-China Foreign Language*, Dec. 2006, Volume 4, No.12(Serial No. 39)。

改译：在不影响按适用法律或分包合同享有任何权利的情况下，承包商有权扣留或暂缓支付承包商应付给分包商的全部或部分到期金额。①

分析：这里对画线部分的误译主要是由于合同术语翻译的不专业造成的。"prejudice"一词在日常英语中有"成见"、"偏见"的含义，然而在法律英语中，"without prejudice to"这一短语具有"在不损害……的原则下"、"在不影响……的情况下"之意。

第二节　商务合同的词汇翻译
Section 2　Translation Strategies on Vocabulary in Business Contracts

2.1 特殊副词
Special Adverbs

为了保证法律的庄重性，法律文本（legal texts）中经常会使用一些古体词（archaism）。商务合同是常见的法律文本之一。因此，在商务合同中不可避免地也会使用这些古体词，常用的主要是一些古旧副词。这类古旧副词主要是由 here, there, where 分别加上 after, by, in, of, on, to, under, upon, with 等介词构成。其作用主要是为了避免重复，使行文显得正式（formal）、准确（accurate）和简洁（concise），同时也起着承接合同条款的作用。这类词通常有其固定的用法和译法。

2.1.1 hereby 特此，因此，兹

"hereby"的英文释义是"by means of, by doing or saying this"，常用于法律文件、合同、协议书等正式文件的开头语，一般置于主语后，紧邻主语。

[例 3]

We hereby certify to the best of our knowledge that the foregoing statement is true and correct and all available information and data have been supplied herein, and that we agree to provide documentary proof upon your request.

译文：特此证明，据我们所知，上述声明内容真实，正确无误，并提供了全部现有的资料和数据，我们同意，应贵方要求出具证明文件。

[例 4]

The parties mutually agree that the said Agreement shall be and is hereby canceled.

译文：缔约双方彼此同意，特此取消该协议。

---

① 李全申：《谈谈商务合同的翻译》，《中国翻译》，1998 年第 2 期。

2.1.2 hereof 关于此点，在本文中

"hereof"的英文释义是"of or belonging to this"，在表示上文已提及的"本合同的、本文件的……"时，使用该词，一般置于所修饰的名词之后。

[例 5]

In the event of conflict between the provisions on arbitration formulated and prepared prior to the effective date of this Law and the provisions of this Law, the provisions hereof shall prevail.

译文：本法施行前制定的有关仲裁的规定与本法的规定相抵触的，以本法为准。

"hereof"与"thereof"的区别是"hereof"强调是"of this"，而"thereof"强调的是"of that"。例如，"the provisions hereof"表示的是"the provisions of this Contract"，而"the provisions thereof"表示的则是"the provisions of that Contract"。

[例 6]

The Party applying for arbitration shall submit to an arbitration commission the arbitration agreement, the application for arbitration and the copies thereof.

译文：当事人申请仲裁，应当向仲裁委员会递交仲裁协议、仲裁申请书及副本。

2.1.3 hereto 至此，于此

"hereto"的英文释义是"to this"，在表示上文已经提及的"本合同的……""本文件的……"时，使用该词，一般置于所修饰的名词之后。例如，"the Parties hereto"表示的是"the Parties to this Contract"。"hereto"与"thereto"的区别类似于"hereof"与"thereof"的区别。

[例 7]

If Party B demands to audit the accounts of Party A, Party B shall, within 10 days after receiving the written notice issued by Party A under Sub-Clause 3.4 of this Contract, notify Party A of the mater in question. The specific contents and procedure of auditing accounts are detailed in Appendix 4 hereto.

译文：乙方如需查核甲方的账目时，应在接到甲方依上述本合同第3.4款规定开出的书面通知后10天之内通知甲方，其具体的查账内容和程序详见本合同附件4。

[例 8]

Joint Venture shall employ competent treasurers and auditors to keep all books of accounts, which are accessible at any time to each Party hereto.

译文：合营企业雇用合格的财务人员和审计员，设立会计账目，合营各方可随时查看有关账目。

2.1.4 herein 此中,于此

"herein"的英文释义是"in this",在表示上文已经提及的"本合同(中)的……","本法(中)的……"等时,使用该词,通常置于所修饰词之后。与之相对应的"therein"强调的则是"in that"。

[例 9]

The term "company" mentioned herein refers to such a limited liability company or such a company limited by shares as are established within the territory of China in accordance with this Law.

译文:本法所称公司是指依照本法在中国境内设立的有限责任公司和股份有限公司。

[例 10]

A certificate of the Borrower shall, substantially, comply with the form set forth in Appendix 4, and the attachments specified therein.

译文:借款人证明书,其格式基本上应遵照附录 4 规定的格式及其规定的附件。

2.1.5 hereinafter 以下,在下文中

"hereinafter"的英文释义是"later in this contract",一般与 referred to as, called 等词组连用,置于这些词组前面。

[例 11]

This Contract is hereby made and concluded by and between YY Co. (hereinafter referred to as Party A) and ZZ Co. (hereinafter referred to as Party B) on (Date), in (Place), China, on the principle of equality and mutual benefit and through amicable consultation.

译文:本合同双方,YY 公司(以下简称甲方)与 ZZ 公司(以下简称乙方),在平等互利基础上,通过友好协商,于×年×月×日在中国××(地点),特签订本合同。

2.1.6 hereunder 在此中

"hereunder"的英文释义是"under this",通常置于所修饰词之后。

[例 12]

The Principal shall not assign or transfer any of its rights, obligations or liabilities hereunder without the express prior written consent of the General Agent.

译文:非经总代理人预先书面同意,委托人不得将本协议规定的任何权利、义务或责任予以转让或转移给他人。[1]

---

[1] 兰天:《国际商务合同翻译教程》,东北财经大学出版社 2007 年版。

2.1.7 thereafter 此后，其后

"thereafter"的英文释义是"after that in time, afterwards"，在表示上文已提及的时间之后时，使用该词，通常置于所修饰词之后。

[例 13]

If the goods do not conform with the contract, the buyer may require the seller to remedy the lack of conformity by repair, unless this is unreasonable having regard to all the circumstances. A request for repair shall be made either in conjunction with notice given under Article 39 or within a reasonable time thereafter.

译文：如货物不符合合同要求，买方可要求卖方修理，以补救与合同不符之处，除非在考虑各种情况之后，认为此要求不合理。该修理要求应是根据第 39 条发出通知中提出的，或在上述通知发出后合理的时间内提出的。（《联合国国际货物销售合同公约》第 46 条）

分析：文中"thereafter"表示"after notice given under Article 39"，它避免了重复，又能准确而严密地表达原意。

2.1.8 whereas 鉴于，就……而论

"whereas"的英文释义是"considering that"，常用于合同、协议书的开头段落，引出合同双方要订立合同的理由或依据。

[例 14]

Whereas Party A and Party B, adhering to the principle of equality and mutual benefit and through friendly consultation, agree to jointly invest to establish a new joint venture company in China（hereinafter referred to as "Joint Venture"）. The Contract hereunder is made and concluded.

译文：鉴于甲方与乙方按照平等互利的原则，经过友好协商，决定共同投资在中国建立合资经营公司（以下称"合资企业"），为此达成如下合同。

2.1.9 whereby 凭借……

"whereby"的英文释义是"by means of which"，用以引出定语从句，相当于"by which"，通常译成"凭此协议"、"凭此条款"。

[例 15]

This Agreement is made and concluded by and between A Corporation（hereinafter called Party A）and B Company（hereinafter called Party B）whereby the Parties hereto agree to enter into the compensation trade under the terms and conditions set forth below.

译文：本协议由 A 公司（以下简称甲方）与 B 公司（以下简称乙方）签订，双方同意按下列条款进行补偿贸易。

2.1.10 构词规则 Rules of word formation

(1)here 代表 this。例如：hereafter= following this; hereby= by this means or by reason of this; herein= in this; hereof= of this; hereto= to this; herewith= with this; hereunder= under this; hereinafter= later in this Contract; hereinbefore= in a preceding part of this Contract 等。

(2)there 代表 that。例如：thereafter= after that; thereby= by that means; therein= in that; thereinafter= in that part of a Contract; thereof= of that; thereto= to that; thereunder= under that part of contract; thereupon= as a result of 等。

(3)where 代表 which，与介词组合，一般为关系副词，引出定语从句，如：whereof= of which。①

2.2 法律惯用语
Legal Phrases

2.2.1 in the event of (that) 在……情况下，在……时，一旦，如果

[例16]

In the event of any conflict between the provisions of this agreement and the provisions of the Articles of Association the provisions of this agreement shall prevail.

译文：如果本协议的规定与章程的规定之间有任何抵触，应以本协议的规定为准。

[例17]

In the event of any difference or dispute arising between the parties as to the construction of this agreement the same shall be determined by an arbitrator appointed in accordance with the Rules of Arbitration of the London Chamber of Commerce.

译文：在双方就本协议的解释发生任何分歧或争议时，应由按照伦敦工商会仲裁规则指定的仲裁员予以决定。

2.2.2 Without the prior (written) consent of 未经……事先（书面）同意

[例18]

Subject to the following sentence, neither party may assign, delegate, sub-contract, mortgage, charge or otherwise transfer any or all of its rights and obligations under this Agreement without the prior written consent of the other party.

译文：在符合下句的规定下，任何一方未经另一方事先书面同意不可

---

① 胡庚申，王春晖，申云帧：《国际商务合同起草与翻译》，外文出版社2001年版。

转让、转授、分包、按揭、抵押或以其他方式转移其在本协议项下的任何或一切权利及义务。

2.2.3 including but not limited/including without limitation 包括但不局限于

[例 19]

Neither party shall be liable for any failure or delay in performance of this agreement which is caused by circumstances beyond the reasonable control of a party including without limitation any labor disputes between a party and its employees.

译文:任何一方均不就超出该方合理控制的情况(包括但不限于一方与其雇员之间的劳动争议)所造成的不履行或延迟履行本协议负责。

2.2.4 ⋯unless⋯otherwise 除⋯⋯/ 另⋯⋯外

在 otherwise 和 unless 搭配使用时,unless 放在从句句首,而 otherwise 放在从句的主语和谓语之间,即:unless+ 主语 +otherwise+ 谓语。如果使用被动语态,则 otherwise 放在主语和 be 动词后面,谓语的过去分词前面,即:unless+ 主语 +be 动词 +otherwise+ 谓语的过去分词。

[例 20]

A notice under subjection （1）shall, unless it otherwise provides, apply to the income from any property specified therein as it applied to the property itself.

译文:根据第(1)款发出的通知书,除其中另有规定外,亦适用于通知书内指明的财产的收入,一如适用于该财产本身。

[例 21]

Unless in any enactment it is otherwise provided⋯

译文:除成文法另有规定外⋯⋯

2.2.5 subject to 在符合⋯⋯的情况下

Subject 在普通日常英语中做名词的情况居多,可以翻译为"主题",但是在法律英语中,subject 常常与 to 连用,构成 subject to 句型,构成条件状语（通常前置）,可以翻译成"根据⋯⋯规定"、"在符合⋯⋯的情况下"、"以⋯⋯为准"或"在不抵触⋯⋯下"。subject to 是形容词,后面直接加名词,而且最常见的是加 agreement, section, contract 等。

[例 22]

Subject to Clause 5, no variation in or modification of the terms to the Contract shall be made except by written amendment signed by the parties.

译文:根据第 5 条规定,合同的任何变更或修改,必须以双方签订的修改本为准。

[例 23]

Subject to the terms of this Agreement, the Producer agrees to be bound by the terms to the following marketing agreement.

译文：在本协议的条件下，制造商同意接受下列销售协议各项条款的约束。

2.2.6 without prejudice to 在不影响……的情况下

这个英文法律短语的功能相当于普通英文中的"without affecting"。与"subject to…"的句法结构相同，跟在"without prejudice to"这个短语之后的通常是一个指代某项法律条款的名词。但对有关事物或条款的规限程度，没有前者那么强硬。前者规限的程度是必须"符合"或"依照"有关条款或规定，后者指不要影响或损害其规限的事物。在汉语中，其意思相当于"在不损害……的原则下"、"在不影响……的情况下"、"……不受影响"、"不妨碍……"以及"不规限……"等等。①

[例 24]

In this event without prejudice to the Buyer's other remedies the Seller shall promptly collect any Goods which have been delivered.

译文：在此种情况下在不影响买方其他补救的原则下，买方应迅速收集已交付的任何有关货物。

2.2.7 provided that 如……，但……

[例 25]

Provided that the acceptance of rent or mesne profits by the Landlord after the expiration of the term of the tenancy hereby created shall not be deemed to operate as a waiver or breach of any of the terms hereof nor as a new periodic tenancy by way of holding over or otherwise. A new Tenancy shall only be created by a fresh tenancy agreement in writing signed by the Landlord and the Tenant.

译文：倘若在本合约规定的租期届满后业主接受租金或中间收益，不应被认为是起了放弃或违背本合约的任何条件的作用，也不应认为是起了作为继续租用或其他的新租期的作用。新租约只能是业主和租户签署的新书面租赁合约。

[例 26]

The Owner may, at its discretion, approve or reject any change proposed by

---

① 李克兴，张新红：《法律文本与法律翻译》，中国对外翻译出版公司 2006 年版。

the Contractor, provided that the Owner shall approve any change proposed by the Contractor to ensure the safety of the Works.

译文：业主可赞成或拒绝由承包人提出的变更，但应接受承包人提出的保证工程安全方面的变更建议。

2.2.8 notwithstanding 尽管……，即使……

该词所引导的并非是一个让步状语从句，因为在习惯用法上该词之后不跟句子，只跟一个名词性短语。虽然该词也可做连词使用，跟一个完整的让步状语从句，例如，He is honest, notwithstanding he is poor（他虽贫穷，却诚实），但这种用法并非是法律英语中的典型用法。

[例 27]

Notwithstanding any other agreement, the Parties shall enter into a new contract with respect to the subject matter.

译文：尽管有任何其他协议，双方仍应就标的签订新合同。

2.2.9 save 除……以外

该词后可跟一个名词性短语，也可以跟一个从句或另一个介词短语。

[例 28]

The Contractor shall not cut or alter the work of any other Contractor save with the consent of the Engineer.

译文：除非得到工程师的同意，该承包商不应削减或改变其他任何承包商的工程。

2.2.10 in respect of 对于，有关，有关……的

[例 29]

For the purpose of the Landlord and the Tenant Ordinance and for the purpose of these presents the rent in respect of the said premises shall be deemed to be in arrear if not paid in advance as stipulated by Clause 1 hereof.

译文：基于租务条例并基于这些通知，有关该楼宇的租金，如果未照合约第一条规定的那样提前缴付，就应该被认为是拖欠。

2.2.11 In Witness Whereof 特立此证，特此证明

作为所协议事项的证据，该短语常用于合同的结尾条款。

[例 30]

In Witness Whereof, the parties have executed this Contract in duplicate by their duly authorized representatives on the date first above written.

译文：特此证明，双方授权代表于上面首次写明的日期正式签订本协议一式两份。

除上述法律惯用语外，英文合同中常出现的短语还有：

prior to(在……之前);in lieu of(作为……代替);in accordance with(根据……);due to(由于,因为);know all men by these presents(根据本文件;特此宣布);now therefore(特此,因此);pertaining to(有关);in question(该,这)等。

第三节 商务合同的句子翻译
Section 3 Translation Strategies on Sentences in Business Contracts

3.1 句子的一般翻译技巧
General Strategies on Sentence Translation

3.1.1 语序调整法 Rearrangement of the word order

由于译文语序和原文语序并不完全一致,所以在将原文翻译成译文时,必须调整一些语序,以使译文符合目的语的表达习惯。在调整语序时,有时必须把在原文中后面表达的词放在译文前面表达,有时要把原文中前面表达的词放在译文后面表达。在调换位置时并没有特别的规律,要视上下文的需要而定。

[例 31]
The Business Plan of the Company shall be established by the Board in view of actual market conditions, expected sales volumes, the employees' ability to absorb new technology and any other factors considered important by the Board.

译文:合营公司的业务计划由董事会在考虑市场实际情况、预计的产品销售额、雇员吸收新技术的能力以及其他董事会认为重要的因素后确定。

分析:原文中"in view of actual market conditions, expected sales volumes, the employees' ability to absorb new technology and any other factors considered important by the Board"等词被放在句子的后面,而在译文中,却被放在了句子的中间。

3.1.2 增词减词法 Amplification and omission

增词减词法指的是根据原文上下文的意思、逻辑关系,以及译文语言的句法特点和表达习惯,在翻译时增加原文字面上没有但实际已包含在内容之内的词,或减去原文中虽有但译文表达已显多余的词的一种方法。[1]在

---

[1] 王道庚:《新编英汉法律翻译教程》,浙江大学出版社 2006 年版。

使用增词减词法时切勿随意添枝加叶或删减,以免使译文违反了准确性原则。

[例32]

Any interim or final Investment Certificate shall be signed by the Chairman and the Vice Chairman of the Board and stamped with the Company seal, and shall certify the amount of registered capital contributed by such Party and the date on which such capital contribution was made.

译文:临时或正式出资证明书应由董事长和副董事长联合签署,加盖合营公司公章,并注明出资方的出资金额和出资日期。

分析:上文是一个增词法的例子。译文中的"联合"一词在原文中并没有对应词,但译者为了使译文更符合中文的表达习惯,所以在译文中加上了"联合"这个词。

[例33]

If any guarantee is required as security for any external financing of the Company approved by the Board in accordance with Article 8.2 (c)(v), and if the Parties agree to provide guarantees in relation to such financing, the Parties shall severally guarantee the obligations of the Company under such external financing in proportion to their respective interests in the registered capital of the Company at such time as the guarantee is given (unless otherwise agreed in writing by the Parties).

译文:如果合营公司董事会依照第8.2(c)(v)条批准的外部融资需要以保证形式提供担保,并且双方同意对该融资提供保证,则(除非双方另有书面协议)双方应按当时在合营公司注册资本中所占份额的比例分别各自对合营公司的义务提供保证。

分析:这是一个减词法的例子。原文中用了"at such time as the guarantee is given"这样一个定语从句,但在译文中,译者根据上下文和逻辑关系把它翻译成了"当时"。原文的意思并没有改变。

3.1.3 转换法 Conversion

在翻译实践中,要做到既忠实于原文又符合译文语言规范,就不能机械地按原文逐字硬译,而需要适当地将英语的某一成分转换为汉语的另一成分或将汉语的某一成分转换为英语的另一成分。

[例34]

The Parties agree that any restructuring shall not adversely affect the economic interests of the Parties.

译文:双方同意,任何重组不得给双方的经济利益带来不利的影响。

分析:原文中的谓语动词"affect"被转换为译文中的宾语"影响",同时做状语的副词"adversely"也被转换为定语"不利的"。

[例 35]

The borrower hereby irrevocably appoints the agent and the receiver to be its attorney in accordance with the provisions of Clause 13.

译文:借款人特此根据第 13 条规定作出一项不可撤销的委任,委任代理人及破产管理人作为其授权人。

分析:原文中做状语的副词"irrevocably"被转换为译文中的定语"不可撤销的",同时译文中增译了"委任"一词。

[例 36]

Partial shipments shall be allowed upon presentation of the clean set of shipping documents.

译文:可以允许分批发货,但须提出一套清洁装运单据。

分析:原文中的主语 shipment 转化为汉语动词,原文中修饰主语的 partial 转化为状语。

3.2 从句的翻译
Translation of Subordinate Clauses

3.2.1 定语从句的翻译 Translation of attributive clauses

英语的定语从句可分为限定性定语从句和非限定性定语从句。一般来说,限定性定语从句和先行词的关系十分紧密,在翻译时可采用合译法,将限定性定语从句译为"……的",置于所修饰词的前面。

[例 37]

Shipment shall be commenced within 10 months counting from the date when the contract has come into force and completed within 16 months.

译文:自合同生效之日起计算,10 个月内装运,16 个月内交付完毕。

如果限定性定语从句太长,放在修饰词前会觉得很拖沓冗长,可采用分译法,把定语从句与主句分离,让定语从句独立出来,或者放在主句的后面,或者与主句完全分离,成为一个独立的分句。

[例 38]

The seller ensures that all the equipment listed in Appendix One to the Contract are brand-new products whose performance shall be in conformity with the Contract and which are manufactured according to current Chinese National Standards or Manufacturer's Standard.

译文:买方保证本合同附件 1 所列全部设备都是新产品,是根据现行的中国国家标准,或生产厂的标准制造的,其性能符合合同规定。

非限定性定语从句与它所修饰的先行词关系并不密切,因此,在翻译非限定性定语从句时可采用分译法。

[例39]

The buyer agrees to buy from the seller and the seller agrees to sell to the buyer the necessary equipment, material design, technical documentation, license, know-how and technical services for construction of a plant with a 54 000 KW phosphorous electric furnace, which will have a production capacity of 30 000 (thirty thousand) metric tons of yellow phosphorus per year and 70,000 (seventy thousand) metric tons of Sodium tripolyphosphate per year with phosphate Rock as raw material by using the process stipulated in Article 10.1 of this Contract.

译文：买方同意向卖方购买、卖方同意向买方出售其建厂所需的设备、材料设计、技术文件、专利许可证、专有技术和技术服务。该工厂将建设 54 000 瓦黄磷电炉一座,以磷酸岩为原料、采用本合同第 10 条第 1 款所规定的工艺,具有年产黄磷 30 000 公吨、三聚磷酸钠 70 000 公吨的生产能力。

3.2.2 状语从句的翻译 Translation of adverbial clauses

商务合同中的状语从句比较常见,主要包括条件状语从句、时间状语从句、让步状语从句等。在翻译这些状语从句时,可以根据逻辑关系和译文的表达习惯来进行翻译,必要时可对译文的语序进行适当的调整。

(1)条件状语从句

引导条件状语从句的连词很多,主要有 if, in case, in the event of, unless 等。这些连词引导的条件状语从句在上文中都有所涉及。在此主要说明由 where 引导的条件状语从句和一种特殊的条件状语从句——"should+ 主语 + 动词"。

由 where 引导的条件状语从句通常可以译为"如果","若"。

[例40]

Where the sum payable is expressed in words and also in figures, and there is a discrepancy between the two, the sum denoted by the words is the amount payable.

译文:如应付金额同时用大小写表示而两者有差异时,应以大写所表示的金额为准。

[例41]

Where a claim has been asserted in legal proceedings within the limitation period in accordance with articles 13, 14, 15 to 16, but such legal proceedings have ended without a decision binding on the merits of the claim, the limitation period shall be deemed to have continued to run.

译文:如依照第 13 条、第 14 条、第 15 条和第 16 条在时效期限内进行法律程序提出请求权,但此种法律程序终结时并未就请求权的是非曲直作出具有拘束力的最后判决时,时效期限应视为持续计算。(《国际货物买卖时效期限公约》第 17 条)

"should+ 主语 + 动词"结构引导的条件句属于非真实条件句。合同英语中使用这种条件句时,其主语一般为陈述语气。该结构表明,发生条件句所述情况的可能性很小,如果该条件句所述情况发生了,那么主句所设的事宜必须完成。

[例 42]

Should the effect of Force Majeure continue more than a hundred and twenty (120) consecutive days, both parties shall settle the further execution of the Contract through friendly negotiations as soon as possible.

译文:如不可抗力事件延续到 120 天以上时,双方应通过友好协商方式尽快解决继续履行合同的问题。

(2)时间状语从句

由 after 引导的时间状语从句一般被译为"……之日起";由 before 引导的时间状语从句一般被译为"……之后,才能……"。

[例 43]

After the Seller receives the relative documents issued by the shipping Company, the Seller shall pay to the Buyer within 20 (twenty) days.

译文:卖方应在收到船舶公司出具的有关单据之日起,20 天内向买方支付款项。

[例 44]

The manufacturers shall, before the goods is delivered over, make a precise and comprehensive inspection of the goods with regard to its quality, specifications, performance and quantity, weight, and issue inspection certificates certifying the technical data and conclusion of the inspection.

译文:制造商应对货物的质量、规格、性能和数量、重量进行一丝不苟和全面的检查,出具检验证明书,证实检验的技术数据和结论后,才能发货。

Part 2 Focusing on Words and Phrases

1. Finding Meaning in Context

Words	Meaning in General English	Meaning in Legal English
exhibit	展出	展示证据,如向法庭、仲裁员等提交的作为证据的文件或物品
hear	听见	听审、审理
immunity	免疫力	豁免权
leave	离开	遗赠、遗留给
proceed	进行	起诉
sentence	句子	判决
presents	礼物	本文件
undo	解开	勾引、诱奸
vacation	假期	(法院)休庭期
warrant	保证	逮捕令
letter	信	许可证、(遗嘱继承中的)证书
battery	电池	殴打、人身攻击

2. Useful Expressions in Legal English

1) In the event of any conflict between the provisions of this agreement and the provisions of the Articles of Association the provisions of this agreement shall prevail.

2) Neither Party may issue any press release concerning the existence or terms of this Agreement without the prior written consent of the other Party, which consent may not be unreasonably withheld or delayed.

3) This agreement shall (except for any obligation fully performed prior to or at the Completion Date) continue in full force and effect after the Completion Date notwithstanding completion.

4) Save as is provided in this Ordinance, no claim within the jurisdiction of the Board shall be actionable in any court.

5) Without prejudice to your powers and discretions, we hereby authorize you or your agents to take any actions including but not limited to the following:

Part 3 Evaluating Your Achievements

词汇日志 Vocabulary Log

personal income tax	个人所得税
Special General Meeting	股东特别大会
subcontract	分包合同
subcontractor	分包商
arbitration commission	仲裁委员会
terms and conditions	条款
London Chamber of Commerce	伦敦工商会
mesne profits	中间收益
partial shipments	分批发货
come into force	生效
limitation period	时效期限
force majeure	不可抗力

章节练习 Check Your Progress

1. Fill in the Blanks

1）The translation principles of international business contract are_____, _____, and _____.

2）In the legal context, the word "_____" shall be translated similarly as its equivalent word "document".

3）In the legal context, the word "_____" shall be translated similarly as its equivalent phrase "considering that".

4）In the legal context, the phrase "_____" is usually translated as "以下简称".

2. Legal Terminology

1）mesne profits

2）force majeure

3）limited liability company

4）extraordinary general meeting

3. Sentence Translation

1）合同是当事人之间设立、变更、终止民事关系的协议。依法成立的合同,受法律保护。

2）依照《中外合资经营企业法》批准在中国境内设立的中外合资经营企业(以下简称合营企业)是中国的法人,受中国法律的管辖和保护。

3）The termination of this Contract shall not in any way affect the outstanding claims and liabilities existing between the Parties hereto upon the expiration of the validity of the Contract and the debtor shall continue to be kept liable for paying the outstanding debts to the creditor.

4）The terms "FOB", "CFR" or "CIF" shall be subject to the "International Rules for the Interpretation of Trade Terms" (INCOTERMS, 2000) provided by International Chamber of Commerce (ICC) unless otherwise specified herein (in this Contract).

5）The decision and award of the arbitration tribunal shall be final, and the judgment on the decision and award in question may, under the request of either party to the Contract, be made by any court having jurisdiction. The parties thereto shall, in good faith, comply with the decision and award of the arbitration tribunal.

自我评价 Self-Assessment Log

In this Chapter, you worked through these activities. How did each of them help you become a better learner? Check A lot, A little, or Not at all.

	A lot	A little	Not at all
I understood the basic legal translation principles.	☐	☐	☐
I learned some typical legal expressions used in international business contracts.	☐	☐	☐
I knew how to translate and use the special adverbs in legal texts.	☐	☐	☐
I understood the translation strategies on subordinate clauses.	☐	☐	☐

（Add something）_____

_____

第五部分
PART V

国际商务合同范本

INTERNATIONAL BUSINESS CONTRACTS SAMPLES

Chapter 9

第九章 国际商务合同范本
International Business Contracts Samples

After the whole term of studying, you have known what a contract is, and what it is, what it must contain and how to write a contract. But have you ever read the CONTRACT in your daily life? Face with this problem, you may find these sample contracts quite useful in your own transactions. However, you will most certainly need to change the clauses to fit your own special situation. Always be careful that your contract covers the rights and risks of your particular purposes.

 Learning Objectives

In this chapter, students will learn how to:
◎ classify sample contracts;
◎ understand and master sample contracts;
◎ practice sample contracts in your own special situation;
◎ identify the context of sample contracts.

 Questions to Consider

1) What are differences between these different sample contracts?
2) How do you use these forms of sample contracts in our daily life?
3) How to deal with the problems that frequently arise because of imprecise or missing terms?

Part 1 Focusing on Legal Knowledge

第一节 销售合同
Section 1 Contracts for Sales of Goods

国际货物销售合同又称国际货物买卖合同,是指营业地处于不同国家的当事人之间就货物买卖所发生的权利义务关系而达成的协议。国际货物销售合同在我国外贸实务中还称外贸合同,或进出口贸易合同,是我国最重要的国际商务合同。

1.1 销售货物合同
Sales Contract

Contract No.:

Signed at:

Date:

The Buyers:

The Sellers:

The Buyers agree to buy and the Sellers agree to sell the following goods on terms and conditions as set forth below:

(1) Name of Commodity, Specifications and Packing:

(2) Quantity:

(3) Unit Price:

(4) Total Value:

(Shipment Quantity___ %more or less allowed)

(5) Time of Shipment:

(6) Port of loading:

(7) Port of Destination:

(8) Insurance: To be covered by the___ for 110% of the invoice value against_____.

(9) Terms of Payment: By confirmed, irrevocable, transferable and divisible letter of credit in favor of _____payable at sight with TT reimbursement

clause/___days'/sight/date allowing partial shipment and transshipment. The covering Letter of Credit must reach the Sellers before _____ and is to remain valid in _____.China until the 15th day after the aforesaid time of shipment, failing which the Sellers reserve the right to cancel this Sales Contract without further notice and to claim from the Buyers for losses resulting there from.

(10)Inspection:The Inspection Certificate of Quality / Quantity / Weight / Packing / Sanitation issued by_____ of China shall be regarded as evidence of the Sellers' delivery.

(11)Shipping Marks:

OTHER TERMS:

1. Discrepancy:In case of quality discrepancy, claim should be lodged by the Buyers within 30 days after the arrival of the goods at the port of destination, while for quantity discrepancy, claim should be lodged by the Buyers within 15 days after the arrival of the goods at the port of destination. In all cases, claims must be accompanied by Survey Reports of Recognized Public Surveyors agreed to by the Sellers. Should the responsibility of the subject under claim be found to rest on the part of the Sellers, the Sellers shall, within 20 days after receipt of the claim, send their reply to the Buyers together with suggestion for settlement.

2. The covering Letter of Credit shall stipulate the Sellers' option of shipping the indicated percentage more or less than the quantity hereby contracted and be negotiated for the amount covering the value of quantity actually shipped. (The Buyers are requested to establish the L/C in amount with the indicated percentage over the total value of the order as per this Sales Contract.)

3. The contents of the covering Letter of Credit shall be in strict conformity with the stipulations of the Sales Contract. In case of any variation there of necessitating amendment of the L/C, the Buyers shall bear the expenses for effecting the amendment. The Sellers shall not be held responsible for possible delay of shipment resulting from awaiting the amendment of the L/C and reserve the right to claim from the Buyers for the losses resulting from there.

4. Except in cases where the insurance is covered by the Buyers as arranged, insurance is to be covered by the Sellers with a Chinese insurance company. If insurance for additional amount and /or for other

insurance terms is required by the Buyers, prior notice to this effect must reach the Sellers before shipment and is subject to the Sellers' agreement, and the extra insurance premium shall be for the Buyers' account.

5. The Sellers shall not be held responsible if they fail, owing to Force Majeure cause or causes, to make delivery within the time stipulated in this Sales Contract or cannot deliver the goods. However, the Sellers shall inform immediately the Buyers by cable. The Sellers shall deliver to the Buyers by registered letter, if it is requested by the Buyers, a certificate issued by the China Council for the Promotion of International Trade or by any competent authorities, attesting the existence of the said cause or causes. The Buyers' failure to obtain the relative Import License is not to be treated as Force Majeure.

6. Arbitration: All disputes arising in connection with this Sales Contract or the execution thereof shall be settled by way of amicable negotiation. In case no settlement can be reached, the case at issue shall then be submitted for arbitration to the China International Economic and Trade Arbitration Commission in accordance with the provisions of the said Commission. The award by the said Commission shall be deemed as final and binding upon both parties.

7. Supplementary Condition(s).(Should the articles stipulated in this Contract be in conflict with the following supplementary condition(s), the supplementary condition(s) should be taken as valid and binding.)

Sellers: Buyers:

销售货物合同

合同编号：

签订地点：

签订日期：

买方：

卖方：

双方同意按下列条款由买方售出下列商品：

(1)商品名称、规格及包装：

(2)数量：

(3)单价：

(4)总值：

(装运数量允许有 _____ %的增减）

（5）装运期限：

（6）装运口岸：

（7）目的口岸：

（8）保险：由 _____ 方负责，按本合同总值 110% 投保 _____ 险。

（9）付款：凭保兑的、不可撤销的、可转让的、可分割的即期有电报套汇条款／见票／出票 ____ 天期付款信用证，信用证以 _____ 为受益人并允许分批装运和转船。该信用证必须在 _____ 前开到卖方，信用证的有效期应为上述装船期后第 15 天，在中国 _____ 到期，否则卖方有权取消本售货合约，不另行通知，并保留因此而发生的一切损失的索赔权。

（10）商品检验：以中国 _____ 所签发的品质／数量／重量／包装／卫生检验合格证书作为卖方的交货依据。

（11）装运唛头：

其他条款：

1. 异议：品质异议须于货到目的口岸之日起 30 天内提出，数量异议须于货到目的口岸之日起 15 天内提出，但均须提供经卖方同意的公证行的检验证明。如责任属于卖方者，卖方于收到异议 20 天内答复买方并提出处理意见。

2. 信用证内应明确规定卖方有权可多装或少装所注明的百分数，并按实际装运数量议付。（信用证之金额按本售货合约金额增加相应的百分数）

3. 信用证内容须严格符合本售货合约的规定，否则修改信用证的费用由买方负担，卖方并不负因修改信用证而延误装运的责任，并保留因此而发生的一切损失的索赔权。

4. 除经约定保险归买方投保者外，由卖方向中国的保险公司投保。如买方需增加保险额及／或需加保其他险，可于装船前提出，经卖方同意后代为投保，其费用由买方负担。

5. 因人力不可抗拒事故使卖方不能在本售货合约规定期限内交货或不能交货，卖方不负责任，但是卖方必须立即以电报通知买方。如果买方提出要求，卖方应以挂号函向买方提供由中国国际贸易促进委员会或有关机构出具的证明，证明事故的存在。买方不能领到进口许可证，不能被认为系属人力不可抗拒范围。

6. 仲裁：凡因执行本合约或有关本合约所发生的一切争执，双方应以友好方式协商解决；如果协商不能解决，应提交中国国际经济贸易仲裁委员会，根据该会的仲裁规则进行仲裁。仲裁裁决是终局的，对双方都有约束力。

7. 附加条款。(本合同其他条款如与本附加条款有抵触时,以本附加条款为准)

卖方: 　　　　　　买方:

1.2 一般货物出口合同
Purchase Contract

Whole Doc.:

Contract No:

Date:

The Buyer:

The Seller:

The Contract, made out, in Chinese and English, both version being equally authentic, by and between the Seller and the Buyer whereby the Seller agrees to sell and the Buyer agrees to buy the under mentioned goods subject to terms and conditions set forth hereinafter as follows:

SECTION 1

1. Name of Commodity and specification
2. Country of Origin & Manufacturer
3. Unit Price (packing charges included)
4. Quantity
5. Total Value
6. Packing (seaworthy)
7. Insurance (to be covered by the Buyer unless otherwise)
8. Time of Shipment
9. Port of Loading
10. Port of Destination
11. Mark shown as below in addition to the port of destination, package number, gross and net weights, measurements and other marks as the Buyer may require stenciled or marked conspicuously with fast and unfailing pigments on each package. In the case of dangerous and/or poisonous cargo(es), the Seller is obliged to take care to ensure that the nature and the generally adopted symbol shall be marked conspicuously on each package.

12. Terms of Payment: One month prior to the time of shipment the Buyer shall open with the Bank of _____ an irrevocable Letter of Credit in favour of the Seller payable at the issuing bank against presentation of documents as stipulated under Clause 18. A. of SECTION II: the Terms of Delivery of this Con-

tract after departure of the carrying vessel. The said Letter of Credit shall remain in force till the 15th day after shipment.

13. Other Terms: Unless otherwise agreed and accepted by the Buyer, all other matters related to this contract shall be governed by Section II, the Terms of Delivery which shall form an integral part of this Contract. Any supplementary terms and conditions that may be attached to this Contract shall automatically prevail over the terms and conditions of this Contract if such supplementary terms and conditions come in conflict with terms and conditions herein and shall be binding upon both parties.

FOR THE SELLER FOR THE BUYER

SECTION 2

14. FOB/FAS TERMS

14.1 The shipping space for the contracted goods shall be booked by the Buyer or the Buyer's shipping agent _____.

14.2 Under FOB terms, the Seller shall undertake to load the contracted goods on board the vessel nominated by the Buyer on any date notified by the Buyer, within the time of shipment as stipulated in Clause 8 of this Contract.

14.3 Under FAS terms, the Seller shall undertake to deliver the contracted goods under the tackle of the vessel nominated by the Buyer on any date notified by the Buyer, within the time of shipment as stipulated in Clause 8 of this Contract.

14.4 10—15 days prior to the date of shipment, the Buyer shall inform the Seller by cable or telex of the contract number, name of vessel, ETA of vessel, quantity to be loaded and the name of shipping agent, so as to enable the Seller to contact the shipping agent direct and arrange the shipment of the goods. The Seller shall advise by cable or telex in time the Buyer of the result thereof. Should, for certain reasons, it become necessary for the Buyer to replace the named vessel with another one, or should the named vessel arrive at the port of shipment earlier or later than the date of arrival as previously notified to the Seller, the Buyer or its shipping agent shall advise the Seller to this effect in due time. The Seller shall also keep in close contact with the agent or the Buyer.

14.5 Should the Seller fail to load the goods on board or to deliver the goods under the tackle of the vessel booked by the Buyer. Within the time as notified by the Buyer, after its arrival at the port of shipment the Seller shall be fully liable to the Buyer and responsible for all losses and expenses such as dead freight, demurrage. Consequential losses incurred upon and/or suffered by the Buyer.

14.6 Should the vessel be withdrawn or replaced or delayed eventually or the cargo be shutout etc., and the Seller be not informed in good time to stop delivery of the cargo, the calculation of the loss in storage expenses and insurance premium thus sustained at the loading port shall be based on the loading date notified by the agent to the Seller (or based on the date of the arrival of the cargo at the loading port in case the cargo should arrive there later than the notified loading date). The abovementioned loss to be calculated from the 16th day after expiry of the free storage time at the port should be borne by the Buyer with the exception of Force Majeure. However, the Seller shall still undertake to load the cargo immediately upon the carrying vessel's arrival at the loading port at its own risk and expenses. The payment of the afore-said expenses shall be effected against presentation of the original vouchers after the Buyer's verification.

15. C&F Terms

15.1 The Seller shall ship the goods within the time as stipulated in clause 8 of this Contract by a direct vessel sailing from the port of loading to China port. Transshipment on route is not allowed without the Buyer's prior consent. The goods shall not be carried by vessels flying flags of countries not acceptable to the Port Authorities of China.

15.2 The carrying vessel chartered by the Seller shall be seaworthy and cargo worthy. The Seller shall be obliged to act prudently and conscientiously when selecting the vessel and the carrier when chartering such vessel. The Buyer is justified in not accepting vessels chartered by the Seller that are not members of the PICLUB.

15.3 The carrying vessel chartered by the Seller shall sail and arrive at the port of destination within the normal and reasonable period of time. Any unreasonable aviation or delay is not allowed.

15.4 The age of the carrying vessel chartered by the Seller shall not exceed 15 years. In case her age exceeds 15 years, the extra average insurance premium thus incurred shall be borne by the Seller. Vessel over 20 years of age shall in no event be acceptable to the Buyer.

15.5 For cargo lots over 1 000 M/T each, or any other lots less than 1 000 metric tons but identified by the Buyer, the Seller shall, at least 10 days prior to the date of shipment, inform the Buyer by telex or cable of the following information: the contract number, the name of commodity, quantity, the name of the carrying vessel, the age, nationality, and particulars of the carrying vessel, the expected date of loading, the expected time of arrival at the port of destination, the name, telex and cable address of the carrier.

15.6 For cargo lots over 1,000 M/T each, or any other lots less than 1,000 metric tons but identified by the Buyer, the Master of the carrying vessel shall notify the Buyer respectively 7 (seven)days and 24(twenty-four)hours prior to the arrival of the vessel at the port of destination, by telex or cable about its ETA(expected time of arrival),contract number, the name of commodity, and quantity.

15.7 If goods are to be shipped per liner vessel under liner Bill of Lading, the carrying vessel must be classified as the highest _____ or equivalent class as per the Institute Classification Clause and shall be so maintained throughout the duration of the relevant Bill of Lading. Nevertheless, the maximum age of the vessel shall not exceed 20 years at the date of loading. The seller shall bear the average insurance premium for liner vessel older than 20 years. Under no circum –stances shall the Buyer accept vessel over 25 years of age.

15.8 For break bulk cargoes, if goods are shipped in containers by the Seller without prior consent of the Buyer, a compensation of a certain amount to be agreed upon by both parties shall be payable to the Buyer by the Seller.

15.9 The Seller shall maintain close contact with the carrying vessel and shall notify the Buyer by fastest means of communication about any and all accidents that may occur while the carrying vessel is on route. The Seller shall assume full responsibility and shall compensate the Buyer for all losses incurred for its failure to give timely advice or notification to the Buyer.

16. CIF Terms:

Under CIF terms, besides Clause 15 C&F Terms of this contract which shall be applied the Seller shall be responsible for covering the cargo with relevant insurance with irrespective percentage.

17. Advice of Shipment:

Within 48 hours immediately after completion of loading of goods on board the vessel the Seller shall advise the Buyer by cable or telex of the contract number, the name of goods, weight (net/gross)or quantity loaded, invoice value, name of vessel, port of loading, sailing date and expected time of arrival(ETA) at the port of destination. Should the Buyer be unable to arrange insurance in time owing to the Seller's failure to give the above mentioned advice of shipment by cable or telex, the Seller shall be held responsible for any and all damages and/or losses attributable to such failure.

18. Shipping Documents

18.A The Seller shall present the following documents to the paying bank for negotiation of payment:

18.A.1 Full set of clean on board, "freight prepaid" for C&F/CIF Terms or "Freight to collect"for FOB/FAS Terms, Ocean Bills of Lading, made out to order and blank endorsed, notifying _____ at the port of destination.

18.A.2 Five copies of signed invoice, indicating contract number L/C number, name of commodity, full specifications, and shipping mark, signed and issued by the Beneficiary of Letter of Credit.

18.A.3 Two copies of packing list and/or weight memo with indication of gross and net weight of each package and/or measurements issued by beneficiary of Letter of Credit.

18.A.4 Two copies each of the certificates of quality and quantity or weight issued by the manufacturer and/or a qualified independent surveyor at the loading port and must indicate full specifications of goods conforming to stipulations in Letter of Credit.

18.A.5 One duplicate copy of the cable or telex advice of shipment as stipulated in Clause 17 of the Terms of Delivery.

18.A.6 A letter attesting that extra copies of abovementioned documents have been dispatched according to the Contract.

18.A.7 A letter attesting that the nationality of the carrying vessel has been approved by the Buyer.

18.A.8 The relevant insurance policy covering, but not limited to at least 110% of the invoice value against all and war risks if the insurance is covered by the Buyer.

18.B Any original document(s)made by rephotographic system, automated or computerized system or carbon copies shall not be acceptable unless they are clearly marked as "ORIGINAL." and certified with signatures in hand writing by authorized officers of the issuing company or corporation.

18.C Through Bill of Lading, Stale Bill of Lading, Short Form Bill of Lading, shall not be acceptable.

18.D Third Party appointed by the Beneficiary as shipper shall not be acceptable unless such Third Party Bill of Lading is made out to the order of shipper and endorsed to the Beneficiary and blank endorsed by the Beneficiary.

18.E Documents issued earlier than the opening date of Letter of Credit shall not be acceptable.

18.F In the case of C&F/CIF shipments, Charter Party Bill of Lading shall not be acceptable unless Beneficiary provides one copy each of the Charter Party, Master's of Mate's receipt, shipping order and cargo or stowage plan and/or other documents called for in the Letter of Credit by the Buyer.

18.G The seller shall dispatch, in care of the carrying vessel, two copies each of the duplicates of Bill of Lading. Invoice and Packing List to the Buyer's receiving agent, _____ at the port of destination.

18.H Immediately after the departure of the carrying vessel, the Seller shall airmail one set of the duplicate documents to the Buyer and three sets of the same to _____ Transportation Corporation at the port of destination.

18.I The Seller shall assume full responsibility and be liable to the Buyer and shall compensate the Buyer for all losses arising from going astray of and/or the delay in the dispatch of the above mentioned documents.

18.J Banking charges outside the People's Republic of China shall be for the Seller's account.

19. If the goods under this Contract are to be dispatched by air, all the terms and conditions of this Contract in connection with ocean transportation shall be governed by relevant air terms.

20. Instruction leaflets on dangerous cargo:

For dangerous and/or poisonous cargo, the Seller must provide instruction leaflets stating the hazardous or poisonous properties, transportation, storage and handling remarks, as well as precautionary and first-air measures and measures against fire. The Seller shall airmail, together with other shipping documents, three copies each of the same to the Buyer and_____ claims:

In case the quality, quantity or weight of the goods be found not in conformity with those as stipulated in this Contract upon re-inspection by the China Commodity Import and Export inspection Bureau within 60 days after completion of the discharge of the goods at the port of destination or, if goods are shipped in containers, 60 days after the opening of such containers, the Buyer shall have the right to request the Seller to take back the goods or lodge claims against the

Seller for compensation for losses upon the strength of the Inspection Certificate issued by the said Bureau, with the exception of those claims for which the insurers or owners of the carrying vessel are liable, all expenses including but not limited to inspection fees, interest, losses arising from the return of the goods or claims shall be borne by the Seller. In such a case, the Buyer may, if so requested, send a sample of the goods in question to the Seller, provided that sampling and sending of such sample is feasible.

22. Damages:

With the exception of late delivery or non-delivery due to "Force Majeure" causes, if the Seller fails to make delivery of the goods in accordance with the terms and conditions, jointly or severally, of this Contract, the Seller shall be liable to the Buyer and indemnify the Buyer for all losses, damages, including but not limited to, purchase price and/or purchase price differentials, dead freight, demurrage, and all consequential direct or indirect losses. The Buyer shall nevertheless have the right to cancel in part or in whole of the contract without prejudice to the Buyer's right to claim compensations.

23. Force Majeure:

Neither the Seller or the Buyer shall be held responsible for late delivery or non-delivery owing to generally recognized "Force Majeure" causes. However in such a case, the Seller shall immediately advise by cable or telex the Buyer of the accident and airmail to the Buyer within 15 days after the accident, a certificate of the accident issued by the competent government authority or the chamber of commerce which is located at the place where the accident occurs as evidence thereof. If the said "Force Majeure" cause lasts over 60 days, the Buyer shall have the right to cancel the whole or the undelivered part of the order for the goods as stipulated in Contract.

24. Arbitration:

Both parties agree to attempt to resolve all disputes between the parties with respect to the application or interpretation of any term hereof of transaction hereunder, through amicable negotiation. If a dispute cannot be resolved in this manner to the satisfaction of the Seller and the Buyer within a reasonable period of time, maximum not exceeding 90 days after the date of the notification of such dispute, the case under dispute shall be submitted to arbitration if the Buyer should decide not to take the case to court at a place of jurisdiction that the Buyer may deem appropriate. Unless otherwise agreed upon by both parties, such arbitration shall be held in _____, and shall be governed by the rules and procedures of arbitration stipulated by the Foreign Trade Arbitration Commission of the China Council for the Promotion of International Trade. The decision by such arbitration shall be accepted as final and binding upon both parties. The arbitration fees shall be borne by the losing party unless otherwise awarded.

号码：

签约日期：

买方：

卖方：

本合同由买卖双方缔结,用中、英文字写成,两种文体具有同等效力,按照下述条款,卖方同意售出买方同意购进以下商品：

第一部分

1. 商品名称及规格
2. 生产国别及制造厂商
3. 单价（包装费用包括在内）
4. 数量
5. 总值
6. 包装（适合海洋运输）
7. 保险（除非另有协议,保险均由买方负责）
8. 装船时间
9. 装运口岸
10. 目的口岸

11. 装运唛头,卖方负责在每件货物上用牢固的不褪色的颜料明显地刷印或标明下述唛头,以及目的口岸、件号、毛重和净重、尺码和其他买方要求的标记。如系危险及／或有毒货物,卖方负责保证在每件货物上明显地标明货物的性质说明及习惯上被接受的标记。

12. 付款条件：买方于货物装船时间前一个月通过_____银行开出以卖方为抬头的不可撤销信用证,卖方在货物装船起运后凭本合同交货条款第18条A款所列单据在开证银行议付贷款。上述信用证有效期将在装船后15天截止。

13. 其他条件：除非经买方同意和接受,本合同其他一切有关事项均按第二部分交货条款之规定办理,该交货条款为本合同不可分的部分,本合同如有任何附加条款将自动地优先执行附加条款,如附加条款与本合同条款有抵触,则以附加条款为准。

第二部分

14. FOB／FAS 条件

14.1 本合同项下货物的装运舱位由买方或买方的运输代理人租订。

14.2 在 FOB 条件下，卖方应负责将所订货物在本合同第 8 条所规定的装船期内按买方所通知的任何日期装上买方所指定的船只。

14.3 在 FAS 条件下，卖方应负责将所订货物在本合同第 8 条所规定的装船期内按买方所通知的任何日期交到买方所指定船只的吊杆下。

14.4 货物装运日前 10–15 天，买方应以电报或电传通知卖方合同号、船只预计到港日期、装运数量及船运代理人的名称。以便卖方与该船运代理人联系及安排货物的装运。卖方应将联系结果通过电报或电传及时报告买方。如买方因故需要变更船只或者船只比预先通知卖方的日期提前或推迟到达装运港口，买方或其船运代理人应及时通知卖方。卖方亦应与买方的运输代理或买方保持密切联系。

14.5 如买方所订船只到达装运港后，卖方不能在买方所通知的装船时间内将货物装上船只或将货物交到吊杆之下，卖方应负担买方的一切费用和损失，如空舱费、滞期费及由此而引起的及／或遭受的买方的一切损失。

14.6 如船只撤换或延期或退关等而未及时通知卖方停止交货，在装港发生的栈租及保险费损失的计算，应以代理通知之装船日期（如货物晚于代理通知之装船日期抵达装港，应以货物抵港日期）为准，在港口免费堆存期满后第 16 天起由买方负担，人力不可抗拒的情况除外。上述费用均凭原始单据经买方核实后支付。但卖方仍应在装载货船到达装港后立即将货物装船，交负担费用及风险。

15. C＆F 条件

15.1 卖方在本合同第 8 条规定的时间之内应将货物装上由装运港到中国口岸的直达船。未经买方事先许可，不得转船。货物不得由悬挂中国港口当局所不能接受的国家旗帜的船装载。

15.2 卖方所租船只应适航和适货。卖方租船时应慎重和认真地选择承运人及船只。买方不接受非保赔协会成员的船只。

15.3 卖方所租载货船只应在正常合理时间内驶达目的港。不得无故绕行或迟延。

15.4 卖方所租载货船只船龄不得超过 15 年。对超过 15 年船龄的船只其超船龄额外保险费应由卖方负担。买方不接受船龄超过 20 年的船只。

15.5 一次装运数量超过 1 000 吨的货载或其他少于 1 000 吨但买方

指明的货载，卖方应在装船日前至少 10 天用电传或电报通知买方合同号、商品名称、数量、船名、船龄、船籍、船只主要规范、预计装货日、预计到达目的港时间、船公司名称、电传和电报挂号。

15.6 一次装运 1 000 吨以上货载或其他少于 1 000 吨但买方指明的货载，其船长应在该船抵达目的港前 7 天和 24 小时分别用电传或电报通知买方预计抵港时间、合同号、商品名称及数量。

15.7 如果货物由班轮装运，载货船只必须是_____船级社最高船级或船级协会条款规定的相同级别的船级，船只状况应保持至提单有效期终了时止，以装船日为准船龄不得超过 20 年。超过 20 年船龄的船只，卖方应负担超船龄外保险费。买方决不接受超过 25 年船龄的船只。

15.8 对于散件货，如果卖方未经买方事前同意而装入集装箱，卖方应负责向买方支付赔偿金，由双方在适当时间商定具体金额。

15.9 卖方应和载运货物的船只保持密切联系，并以最快的手段通知买方船只在途中发生的一切事故，如因卖方未及时通知买方而造成买方的一切损失卖方应负责赔偿。

16. CIF 条件

在 CIF 条件下，除本合同第 15 条 C&F 条件适用之外卖方负责货物的保险，但不允许有免赔率。

17. 装船通知

货物装船完毕后 48 小时内，卖方应即以电报或电传通知买方合同号、商品名称、所装重量(毛／净)或数量、发票价值、船名、装运口岸、开船日期及预计到达目的港时间。如因卖方未及时用电报或电传给买方以上述装船通知而使买方不能及时保险，卖方负责赔偿买方由此而引起的一切损害及／或损失。

18. 装船单据

18.A 卖方凭下列单据向付款银行议付货款：

18.A.1 填写通知目的口岸的_____运输公司的空白抬头、空白背书的全套已装运洋轮的清洁提单（如系 C&F／CIF 条款则注明"运费已付"，如系 FOB／FAS 条款则注明"运费待收"）。

18.A.2 由信用证受益人签名出具的发票 5 份，注明合同号、信用证号、商品名称、详细规格及装船唛头标记。

18.A.3 两份由信用证受益人出具的装箱单及／或重量单，注明每件货物的毛重和净重及／或尺码。

18.A.4 由制造商及／或装运口岸的合格、独立的公证行签发的品质检验证书及数量或重量证书各两份，必须注明货物的全部规格与信用证规定相符。

18.A.5 本交货条件第 17 条规定的装船通知电报或电传副本一份。

18.A.6 证明上述单据的副本已按合同要求寄出的书信一封。

18.A.7 运货船只的国籍已经买主批准的书信一封。

18.A.8 如系卖方保险需提供投保不少于发票价值 110% 的一切险和战争险的保险单。

18.B 不接受影印、自动或电脑处理、或复印的任何正本单据,除非这些单据印有清晰的"正本"字样,并经发证单位授权的领导人手签证明。

18.C 联运提单、迟期提单、简式提单不能接受。

18.D 受益人指定的第三者为装船者不能接受,除非该第三者提单由装船者背书转受益人,再由受赠人背书后方可接受。

18.E 信用证开立日期之前出具的单据不能接受。

18.F 对于 C&F/CIF 货载,不接受租船提单,除非受益人提供租船合同、船长或大副收据、装船命令、货物配载图及或买方在信用证内所要求提供的其它单据副本各一份。

18.G 卖方须将提单、发票及装箱单各两份副本随船带交目的口岸的买方收货代理人＿＿＿＿＿＿＿＿＿＿。

18.H 载运货船启碇后,卖方须立即航空邮寄全套单据副本一份给买方,三份给目的口岸的对外贸易运输公司分公司。

18.I 卖方应负责赔偿买方因卖方失寄或迟寄上述单据而使买方遭受的一切损失。

18.J 中华人民共和国境外的银行费用由卖方负担。

19. 合同所订货物如用空运,则本合同有关海运的一切条款均按空运条款执行。

20. 危险品说明书

凡属危险品及/或有毒,卖方必须提供其危险或有毒性能、运输、仓储和装卸注意事项以及防治、急救、消防方法的说明书,卖方应将此项说明书各三份随同其他装船单据航空邮寄给买方及目的口岸的运输公司。

21. 检验和索赔

货物在目的口岸卸毕 60 天内(如果用集装箱装运则在开箱后 60 天)经中国进出口商品检验局复验,如发现品质、数量或重量以及其他任何方面与本合同规定不符,除属于保险公司或船行负责者外,买方有权凭上述检验局出具的检验证书向卖方提出退货或索赔。因退货或索赔引起的一切费用包括检验费、利息及损失均由卖方负担。在此情况下,凡货物适于抽样及寄送时如卖方要求,买方可将样品寄交卖方。

22. 赔偿费

因"人力不可抗拒"而推迟或不能交货者除外,如果卖方不能交货或不能按合同规定的条件交货,卖方应负责向买方赔偿由此而引起的一切损失和遭受的损害,包括买价及／或买价的差价、空舱费、滞期费,以及由此而引起的直接或间接损失。买方有权撤销全部或部分合同,但并不妨碍买方向卖方提出索赔的权利。

23. 不可抗力(赔偿例外)

由于一般公认的"人力不可抗拒"原因而不能交货或延迟交货,卖方或买方都不负责任。但卖方应在事故发生后立即用电报或电传告知买方并在事故发生后15天内航空邮寄买方灾害发生地点之有关政府机关或商会所出具的证明,证实灾害存在。如果上述"人力不可抗拒"继续存在60天以上,买方有权撤销合同的全部或一部。

24. 仲裁

双方同意对一切因执行和解释本合同条款所发生的争议,努力通过友好协商解决。在争议发生之日起一个合理的时间内,最多不超过90天,协商不能取得对买卖双方都满意的结果时,如买方决定不向他认为合适的有管辖权的法院提出诉讼,则该争议应提交仲裁。除双方另有协议,仲裁应在中国北京举行,并按中国国际贸易促进委员会对外贸易仲裁委员会所制定的仲裁规则和程序进行仲裁,该仲裁为终局裁决,对双方均有约束力。仲裁费用除非另有决定,由败诉一方负担。

卖方: 买方:

第二节 合资经营企业合同

Section 2　Contracts for Joint Ventures

合资经营企业合同是指合营各方为设立合营企业,在合营协议的基础上,经过合营各方调查研究、考察、谈判、协商,就举办合营企业各有关事项明确相互权利义务关系的协议。

2.1 合资经营企业协议

Joint Ventures Agreement

This Agreement made this＿＿ day of＿＿ , ＿＿ by ABC Corporation (hereinafter called "Party A"), a Chinese corporation having its registered office at＿＿, China, and XYZ Company (hereinafter called "Party B"), an American company having its registered office at＿＿, USA.

WITNESSES

WHEREAS Party A is engaged in manufacturing and selling _____ in China; andWHEREAS Party B is engaged in manufacturing and selling ____ (hereinafter called "Licensed Product") and has American patent rights to Licensed Product (hereinafter called "Patents") and registered Trademark No.____ (hereinafter called "Trademark"); and

WHEREAS the Parties consider it mutually advantageous to organize a jointly owned corporation (hereinafter called "Joint Venture") under the laws of the People's Republic of China to engage in the manufacture, sale and development of Licensed Product in_____.

NOW THEREFORE, in consideration of the premises and convenance described hereinafter Party A and Party B agree as follows:

Article 1 Definitions

...

In this Agreement, the following terms have the following meanings unless the context clearly dictates otherwise.

1. "Joint Venture" means the corporation to be organized pursuant to the provisions of Article 2 hereto.

2. "Licensed Product" means_____.

3. "Patents" means_____.

4. "Trademark" means_____.

...

Article 2 Formation of Joint Venture

1. Party A and Party B shall spare no efforts for the organization of Joint Venture under the laws of the People's Republic of China.

2. The name of Joint Venture is_____ with its legal address:_____.

3. All activities of Joint Venture shall comply with the provisions of the laws, decrees and pertinent regulations of the People's Republic of China.

4. Joint Venture shall take the form of a limited liability company. The profits, risks and losses of Joint Venture shall be shared by both Party A and Party B in proportion to the contributions to the registered capital.

5. The expenses of organizing Joint Venture shall be equally borne by Party A and Party B.

Article 3 Purpose, Scope and Size of Business

1. In line with the spirit of strengthening economic cooperation and ex-

panding technical exchange, Joint Venture is to use state-of-the-art and appropriate technology and equipment, with efficient management systems, to produce Licensed Product which shall be of top quality and competitive in the world markets, so as to achieve satisfactory economic returns.

2. Joint Venture is to product _____ (Licensed Product) with a production capacity of_____ per year.? Joint Venture shall do its best to improve Licensed Product and management so as to be able to meet competition worldwide.

3. Joint Venture shall, if possible, develop new varieties of Licensed Product in order to keep up with market developments both in the host country and in the world.

Article 4 Capital Structure

1. The registered capital of Joint Venture shall be (amount of capital), of which half (50%) will be contributed by each Party.

2. Party A's contributions include

(1) Buildings and premises:_____(value);

(2) Domestically-made equipment:_____(value);

(3) Cash:_____;

(4) The site of Joint Venture:_____(value).

3. Party B's contributions include

(1) Cash:_____;

(2) Sophisticated equipment:_____(value);

(3) Industrial property: _____(value).

Party B shall present to Party A the relevant documentation on the industrial property including photocopies of the patent certificates and trademark registration certificates, statements of validity, their technical characteristics, practical value, the basis for calculating the price, etc.

4. Each Party to Joint Venture shall pay in its contributions before_____ (time limit).Any delay in payment will be subject to a payment of interest or a compensation for the loss occurred therein.

5. The transfer of one Party's share in the registered capital shall be effected with the prior consent of the other Party and approval of its government and the latter shall enjoy priority to purchase it.

Article 5 Patent Licensing Arrangement

1. Party B agrees to grant Joint Venture the following exclusive licenses:

(1) An exclusive license to manufacture, use and sell Licensed Product

under Party B's Patents according to the terms and conditions of the Patent License Agreement attached hereto.

(2) An exclusive license to use Trademark in marketing Licensed Product according to the terms and conditions of the Trademark License Agreement attached hereto.

(3) An exclusive license to practice Party B's know-how for manufacturing and marketing Licensed Product according to the terms and conditions of the Technical Assistance Agreement attached hereto.

2. Party A and Party B agree that simultaneously with the execution of this Agreement, they shall carry out, the above three agreements – the Patent License Agreement, the Trademark License Agreement and the Technical Assistance Agreement.

Article 6　Marketing Arrangements

1. Party A and Party B shall be responsible for the sales of Licensed Product.

2. The initial amount of Licensed Product to be sold on the foreign markets is_____% of the total production through Party B's marketing system worldwide. Meanwhile Party A shall help Joint Venture to export Licensed Product through China's trade establishments.

3. Licensed Product may also be distributed on the Chinese market.

4. In purchase of the required raw materials and semiprocessed products, fuels, auxiliary equipment etc., Joint Venture shall give first priority to Chinese sources where conditions are the same, but may also acquire them directly from the world market with its own foreign exchange funds.

Article 7　Board of Directors

1. The Board of Directors is the top leadership of Joint Venture. It is responsible for all major issues concerning Joint Venture.

2. The Board of Directors consists of_____(number) directors, of whom _____ (number) including the chairman shall be appointed by party A, and_____(number) including the deputy chairman shall be appointed by Party B.?The office term for the directors is 4 years, which may be renewed with the consent of the Parties to Joint Venture.

3. Board meetings shall generally be held at the location of Joint Venture's legal address, once each year. A quorum for a meeting shall consist of not fewer than two thirds (2/3) of the directors. Should any director be unable to attend

the meeting, he shall authorize a representative to be present at the meeting and vote for him.

In case a director dies, resigns, or is otherwise unable to fulfill his duties prior to the fulfillment of his term, the Parties agree to cooperate fully to have as his replacement a director nominated by the Party that nominated the director whose death, resignation or other conditions created the vacancy.

4. Decisions on the following items shall be made only when unanimously agreed upon by the directors present at the Board meeting.

(1) Amendment to the articles of incorporation of Joint Venture;

(2) Termination and dissolution of Joint Venture;

(3) Increase or assignment of the registered capital of Joint Venture;

(4) Merger of Joint Venture with another economic organization.

Decisions on other items shall be made by a simple majority vote of the directors present at the meeting.

Article 8 Management

1. Joint Venture shall establish a management office which shall be responsible for daily management of Joint Venture.

2. The management office shall have a general manager and two deputy general managers, whose term is 4 years. The general manager nominated by Party A is responsible for the implementation of the decisions of the Board of Directors and daily operation. The deputy managers, one of whom is nominated by each Party, shall assist the general manager in his duties.

3. The management office may have its subdivisions, the duties of which are to manage different business departments under the leadership of the general manager or deputy general managers.

Article 9 Labor management

1. Party A agrees to help Joint Venture to invite and recruit Chinese experts, technicians, workers and other personnel and Party B agree to help Joint Venture to invite and recruit foreign experts.

2. The employment and dismissal, wages, insurance, welfare, awards, and fines of its experts, staff members and workers shall be decided by the Board of Directors according to "Regulations for the Implementation of the Law of the People's Republic of China on Chinese Foreign Joint Venture".

Article 10 Financial Affairs and Accounting

1. The parties hereto are fully aware that the best interests of their own

and Joint Venture will be served by taking all reasonable measures to ensure increase in production and in order to achieve this goal, the Parties agree to retain sufficient earnings in Joint Venture for the expansion of production and other requirements, such as bonus and welfare funds.The annual proportion of the earnings to be retained shall be decided by the Board of Directors.

2. Joint Venture shall employ competent treasurers and auditors to keep all books of accounts, which are accessible at any time to each Party hereto.

3. The fiscal year of Joint Venture shall begin on January 1st and end on December 31st.The net profit of Joint Venture shall be distributed between the Parties to Joint Venture in proportion to their respective shares in the registered capital after the deduction therefrom of the reserve funds, the bonus and the expansion funds of Joint Venture.Dividends shall be paid in (currency).

Article 11　Tax

1. Joint Venture shall pay taxes in accordance with the relevant laws of the People's Republic of China.

2. The staff members and workers employed by Joint Venture shall pay individual income tax according to the Individual Income Tax Law of the People's Republic of China.

3. Joint Venture shall pay or exempt from customs duty and industrial and commercial consolidated tax on goods imported or exported in accordance with the relevant laws of the People's Republic of China.

Article 12　Duration of Joint Venture

1. The duration of Joint Venture is_____ years, which begins on the date when Joint Venture is issued the business license.

2. When both Parties to Joint Venture agree to extend the duration, Joint Venture shall file an application for extending the duration to the relevant authority of the Chinese government 6 months before its expiration date.

Article 13　Dissolution and Liquidation

Upon announcement of the dissolution of Joint Venture, its Board of Directors shall work out procedures and principles for the liquidation and set up a liquidation committee.

All matters concerning the dissolution and liquidation of Joint Venture shall be dealt with in accordance with the relevant laws of the People's Republic of China.

Article 14 Insurance

Insurance against various risks shall be effected by Joint Venture with the People's Insurance Company of China.

Article 15 Arbitration

All disputes, controversies or differences which may arise between the Parties hereto, out of or in relation to this Agreement and which the Board of Directors fails to settle through consultation, shall finally be submitted to arbitration which shall be conducted by the Foreign Trade Arbitration Commission of the China Council for the Promotion of International Trade in accordance with the Provisional Rules of Procedure of Arbitration of the said commission, the decision of which shall be final and binding upon both parties.

Article 16 Amendment

This Agreement may be amended during the duration of this Agreement by the Parties, provided that such amendment shall be in writing and signed by both Parties and shall be approved by the competent agency of the government of the People's Republic of China.

Article 17 Force Majeure

1. Any failure or delay in the performance by either Party hereto of its obligations under this Agreement shall not constitute a breach hereof or give rise to any claims for damages if it is caused by the following occurrences beyond the control of the Party: earthquake, fire, floods, explosions, storms, accidents, war.

2. The Party affected by force majeure event shall immediately cable the other Party about the event, and submit within_____ days after the cable the certified documents issued by a public competent organization at the place where the force majeure event has taken place, with which the two Parties hereto shall settle the problem in a friendly and reasonable way.

Article 18 Notice

Any notice required or permitted under the provisions of this Agreement shall be in writing and addressed as follows:

To ABC Corporation: at_____.

To XYZ Company: at_____.

To Joint Venture: at_____.

Notice shall be deemed to have been given on the date of mailing except the notice of change of address which shall be deemed to have been given when received. The time shall be calculated according to that of the time zone of the addresser or sender.

Article 19 Sole Agreement

This Agreement constitutes the entire and only Agreement between the Parties hereto and supersedes and nullifies all prior agreements, commitments, expressed or implied, between the Parties hereto.

Article 20 Governing Law

The formation, validation, interpretation and performance of this Agreement are governed by the laws of the People's Republic of China.

Article 21 Language

This Agreement shall be executed by the Parties hereto in both Chinese version and English version, each of which shall be binding upon both Parties. But the Chinese version shall prevail in the event of any discrepancy between the two said versions.

IN WITNESS WHEREOF, the Parties hereto have executed this Agreement in duplicate by their duly authorized representatives as of the date first above written.

ABC Co.   XYZ Co.

By _____   By _____

本协议于19XX年X月X日签订。

  签约第一方:ABC公司,该公司系中国公司,在中国XX注册(以下简称"甲方");

  签约第二方:XYZ公司,系美国公司,在美国XX注册(以下简称"乙方")。

  兹证明

  甲方在中国生产和销售XX产品;

  乙方生产和销售XX产品(以下称"许可产品"),拥有许可产品的美国专利(以下称"专利")和X号注册商标;

  甲乙双方认为按照中华人民共和国的法律成立共同所有的公司(以下称"合营公司"),在XX地从事生产、销售和开发许可产品,对双方都是有利的;

  为此,鉴于本协议所述的前提与约定,特此立约如下:

  第一条　定义

  在本协议中,除非文中另有明确规定,下列短语具有以下意思:

  1."合营企业",系指根据本协议建立的公司。

  2."许可产品",系指XXXX。

  3."专利",系指XXXX。

4. "商标",系指XXXX。

第二条　建立合营企业

1. 甲方和乙方按照中华人民共和国的法律建立合营企业。

2. 合营企业称为XXXX,地址为XXXX。

3. 合营企业的一切活动,必须遵守中华人民共和国的法律、法令和有关条例规定。

4. 合营企业的组织形式为有限责任公司。甲乙双方以各自认缴的出资额对合营公司的债务承担责任。各方按其出资额在注册资本中的比例分享利润和分担风险及亏损。

5. 合营企业的组建费用由甲乙双方平均分担。

第三条　生产经营的目的、范围和规模

1. 甲、乙双方合资经营的目的是:本着加强经济合作和扩大技术交流的愿望,采用先进而适用的技术和科学的经营管理方法,提高产品质量,开发新产品,并在质量、价格等方面具有国际市场上的竞争能力,提高经济效益,使投资各方获得满意的经济利益。

2. 合营企业生产XXXX(许可产品),生产能力为每年XXXX。合营企业将努力改进许可产品,改善管理,以适应国际竞争。

3. 合营企业尽可能开发许可产品的新品种,以满足国内外市场的发展需要。

第四条　资本结构

1. 合营企业的注册资本为XXXX,其中甲、乙双方各出资XX,即各占50%。

2. 甲方出资

(1)厂房:XXXX;

(2)国产设备:XXXX;

(3)现金:XXXX;

(4)合资企业厂地:XXXX;

3. 乙方出资

(1)现金:XXXX;

(2)先进设备:XXXX;

(3)工业产权:XXXX。

乙方向甲方提供工业产权的技术资料包括影印本的专利证书和注册商标证书、有效期说明、技术特点、实际价值、价格计算依据等。

4. 合营企业各方必须在19XX年X月X日前交付其出资。迟交必须交纳利息或赔偿因此而造成的损失。

5. 甲乙双方中任何一方转让其出资额,须经另一方同意和其政府批准,该方享有优先购买权。

第五条 专利许可

1. 乙方同意向合营企业转让下列独家许可:

(1)专利独占许可——依据本协议的专利许可协议,用乙方专利生产、使用和销售许可产品。

(2)商标独占许可——依据本协议的专利许可协议,用乙方商标销售许可产品。

(3)专有技术独占许——根据本协议的技术援助协议,用乙方专有技术生产和销售专利产品。

2. 甲乙双方同意,在执行本协议的同时,将全面贯彻执行上述三个协议:专利许可协议、商标许可协议和技术援助协议。

第六条 产品销售

1. 甲乙双方共同负责销售许可产品。

2. 通过乙方世界销售系统销售的产品初期销售量为总产量的XX%。同时,甲方将协助合营企业通过中国的外贸公司出口许可产品。

3. 许可产品也可以在中国市场出售。

4. 中营企业所需购买的原材料、半成品、燃料和配套件等,在条件相同的情况下,应首先在中国购买。当然,也可使用自己的外汇直接从世界市场购进。

第七条 董事会

1. 董事会是合营企业的最高领导机构,负责合营企业的主要事宜。

2. 董事会由XX名董事组成,其中X名(包括董事长)由甲方指定;X名(包括副董事长)由乙方指定。董事的任期为4年,若双方同意,任期可以延长。

3. 董事会每年召开一次,原则上在合营企业的法定地址举行。出席会议的法定人数不得少于董事人数的2/3。若董事不能出席会议,应授权代表出席会议,代表他投票。

若在任期内,因死亡、退休或其他原因,董事在任期届满前不能履行职责者,双方同意充分合作,并由因其指定的董事死亡、退休或其他原因造成空位的一方给予更换。

4. 对于下列问题,必须经出席会议的董事一致通过,方可作出决定:

(1)修改合营企业章程;

(2)终止和解散合营企业;

(3)增加或转让合营企业的注册资本;

(4)合营企业同其他经济组织合并。

其他问题的决定,以出席会议董事人数的微弱多数票作出。

第八条 管理

1. 合营企业设经营管理机构,负责企业的日常经营管理工作。

2. 经营管理机构设经理1人、副经理2人,任期4年。总经理由甲方指定,负责执行董事会的决议和日常管理工作。副总经理由双方各指定1人,协助总经理工作。

3. 管理机构设若干部门,在总经理和副总经理的领导下,负责企业各部门的工作。

第九条 劳动管理

1. 合营企业的中方专家、技术人员、工人和其他人员由甲方招聘;合营企业的外方专家由乙方招聘。

2. 合营企业的专家、职员或工人的雇用、辞退、工资、劳动保险、生活福利和奖惩等项,由董事会按照《中华人民共和国中外合资经营企业法实施条例》决定。

第十条 财务与会计

1. 协议双方充分认识到,为了他们自己和合营企业的最大利益,必须尽一切可能增加生产。因此,双方同意合营企业应保留足够的收益,用于扩大生产的其他需要,如奖金和福利基金。合营企业的年留用奖金比率由董事会决定。

2. 合营企业雇用合格的财务人员和审计员,设立会计账目,合营各方可随时查看有关账目。

3. 合营企业的财政年度自1月1日至12月31日。合营企业的净收入,在扣除储备金、奖金和企业发展奖金以后,根据各方出资在注册项目中占的比例进行分配。红利以XX(货币)支付。

第十一条 税费

1. 合营企业必须按照中华人民共和国的法律纳税。

2. 合营公司的职员和工人必须按照《中华人民共和国个人所得税》纳税。

3. 合营企业进出口货物根据中华人民共和国的法律缴纳或减免关税。

第十二条 合营期限

1. 合营期限为X年。合营企业的成立日期为合营公司营业执照签发之日。

2. 若双方同意延期,合营企业必须在期满前6个月向中国政府的主管部门提出延长期限的申请。

第十三条　解散与清算

董事会宣布解散合营企业,必须制定清算程序和原则,并成立清算委员会。

合营企业解散和清算的一切事宜均按中华人民共和国法律办理。

第十四条　保险

合营企业的各项保险均在中保财产保险公司投保。

第十五条　仲裁

有关本协议的一切分歧与争议,若董事会不能通过协商解决,则提交中国国际贸易促进委员会对外贸易仲裁委员会,根据该会仲裁程序暂行规则进行仲裁。该委员会的裁决是终局的,对双方均具有约束力。

第十六条　协议的修改

本协议的修改,必须经甲乙双主同意,签署书面协议,并报中华人民共和国主管部门批准。

第十七条　不可抗力

1. 本协议任何一方因地震、火灾、洪水、爆炸、风暴、事故和战争等不可抗力事件,未能履行协议,不构成违约或索赔之缘由。

2. 遭受不可抗力事件一方必须立即电报通知另一方,并在发报后 X 天内提交当地主管部门出具的证明文件,供双方据以友好合理地解决有关问题。

第十八条　通知

一切有关本协议的通知必须采用书面形式,其地址如下:

ABC 公司地址:

XYZ 公司地址:

合营企业地址:

通知日期以通知发出日为准,但改变地址的通知以通知收到日为准。时间按通知方所在的时区计算。

第十九条　唯一协议

本协议是当事人的唯一协议,并取代当事人双方以前明确表示和暗示方式所达成的一切协议和承诺。

第二十条　适用法律

本协议的形式、有效期、解释和履行,均以中华人民共和国法律为准。

第二十一条　文字

本协议以中、英文书写,两种文本对双方均具有约束力,但在产生分歧时,以中文本为准。

兹证明,双方委派各自代表,在以下开首语中注明的日期签署盖章。

本协议一式两份。

ABC 公司:_____(签字)
XYZ 公司:_____(签字)

2.2 中外合作经营合同
Contract for Sino-foreign Joint Ventures

Chapter 1 General Provisions

In accordance with the Law of the People's Republic of China on Chinese-Foreign Cooperative Joint Ventures and other relevant Chinese laws and regulations, _____Company and _____Company, in accordance with the principle of equality and mutual benefit and through friendly consultations, agree to jointly set up a Cooperative venture in _____the People's Republic of China.

Chapter 2 Parties of the Cooperative Venture Article

Article 1 Parties to this contract are as follows: _____ Company (hereinafter referred to as Party A), registered with _____ in China, and its legal address is at_____ (street)_____ (district) _____(city)_____China. Legal representative: Name: Position: Nationality: _____Company (hereinafter referred to as Party B), registered with_____. Its legal address is at _____.

Legal representative: Name: Position: Nationality: (Note: In case there are more than two investors, they will be called Party C, D… in proper order).

Chapter 3 Establishment of the Cooperative Venture Company

Article 2 In accordance with the Cooperative Venture Law and other relevant Chinese laws and regulations, both parties of the Cooperative venture agree to set up _____Cooperative venture limited liability company(hereinafter referred to as the Cooperative venture company).

Article 3 The name of the Cooperative venture company is_____ Limited Liability Company. The name in foreign language is _____. The legal address of the joint venture company is at_____ street_____ (city)_____province.

Article 4 All activities of the Cooperative venture company shall be governed by the laws, decrees and pertinent rules and regulations of the People's Republic of China.

Article 5 The organization form of the Cooperative venture company is a limited liability company. The profits, risks and losses of the Cooperative venture company shall be shared by the parties according to the relevant provisions thereafter.

Chapter 4 The Purpose, Scope and Scale of Production and Business

Article 6 The goals of the parties to the Cooperative venture are to enhance economic cooperation technical exchanges, to improve the product quality, develop new products, and gain a competitive position in the world marketing quality and price by adopting advanced and appropriate technology and scientific management methods, so as to raise economic results and ensure satisfactory economic benefits for each Cooperator. (Note: This article shall be written according to the specific situations in the contract)

Article 7 The productive and business scope of the Cooperative venture company is to produce _____products; provide maintenance service after the sale of the products; study and develop new products. (Note: It shall be written in the contract according to the specific conditions)

Article 8 The production scale of the Cooperative venture company is as follows: 1. The production capacity after the Cooperative venture is put into operation is _____. 2. The production scale may be increased up to_____ with the development of the production and operation. The product varieties may be developed into _____. (Note: It shall be written according to the specific situation)

Chapter 5 Total Amount of Investment and the Registered Capital

Article 9 The total amount of investment of the Cooperative venture company is RMB_____ (or a foreign currency agreed upon by both parties).

Article 10 The registered capital of the joint venture company is RMB _____. (Exclusive of the right to the use of the site or the right to the exploitation of the natural resources and premises contributed by Party A)

Article 11 Party A and Party B will contribute the following to the cooperative venture: Party A: premises_____m² the right to the use of the site_____m² Party B: cash _____Yuan machines and equipment _____Yuan industrial property _____Yuan others _____Yuan, _____Yuan in all. (Note: When contributing industrial property as investment, Party A and Party B shall conclude a separate contract to be a part of this main contract)

Article 12 The right to the use of site contributed by Party A shall be for the use of the cooperative venture company within _____ days after the approval of the contract. The cash contributed by Party B shall be paid in_____ installment. Each installment shall be as follows: (Note: it shall be written according to the concrete conditions)

Article 13 The machines and equipment contributed by Party B as investment shall meet the needs of the cooperative venture company, and shall be carried to he Chinese port_____ days before the completion of the premises construction.

Chapter 6 Responsibilities of Each Party to the Joint Venture

Article 14 Party A and Party B shall be respectively responsible for the following matters:

1) Responsibilities of Party A: Handling of applications for approval, registration, business license and other matters concerning the establishment of the cooperative venture company from relevant departments in charge of China; Processing the application for the right to the use of a site to the authority in charge of the land; Organizing the design and construction of the premises and other engineering facilities of the cooperative venture company; Assisting Party B to process import customs declaration for the machinery and equipment contributed by Party B as investment and arranging the transportation within the Chinese territory; Assisting the cooperative venture company in purchasing or leasing equipment, materials, raw materials, articles for office use, means of transportation and communication facilities etc.; Assisting the cooperative venture company in contacting and settling the fundamental facilities such as water, electricity, transportation; Assisting the cooperative venture in recruiting Chinese management personnel, technical personnel, workers and other personnel needed; Assisting foreign workers and staff in applying for entry visas, work licenses and handling their travel procedures; Responsible for handling other matters entrusted by the cooperative venture company.

2) Responsibilities of Party B: Providing cash, machinery and equipment, industrial property... in accordance with the provisions of Article 11 and Article 12, 13, and responsible for shipping capital goods such as machinery and equipment etc. contributed as investment to a Chinese port; Handling the matters entrusted by the cooperative venture company, such as selecting and purchasing machinery and equipment outside China,etc.; Providing necessary technical personnel for installing, testing and trial production of the equipment as well as the

technical personnel for production and inspecting; Training the technical personnel and workers of the cooperative venture company; In case Party B is the licensor, it shall be responsible for the stable production of qualified products of the cooperative venture company in the light of design capacity within the specified period; Responsible for other matters entrusted by the joint venture company. (Note: It shall be written according to the specific situation)

Chapter 7 Distribution of Profits and Repayment for Party B's Investment

Article 15 The cooperative venture company shall distribute its profits in accordance with the following procedure after paying the income tax: _____% as allocations for reserve funds, expansion funds, welfare funds and bonuses for staff and workers of the cooperative venture company; _____% as repayment for Party B's Investment and_____Years scheduled to pay back all Party B's Investment; _____% of the left distributed to Party A and _____% to Party B.

Chapter 8 Selling of Products

Article 16 The products of cooperative venture company will be sold both on the Chinese and the overseas market, the export portion accounts for_____%, _____% for the domestic market. (Note: An annual percentage and amount for outside and domestic selling will be written out according to practical operations, in normal conditions, the amount for export shall at least meet the needs of foreign exchange expenses of the joint venture company)

Article 17 Products may be sold on overseas markets through the following channels: The cooperative venture company may directly sell its products on the international market, accounting for _____%. The cooperative venture company may sign sales contracts with Chinese foreign trade companies, entrusting them to be the sales agencies or exclusive sales agencies, accounting for _____%. The cooperative venture company may entrust Party B to sell its products, accounting for _____%.

Article 18 The cooperative venture's products to be sold in China may be handled by the Chinese materials and commercial departments by means of agency or exclusive sales, or may be sold by the cooperative venture company directly.

Article 19 In order to provide maintenance service to the products sold both in China or abroad, the cooperative venture company may set up sales branches for maintenance service both in China or abroad subject to the approval of the relevant Chinese department.

Chapter 9 The Board of Directors.

Article 20 The date of registration of the cooperative venture company shall be the date of the establishment of the board of directors of the cooperative venture company.

Article 21 The board of directors is composed of _____ directors, of which _____ shall be appointed by Party A, _____ by Party B. The chairman of the board shall be appointed by Party A, and its vice-chairman by Party B. The term of office for the directors, chairman and vice-chairmen four years, their term of office may be renewed if continuously appointed by the relevant party.

Article 22 The highest authority of the cooperative venture company shall be its board of directors. It shall decide all major issues concerning the cooperative venture company. Unanimous approval shall be required for any decisions concerning major issues. As for other matters, approval by majority or a simple majority shall be required. (Note: It shall be explicitly set out in the contract)

Article 23 The chairman of the board is the legal representative of the cooperative venture company. Should the chairman be unable to exercise his responsibilities for any reason, he shall authorize the vice-chairman or any other directors to represent the joint venture company temporarily.

Article 24 The board of directors shall convene at least one meeting every year. The meeting shall be called and presided over by the chairman of the board. The chairman may convene an interim meeting based on a proposal made by more than one third of the total number of directors. Minutes of the meetings shall be placed on file.

Article 25 The meeting shall be valid only when more than two thirds of the total number of directors attend. In case of absence, the director shall entrust another person to attend and vote for him with a trust deed.

Chapter 10 Business Management Office

Article 26 The cooperative venture company shall establish a management office which shall be responsible for its daily management. The management office shall have a general manager, appointed by Party _____, _____ deputy general managers, _____ by Party _____; _____ by Party _____. The general manager and deputy general managers whose terms of office is _____ years shall be appointed by the board of directors.

Article 27 The responsibility of the general manager is to carry out the decisions of the board and organize and conduct the daily management of the cooperative venture company. The deputy general managers shall assist the general manager in his work.

Article 28 The general manager shall report to the board of directors the operation conditions of the cooperative company every three months, and make a financial report every six months.

Article 29 In case of graft or serious dereliction of duty on the part of the general manager and deputy general managers, the board of directors shall have the power to dismiss them at any time.

Chapter 11 Labor Management

Article 30 Labor contract covering the recruitment, employment, dismissal and resignation, wages, labor insurance, welfare, rewards, penalties and other matters concerning the staff and workers of the cooperative venture company shall be drawn up between the cooperative venture company and the trade union of the cooperative venture company as a whole, or the individual employees in the cooperative venture company as a whole or individual employees in accordance with the law of the People's Republic of China on Chinese-Foreign Cooperative Joint Ventures. The labor contracts shall, after being signed, be filed with the local labor management department.

Article 31 The appointment of high-ranking administrative personnel recommended by both parties, their salaries, social insurance, welfare and the standard of traveling expenses etc. shall be decided by the meeting of the board of directors.

Chapter 12 Taxes, Finance and Audit

Article 32 The cooperative venture company shall pay taxes in accordance with the provisions of Chinese laws and other relative regulations.

Article 33 Staff members and workers of the cooperative venture company shall pay individual income tax according to the Individual Income Tax Law of the People's Republic of China.

Article 34 The fiscal year of the joint venture company shall be from January 1to December 31. All vouchers, receipts, statistic statements and reports shall be written in Chinese. (Note: A foreign language can be used concurrently with mutual consent)

Article 35 Financial checking and examination of the cooperative venture company shall be conducted by an auditor registered in China and reports shall be submitted to the board of directors and the general manager. In case Party B considers it necessary to employ a foreign auditor registered in another country to undertake annual financial checking and examination, Party A shall give its consent. All the expenses thereof shall be borne by Party B.

Article 36 In the first three months of each fiscal year, the manager shall prepare the previous year's balance sheet, profit and loss statement and proposal regarding the disposal of profits, and submit them to the board of directors for examination and approval.

Chapter 13 Duration of the Cooperative Venture

Article 37 The duration of the cooperative venture company is_____ years. The establishment date of the joint venture company shall be the date on which the business license of the cooperative venture company is issued. An application for the extension of the duration, proposed by one party and unanimously approved by the board of directors, shall be submitted to the Ministry of Foreign Trade and Economic Cooperation (or the examination and approval authority entrusted by it) six months prior to the expiry date of the joint venture.

Chapter 14 The Disposal of Assets after the Expiration of the Duration

Article 38 Upon the expiration of the duration, the assets shall belong to Party A.

Chapter 15 Insurance

Article 39 Insurance policies of the joint venture company on various kinds of risks shall be underwritten with the People's Republic of China. Types, value and duration of insurance shall be decided by the board of directors in accordance with the provisions of the People's Insurance Company of China.

Chapter 16 The Amendment, Alteration and Termination of the Contract

Article 40 The amendment of the contract or other appendices shall come into force only after a written agreement has been signed by Party A and Party B and approved by the original examination and approval authority.

Article 41 In case of inability to fulfill the contract or to continue operation due to heavy losses in successive years as a result of force majeure, the duration of the cooperative venture and the contract shall be terminated before the time of expiration after being unanimously agreed upon by the board of directors and approved by the original examination and approval authority.

Chapter 17 Liability for Breach of Contract

Article 42 Should the cooperative venture company be unable to continue its operation or achieve its business purpose due to the fact that one of the contracting parties fails to fulfill the obligations prescribed by the contract and articles of association, or seriously violates the provisions of the contract and articles of association, that party shall be deemed to have unilaterally terminated the contract. The other party shall have the right to terminate the contract in accordance with the provisions of the contract after approval by the original examination and approval authority, and to claim damages. In case Party A and Party B of the cooperative venture company agree to continue the operation, the party who fails to fulfill its obligations shall be liable for the economic losses caused thereby to the joint venture company.

Article 43 Should either Party A or Party B fail to provide on schedule the contributions in accordance with the provisions defined in Chapter 5 of this contract, the party in breach shall pay to the other party_____ Yuan, or _____% of the contribution starting from the first month after exceeding the time limit. Should the party in breach fail to provide after _____months, _____Yuan, or _____% of the contribution shall be paid to the other party, who shall have the right to terminate the contract and to claim damages from the party in breach in accordance with the provisions of Article 42 of the contract.

Article 44 Should all or part of the contract and its appendices be unable to be fulfilled owing to the fault of one party, the party in breach shall bear the liability therefore. Should it be the fault of both parties, they shall bear their respective liabilities according to the actual situation.

Article 45 In order to guarantee the performance of the contract and its appendices, both Party A and Party B shall provide each other with bank guarantees for performance of the contract within _____days after the contract comes into force.

Chapter 18 Force Majeure

Article 46 Should either of the parties to the contract be prevented from executing the contract by force majeure, such as earthquake, typhoon, flood, fire, war or other unforeseen events, and their occurrence and consequences are unpreventable and unavoidable, the prevented party shall notify the other party by telegram without any delay, and within 15 days thereafter provide detailed information of the events and a valid document for evidence issued by the relevant public notary organization explaining the reason of its inability to execute or delay the execution of all or part of the contract. Both parties shall, through consultations, decide whether to terminate the contract or to exempt part of the obligations for implementation of the contract or whether to delay the execution of the contract according to the effects of the events on the performance of the contract.

Chapter 19 Applicable Law

Article 47 The formation, validity, interpretation, execution and settlement of disputes in respect of, this contract shall be governed by the relevant laws of the People's Republic of China.

Chapter 20 Settlement of Disputes

Article 48 Any disputes arising from the execution of, or in connection with, the contract shall be settled through friendly consultations between both parties. In case no settlement can be reached through consultations, the disputes shall be submitted to the Foreign Economic and Trade Arbitration Commission of the China Council for the Promotion of International Trade or arbitration in accordance with its rules of procedure. The arbitral award is final and binding upon both parties.

Article 49 During the arbitration, the contract shall be observed and enforced by both parties except for the matters in dispute.

Chapter 21 Language

Article 50 The contract shall be written in Chinese and in _____. Both language versions are equally authentic. In the event of any discrepancy between the two aforementioned versions, the Chinese version shall prevail.

Chapter 22 Effectiveness of the Contract and Miscellaneous

Article 51 The appendices drawn up in accordance with the principles of this contract are integral parts of this contract, including: the project agreement, the technology transfer agreement, the sales agreement etc.

Article 52 The contract and its appendices shall come into force commencing from the date of approval of the Ministry of Foreign Trade and Economic Cooperation of the People's Republic of China (or its entrusted examination and approval authority).

Article 53 Should notices in connection with any party's rights and obligations be sent by either Party A or Party B by telegram or telex, etc., the Written letter notices shall be also required afterwards. The legal addresses of Party A and Party B listed in this contract shall be the posting addresses.

Article 54 The contract is signed in _____, China by the authorized representatives of both parties on _____, 19_____.

For Party A For Party B
（Signature）（Signature）

第三节　劳务合同
Section 3　Contracts for Labor Services

3.1 劳动合同
Labor Contract

Employer:

Legal Representative:

Position:

Address:

Post code:

Employee:

Name:

Gender:

Address:

Nationality:

ID Card No.:

Date of Birth:

Education Degree:

This Contract is signed on a mutuality voluntary basis by and between the following Employer and Employee in accordance with the Labor Law of People's Republic of China.

1. Term of the Contract

The term of this contract is for _____ years and shall commence on _____, _____, and shall continue until _____, _____, unless earlier terminated pursuant to this Contract. The Employee shall undergo a probationary period of ___months.

2. Job Description

The Employer agrees to employ Mr./Ms._____ (name) as _____

(job title) in _____ Department, located in _____ (office location and city).

3. Remuneration of Labor

a. The salary of the Employee shall be monthly paid by the Employer in accordance with applicable laws and regulations of P.R.C. It shall be paid by legal tender and not less than the standard minimum salary in Tianjin.

b. The salary of the Employee is RMB/$_____ per month in the probationary period and RMB/$ _____ after the probationary period.

c. If the delay or default of salary takes place, the Employer shall pay the economic compensation except the salary itself in accordance with the relevant laws and regulations.

4. Working Hours & Rest & Vocation

a. The normal working hours of the Employee shall be eight hours each day, excluding meals and rest for an average of five days per week, for an average of forty hours per week.

b. The Employee is entitled to all legal holidays and other paid leaves of absence in accordance with the laws and regulations of the P.R.C. and the company's work rules.

c. The Employer may extend working hours due to the requirements of its production or business after consultation with the trade union and the Employee, but the extended working hour for a day shall generally not exceed one hour; if such extension is called for due to special reasons, the extended hours shall not exceed three hours a day. However, the total extension in a month shall not exceed thirty-six hours.

5. Social Security & Welfare

a. The Employer will pay for all mandatory social security programs such pension insurance, unemployment insurance, medical insurance of the Employee according to the relevant government and city regulations.

b. During the period of the Contract, the Employee's welfare shall be implemented accordance with the laws and relevant regulations of P.R.C.

6. Working Protection & Working Conditions

a. The Employer should provide the Employee with occupational safety and health conditions conforming to the provisions of the State and necessary articles of labor protection to guarantee the safety and health during the working process.

b. The Employer should provide the Employee with safety education and technique training; The Employee to be engaged in specialized operations should receive specialized training and acquire qualifications for such special operations.

c. The Employee should strictly abide by the rules of safe operation in the process of their work.

7. Labour Discipline

a. The Employer may draft bylaws and labor disciplines of the Company, According to which, the Employer shall have the right to give rewards or take disciplinary actions to the Employee; b.The Employee shall comply with the management directions of the Employer and obey the bylaws and labor disciplines of the Employer.

c. The Employee shall undertake the obligation to keep and not to disclose the trade secret for the Employer during the period of this Contract; This obligation of confidentiality shall survive the termination of this Contract for a period of two (2) years.

8. Termination, Modification, Renew and Discharge of the Contract

a. The relevant clauses of the Contract may be modified by the parties:

Ⅰ) The specific clause is required to be modified by the parties through consultation;

Ⅱ) Due to the force majeure, the Contract can not be executed;

Ⅲ.)The relevant laws and regulations have been modified or abolished by the time of signing the Contract.

b. The Contract may be automatically terminated:

Ⅰ) This Contract is not renewed at the expiration of this Contract;

Ⅱ)The Employer is legally announced to be bankruptcy, dismissed, or canceled;

Ⅲ)The death of the Employee occurs;

Ⅳ)The force majeure takes place;

Ⅴ)The conditions of termination agreed in the Contract by the parties arise.

c. The Contract may be renewed at the expiration through consultation by the parties with the fulfillment of the procedure within 15 days to the expiration;

d. The Contract may be discharged through consultation by the parties;

e. The Contract may be discharged by the Employer with immediate effect and the Employee will not be compensated:

Ⅰ) The Employee does not meet the job requirements during the probationary period;

Ⅱ) The Employee seriously violates disciplines or bylaws of the Employer;

Ⅲ) The Employee seriously neglects his duty, engages in malpractice for selfish ends and brings significant loss to the Employer;

Ⅳ) The Employee is being punished by physical labour for its misfeasance;

Ⅴ) The Employee is being charged with criminal offences;

f. The Contract may be terminated by the Employer by giving notice in written form 30(thirty) days in advance;

Ⅰ) The Employee fails ill or is injured to (other than due to work) and after completion of medical treatment, is not able to perform his previous function or any other function the Employer assigns to him;

Ⅱ) The Employee does not show satisfactory performance and after training and adjusting measures is still not able to perform satisfactorily;

Ⅲ) The circumstances have materially changed from the date this Contract was signed to the extent that it is impossible to execute the Contract provided, however, that the parties cannot reach an agreement to amend the contract to reflect the changed circumstances.

Ⅳ) The Employer is being consolidated in the legal consolidation period on the brink of bankruptcy or the situation of business is seriously in trouble, under such condition, it is required to reduce the employee.(in legal procedure)

g. The Employee shall not be dismissed :

Ⅰ) The Contract has neither expired nor conformed to 8.d,8.e,8.f,8.g;

Ⅱ) The Employee is ill with occupational disease or injured due to work and has been authenticated fully or partly disabled by the Labor Authentication Commission in Baodi County, Tianjin.

Ⅲ) The Employee is ill or injured (other than due to work) and is within the period of medical leave provided for by applicable P.R.C. law and regulations and Company policy;

Ⅳ) The Employee is woman who is pregnant, on maternity leave, or nursing a baby under one year of age; or

Ⅴ) The applicable P.R.C.laws and regulations otherwise prohibit the termination of this Contract.

h. The Contract may be discharged by the Employee by giving notice in written form 30 (thirty) days in advance. However, the Employee may inform the Employer to discharge the Contract at random under the following occasions;

I) The Employee is still in the probationary period;

II) The Employer force the Employee to work by violence, duress or illegal restriction to physical freedom;

III) The Employer does not pay the remuneration of the Employee accordance with the relevant clause in the Contract;

IV) The Employer violates the relevant regulations of State or Tianjin for its terrible safe and health condition, which is harmful to the Employee's health.

i. The Contract can not be terminated by the Employee before the expiration if not conforming to 8.d, 8.h;

j. The Employer shall pay the economic compensation to the Employer if the Contract is terminated conforming to 8.d,8.f,8.h.i–8.h.iv. Additional fee for medical allowance should be paid to the Employee if the Contract is terminated conforming to 8.f.i.

9.Breach Liabilities

a. Due to either party's fault, if breaching the Contract, that party shall undertake the breach liability according to the extent to the performance of the Contract; if the parties both breach the Contract, they shall undertake its separate liability according to the concrete situation.

b. Due to either party's fault, if breaching the Contract to damage the other party. The damage should be compensated by the faulty party accordance with the relevant laws and regulations of P.R.C. .

c. Due to the force majeure, causing the non-performance or the damages to either party, the other party may not undertake the breach liability;

d. The Employee wants to resign and has received training provided by the Employer, the Employee shall compensate for the training cost. The method of compensation should be fixed according to the relevant company regulations as follows:

The Employee shall compensate RMB_____ within ___year (s) in the Company if the Contract is terminated by the Employee at his cause;

The Employee shall compensate RMB_____ within ___year (s) in the Company if the Contract is terminated by the Employee at his cause;

The Employee shall compensate RMB_____ within ___year (s) in the Company if the Contract is terminated by the Employee at his cause.

10. Labor Disputes

Where a labor dispute between the parties takes place during the performance of this Contract, the parties concerned may seek for a settlement through consultation; or either party may apply to the labor dispute mediation committee of their unit for mediation; if the mediation fails and one of the parties requests for arbitration, that party may apply to the labor dispute arbitration committee for arbitration. Either party may also directly apply to the labor dispute arbitration committee for arbitration within 60 days starting from the date of the occurrence of a labor dispute. If one of the parties is not satisfied with the adjudication of arbitration, the party may bring the case to a people's court within 15 days of the date of receiving the ruling of arbitration

11. The verification of this Contract shall be made in Baodi Labor Bureau, Tianjin within 30 days after being signed by the parties.

Employer: (official stamp) Employee:
Representative :
Address: Address:

Date: July ,2003

It's verified herein that the Contract conforms to the relevant laws and regulations through examination and review.

Authority:

Clerk:

3.2 聘用契约书
Employment Agreement

This Agreement is made and entered into on the _____day of _____, _____by and between _____ (Institute or Preparatory Office), Academia Sinica (hereinafter referred to as "A") and_____(hereinafter "B").

Whereas, A is willing to offer B employment, and B is willing to accept such employment subject to the following terms and conditions:

1. Term of Employment

The parties agree that the term of this agreement shall be commencing from this _____ day of _____ , _____ to the_____ day of _____ , _____.

2. Remuneration

A shall pay B a salary of N.T. $ _____ per month.

3. B's duties (in specific description)

B's duties shall include _____.

4. B's Obligations and Termination

4.1 B shall handle in a confidential manner all matters relating to A's business. This confidentiality obligation shall remain effective during the period specified in the regulations or working rules concerned. In case that no time period is specified, it remains effective for successive _____ years' terms after B's termination of this employment. In the event that B violates any law or regulation, or breaches this Agreement or working rules concerned, A may in its discretion reprimand B or terminate this Agreement. A also reserves the right to institute suit against B for civil compensation or to impose criminal liability.

4.2 During the term of this Agreement, B shall comply with the directions and instructions of his/her supervisors, perform his/her duties in accor dance with all regulations and relevant working rules. Where B violates any obligation specified in this paragraph and the case is considered to be serious in nature, A may in its discretion terminate this Agreement. If at any time the parties intend to terminate this Agreement due to causes beyond the reasonable control of such party, either shall give thirty (30) days' notice of cancellation to the other party prior to the intended termination date. B shall vacate his/her office under and pursuant to the stipulations agreed upon by both parties. B shall submit to the proceedings in prescribed manner as to be vacated of his/her office. In case of any one of the following conditions which is due to B's fault, B shall be responsible for compensation: (1) Where B inflicts damage to or exces sively abuses machinery, equipment, tools, raw materials, products or other article belonging to Academia Sinica; (2) Where B commits torts; (3) Where B violates A's ownership of intellectual property rights.

5. B shall comply with any ad ministrative regulations and rules provided by A. In regard to the matters of absence on leave, "pay-as-you-go" contribution benefit, labor insurance and national health insurance, the following terms and conditions shall be applicable.

5.1 "Absence on leave" shall be operated pursuant to "Regulation of Absence on leave for Personnel served in all Executive Yuan organizations under Civil Contractual Relationship".

5.2 The deduction and grant of "pay-as-you-go" contribution benefit shall be operated pursuant to "Regulation of 'pay-as-you-go' contribution benefit for Personnel served in all organizations and schools under Civil Contractual Relationship". Certain amount of salary shall be deducted per month and accrue on the financial institute over the term of this employment.

5.2.1 An amount equal to seven percent (7%) of the monthly salary shall be contributed. Fifty percent (50%) of the contribution shall be drawn from B's monthly salary. (hereinafter called "personal contribution benefit") A shall provide the other fifty percent (50%) of the contribution (hereinafter called "public contribution benefit"), and shall open a special account on financial institute as to accumulate and manage this contribution (personal plus public).

5.2.2 The total amount of the contribution benefits (personal plus public) shall be granted to B, if at any time (a) B leaves the office on the expiry of this Agreement, (b) B vacates the office prior to the expiration date with the consent of A, and (c) B deceases due to undertaking of duty, illness or accident.

5.2.3 The amount of personal contribution benefits accumulated shall be granted to B, if at any time (a) A terminates this Agreement inasmuch as B breaches any obligation, and (b) B resigns from the office prior to the expiration date without the consent of A.

5.2.4 Any matter or event not provided in the context of this Article shall be operated pursuant to "Regulation of 'pay-as-you-go' contribution benefit for Personnel served in all organizations and schools under Civil Contractual Relationship" and relevant regulations.

5.3 During the term of this Agreement, A shall insure B subject to the terms and conditions pursuant to labor insurance regulations and national health insurance regulations.

6. Both parties agree that A shall own proprietary right pertaining to the literary works or achievements completed by B under the projects initiated or coordinated by A during the term of this Agreement. The ownership of intellectual property rights (including but not limited to certain patents, trademarks, copyrights, technical information and know-how) accrued from the literary works or achievements herein contained is subject to the relevant regulations and rules provided by A.

7. Expiration

At the expiration of the term of this agreement, the employment relationship shall automatically terminate without any condition. A new employment agreement shall be signed for the renewal and continuance of such relationship, if agreed to any by both parties.

8. Any matter or event not provided in the context of this Agreement shall be governed by and interpreted in accordance with "Employment Regulation for Personnel under Civil Contractual Relationship" (stipulated by Academia Sinica) & "Employment Regulation for Personnel served in all Executive Yuan organizations under Civil Contractual Relationship".

9. Governing Language

The Chinese text of this Agreement shall be deemed the original. In the event of any dispute or misunderstanding as to the interpretation of the language or terms of this Agreement, the Chinese language version shall control.

10. Governing Law

Any dispute or controversy between the parties with respect to this agreement shall be determined in accordance with the laws of the Republic of China. The parties hereby submit and consent to the non-exclusive jurisdiction of the Shih-Lin District Court.

11. In Witness whereof, the parties hereto have executed this Agreement in three (3) counterparts on the date first above indicated, each such counterpart being deemed an original and all such counterparts together constituting one single instrument. The parties have delivered this Agreement, two for A (the Central Administration Office and the Institute or Preparatory Office hereto) and one for B.

Party A (signature): _____ Party B (signature): _____
Date: _____ Date: _____

_____(以下简称甲方)为应业务需要,聘(雇)用_____先生(女士)(以下简称乙方)为约聘(雇)人员,双方订立契约条款如下:

一、聘(雇)用期间:自_____年_____月_____日起至_____年_____月_____日止。

二、聘(雇)用报酬:甲方按月支给乙方报酬_____薪点(_____元)。

三、工作内容(具体叙明):_____。

四、受聘(雇)责任：

乙方受聘(雇)后须确保甲方公务机密，有保密期限者从其规定，无保密期限者自离职日起＿＿＿＿＿＿＿年为限[解聘(雇)者亦同]。乙方不得有不法行为或违背约定义务，如有违背者，除涉及民、刑事责任，由甲方依法追究外，并得随时解聘(雇)。

在聘(雇)用期间，乙方愿接受与甲方约定之工作上的指派调遣，并遵守此工作上之相关规定。若乙方违背上述相关规定确属情节重大，甲方得随时终止契约；甲、乙双方如因特别事故须提前终止契约时，应于一个月前提出预告，经甲、乙双方协议后乙方始得离职。乙方离职时，应先依照规定办妥离职手续。如有损害公物，或侵权情事(或违反甲方智能财产权规定)，应负责赔偿。

五、乙方在受聘(雇)用期间，除应遵守甲方一切行政法规之规定外，其假期、离职储金给予、劳工保险及全民健保等，依下列约定：

假期核给：依＿＿＿＿＿＿＿办理。

离职储金之扣缴及给予依＿＿＿＿＿＿＿规定办理，按月扣缴储存生息，并于离职时依规定发给。

按乙方每月支报酬之百分之＿＿＿＿＿＿＿提存储金，其中百分之＿＿＿＿＿＿＿由乙方于每月报酬中扣缴作为自提储金，另百分之＿＿＿＿＿＿＿由甲方提拨作为公提储金，并由甲方在金融机构开立专户储存孳息，列账管理。

乙方因契约期满离职、或经甲方同意于契约期限届满前离职、或在职因公、因病或意外死亡者，发给公、自提储金本息。

乙方因违反契约所定义务而经甲方予以解聘，或未经甲方同意而于契约期限届满前离职者，仅发给自提储金之本息。

其余未尽事宜请参考＿＿＿＿＿＿＿有关规定。

乙方受聘(雇)用期间，甲方应善尽投保劳工保险及全民健康保险之义务。

六、乙方于受聘(雇)期间之著作或工作成果，如系于甲方企划下，或法定工作期间完成者，其所有权归属甲方。因前开著作或工作成果所生之智能财产权，应依本院之相关规定办理。

七、本契约期间届满当然失效，如因业务需要须续聘时，另行签订新契约。

八、本契约未订定事项，悉依《聘用人员聘用条例》及＿＿＿＿＿＿＿相关规定办理。

九、本契约以中文本为准。如中、英文二本互相歧义或抵触时，以中文本为准。

十、本契约法律纠纷以＿＿＿＿＿＿＿法院为第一审管辖法院。

十一、本契约一式三份，除一份由甲方报院备查外，另由双方各执一份。

甲方（签章）：＿＿＿＿＿＿　　乙方（签章）：＿＿＿＿＿＿

＿＿＿＿＿年＿＿月＿＿日　　＿＿＿＿＿年＿＿月＿＿日

3.3 聘请法律顾问合同
Contract for Legal Counsel Employment

＿＿＿＿＿＿＿＿＿（"A" hereinafter） would like to retain ＿＿＿＿＿＿＿（"B" hereinafter） as its legal counsel, according to "Provisional Rules on Legal Counsel of the People's Republic of China". The two parties through consultation hereby agree upon, and shall be bound by, the following terms:

1. B will designate ＿＿＿＿＿＿, the lawyer employed by A, to work as B's legal counsel. ＿＿＿＿＿＿ will provide legal assistance and protect B's interests vested by law.

2. The legal counsel will provide the following services:

a. Providing answers to legal questions, and issuing written legal opinion when necessary;

b. Assisting in drafting and reviewing contracts and other legal document;

c. Participating in contract negotiation on A's behalf;

d. Participating in litigation, non-litigation activities, arbitration, and intermediation;

e. Handling other legal matters on behalf of A.

3. A will contact the legal counsel to decide the time and location each time when service is needed.

4. A shall pay B an annual fee of $ ＿＿＿＿＿＿. Additional fee will be charged on an hourly basis for the service of litigation, intermediation, arbitration, and contract negotiation.

5. Whenever the legal counsel is on business trip on behalf of A, all his/her living and travelling expense shall be paid by A.

6. A shall provide the legal counsel with relevant information, material and appropriate working conditions.

7. This contract shall come into effect on the date when it is signed by both

parties. The term of this contract is _____ years.

8. This contract shall have two originals and each party will have one. Both copies shall be equally valid.

Party A (official stamp) Party B (official stamp)

Representative of party A Representative of party B

(signature) (signature)

_____ _____

Our Contract Template Database is complied in accordance with laws of P. R.China. This English document is translated according to its Chinese version. In case of discrepancy, the original version in Chinese shall prevail.

第四节 租赁合同
Section 4　Lease Contracts

This lease agreement is made and entered into on _____, _____, _____ (M/D/Y), by and between AAA, a public corporation, ("Lessor"), and BBB, a _____ partnership, ("Lessee").

ARTICLE 1.DEMISE, DESCRIPTION, USE, TERM, AND RENTLessor hereby leases to Lessee, and Lessee hereby leases from Lessor, that certain property, hereinafter called the "leased premises", situated in the City of Anniston, _____ County, _____ (STATE), and described as follows: SEE ATTACHED PROPERTY DESCRIPTION commencing on _____, _____, _____ (M/D/Y), and ending on _____, _____, _____ (M/D/Y) for the rent payable as specified in Article 2.

ARTICLE 2.RENTMINIMUM RENT2.01. Lessee shall pay Lessor at _____, or at such other place as the Lessor shall designate from time to time in writing, as rent for the leased premises, as follows: (a) $ _____ per month, payable on the first day of each month during the term of this Lease.

EFFECT OF DEFAULT IN RENT AND OTHER PAYMENTS2.02. If Lessee defaults in the payment of any installment of rent hereunder, such installment shall bear interest at the rate of 12 percent per annum from the day it is due until actually paid. In like manner, all other obligations, benefits, and moneys which may become due to Lessor from Lessee under the terms hereof, or which are paid by Lessor because of Lessee's default hereunder, shall bear interest at the rate of 12 percent per annum from the due date until paid, or, in the case of sums paid by Lessor, because of Lessee's default hereunder, from the date such payments are made by Lessor until the date Lessor is reimbursed by Lessee therefor.

ARTICLE 3.TAXES AND ASSESSMENTSADDITIONAL RENT – PAYMENTS IN LIEU OF SCHOOL TAXES3.01. (a) Lessor and Lessee acknowledge that, under present law, the leased premises, so long as it is owned by the Lessor is exempt from ad valorem taxation by the State of _____ ﹒(STATE) or any other political or taxing subdivision thereof, including _____ County. Nonetheless, the Lessee hereby agrees to make annual additional rent payments to the Anniston City School System and the _____ County School System in amounts equal to the respective ad valorem school systems. Such annual payments shall be due on _____ , _____ , _____ (M/D/Y) and on each _____ , _____ (M/D) thereafter so long as the Lease remains in effect. The amount of each such annual payment shall be determined by the Tax Assessor of _____ County, _____ (STATE). Lessor shall provide the Lessee with written notice of the amount of each such annual payment at least thirty (30) days prior to the due date thereof. Lessor acknowledges that the obligation of the Lessee to make the payment of additional rent provided for in this section is conditioned upon the Leased premises remaining exempt from ad valorem taxation throughout the period of time to which such payment is referable. If, as a result of a change in law prior to the termination of this Lease Agreement, the Leased premises become subject to ad valorem taxes, the Lessee shall pay such taxes as additional rent.

HOLD HARMLESS CLAUSE3.02. Lessee agrees to and shall protect and hold harmless Lessor and the leased premises for liability for any and all personal property taxes, personal property assessments, and personal property charges, together with any interest, penalties, or other sums thereby imposed, and from any sale or other proceeding to enforce payment thereof. This section is for the benefit of the parties hereto and is not given to protect third parties.

SEPARATE ASSESSMENTS OF PERSONAL PROPERTY3.03. During the term hereof, Lessee shall cause all taxes, assessments, and other charges levied on or imposed on any of its personal property situated in, on or about the leased premises to be levied on Lessee.

TAXES EXCLUDED3.04. Nothing herein contained requires, or shall be construed to require, Lessee (or any of its subtenants) to pay any property, gift, estate, inheritance, or other tax assessed against Lessor or its heirs or successors and assigns, or any income or other tax, assessment, charge, or levy on the rent payable by Lessor under this lease.

ARTICLE 4.INSURANCE4.01. Lessee agrees to and shall, within seven (7) days from the date hereof, secure from a good and responsible company or companies doing insurance business in the State of _____ (STATE) and maintain during the entire term of this lease, the following insurance coverage:

1) Public liability insurance in the minimum amount of _____ Dollars ($ _____) for loss from an accident resulting in bodily injury to or death of persons, and _____ Dollars ($ _____) for loss from an accident resulting in damage to or destruction of property; and umbrella insurance coverage in the amount of an additional _____ Dollars ($ _____).

2) Fire and extended coverage insurance on Lessee's fixtures, goods, wares, and merchandise in or on the leased premises, with coverage in an amount of not less than its full replacement value.

4.02. Lessor agrees to and shall, within seven (7) days from the date hereof, secure from a good and responsible company or companies doing insurance business in the State of _____ (STATE) and maintain during the entire term of this lease, the following insurance coverage:

1) Fire and extended coverage insurance in an amount of not less than 100% of the value of the leased premises and other improvements on the leased premises, provided that insurance in that percentage can be obtained, and, if not, then to the highest percentage that can be obtained less than the said 100%, but in no event will said coverage be less than _____ Dollars ($ _____).

2) In the event that Lessor shall cause any work on the leased premises to

be done pursuant to the provisions of this Article 4, before said work shall commence, it shall secure public liability insurance in the minimum amount of _____ Dollars ($ _____) for loss from an accident resulting in bodily injury to or death of persons, and _____ Dollars ($ _____) for loss from an accident resulting in damage to or destruction of property; and umbrella insurance coverage to aggregate at least an additional _____ Dollars ($ _____).

第五节 国际技术转让合同与国际许可合同
Section 5 Contracts for International Technology Transfer and Contracts for International Licensing

国际技术转让合同是技术出让方越过国界将技术或技术使用权转让给受让方，受让方取得技术或技术使用权并支付价款或技术费用，或越过国界以技术为另一方完成一定工作任务，使其获得劳动成果并支付报酬的协议。技术转让合同包括专利权转让、专利申请权转让、技术秘密转让、专利实施许可合同等。

国际许可合同(international-licensing-contract)亦称国际许可协议(international- licensing-agreement)，是指其中规定技术供方亦即许可方(licensor)向技术受方亦即被许可方(licensee)转让技术的使用权，而被许可方则须为此向许可方支付技术使用费，以及双方当事人其他权利义务的、具有法律所规定的国际性的协议。

5.1 技术合作协议
Contract for Technology Corporation

BETWEEN

XXX

("XX")

and

ZHEJIANG XXX

A limited liability comp XXX any incorporated under the laws of China, and located in ("XXXX")

WHEREAS XXXX possesses the knowhow ("the Product Knowhow" as defined below) for a process for the manufacture of the bulk unformulated active pharmaceutical ingredient XXXXXX.

WHEREAS XXXX has the facilities, personnel, capacity and infrastructure necessary to manufacture the chemical compound XXXXXXXX, which is used as a chemical intermediate for manufacturing XXXXXX ("the intermediated")

WHEREAS XXXX and XX desire that Jizhou shall transfer to XX the right to use the product Knowhow in accordance with the terms and conditions of this agreement;

WHEREAS XXXX desires to supply XX with its requirements of intermediate which XX is willing to purchase from XXXX in accordance with the terms and conditions of this Agreement.

NOW THEREFORE THE PARTIES AGREE AS FOLLOWS:

1. DEFINITIONS

The preamble to this Agreement forms an integral part hereof. Clause headings in this Agreement are intended solely for convenience of reference and shall be given no effect in the interpretation of this Agreement. All agreed upon annexes to this Agreement, whether attached at the time of signature hereof or at any time thereafter, shall be construed as an integral part of this Agreement. In this agreement, the following expressions shall bear the meanings assigned to them below ad cognate expressions shall bear corresponding meaning:

1.1 "Affiliate"-shall mean with respect to each of the parties, any person, corporation, company, partnership, joint venture or other entity controlling, controlled by or under common control with such party. For such purpose the term "control" means the holding of 50% or more of the common voting stock or ordinary shares in, or the right to appoint 50% or more of the directors of, or the right to share in 50% or more of the profits of, the said corporation, company, partnership, joint venture, or entity.

1.2 "Effective Date"— shall mean the date on which this Agreement is signed by the latter of the parties to sign this Agreement.

1.3 "Product"— shall mean XXXXXX manufactured in accordance with the Product Knowhow received from XXXX using the Intermediate.

1.4 "Product Knowhow"—shall mean any and all data, information, documentation, and/or knowhow related to the process for manufacture of the Product in possession or control of XXXX, including without limitation, any analytical data and/or methods or procedure.

2. PRODUCT KNOWHOW

XXXX shall provide XX upon the Effective Date a complete written technical package containing the Product Knowhow. XX shall have the irrevocable right and license to use the Product Knowhow.

3. SUPPLY AND PURCHASE OF INTERMEDIATE

XXXX undertakes to manufacture the intermediate in accordance with the terms and conditions of this Agreement and to supply XX with its requirements of the Intermediated in accordance with XX firm orders pursuant to clause 6 below. XX undertakes, subject to clause 6 and 7, to purchase its requirements of the Intermediate that are to be used for manufacturing the Product Knowhow, only from XXXX.

4. MANUFACTURE OF INTERMEDIATE

4.1 XXXX represents and warrants to XX that all intermediate supplied by XXXX hereunder shall be manufactured and supplied by XXXX to XX or its nominee in strict accordance with (Ⅰ) the specifications to be agreed to by the parties before the commencement of supply and when agreed to be attached hereto as Annex A ("the Specifications")

4.2 Each shipment of Intermediate supplied hereunder by XXXX shall be accompanied by a packing list, inspection certificate by and authoritative mutually recognized organization and a certificate of analysis signed by a representative of XXXX for each batch.

5. ORDERS AND PRICE

5.1 XX shall provide to XXXX at least forty five (45) days in advance a firm order setting forth XX's total requirements of Intermediated. The order shall state in detail the quantities of Intermediate ordered, dates for delivery of the intermediated, and reasonable instructions for shipping and destinations. XXXX undertakes to deliver such quantities of Intermediate ordered by XX in accordance with the terms and Instructions set forth in each such firm order.

5.2 XXXX and XX shall from time to time set the price of the intermediate based upon their good faith discussions, provided that such price:

a. is competitive with the world market price of the intermediate;

b. shall be such that the Product manufactured by XX using such intermediate can be sole at a price which is competitive with the world market price of the Product.

6. FAILURE TO SUPPLY

If XXXX fails to supply XX its requirements of the intermediate for any continuous three (3) month period or for three (3) months in the aggregate during any one calendar year, including without limitation, due to a force majeure event, XX shall have the right to source the intermediated from a third party without penalty.

7. TERM AND TERMINATION OF AGREEMENT

7.1 This agreement shall have an initial term of ten (10) years from the Effective Date. The initial term shall be extended automatically for additional successive two (2) year terms unless either one of the parties hereto will have sent the other party a written notice indicating that the first party dose not wish the Agreement to be extended. Such termination notice shall be given at least six (6) months prior to the end of initial term of renewal term, as the case may be.

7.2 Either party may terminate this agreement for a material breach of any term or condition of this agreement, by the non-breaching party providing the breaching party written notice, specifying the breach rolled on, and affording the breaching party sixty (60) days to cure such breach. If the breach has not been cured at the end of sixty (60) days period, then, upon notice thereof to the breaching party by the non-breaching party, this Agreement shall terminate.

7.3 Either party shall have the right to terminate this Agreement at any time during the term of this Agreement in the event that it shall in good faith form the opinion that the continuation of this agreement as contemplated hereunder is not commercially viable, such termination to the other party.

8. CONSEOUENCES ON TERMINATION

In the event of termination of this Agreement for whatever reason (by expiration of term or otherwise) (I) neither party shall be entitled as a result of such termination to any compensation or damages or other payment from the other payment from the other.

9. CONFIDENTIALITY

Each party agrees that it will keep the existence of this Agreement and the terms and conditions contained herein secret during the term of this Agreement and for a period of five (5) years after its termination.

10. MISCELLANEOUS

10.1 This Agreement does not constitute either party as the agent or legal representative of the other for any purpose whatsoever.

10.2 Except for XX to Affiliates, neither party may, without the written consent of the other, assign, mortgage charge (otherwise that by floating charge) or dispose of any of its rights hereunder or subcontract or otherwise delegate any of its obligations under this Agreement, during or after the duration of the present contract.

10.3 Any dispute between the parties shall be referred to arbitration to be conducted under the Rules of China International Economic and Trade Arbitration Commission. The parties agree that the arbitration as aforesaid shall be conducted in Shanghai, China. And the substantive law to be applied by the arbitrator in considering and resolving the dispute referred to arbitration in terms hereof, shall be the Chinese law. The parties further agree to exclude any right of application or appeal to any courts arising in the course of such arbitration and with respect to any award made in such arbitration, which award shall be final and binding on the parties.

If to XX

5 Basel Street, Petah Tiqva 49131, Israel

Attention: Vice President, API Division

Telephone: 972-3-9267338 facsimile:972-3-9267477

If to XXXX:

Waisha 99#, Jiaojiang, Taizhou, Zhejiang,318000, China

Attention: Vice President, Sale Dept.

Telephone: 0086-576-8827561 Fax: 0086-576-8827681

Or to such other addresses or facsimile numbers as either party shall designate by notice, similarly given, to the other party. Notices or written communications shall be deemed to have been sufficiently made or given if by air courier or by facsimile with confirmed transmission, within 3 days of such transmission or if by first class airmail within 10 days of being sent.

10.4 Should any part or provision of the Agreement be held unenforceable or in conflict with the applicable laws or regulations of any jurisdiction, the invalid or unenforceable part or provision shall, provided that it does not go the essence of this Agreement, be replaced with a revision which accomplishes to the extent possible, the original business purpose of such part or provision in a valid and enforceable manner, and the balance of this agreement shall remain in full force and effect and binding upon the parties hereto.

10.5 This Agreement and the other agreements contemplated hereby constitute the entire agreement between the parties with respect to its subject matter and supersede all prior agreement, arrangements, dealings or writings between the parties. This Agreement may not be varied except in writhing signed by the parties' authorized representatives.

10.6 No waiver of a breach or default hereunder shall be considered valid unless in writing and signed by the party giving such waiver, and no such waiver shall be deemed a waiver of any subsequent breach or default of the same or similar nature.

IN WITNESS WHEREOF, each of the parties has executed this Agreement and the Annex hereto as of the date below,

XXX

Israel

_____

(signatures, date)

ZHEJAING XXXX PHARMACEUTICAL CO.,LTD

China

_____

(signature, date)

5.2 国际商标许可合同
Trademark Licensing Contract

Agreement made this _____ day of _____, between _____ (hereinafter called "Licensor"), and _____ (hereinafter called "Licensee"):

WITNESSETH

Whereas Licensor owns certain valuable registered trademarks and service marks, and owns and has merchandising rights to various other Licensor properties as defined in paragraph 1 of the Rider attached hereto and hereby made a part hereof (hereinafter called "Name"), said Name having been used over the facilities of numerous stations in radio and/or television broadcasting in allied fields, and in promotional and advertising material in different businesses and being well Known and recognized by the general public and associated in the public mind with Licensor, and Whereas Licensee desires to utilize the Name upon and in connection with the manufacture, sale and distribution of articles hereinafter described,

Now, Therefore, in consideration of the mutual promises herein contained, it is hereby agreed:

1.Grant of License

(a) Articles

Upon the terms and conditions hereinafter set forth, Licensor hereby grants to Licensee as a related company, and Licensee hereby accepts the right, license and privilege of utilizing the Name solely and only upon and in connection with the manufacture, sale and distribution of the

following articles.

(insert description)

(b) Territory

The license hereby granted extends only to ＿＿＿＿＿＿＿＿. Licensee agrees that it will not make, or authorize, any use, direct or indirect, of the Name in any other area, and that it will not knowingly sell articles covered by this agreement to persons who intend or are likely to resell them in any other area.

(c) Term

The term of the license hereby granted shall be effective on the ＿＿＿＿＿day of ＿＿＿＿＿＿ and shall continue until the ＿＿＿＿＿ day of ＿＿＿＿＿＿, unless sooner terminated in accordance with the provisions hereof. The term of this license may be automatically renewed from year to year upon all the terms and conditions contained herein, with the final renewal to expire on December 31st, ＿＿＿＿＿＿. At the end of each term, beginning with December 31st, ＿＿＿＿＿＿＿, this license shall be automatically renewed for a one-year term expiring December 31st of the following year, unless either party hereto shall be given written notice to the contrary at least thirty (30) days prior to the expiration date.

2. Terms of Payment

(a) Rate

Licensee agrees to pay to Licensor as royalty a sum equal to ＿＿＿＿＿＿percent of all net sales by Licensee or any of its affiliated, associated or subsidiary companies of the articles covered by this agreement. The term "net sales" shall mean gross sales less quantity discounts and returns, but no deduction shall be made for cash or other discounts or uncollectible accounts. No costs incurred in the manufacture, sale, distribution or exploitation of the articles shall be deducted from any royalty payable by Licensee. Licensee agrees that in the event it should pay any other Licensor a higher royalty or licensing rate or commission than that provided herein for the use of the Name, than said higher rate shall automatically and immediately apply to this contract.

(b) Minimum Royalties

Licensee agrees to pay to Licensor a minimum royalty of _____ Dollars ($_____) as a minimum guarantee against royalties to be paid to Licensor during the first contract term, said minimum royalty to be paid on or before the last day of the initial term hereof. The advance sum of _____ dollars ($_____) paid on the signing hereof shall be applied against such guarantee. No part of such minimum royalty shall in any event be repayable to Licensee.

(c) Periodic Statements

Within _____ days after the initial shipment of the articles covered by this agreement, and promptly on the _____ of each calendar _____ thereafter, Licensee shall furnish to Licensor complete and accurate statements certified to be accurate by Licensee showing the number, description and gross sales price, itemized deductions from gross sales price and net sales price of the articles covered by this agreement distributed and/or sold by Licensee during the preceding calendar _____, together with any returns made during the preceding calendar _____ For this purpose, Licensee shall use the statement form attached hereto, copies of which form may be obtained by Licensee from Licensor. Such statements shall be furnished to Licensor whether or not any of the articles have been sold during the preceding calendar _____.

(d) Royalty payments

Royalties in excess of the aforementioned minimum royalty shall be due on the _____ day of the _____ following the calendar _____ in which earned, and payment shall accompany the statements furnished as required above. The receipt or acceptance by Licensor of any of the statements furnished pursuant to this agreement or of any royalties paid hereunder (or the cashing of any royalty checks paid hereunder) shall not preclude Licensor from questioning the correctness thereof at any time, and in the event that any inconsistencies or mistakes are discovered in such statements or payments, they shall immediately be rectified and the appropriate payment made by Licensee. Payment shall be in _____. Domestic taxes payable in the licensed territory shall be payable by Licensee.

3. Exclusivity

(a) Nothing in this agreement shall be construed to prevent Licensor from granting any other licenses for the use of the Name or from utilizing the Name in any manner whatsoever, except that Licensor agrees that except as provided herein it will grant no other licenses for the territory to which this license extends effective during the term of this agreement, for the use of the Name in connection with the sale of the articles described in paragraph 1.

(b) It is agreed that if Licensor should convey an offer to Licensee to purchase any of the articles listed in paragraph 1, in connection with a premium, giveaway or other promotional arrangement, Licensee shall have _____ days within which to accept or reject such an offer. In the event that Licensee fails to accept such offer within the specified _____ days, Licensor shall have the right to enter into the proposed premium, giveaway or promotional arrangement using the services of another manufacturer, provided, however, that in such event Licensee shall have a three (3) day period within which to meet the best offer of such manufacturer for the production of such articles if the price of such manufacturer is higher than the price offered to Licensee by Licensor. Licensee agrees that it shall not, without the prior written consent of Licensor, (i) offer the articles as a premium in connection with any other product or service, or (ii) sell or distribute the articles in connection with another product or service which product or service is a premium.

4. Good Will

Licensee recognizes the great value of the good will associated with the Name, and acknowledges that the Name and all rights therein and good will pertaining thereto belong exclusively to Licensor, and that the Name has a secondary meaning in the mind of the public.

5. Licensor's Title and Protection of Licensor's Rights

(a) Licensee agrees that it will not during the term of this agreement, or thereafter, attack the title or any rights of Licensor in and to the Name or attack the validity of this license. Licensor hereby indemnifies Licensee and undertakes to hold it harmless against any claims or suits arising solely out of the use by Licensee of the Name as authorized in this agreement, provided that prompt notice is given to Licensor of any such claim or suit and provided, further, that Licensor shall have the option to undertake and conduct the defense of any suit so brought and no settlement of any such claim or suit is made without the prior written consent of Licensor.

(b) Licensee agrees to assist Licensor to the extent necessary in the procurement of any protection or to protect any of Licensor's rights to the Name, and Licensor, if it so desires may commence or prosecute any claims or suits in its own name or in the name of licensee or join Licensee as a party thereto. Licensee shall notify Licensor in writing of any infringements or imitations by others in the Name on articles the same as or similar to those covered by this agreement which may come to Licensee's attention, and Licensor shall have the sole right to determine whether or not any action shall be taken on account of any such infringements or imitations. Licensee shall not institute any suit or take any action on account of any such infringements or imitations without first obtaining the written consent of the Licensor so to do.

6.Indemnification by Licensee and Product Liability Insurance

Licensee hereby indemnifies Licensor and undertakes to defend Licensee and/or Licensor against and hold Licensor harmless from any claims, suits, loss and damage arising out of any allegedly unauthorized use of any trademark, patent, process, idea, method or device by Licensee in connection with the articles covered by this agreement or any other alleged action by Licensee and also from any claims, suits, loss and damage arising out of alleged defects in the articles. Licensee agrees that it will obtain, at its own expense, product liability insurance from a recognized insurance company which has qualified to do business in _____, providing adequate protection (at least in the amount of _____) for Licensor (as well for Licensee) against any claims, suits, loss or damage arising out of any alleged defects in the articles. As proof of such insurance, a fully paid certificate of insurance naming Licensor as an insured party will be submitted to Licensor by Licensee for Licensor's prior approval before any article is distributed or sold, and at the latest within _____ days after the date first written above; any proposed change in certificates of insurance shall be submitted to Licensor for its prior approval. Licensor shall be entitled to a copy of the then prevailing certificate of insurance, which shall be furnished Licensor by Licensee. As Used in the first 2 sentences of this paragraph 6, "Licensor" shall also include the officers, directors, agents, and employees of the Licensor, or any of its subsidiaries or affiliates, any person(s) the use of whose name may be licensed hereunder, the package producer and the cast of the radio and/or television program whose name may be licensed hereunder, the stations over which the programs are transmitted, any sponsor of said programs and its advertising agency, and their respective officers, directors, agents and employees.

7.Quality of Merchandise

Licensee agrees that the articles covered by this agreement shall be of high standard and of such style, appearance and quality as to be adequate and suited to their exploitation to the best advantage and to the protection and enhancement of the Name and the good will pertaining thereto, that such articles will be manufactured, sold and distributed in accordance with all applicable Federal, State and local laws, and that the same shall not reflect adversely upon the good name of Licensor or any of its programs or the Name. To this end Licensee shall, before selling or distributing any of the articles, furnish to Licensor free of cost, for its written approval, a reasonable number of samples of each article, its cartons, containers and packing and wrapping material. The quality and style of such articles as well as of any carton, container or packing or wrapping material shall be subject to the approval of Licensor. Any item submitted to Licensor shall not be deemed approved unless and until the same shall be approved by Licensor in writing. After samples have been approved pursuant to this paragraph, Licensee shall not depart therefrom in any material respect without Licensor's prior written consent, and Licensor shall not withdraw its approval of the approved samples except on _____ days' prior written notice to Licensee. From time to time after Licensee has commenced selling the articles and upon Licensor's written request, Licensee shall furnish without cost to Licensor not more than additional random samples of each article being manufactured and sold by Licensee hereunder, together with any cartons, containers and packing and wrapping material used in connection therewith.

8.Labeling

(a) Licensee agrees that it will cause to appear on or within each article sold by it under this license and on or within all advertising, promotional or display material bearing the Name the notice "Copyright (c) _____ (year)" in connection with Name properties (e) and (f) in Rider, paragraph 1, and any other notice desired by Licensor and, where such article or advertising, promotional or display material bears a trademark or service mark, appropriate statutory notice of registration or application for registration thereof. In the event that any article is marketed in a carton, container and/or packing or wrapping material bearing the Name, such notice shall also appear upon the said carton, container and/or packing or wrapping material. Each and every tag, label, imprint or other device containing any such notice and all advertising, promotional or display material bearing the Name shall be submitted by Licensor for its written approval prior to use by Licensee. Approval by Licensor shall not constitute waiver of Licensor's rights or Licensee's duties under any provision of this agreement.

(b) Licensee agrees to cooperate fully and in good faith with Licensor for the purpose of securing and preserving Licensor's (or any grantor of Licensor's) rights in and to the Name. In the event there has been no previous registration of the Name and/or articles and/or any material relating thereto, Licensee shall, at Licensor's request and expense, register such a copyright, trademark and/or service mark in the appropriate class in the name of Licensor or, if Licensor so requests, in Licensee's own name. However, it is agreed that nothing contained in this agreement shall be construed as an assignment or grant to the Licensee of any right, title or interest in or to the Name, it being understood that all rights relating thereto are reserved by Licensor, except for the license hereunder to Licensee of the right to use and utilize the Name only as specifically and expressly provided in this agreement. Licensee hereby agrees that at the termination or expiration of this agreement Licensee will be deemed to have assigned, transferred and conveyed to Licensor any rights, equities, good will, titles or other rights in and to the Name which may have been obtained by Licensee or which may have vested in Licensee in pursuance of any endeavors covered hereby, and that Licensee will execute any instruments requested by Licensor to accomplish or confirm the foregoing. Any such assignment, transfer or conveyance shall be without other consideration than the mutual covenants and considerations of this agreement.

(c) Licensee hereby agrees that its every use of such name shall inure to the benefit of Licensor and that Licensee shall not at any time acquire any rights in such name by virtue of any use it may make of such name.

9.Promotional Material

(a) In all cases where Licensee desires artwork involving articles which are the subject of this license to be executed, the cost of such artwork and the time for the production thereof shall be borne by Licensee. All artwork and designs involving the Name, or any reproduction thereof, shall, notwithstanding their invention or use by Licensee, be and remain the property of Licensor and Licensor shall be entitled to use the same and to license the use of the same by others.

(b) Licensor shall have the right, but shall not be under any obligation, to use the Name and/or the name of Licensee so as to give the Name, Licensee, Licensor and/or Licensor's programs full and favorable prominence and publicity. Licensor shall not be under any obligation whatsoever to continue broadcasting any radio or television program or use the Name or any person, character, symbol, design or likeness or visual representation thereof in any radio or television program.

(c) Licensee agrees not to offer for sale or advertise or publicize any of the articles licensed hereunder on radio or television without the prior written approval of Licensor, which approval Licensor may grant or withhold in its unfettered discretion.

10. Distribution

(a) Licensee agrees that during the term of this license it will diligently and continuously manufacture, distribute and sell the articles covered by this agreement and that it will make and maintain adequate arrangement for the distribution of the articles.

(b) Licensee shall not, without prior written consent of Licensor, sell or distribute such articles to jobbers, wholesalers, distributors, retail stores or merchants whose sales or distribution are or will be made for publicity or promotional tie-in purposes, combination sales, premiums, giveaways, or similar methods of merchandising, or whose business methods are questionable.

(c) Licensee agrees to sell to Licensor such quantities of the articles at as low a rate and on as good terms as Licensee sells similar quantities of the articles to the general trade.

11. Records

Licensee agrees to keep accurate books of account and records covering all transactions relating to the license hereby granted, and Licensor and its duly authorized representatives shall have the right at all reasonable hours of the day to an examination of said books of account and records and of all other documents and materials in the possession or under the control of Licensee with respect to the subject matter and terms of this agreement, and shall have free and full access thereto for said purposes and for the purpose of making extracts therefrom. Upon demand of Licensor, Licensee shall at its own expense furnish to Licensor a detailed statement by an independent certified public accountant showing the number, description, gross sales price, itemized deductions from gross sales price and net sale price of the articles covered by this agreement distributed and/or sold by Licensee to the date of Licensor's demand. All books of account and records shall be kept available for at least _____ years after the termination of this license.

12. Bankruptcy, Violation, etc.

(a) If Licensee shall not have commenced in good faith to manufacture and distribute in substantial quantities all the articles listed in paragraph 1 within _____ months after the date of this agreement or if at any time thereafter in any calendar month Licensee fails to sell any of the articles (or any class or category of the articles), Licensor in addition to all other remedies available to it hereunder may terminate this license with respect to any articles or class or category thereof which have not been manufactured and distributed during such month, by giving written notice of termination to Licensee. Such notice shall be effective when mailed by Licensor.

(b) If Licensee files a petition in bankruptcy or is adjudicated a bankrupt or if a petition in bankruptcy is filed against Licensee or if it becomes insolvent, or makes an assignment for the benefit of its creditors or an arrangement pursuant to any bankruptcy law, or if Licensee discontinues its business or if a receiver is appointed for it or its business, the license hereby granted shall automatically terminate forthwith without any notice whatsoever being necessary. In the event this license is so terminated, Licensee, its receivers, representatives, trustees, agents, administrator, successors and/or assigns shall have no right to sell, exploit or in any way deal with or in any articles covered by this agreement or any carton, container, packing or wrapping material, advertising, promotional or display material pertaining thereto, except with and under the special consent and instructions of Licensor in writing, which they shall be obligated to follow.

(c) If Licensee shall violate any of its other obligations under the terms of this agreement, Licensor shall have the right to terminate the license hereby granted upon _____ days' notice in writing, and such notice of termination shall become effective unless Licensee shall completely remedy the violation within the _____ day period and satisfy Licensor that such violation has been remedied.

(d) Termination of the license under the provisions of paragraph 12 shall be without prejudice to any rights which Licensor may otherwise have against Licensee. Upon the termination of this license, notwithstanding anything to the contrary herein, all royalties on sales theretofore made shall become immediately due and payable and no minimum royalties shall be repayable or avoidable.

13. Sponsorship by Competitive Product

In the event that any of the articles listed in paragraph 1 conflicts with any product of a present or future sponsor of a program on which the Name appears or is used, or with any product of a subsidiary or affiliate of such sponsor, then Licensor shall have the right to terminate this agreement as to such article or articles by written notice to Licensee effective not less than _____ days after the date such notice is given. In the event of such termination, Licensee shall have _____ days after the effective date of such termination to dispose of all of such articles on hand or in process of manufacture prior to such notice, in accordance with the provisions of paragraph 15. However, in the event such termination is effective as to all the articles subject to this agreement and the advance guarantee for the then current year has not been fully accounted for by actual royalties by the end of the _____ disposal period, Licensor shall refund to Licensee the difference between the advance guarantee which has been paid for such contract year and the actual royalties. The refund provision contained in the preceding sentence pertains only to termination occurring pursuant to this paragraph 13, and shall not affect the applicability of any other paragraph to such termination except as expressly contradicted herein.

14. Final Statement Upon Termination or Expiration

_____ days before the expiration of this license and, in the event of its termination, _____ days after receipt of notice of termination or the happening of the event which terminates this agreement where no notice is required, a statement showing the number and description of articles covered by this agreement on hand or in process shall be furnished by Licensee to Licensor. Licensor shall have the right to take a physical inventory to ascertain or verify such inventory and statement, and refusal by Licensee to submit to such physical inventory by Licensor shall forfeit Licensee's right to dispose of such inventory, Licensor retaining all other legal and equitable rights Licensor may have in the circumstances.

15. Disposal of Stock Upon Termination or Expiration

After termination of the license under the provisions of paragraph 12, Licensee, except as otherwise provided in this agreement, may dispose of articles covered by this agreement which are on hand or in process at the time notice of termination is received for a period of _____ days after notice of termination, provided advances and royalties with respect to that period are paid and statements are furnished for that period in accordance with paragraph 2. Notwithstanding anything to the contrary herein, Licensee shall not manufacture, sell or dispose of any articles covered by this license after its expiration or its termination based on the failure of Licensee to affix notice of copyright, trademark or service mark registration or any other notice to the articles, cartons, containers, or packing or wrapping material or advertising, promotional or display material, or because of the departure by Licensee from the quality and style approved by Licensor pursuant to paragraph 7.

16. Effect of Termination or Expiration

Upon and after the expiration or termination of this license, all rights granted to Licensee hereunder shall forthwith revert to Licensor, who shall be free to license others to use the Name in connection with the manufacture, sale and distribution of the articles covered hereby and Licensee will refrain from further use of the Name or any further reference to it, direct or indirect, or anything deemed by Licensor to be similar to the Name in connection with the manufacture, sale or distribution of Licensee's products, except as provided in paragraph 15.

17. Licensor's Remedies

(a) Licensee acknowledges that its failure (except as otherwise provided herein) to commence in good faith to manufacture and distribute in substantial quantities any one or more of the articles listed in paragraph 1 within _____ months after the date of this agreement and to continue during the term hereof to diligently and continuously manufacture, distribute and sell the articles covered by this agreement or any class or category thereof will result in immediate damages to Licensor.

(b) Licensee acknowledges that its failure (except as otherwise provided herein) to cease the manufacture, sale or distribution of the articles covered by this agreement or any class or category thereof at the termination or expiration of this agreement will result in immediate and irremediable damage to Licensor and to the rights of any subsequent licensee. Licensee acknowledges and admits that there is no adequate remedy at law for such failure to cease manufacture, sale or distribution, and Licensee agrees that in the event of such failure Licensor shall be entitled to equitable relief by way of temporary and permanent injunctions and such other further relief as any court with jurisdiction may deem just and proper.

(c) Resort to any remedies referred to herein shall not be construed as a waiver of any other rights and remedies to which Licensor is entitled under this agreement or otherwise.

18. Excuse For Nonperformance

Licensee shall be released from its obligations hereunder and this license shall terminate in the event that governmental regulations or other causes arising out of a state of national emergency or war or causes beyond the control of the parties render performance impossible and one party so informs the other in writing of such causes and its desire to be so released. In such events, all royalties on sales theretofore made shall become immediately due and payable and no minimum royalties shall be repayable.

19. Notices

All notices and statements to be given, and all payments to be made hereunder, shall be given or made at the respective addresses of the parties as set forth above unless notification of a change of address is given in writing, and the date of mailing shall be deemed the date the notice or statement is given.

20. No Joint Venture

Nothing herein contained shall be construed to place the parties in the relationship of partners or joint venturers, and Licensee shall have no power to obligate or bind Licensor in any manner whatsoever.

21. No Assignment or Sublicense by Licensee

This agreement and all rights and duties hereunder are personal to Licensee and shall not, without the written consent of Licensor, be assigned, mortgaged, sublicensed or otherwise encumbered by Licensee or by operation of law. Licensor may assign but shall furnish written notice of assignment.

22. No Waiver

None of the terms of this agreement can be waived or modified except by an express agreement in writing signed by both parties. There are no representations, promises, warranties, covenants or undertakings other than those contained in this agreement, which represents the entire understanding of the parties. The failure of either party hereto to enforce, or the delay by either party in enforcing, any of its rights under this agreement shall not be deemed a continuing waiver or a modification thereof and either party may, within the time provided by applicable law, commence appropriate legal proceeding to enforce any or all of such rights. No person, firm, group or corporation （whether included in the Name or otherwise） other than Licensee and Licensor shall be deemed to have acquired any rights by reason of anything contained in this agreement, except as provided in paragraphs 6 and 21.

In witness whereof, the parties have caused this instrument to be duly executed as of the day and year first above written.

_____, Licensor

By_____

Title:

_____, Licensee

By_____

Title:

协议由_____公司（以下称为许可方）和_____（以下称为被许可方）于_____年_____月_____日签订。

鉴于许可方拥有具有一定价值并经注册的商标和服务标志，且拥有并可出售其他如附文第一节所述的许可方财产，其中包括"商标"。这一商标在广播或电视中经常使用，并出现在各种促销和广告业务中，得到公众的广泛认可，在公众印象中与许可方有密切关系；

鉴于被许可方意于在制造、出售、分销产品时使用这一商标；

因此考虑到双方的保证，达成如下协议：

一、授予许可

1．产品

根据以下规定的条款，许可方授予被许可方，被许可方接受单独使用这一商标的许可权力，且只在制造和出售、分销以下产品时使用。

（加入产品描述）

2．地域

许可协议只在_____地区有效。被许可方同意不在其他地区直接或间接使用或授权使用这一商标，且不在知情的情况下向有意或有可能在其他地区出售协议下产品的第三者销售该产品。

3．期限

许可协议自_____日生效,如未提前终止,至_____日期满。若满足协议条件,本协议期限每年自动续展,直至最后一次续展终止于_____年1X月31日。始于_____年1X月31日,本许可协议在每一期末自动续展一年,到下一年的1X月31日止,除非一方在协议到期前30天以前书面通知另一方终止协议的执行。

二、付款方式

1. 比例

被许可方同意向许可方支付其或其附属公司、子公司等出售协议产品的净销售额的_____%作为使用费。"净销售额"指总销售额减去数量折扣和利润,但不包括现金折扣和不可收账目折扣。在制造、出售或利用产品时的费用均不可从被许可方应支付的使用费中折扣。被许可方同意如向其他许可方支付更高的使用费或更高比例的许可使用费,将自动马上适用于本协议。

2. 最低限度使用费

被许可方同意向许可方支付最低限度使用费_____美元,作为对合同第一期应支付使用费的最低保证,上述最低限度使用费将在第一期的最后一天或此前支付。在协议签字时支付的预付款将不包括在内。此最低限度使用费在任何情况下都不会再归还给被许可方。

3. 定期报告

第一批协议产品装运后,被许可方应立即向许可方提供完整、精确的报告,说明被许可方在前一期售出的产品数量、概况、总销售额、详细列明的总销售额折扣、净销售额及前一期中的利润。被许可方将使用后附的,由许可方提供给其的报告样本。无论被许可方在前一期中是否销售了产品,均应向许可方提供报告。

4. 使用费支付

除上述最低使用费以外的使用费需在销售期后_____日交付,同时提交的还有上述要求的报告。许可方接受被许可方按协议要求提供的报告和使用费(或兑现支付使用的支票)后,如发现报告或支付中有不一致或错误,可以在任何时间提出质疑,被许可方须及时改正、支付。支付应用美元。在许可地内的应缴国内税由被许可方支付。

三、专有权

1. 除非许可方认可在协议有效期内不在协议有效区域内再授予别人销售第一节所述产品时使用这一商标,本协议不限制许可方授予其他人使用这一商标的权力。

2. 协议规定如果许可方向被许可方提出购买第一节所述产品,用于奖励、赠给或其他促销安排,被许可方有10天时间决定是否同意。如果被许可方在10天内未接受这一要求,许可方有权通过其他生产者进行奖励、赠给或其他促销安排。在这种情况下,当其他生产者的价格比许可方向被许可方支付的高时,被许可方有3天时间去满足生产者生产此种产品的要求。被许可方保证在未得到许可方书面同意前,不把协议产品与其他产品或服务一起作为奖励,不与其他作为奖励的产品或服务一起出售协议产品。

四、信誉

被许可方承认与该商标相关联的信誉的价值,确认这一商标、相关权力及与该商标相关联的信誉只属于许可方,这一商标在公众印象中有从属的含义。

五、许可方的所有权及许可方权利的保护

1. 被许可方同意在协议有效期内及其后,不置疑许可方就该商标享有的所有权和其他权利,不质疑本协议的有效性。如果许可方能及时收到索赔和诉讼的通知,许可方保护被许可方,使其不受仅由本协议所授权的商标使用引起的索赔和诉讼的损害,许可方可选择就这样的诉讼进行辩护。在未得到许可方的同意之前,不应就这样的索赔和诉讼达成解决办法。

2. 被许可方同意向许可方提供必要的帮助来保护许可方就该商标拥有的权利。许可方根据自己的意愿,可以自己的名义、被许可方的名义或双方的名义针对索赔和诉讼应诉。被许可方在可知范围内将书面告知许可方就协议产品的商标的侵权和仿制行为;只有许可方有权决定是否对这样的侵权和仿制行为采取行动。若事先未得到许可方的书面同意,被许可方不应就侵权和仿制行为提出诉讼或采取任何行动。

六、被许可方提供的保证及产品责任保险

被许可方负责为自己和／或许可方就其非经授权使用协议产品商标、专利、工艺、设计思想、方法引起的索赔、诉讼或损失,就其他行为或产品瑕疵导致的索赔、诉讼或损失进行辩护,并使许可方免受损失。被许可方将自己负担费用,向一家在_____地区有经营资格的XX公司承保产品责任险,为许可方(同时也为被许可方)因产品瑕疵导致的索赔、诉讼或损失提供合理的保护。被许可方将向许可方提交以许可方为被保险人的已付款保险单,在此基础上,许可方才能同意产品出售。如果对保险单有所改动,需事先得到许可方的同意。许可方有权要求被许可方向其提供新的保险单。许可方一词包括其官员、董事、代理人、雇员、下属和附属机构,名字被许可使用的人,包装制造人,名字被许可使用的广播、电视节目制作人、节目转播台、节目主办者和其广告代理,及这些人的官员、董事、代理人和雇员。

七、商品质量

被许可方同意协议产品将符合高标准,其式样、外观和质量将能发挥其最好效益,将保护并加强商标名誉及其代表的信誉。同时协议产品的生产、出售、分销将遵守适用的联邦、州、地方法律,并不得影响许可方、其计划及商标本身的名声。为了达到这一目标,被许可方应在出售协议产品之前,免费寄给许可方一定量的产品样品,其包装纸箱、集装箱和包装材料,以取得许可方的书面同意。协议产品及其纸箱、集装箱和包装材料的质量和式样需得到许可方的同意。向许可方提交的每份产品在得到其书面同意前不能视作通过。样品按本节所述得到同意后,被许可方在未得到许可方的书面同意前不能作实质变动。而许可方除非提前60天书面通知被许可方,不能撤销其对样品的同意。在被许可方开始出售协议产品后,应许可方的要求,将免费向许可方提供不超过_____件的随机抽样样品及相关的纸箱、包装箱和包装材料。

八、标签

1. 被许可方同意在出售许可合同项下产品或在产品广告、促销和展示材料中将根据第一节附文中商标权第五、六条的规定标明"注册商标公司_____年",或其他许可方要求的标志。如果产品、或其广告、促销、展示材料含有商标或服务标志,应标明注册的法律通知及申请。如果产品在市场出售时其包装纸箱、集装箱或包装材料上带有商标,在上述物品上也应标明相应标志。被许可方在使用小牌、标签、标记或其他标志时,在广告、促销和展示材料中标明商标,需事先得到许可方的同意。许可方的同意不构成此协议下许可方权力和被许可方责任的放弃。

2. 被许可方同意与许可方真诚合作,确保和维护许可方(或许可方的授予人)对商标拥有的权力。如果商标、产品、相关材料事先未注册,被许可方应许可方的要求,由许可方承担费用,以许可方的名义对版权、商标、服务标志进行恰当注册,或应许可方的要求,以被许可方自己的名义注册。但是,双方确认本协议不能视作向被许可方转让了任何与商标有关的权利、所有权和利益。双方确认除根据本许可协议,被许可方享有严格按协议使用商标的权利外,其他相关权利都由许可方保留。被许可方同意协议终止或期满时,将其已获得的或在执行协议项下行为而获得的有关商标的一切权利、权益、信誉、所有权等交回给许可方。被许可方将采取一切许可方要求的方式来完成上述行为。此种交回的权利范围只能基于本协议或双方的契约而产生。

3．被许可方同意其对商标的使用不损害许可方的利益,而且不因为其使用该商标而取得关于商标的任何权利。

九、促销资料

1．在任何情况下,被许可方如果期望得到本协议产品的宣传材料,那么生产该宣传材料的成本和时间由被许可方承担。所有涉及本协议商标或其复制品的宣传材料的产权应归被许可方所有,尽管该宣传材料可能由被许可方发明或使用,而许可方应有权使用或将其许可给其他方。

2．许可方有权,但没有义务使用本协议商标或被许可方的商标,以使本协议商标、许可方或被许可方或其项目能够完满或卓越。许可方没有义务继续在电台或电视台节目中宣传本协议商标或其数字、符号或设计等。

3．被许可方同意,在没有得到许可方的事先书面批准的情况下,不在电台或电视台作使用本协议商标的产品的宣传或广告。许可方可以自由决定同意批准或不批准。

十、分销

1．被许可方同意将恪尽勤勉,并且持续制造、分销或销售本协议产品,而且还将为此作出必要和适当的安排。

2．被许可方在没有得到许可方的书面同意前,不得将本协议产品销售给那些以获取佣金为目的的、有可能将本协议产品当做促销赠品的、以促进其搭售活动目的的及销售方式有问题的批发商、零售商、零售店及贸易商等。

十一、会计记录

被许可方同意建立和保留所有有关本协议项下交易活动的会计账本和记录。许可方或其全权代表有权在任何合理的时间内查询该会计账本或记录及其他所有与交易有关的、在被许可方控制之下的文件和资料。许可方或其全权代表为上述目的可摘录其中的内容。应许可方的要求,被许可方应自行承担费用,将其至许可方提出要求之日止的所有销售活动情况,包括数量、规格、毛价格和净价格等以独立的、公开账本方式,向被许可方提供一份详细的会计报告声明。所有的会计账本和记录应保留至本协议终止两年之后。

十二、破产、违约等

1．如果被许可方在达成协议后3个月内未开始生产和销售一定量的第一节所述的产品,或者3个月后的某个月未销售产品(或类产品),许可方在采取其他补偿措施以外,可书面通知被许可方因其该月未生产销售协议产品(或类产品)而终止合同。通知自许可方寄出之日起生效。

2．如果被许可方提出破产陈诉,或被判破产,或对被许可方提起破产诉状，或被许可方无偿还能力，或被许可方为其债权人的利益而转让，或依照破产法作出安排，或被许可方停止经营，或有人接收其经营，则此许可合同自动终止。除非得到许可方书面表示的同意意见，被许可方、其接收者、代表、受托人、代理人、管理人、继承人或被转让人无权出售、利用或以任何方式经营协议产品，或相关的纸箱、集装箱、包装材料、广告、促销和陈列材料。这是必须遵守的。

3. 如果被许可方违反了本协议条款下的义务，许可方在提前10天书面通知后有权终止合同，除非被许可方在10天内对其违约行为作出全部补偿，令许可方满意。

4. 根据第十二条所述条款，终止许可合同将不影响许可方对被许可方拥有的其他权利。当协议终止时，基于销售额的使用费即刻到期须马上支付，不能缺交最低限度使用费，且最低限度使用费将不返还。

十三、竞争产品

如果协议第一节所述的产品与目前、今后生产的使用该商标的产品，或其下属、附属机构生产的使用该商标的产品相矛盾，许可方有权终止协议。许可方书面通知被许可方后30天此通知生效。根据第十五条的条款，被许可方在协议终止后有60天时间来处理手中的协议产品和在接到终止协议通知前正在生产的产品。然而，如果在60天期间，对协议产品的终止有效，被许可方应缴纳的实际使用费少于当年的预付保证金，许可方将把签约当年已付的预付保证金与实际使用费之间的差额退还给被许可方。上句所述的退还条款仅适用于第十三条规定的协议终止情况，而不影响除表述相矛盾的条款外其他所有条款的适用性。

十四、最后报告

在协议期满前60天内，或收到终止通知的10天以内，或是在无须通知的协议终止情况下10天以内，被许可方应向许可方出具一份报告以说明手中的和正在加工中的协议产品的数量和种类。许可方有权进行实地盘存以确认存货情况和报告的准确。若被许可方拒绝许可方的核查，将失去处理存货的权利。许可方保留其拥有的其他法律权利。

十五、存货处理

协议根据第十二条的条款终止后，在被许可方已支付预付款和使用费，并已按第二条要求提供报告的情况下，如协议中无另外规定，被许可方可以在收到终止协议通知后60天内处理其手中的和正在加工中的协议产品。合同到期后，或因被许可方未在产品，或其包装纸箱、集装箱、包装材料和广告、促销、展示材料上加贴版权、商标和服务标志注册标签，或因被许可方生产的产品的质量、式样不符合第七条所述许可方的要求，而导致协议终止,被许可方不得再生产、出售、处理任何协议产品。

十六、协议终止或期满的效果

协议终止或期满后,授予被许可方的一切权利即刻返还许可方。许可方可自由地向他人转让在生产、出售、分销协议产品过程中使用该商标的权利。被许可方不得再使用该商标,或直接、间接地涉及该商标。除第十五条所述的情况外,被许可方不得在制造、出售、分销其自己的产品时使用类似的商标。

十七、对许可方的补偿

1. 被许可方认识到(除另有规定外),如果其在协议生效后 3 个月内未开始生产、分销一定量的协议产品,或在协议期内未能持续地生产、分销、出售协议产品,将立即导致许可方的损失。

2. 被许可方认识到(除另有规定外),如果在协议终止或期满后,未能停止生产、出售、分销协议产品,将导致许可方不可弥补的损失,并损害后继被许可方的权利。被许可方认识到,对此没有恰当的法律补偿。被许可方同意在此情况下,许可方有权获得衡平法上的救济,对被许可方实施暂时或永久禁令,或实施其他法庭认为公正、恰当的裁决。

3. 实施这些补偿措施,不影响许可方在协议中规定享有的其他权利和补偿。

十八、无法执行协议的原因

若由于政府法规的变化,或因国家紧急状态、战争状态和其他无法控制的原因,一方无法执行协议,书面通知对方原因和希望解除协议的意愿,则被许可方将被免除协议下的义务,本协议将终止,而基于销售额的使用费将立即到期应付,最低限度使用费将不会返还。

十九、通知

除非有更改地址的书面通知,所有的通知、报告、声明及款项均应寄至协议记载的双方正式地址。邮寄日视作通知、报告等发出之日。

二十、不允许合资企业

根据本协议,双方不应组成合伙人关系或合资企业。被许可方无权要求或限制许可方的行为。

二十一、被许可方不得再行转让、许可

本协议和协议下被许可方的权利、义务,未经许可方书面同意,不得转让、抵押、再许可,不因法律的实施或被许可方的原因而受到阻碍。

许可方可以进行转让,但需向被许可方提供书面通知。

二十二、无免责

除非有双方签字的书面契约,本协议的任何条款不得被放弃或修改。

本协议以外的陈述、允诺、保证、契约或许诺都不能代表双方全部的共识。任一方不行使或延误行使其协议下的权利，将不被视作对协议权利的放弃或修改。任一方可在适用法律允许的时间内采取恰当的法律程序强制行使权利。除了如第六条和第十二条的规定，被许可方和许可方以外的任何人、公司、集团（无论是否涉及该商标），都不因本协议而获得任何权利。

按契约规定时间执行协议的双方：

许可方　　　　　　　　　　被许可方

签字人：　　　　　　　　　签字人：

职务：　　　　　　　　　　职务：

【名称】

自我评价 Self-Assessment Log

In this Chapter, you worked through these activities. How did each of them help you become a better learner? Check A lot, A little, or Not at all.

	A lot	A little	Not at all
I gathered information about Contracts for Sales of Goods from the Internet.	❑	❑	❑
I knew the details about Contracts for Joint Ventures.	❑	❑	❑
I got key terms and articles for Contracts for Labor Services.	❑	❑	❑
I learned words and expressions on Contracts for Lease.	❑	❑	❑
I understood the importance related to contract for International Technology Transfer and International Licensing.	❑	❑	❑

(Add something) _____

_____

附录一
APPENDIX I

CISG
联合国国际货物销售合同公约

United Nations Convention on Contracts for the International Sale of Goods (1980)

Preamble

The States Parties to this Convention

Bearing in Mind the broad objectives in the resolutions adopted by the sixth special session of the General Assembly of the United Nations on the establishment of a New International Economic Order,

Considering that the development of international trade on the basis of equality and mutual benefit is an important element in promoting friendly relations among States,

Beeing of the Opinion that the adoption of uniform rules which govern contracts for the international sale of goods and take into account the different social, economic and legal systems would contribute to the removal of legal barriers in international trade and promote the development of international trade, have decreed as follows:

PART I
Sphere of Application and General Provisions

Chapter I Sphere of Application

● Article 1

(1) This Convention applies to contracts of sale of goods between parties whose places of business are in different States:

(a) when the States are Contracting States; or

(b) when the rules of private international law lead to the application of the law of a Contracting State.

(2) The fact that the parties have their places of business in different States is to be disregarded whenever this fact does not appear either from the contract or from any dealings between, or from information disclosed by, the parties at any time before or at the conclusion of the contract.

(3) Neither the nationality of the parties nor the civil or commercial character of the parties or of the contract is to be taken into consideration in determining the application of this Convention.

● Article 2

This Convention does not apply to sales:

(a) of goods bought for personal, family or household use, unless the seller, at any time before or at the conclusion of the contract, neither knew nor ought to have known that the goods were bought for any such use;

(b) by auction;

(c) on execution or otherwise by authority of law;

(d) of stocks, shares, investment securities, negotiable instruments or money;

(e) of ships, vessels, hovercraft or aircraft;

(f) of electricity.

● Article 3

(1) Contracts for the supply of goods to be manufactured or produced are to be considered sales unless the party who orders the goods undertakes to supply a substantial part of the materials necessary for such manufacture or production.

(2) This Convention does not apply to contracts in which the preponderant part of the obligations of the party who furnishes the goods consists in the supply of labour or other services.

● Article 4

This Convention governs only the formation of the contract of sale and the rights and obligations of the seller and the buyer arising from such a contract. In particular, except as otherwise expressly provided in this Convention, it is not concerned with:

(a) the validity of the contract or of any of its provisions or of any usage;

(b) the effect which the contract may have on the property in the goods sold.

● Article 5

This Convention does not apply to the liability of the seller for death or personal injury caused by the goods to any person.

● Article 6

The parties may exclude the application of this Convention or, subject to article 12, derogate from or vary the effect of any of its provisions.

Chapter II   General Provisions

● Article 7

(1) In the interpretation of this Convention, regard is to be had to its international character and to the need to promote uniformity in its application and the observance of good faith in international trade.

(2) Questions concerning matters governed by this Convention which are not expressly settled in it are to be settled in conformity with the general principles on which it is based or, in the absence of such principles, in conformity with the law applicable by virtue of the rules of private international law.

● Article 8

(1) For the purposes of this Convention statements made by and other conduct of a party are to be interpreted according to his intent where the other party knew or could not have been unaware what that intent was.

(2) If the preceding paragraph is not applicable, statements made by and other conduct of a party are to be interpreted according to the understanding that a reasonable person of the same kind as the other party would have had in the same circumstances.

(3) In determining the intent of a party or the understanding a reasonable person would have had, due consideration is to be given to all relevant circumstances of the case including the negotiations, any practices which the parties have established between themselves, usages and any subsequent conduct of the parties.

● Article 9

(1) The parties are bound by any usage to which they have agreed and by any practices which they have established between themselves.

(2) The parties are considered, unless otherwise agreed, to have impliedly made applicable to their contract or its formation a usage of which the parties knew or ought to have known and which in international trade is widely known to, and regularly observed by, parties to contracts of the type involved in the particular trade concerned.

● Article 10

For the purposes of this Convention:

(a) if a party has more than one place of business, the place of business is that which has the closest relationship to the contract and its performance, having regard to the circumstances known to or contemplated by the parties at any time before or at the conclusion of the contract;

(b) if a party does not have a place of business, reference is to be made to his habitual residence.

● Article 11

A contract of sale need not be concluded in or evidenced by writing and is not subject to any other requirement as to form. It may be proved by any means, including witnesses.

● Article 12

Any provision of article 11, article 29 or Part II of this Convention that allows a contract of sale or its modification or termination by agreement or any offer, acceptance or other indication of intention to be made in any form other than in writing does not apply where any party has his place of business in a Contracting State which has made a declaration under article 96 of this Convention. The parties may not derogate from or vary the effect or this article.

● Article 13

For the purposes of this Convention "writing" includes telegram and telex.

PART II
Formation of the Contract

● Article 14

(1) A proposal for concluding a contract addressed to one or more specific persons constitutes an offer if it is sufficiently definite and indicates the intention of the offeror to be bound in case of acceptance. A proposal is sufficiently definite if it indicates the goods and expressly or implicitly fixes or makes provision for determining the quantity and the price.

(2) A proposal other than one addressed to one or more specific persons is to be considered merely as an invitation to make offers, unless the contrary is clearly indicated by the person making the proposal.

● Article 15

(1) An offer becomes effective when it reaches the offeree.

(2) An offer, even if it is irrevocable, may be withdrawn if the withdrawal reaches the offeree before or at the same time as the offer.

● Article 16

(1) Until a contract is concluded an offer may be revoked if the revocation reaches the offeree before he has dispatched an acceptance.

(2) However, an offer cannot be revoked:

(a) if it indicates, whether by stating a fixed time for acceptance or otherwise, that it is irrevocable; or

(b) if it was reasonable for the offeree to rely on the offer as being irrevocable and the offeree has acted in reliance on the offer.

● Article 17

An offer, even if it is irrevocable, is terminated when a rejection reaches the offeror.

● Article 18

(1) A statement made by or other conduct of the offeree indicating assent to an offer is an acceptance. Silence or inactivity does not in itself amount to acceptance.

(2) An acceptance of an offer becomes effective at the moment the indication of assent reaches the offeror. An acceptance is not effective if the indication of assent does not reach the offeror within the time he has fixed or, if no time is fixed, within a reasonable time, due account being taken of the circumstances of the transaction, including the rapidity of the means of communication employed by the offeror. An oral offer must be accepted immediately unless the circumstances indicate otherwise.

(3) However, if, by virtue of the offer or as a result of practices which the parties have established between themselves or of usage, the offeree may indicate assent by performing an act, such as one relating to the dispatch of the goods or payment of the price, without notice to the offeror, the acceptance is effective at the moment the act is performed, provided that the act is performed within the period of time laid down in the preceding paragraph.

● Article 19

(1) A reply to an offer which purports to be an acceptance but contains additions, limitations or other modifications is a rejection of the offer and constitutes a counter-offer.

(2) However, a reply to an offer which purports to be an acceptance but con-

tains additional or different terms which do not materially alter the terms of the offer constitutes an acceptance, unless the offeror, without undue delay, objects orally to the discrepancy or dispatches a notice to that effect. If he does not so object, the terms of the contract are the terms of the offer with the modifications contained in the acceptance.

(3) Additional or different terms relating, among other things, to the price, payment, quality and quantity of the goods, place and time of delivery, extent of one party's liability to the other or the settlement of disputes are considered to alter the terms of the offer materially.

● Article 20

(1) A period of time for acceptance fixed by the offeror in a telegram or a letter begins to run from the moment the telegram is handed in for dispatch or from the date shown on the letter or, if no such date is shown, from the date shown on the envelope. A period of time for acceptance fixed by the offeror by telephone, telex or other means of instantaneous communication, begins to run from the moment that the offer reaches the offeree.

(2) Official holidays or non-business days occurring during the period for acceptance are included in calculating the period. However, if a notice of acceptance cannot be delivered at the address of the offeror on the last day of the period because that day falls on an official holiday or a non-business day at the place of business of the offeror, the period is extended until the first business day which follows.

● Article 21

(1) A late acceptance is nevertheless effective as an acceptance if without delay the offeror orally so informs the offeree or dispatches a notice to that effect.

(2) If a letter or other writing containing a late acceptance shows that it has been sent in such circumstances that if its transmission had been normal it would have reached the offeror in due time, the late acceptance is effective as an acceptance unless, without delay, the offeror orally informs the offeree that he considers his offer as having lapsed or dispatches a notice to that effect.

● Article 22

An acceptance may be withdrawn if the withdrawal reaches the offeror before or at the same time as the acceptance would have become effective.

● Article 23

A contract is concluded at the moment when an acceptance of an offer becomes effective in accordance with the provisions of this Convention.

● Article 24

For the purposes of this Part of the Convention, an offer, declaration of acceptance or any other indication of intention "reaches" the addressee when it is made orally to him or delivered by any other means to him personally, to his place of business or mailing address or, if he does not have a place of business or mailing address, to his habitual residence.

PART III
Sale of Goods

Chapter I General Provisions

● Article 25

A breach of contract committed by one of the parties is fundamental if it results in such detriment to the other party as substantially to deprive him of what he is entitled to expect under the contract, unless the party in breach did not foresee and a reasonable person of the same kind in the same circumstances would not have foreseen such a result.

● Article 26

A declaration of avoidance of the contract is effective only if made by notice to the other party.

● Article 27

Unless otherwise expressly provided in this Part of the Convention, if any notice, request or other communication is given or made by a party in accordance with this Part and by means appropriate in the circumstances, a delay or error in the transmission of the communication or its failure to arrive does not deprive that party of the right to rely on the communication.

● Article 28

If, in accordance with the provisions of this Convention, one party is entitled to require performance of any obligation by the other party, a court is not bound to enter a judgement for specific performance unless the court would do so under its own law in respect of similar contracts of sale not governed by this Convention.

● Article 29

(1) A contract may be modified or terminated by the mere agreement of the parties.

(2) A contract in writing which contains a provision requiring any modification or termination by agreement to be in writing may not be otherwise modified or terminated by agreement. However, a party may be precluded by his conduct from asserting such a provision to the extent that the other party has relied on that conduct.

Chapter II Obligations of the Seller
● Article 30

The seller must deliver the goods, hand over any documents relating to them and transfer the property in the goods, as required by the contract and this Convention.

Section I. Delivery of the goods and handing over of documents
● Article 31

If the seller is not bound to deliver the goods at any other particular place, his obligation to deliver consists:

(a) if the contract of sale involves carriage of the goods—in handing the goods over to the first carrier for transmission to the buyer;

(b) if, in cases not within the preceding subparagraph, the contract related to specific goods, or unidentified goods to be drawn from a specific stock or to be manufactured or produced, and at the time of the conclusion of the contract the parties knew that the goods were at, or were to be manufactured or produced at, a particular place—in placing the goods at the buyer's disposal at that place;

(c) in other cases—in placing the goods at the buyer's disposal at the place where the seller had his place of business at the time of the conclusion of the contract.

● Article 32

(1) If the seller, in accordance with the contract or this Convention, hands the goods over to a carrier and if the goods are not clearly identified to the contract by markings on the goods, by shipping documents or otherwise, the seller must give the buyer notice of the consignment specifying the goods.

(2) If the seller is bound to arrange for carriage of the goods, he must make such contracts as are necessary for carriage to the place fixed by means of

transportation appropriate in the circumstances and according to the usual terms for such transportation.

(3) If the seller is not bound to effect insurance in respect of the carriage of the goods, he must, at the buyer's request, provide him with all available information necessary to enable him to effect such insurance.

● Article 33

The seller must deliver the goods:

(a) if a date is fixed by or determinable from the contract, on that date;

(b) if a period of time is fixed by or determinable from the contract, at any time within that period unless circumstances indicate that the buyer is to choose a date; or

(c) in any other case, within a reasonable time after the conclusion of the contract.

● Article 34

If the seller is bound to hand over documents relating to the goods, he must hand them over at the time and place and in the form required by the contract. If the seller has handed over documents before that time, he may, up to that time, cure any lack of conformity in the documents, if the exercise of this right does not cause the buyer unreasonable inconvenience or unreasonable expense. However, the buyer retains any right to claim damages as provided for in this Convention.

Section II. Conformity of the goods and third party claims

● Article 35

(1) The seller must deliver goods which are of the quantity, quality and description required by the contract and which are contained or packaged in the manner required by the contract.

(2) Except where the parties have agreed otherwise, the goods do not conform with the contract unless they:

(a) are fit for the purposes for which goods of the same description would ordinarily be used;

(b) are fit for any particular purpose expressly or impliedly made known to the seller at the time of the conclusion of the contract, except where the circumstances show that the buyer did not rely, or that it was unreasonable for him to rely, on the seller's skill and judgement;

(c) possess the qualities of goods which the seller has held out to the buyer as a sample or model;

(d) are contained or packaged in the manner usual for such goods or, where there is no such manner, in a manner adequate to preserve and protect the goods.

(3) The seller is not liable under subparagraphs (a) to (d) of the preceding paragraph for any lack of conformity of the goods if at the time of the conclusion of the contract the buyer knew or could not have been unaware of such lack of conformity.

● Article 36

(1) The seller is liable in accordance with the contract and this Convention for any lack of conformity which exists at the time when the risk passes to the buyer, even though the lack of conformity becomes apparent only after that time.

(2) The seller is also liable for any lack of conformity which occurs after the time indicated in the preceding paragraph and which is due to a breach of any of his obligations, including a breach of any guarantee that for a period of time the goods will remain fit for their ordinary purpose or for some particular purpose or will retain specified qualities or characteristics.

● Article 37

If the seller has delivered goods before the date for delivery, he may, up to that date, deliver any missing part or make up any deficiency in the quantity of the goods delivered, or deliver goods in replacement of any non-conforming goods delivered or remedy any lack of conformity in the goods delivered, provided that the exercise of this right does not cause the buyer unreasonable inconvenience or unreasonable expense. However, the buyer retains any right to claim damages as provided for in this Convention.

● Article 38

(1) The buyer must examine the goods, or cause them to be examined, within as short a period as is practicable in the circumstances.

(2) If the contract involves carriage of the goods, examination may be deferred until after the goods have arrived at their destination.

(3) If the goods are redirected in transit or redispatched by the buyer without a reasonable opportunity for examination by him and at the time of the conclusion of the contract the seller knew or ought to have known of the possibility of such redirection or redispatch, examination may be deferred until after the goods have arrived at the new destination.

Article 39

(1) The buyer loses the right to rely on a lack of conformity of the goods if he does not give notice to the seller specifying the nature of the lack of conformity within a reasonable time after he has discovered it or ought to have discovered it.

(2) In any event, the buyer loses the right to rely on a lack of conformity of the goods if he does not give the seller notice thereof at the latest within a period of two years from the date on which the goods were actually handed over to the buyer, unless this time-limit is inconsistent with a contractual period of guarantee.

Article 40

The seller is not entitled to rely on the provisions of articles 38 and 39 if the lack of conformity relates to facts of which he knew or could not have been unaware and which he did not disclose to the buyer.

Article 41

The seller must deliver goods which are free from any right or claim of a third party, unless the buyer agreed to take the goods subject to that right or claim. However, if such right or claim is based on industrial property or other intellectual property, the seller's obligation is governed by article 42.

Article 42

(1) The seller must deliver goods which are free from any right or claim of a third party based on industrial property or other intellectual property, of which at the time of the conclusion of the contract the seller knew or could not have been unaware, provided that the right or claim is based on industrial property or other intellectual property:

(a) under the law of the State where the goods will be resold or otherwise used, if it was contemplated by the parties at the time of the conclusion of the contract that the goods would be resold or otherwise used in that State; or

(b) in any other case, under the law of the State where the buyer has his place of business.

(2) The obligation of the seller under the preceding paragraph does not extend to cases where:

(a) at the time of the conclusion of the contract the buyer knew or could not have been unaware of the right or claim; or

(b) the right or claim results from the seller's compliance with technical drawings, designs, formulae or other such specifications furnished by the buyer.

● Article 43

(1) The buyer loses the right to rely on the provisions of article 41 or Article 42 if he does not give notice to the seller specifying the nature of the right or claim of the third party within a reasonable time after he has become aware or ought to have become aware of the right or claim.

(2) The seller is not entitled to rely on the provisions of the preceding paragraph if he knew of the right or claim of the third party and the nature of it.

● Article 44

Notwithstanding the provisions of paragraph (1) of article 39 and paragraph (1) of article 43, the buyer may reduce the price in accordance with Article 50 or claim damages, except for loss of profit, if he has a reasonable excuse for his failure to give the required notice.

Section III. Remedies for breach of contract by the seller

● Article 45

(1) If the seller fails to perform any of his obligations under the contract or this Convention, the buyer may:

(a) exercise the rights provided in articles 46 to 52;

(b) claim damages as provided in articles 74 to 77.

(2) The buyer is not deprived of any right he may have to claim damages by exercising his right to other remedies.

(3) No period of grace may be granted to the seller by a court or arbitral tribunal when the buyer resorts to a remedy for breach of contract.

● Article 46

(1) The buyer may require performance by the seller of his obligations unless the buyer has resorted to a remedy which is inconsistent with this requirement.

(2) If the goods do not conform with the contract, the buyer may require delivery of substitute goods only if the lack of conformity constitutes a fundamental breach of contract and a request for substitute goods is made either in conjunction with notice given under article 39 or within a reasonable time thereafter.

(3) If the goods do not conform with the contract, the buyer may require the seller to remedy the lack of conformity by repair, unless this is unreasonable having regard to all the circumstances. A request for repair must be made either in conjunction with notice given under article 39 or within a reasonable time thereafter.

●Article 47

(1) The buyer may fix an additional period of time of reasonable length for performance by the seller of his obligations.

(2) Unless the buyer has received notice from the seller that he will not perform within the period so fixed, the buyer may not, during that period, resort to any remedy for breach of contract. However, the buyer is not deprived thereby of any right he may have to claim damages for delay in performance.

●Article 48

(1) Subject to article 49, the seller may, even after the date for delivery, remedy at his own expense any failure to perform his obligations, if he can do so without unreasonable delay and without causing the buyer unreasonable inconvenience or uncertainty of reimbursement by the seller of expenses advanced by the buyer. However, the buyer retains any right to claim damages as provided for in this Convention.

(2) If the seller requests the buyer to make known whether he will accept performance and the buyer does not comply with the request within a reasonable time, the seller may perform within the time indicated in his request. The buyer may not, during that period of time, resort to any remedy which is inconsistent with performance by the seller.

(3) A notice by the seller that he will perform within a specified period of time is assumed to include a request, under the preceding paragraph, that the buyer make known his decision.

(4) A request or notice by the seller under paragraph (2) or (3) of this Article is not effective unless received by the buyer.

●Article 49

(1) The buyer may declare the contract avoided:

(a) if the failure by the seller to perform any of his obligations under the contract or this Convention amounts to a fundamental breach of contract; or

(b) in case of non-delivery, if the seller does not deliver the goods within the additional period of time fixed by the buyer in accordance with paragraph (1) of article 47 or declares that he will not deliver within the period so fixed.

(2) However, in cases where the seller has delivered the goods, the buyer loses the right to declare the contract avoided unless he does so:

(a) in respect of late delivery, within a reasonable time after he has become aware that delivery has been made;

(b) in respect of any breach other than late delivery, within a reasonable time:

(i) after he knew or ought to have known of the breach;

(ii) after the expiration of any additional period of time fixed by the buyer in accordance with paragraph (1) of article 47, or after the seller has declared that he will not perform his obligations within such an additional period; or

(iii) after the expiration of any additional period of time indicated by the seller in accordance with paragraph (2) of article 48, or after the buyer has declared that he will not accept performance.

● Article 50

If the goods do not conform with the contract and whether or not the price has already been paid, the buyer may reduce the price in the same proportion as the value that the goods actually delivered had at the time of the delivery bears to the value that conforming goods would have had at that time. However, if the seller remedies any failure to perform his obligations in accordance with article 37 or article 48 or if the buyer refuses to accept performance by the seller in accordance with those Articles, the buyer may not reduce the price.

● Article 51

(1) If the seller delivers only a part of the goods or if only a part of the goods delivered is in conformity with the contract, articles 46 to 50 apply in respect of the part which is missing or which does not conform.

(2) The buyer may declare the contract avoided in its entirety only if the failure to make delivery completely or in conformity with the contract amounts to a fundamental breach of the contract.

● Article 52

(1) If the seller delivers the goods before the date fixed, the buyer may take delivery or refuse to take delivery.

(2) If the seller delivers a quantity of goods greater than that provided for in the contract, the buyer may take delivery or refuse to take delivery of the excess quantity. If the buyer takes delivery of all or part of the excess quantity, he must pay for it at the contract rate.

Chapter III Obligations of the Buyer

● Article 53

The buyer must pay the price for the goods and take delivery of them as required by the contract and this Convention.

Section I. Payment of the price

● Article 54

The buyer's obligation to pay the price includes taking such steps and complying with such formalities as may be required under the contract or any laws and regulations to enable payment to be made.

● Article 55

Where a contract has been validly concluded but does not expressly or implicitly fix or make provision for determining the price, the parties are considered, in the absence of any indication to the contrary, to have impliedly made reference to the price generally charged at the time of the conclusion of the contract for such goods sold under comparable circumstances in the trade concerned.

● Article 56

If the price is fixed according to the weight of the goods, in case of doubt it is to be determined by the net weight.

● Article 57

(1) If the buyer is not bound to pay the price at any other particular place, he must pay it to the seller:

(a) at the seller's place of business; or

(b) if the payment is to be made against the handing over of the goods or of documents, at the place where the handing over takes place.

(2) The seller must bear any increases in the expenses incidental to payment which is caused by a change in his place of business subsequent to the conclusion of the contract.

● Article 58

(1) If the buyer is not bound to pay the price at any other specific time, he must pay it when the seller places either the goods or documents controlling their disposition at the buyer's disposal in accordance with the contract and this Convention. The seller may make such payment a condition for handing over the goods or documents.

(2) If the contract involves carriage of the goods, the seller may dispatch the goods on terms whereby the goods, or documents controlling their disposition, will not be handed over to the buyer except against payment of the price.

(3) The buyer is not bound to pay the price until he has had an opportunity to examine the goods, unless the procedures for delivery or payment agreed upon by the parties are inconsistent with his having such an opportunity.

●Article 59

The buyer must pay the price on the date fixed by or determinable from the contract and this Convention without the need for any request or compliance with any formality on the part of the seller.

Section II. Taking delivery

●Article 60

The buyer's obligation to take delivery consists:

(a) in doing all the acts which could reasonably be expected of him in order to enable the seller to make delivery; and

(b) in taking over the goods.

Section III. Remedies for breach of contract by the buyer

●Article 61

(1) If the buyer fails to perform any of his obligations under the contract or this Convention, the seller may:

(a) exercise the rights provided in articles 62 to 65;

(b) claim damages as provided in articles 74 to 77.

(2) The seller is not deprived of any right he may have to claim damages by exercising his right to other remedies.

(3) No period of grace may be granted to the buyer by a court or arbitral tribunal when the seller resorts to a remedy for breach of contract.

●Article 62

The seller may require the buyer to pay the price, take delivery or perform his other obligations, unless the seller has resorted to a remedy which is inconsistent with this requirement.

●Article 63

(1) The seller may fix an additional period of time of reasonable length for performance by the buyer of his obligations.

(2) Unless the seller has received notice from the buyer that he will not perform within the period so fixed, the seller may not, during that period, resort to any remedy for breach of contract. However, the seller is not deprived thereby of any right he may have to claim damages for delay in performance.

●Article 64

(1) The seller may declare the contract avoided:

(a) if the failure by the buyer to perform any of his obligations under the contract or this Convention amounts to a fundamental breach of contract; or

(b) if the buyer does not, within the additional period of time fixed by the seller in accordance with paragraph (1) of article 63, perform his obligation to pay the price or take delivery of the goods, or if he declares that he will not do so within the period so fixed.

(2) However, in cases where the buyer has paid the price, the seller loses the right to declare the contract avoided unless he does so:

(a) in respect of late performance by the buyer, before the seller has become aware that performance has been rendered; or

(b) in respect of any breach other than late performance by the buyer, within a reasonable time:

(i) after the seller knew or ought to have known of the breach; or

(ii) after the expiration of any additional period of time fixed by

the seller in accordance with paragraph (1) or article 63, or after the buyer has declared that he will not perform his obligations within such an additional period.

● Article 65

(1) If under the contract the buyer is to specify the form, measurement or other features of the goods and he fails to make such specification either on the date agreed upon or within a reasonable time after receipt of a request from the seller, the seller may, without prejudice to any other rights he may have, make the specification himself in accordance with the requirements of the buyer that may be known to him.

(2) If the seller makes the specification himself, he must inform the buyer of the details thereof and must fix a reasonable time within which the buyer may make a different specification. If, after receipt of such a communication, the buyer fails to do so within the time so fixed, the specification made by the seller is binding.

Chapter IV Passing of Risk

● Article 66

Loss of or damage to the goods after the risk has passed to the buyer does not discharge him from his obligation to pay the price, unless the loss or damage is due to an act or omission of the seller.

● Article 67

(1) If the contract of sale involves carriage of the goods and the seller is not

bound to hand them over at a particular place, the risk passes to the buyer when the goods are handed over to the first carrier for transmission to the buyer in accordance with the contract of sale. If the seller is bound to hand the goods over to a carrier at a particular place, the risk does not pass to the buyer until the goods are handed over to the carrier at that place. The fact that the seller is authorized to retain documents controlling the disposition of the goods does not affect the passage of the risk.

(2) Nevertheless, the risk does not pass to the buyer until the goods are clearly identified to the contract, whether by markings on the goods, by shipping documents, by notice given to the buyer or otherwise.

● Article 68

The risk in respect of goods sold in transit passes to the buyer from the time of the conclusion of the contract. However, if the circumstances so indicate, the risk is assumed by the buyer from the time the goods were handed over to the carrier who issued the documents embodying the contract of carriage. Nevertheless, if at the time of the conclusion of the contract of sale the seller knew or ought to have known that the goods had been lost or damaged and did not disclose this to the buyer, the loss or damage is at the risk of the seller.

● Article 69

(1) In cases not within articles 67 and 68, the risk passes to the buyer when he takes over the goods or, if he does not do so in due time, from the time when the goods are placed at his disposal and he commits a breach of contract by failing to take delivery.

(2) However, if the buyer is bound to take over the goods at a place other than a place of business of the seller, the risk passes when delivery is due and the buyer is aware of the fact that the goods are placed at his disposal at that place.

(3) If the contract relates to goods not then identified, the goods are considered not to be placed at the disposal of the buyer until they are clearly identified to the contract.

● Article 70

If the seller has committed a fundamental breach of contract, articles 67, 68 and 69 do not impair the remedies available to the buyer on account of the breach.

Chapter V Provisions Common to the Obligations of the Seller and of the Buyer

Section I. Anticipatory breach and instalment contracts

● Article 71

(1) A party may suspend the performance of his obligations if, after the conclusion of the contract, it becomes apparent that the other party will not perform a substantial part of his obligations as a result of:

(a) a serious deficiency in his ability to perform or in his creditworthiness; or

(b) his conduct in preparing to perform or in performing the contract.

(2) If the seller has already dispatched the goods before the grounds described in the preceding paragraph become evident, he may prevent the handing over of the goods to the buyer even though the buyer holds a document which entitles him to obtain them. The present paragraph relates only to the rights in the goods as between the buyer and the seller.

(3) A party suspending performance, whether before or after dispatch of the goods, must immediately give notice of the suspension to the other party and must continue with performance if the other party provides adequate assurance of his performance.

● Article 72

(1) If prior to the date for performance of the contract it is clear that one of the parties will commit a fundamental breach of contract, the other party may declare the contract avoided.

(2) If time allows, the party intending to declare the contract avoided must give reasonable notice to the other party in order to permit him to provide adequate assurance of his performance.

(3) The requirements of the preceding paragraph do not apply if the other party has declared that he will not perform his obligations.

● Article 73

(1) In the case of a contract for delivery of goods by instalments, if the failure of one party to perform any of his obligations in respect of any instalment constitutes a fundamental breach of contract with respect to that instalment, the other party may declare the contract avoided with respect to that instalment.

(2) If one party's failure to perform any of his obligations in respect of any instalment gives the other party good grounds to conclude that a fundamental breach of contract will occur with respect to future instalments, he may declare the contract avoided for the future, provided that he does so within a reasonable time.

(3) A buyer who declares the contract avoided in respect of any delivery may,

at the same time, declare it avoided in respect of deliveries already made or of future deliveries if, by reason of their interdependence, those deliveries could not be used for the purpose contemplated by the parties at the time of the conclusion of the contract.

Section II. Damages

● Article 74

Damages for breach of contract by one party consist of a sum equal to the loss, including loss of profit, suffered by the other party as a consequence of the breach. Such damages may not exceed the loss which the party in breach foresaw or ought to have foreseen at the time of the conclusion of the contract, in the light of the facts and matters of which he then knew or ought to have known, as a possible consequence of the breach of contract.

● Article 75

If the contract is avoided and if, in a reasonable manner and within a reasonable time after avoidance, the buyer has bought goods in replacement or the seller has resold the goods, the party claiming damages may recover the difference between the contract price and the price in the substitute transaction as well as any further damages recoverable under article 74.

● Article 76

(1) If the contract is avoided and there is a current price for the goods, the party claiming damages may, if he has not made a purchase or resale under article 75, recover the difference between the price fixed by the contract and the current price at the time of avoidance as well as any further damages recoverable under article 74. If, however, the party claiming damages has avoided the contract after taking over the goods, the current price at the time of such taking over shall be applied instead of the current price at the time of avoidance.

(2) For the purposes of the preceding paragraph, the current price is the price prevailing at the place where delivery of the goods should have been made or, if there is no current price at that place, the price at such other place as serves as a reasonable substitute, making due allowance for differences in the cost of transporting the goods.

● Article 77

A party who relies on a breach of contract must take such measures as are reasonable in the circumstances to mitigate the loss, including loss of profit, resulting from the breach. If he fails to take such measures, the party in breach may claim a reduction in the damages in the amount by which the loss should have been mitigated.

Section III. Interest

● Article 78

If a party fails to pay the price or any other sum that is in arrears, the other party is entitled to interest on it, without prejudice to any claim for damages recoverable under article 74.

Section IV. Exemptions

● Article 79

(1) A party is not liable for a failure to perform any of his obligations if he proves that the failure was due to an impediment beyond his control and that he could not reasonably be expected to have taken the impediment into account at the time of the conclusion of the contract or to have avoided or overcome it or its consequences.

(2) If the party's failure is due to the failure by a third person whom he has engaged to perform the whole or a part of the contract, that party is exempt from liability only if:

(a) he is exempt under the preceding paragraph; and

(b) the person whom he has so engaged would be so exempt if the provisions of that paragraph were applied to him.

(3) The exemption provided by this article has effect for the period during which the impediment exists.

(4) The party who fails to perform must give notice to the other party of the impediment and its effect on his ability to perform. If the notice is not received by the other party within a reasonable time after the party who fails to perform knew or ought to have known of the impediment, he is liable for damages resulting from such non-receipt.

(5) Nothing in this article prevents either party from exercising any right other than to claim damages under this Convention.

● Article 80

A party may not rely on a failure of the other party to perform, to the extent that such failure was caused by the first party's act or omission.

Section V. Effects of avoidance

● Article 81

(1) Avoidance of the contract releases both parties from their obligations under

it, subject to any damages which may be due. Avoidance does not affect any provision of the contract for the settlement of disputes or any other provision of the contract governing the rights and obligations of the parties consequent upon the avoidance of the contract.

(2) A party who has performed the contract either wholly or in part may claim restitution from the other party of whatever the first party has supplied or paid under the contract. If both parties are bound to make restitution, they must do so concurrently.

● Article 82

(1) The buyer loses the right to declare the contract avoided or to require the seller to deliver substitute goods if it is impossible for him to make restitution of the goods substantially in the condition in which he received them.

(2) The preceding paragraph does not apply:

(a) if the impossibility of making restitution of the goods or of making restitution of the goods substantially in the condition in which the buyer received them is not due to his act or omission;

(b) if the goods or part of the goods have perished or deteriorated as a result of the examination provided for in article 38; or

(c) if the goods or part of the goods have been sold in the normal course of business or have been consumed or transformed by the buyer in the course normal use before he discovered or ought to have discovered the lack of conformity.

● Article 83

A buyer who has lost the right to declare the contract avoided or to require the seller to deliver substitute goods in accordance with article 82 retains all other remedies under the contract and this Convention.

● Article 84

(1) If the seller is bound to refund the price, he must also pay interest on it, from the date on which the price was paid.

(2) The buyer must account to the seller for all benefits which he has derived from the goods or part of them:

(a) if he must make restitution of the goods or part of them; or

(b) if it is impossible for him to make restitution of all or part of the goods or to make restitution of all or part of the goods substantially in the condition in which he received them, but he has nevertheless declared the contract avoided or required the seller to deliver substitute goods.

Section VI. Preservation of the goods
● Article 85

If the buyer is in delay in taking delivery of the goods or, where payment of the price and delivery of the goods are to be made concurrently, if he fails to pay the price, and the seller is either in possession of the goods or otherwise able to control their disposition, the seller must take such steps as are reasonable in the circumstances to preserve them. He is entitled to retain them until he has been reimbursed his reasonable expenses by the buyer.

● Article 86

(1) If the buyer has received the goods and intends to exercise any right under the contract or this Convention to reject them, he must take such steps to preserve them as are reasonable in the circumstances. He is entitled to retain them until he has been reimbursed his reasonable expenses by the seller.

(2) If goods dispatched to the buyer have been placed at his disposal at their destination and he exercises the right to reject them, he must take possession of them on behalf of the seller, provided that this can be done without payment of the price and without unreasonable inconvenience or unreasonable expense. This provision does not apply if the seller or a person authorized to take charge of the goods on his behalf is present at the destination. If the buyer takes possession of the goods under this paragraph, his rights and obligations are governed by the preceding paragraph.

● Article 87

A party who is bound to take steps to preserve the goods may deposit them in a warehouse of a third person at the expense of the other party provided that the expense incurred is not unreasonable.

● Article 88

(1) A party who is bound to preserve the goods in accordance with article 85 or 86 may sell them by any appropriate means if there has been an unreasonable delay by the other party in taking possession of the goods or in taking them back or in paying the price or the cost of preservation, provided that reasonable notice of the intention to sell has been given to the other party.

(2) If the goods are subject to rapid deterioration or their preservation would involve unreasonable expense, a party who is bound to preserve the goods in accordance with article 85 or 86 must take reasonable measures to sell them. To the extent possible he must give notice to the other party of his intention to sell.

(3) A party selling the goods has the right to retain out of the proceeds of sale an amount equal to the reasonable expenses of preserving the goods and of selling them. He must account to the other party for the balance.

PART IV
Final Provisions

●Article 89
The Secretary-General of the United Nations is hereby designated as the depositary for this Convention.

●Article 90
This Convention does not prevail over any international agreement which has already been or may be entered into and which contains provisions concerning the matters governed by this Convention, provided that the parties have their places of business in States parties to such agreement.

●Article 91
(1) This Convention is open for signature at the concluding meeting of the United Nations Conference on Contracts for the International Sale of Goods and will remain open for signature by all States at the Headquarters of the United Nations, New York until 30 September 1981.
(2) This Convention is subject to ratification, acceptance or approval by the signatory States.
(3) This Convention is open for accession by all States which are not signatory States as from the date it is open for signature.
(4) Instruments of ratification, acceptance, approval and accession are to be deposited with the Secretary-General of the United Nations.

●Article 92
(1) A Contracting State may declare at the time of signature, ratification, acceptance, approval or accession that it will not be bound by Part II of this Convention or that it will not be bound by Part III of this Convention.
(2) A Contracting State which makes a declaration in accordance with the preceding paragraph in respect of Part II or Part III of this Convention is not to be considered a Contracting State within paragraph (1) of article 1 of this Convention in respect of matters governed by the Part to which the declaration applies.

● Article 93

(1) If a Contracting State has two or more territorial units in which, according to its constitution, different systems of law are applicable in relation to the matters dealt with in this Convention, it may, at the time of signature, ratification, acceptance, approval or accession, declare that this Convention is to extend to all its territorial units or only to one or more of them, and may amend its declaration by submitting another declaration at any time.

(2) These declarations are to be notified to the depositary and are to state expressly the territorial units to which the Convention extends.

(3) If, by virtue of a declaration under this article, this Convention extends to one or more but not all of the territorial units of a Contracting State, and if the place of business of a party is located in that State, this place of business, for the purposes of this Convention, is considered not to be in a Contracting State, unless it is in a territorial unit to which the Convention extends.

(4) If a Contracting State makes no declaration under paragraph (1) of this Article, the Convention is to extend to all territorial units of that State.

● Article 94

(1) Two or more Contracting States which have the same or closely related legal rules on matters governed by this Convention may at any time declare that the Convention is not to apply to contracts of sale or to their formation where the parties have their places of business in those States. Such declarations may be made jointly or by reciprocal unilateral declarations.

(2) A Contracting State which has the same or closely related legal rules on matters governed by this Convention as one or more non-Contracting States may at any time declare that the Convention is not to apply to contracts of sale or to their formation where the parties have their places of business in those States.

(3) If a State which is the object of a declaration under the preceding paragraph subsequently becomes a Contracting State, the declaration made will, as from the date on which the Convention enters into force in respect of the new Contracting State, have the effect of a declaration made under paragraph (1), provided that the new Contracting State joins in such declaration or makes a reciprocal unilateral declaration.

● Article 95

Any State may declare at the time of the deposit of its instrument of ratification, acceptance, approval or accession that it will not be bound by subparagraph (1)

(b) of article 1 of this Convention.
Article 96
A Contracting State whose legislation requires contracts of sale to be concluded in or evidenced by writing may at any time make a declaration in accordance with article 12 that any provision of article 11, article 29, or Part II of this Convention, that allows a contract of sale or its modification or termination by agreement or any offer, acceptance, or other indication of intention to be made in any form other than in writing, does not apply where any party has his place of business in that State.
Article 97
(1) Declarations made under this Convention at the time of signature are subject to confirmation upon ratification, acceptance or approval.

(2) Declarations and confirmations of declarations are to be in writing and be formally notified to the depositary.

(3) A declaration takes effect simultaneously with the entry into force of this Convention in respect of the State concerned. However, a declaration of which the depositary receives formal notification after such entry into force takes effect on the first day of the month following the expiration of six months after the date of its receipt by the depositary. Reciprocal unilateral declarations under article 94 take effect on the first day of the month following the expiration of six months after the receipt of the latest declaration by the depositary.

(4) Any State which makes a declaration under this Convention may withdraw it at any time by a formal notification in writing addressed to the depositary. Such withdrawal is to take effect on the first day of the month following the expiration of six months after the date of the receipt of the notification by the depositary.

(5) A withdrawal of a declaration made under article 94 renders inoperative, as from the date on which the withdrawal takes effect, any reciprocal declaration made by another State under that article.
Article 98
No reservations are permitted except those expressly authorized in this Convention.
Article 99
(1) This Convention enters into force, subject to the provisions of paragraph (6) of this article, on the first day of the month following the expiration of

twelve months after the date of deposit of the tenth instrument of ratification, acceptance, approval or accession, including an instrument which contains a declaration made under article 92.

(2) When a State ratifies, accepts, approves or accedes to this Convention after the deposit of the tenth instrument of ratification, acceptance, approval or accession, this Convention, with the exception of the Part excluded, enters into force in respect of that State, subject to the provisions of paragraph (6) of this article, on the first day of the month following the expiration of twelve months after the date of the deposit of its instrument of ratification, acceptance, approval or accession.

(3) A State which ratifies, accepts, approves or accedes to this Convention and is a party to either or both the Convention relating to a Uniform Law on the Formation of Contracts for the International Sale of Goods done at The Hague on 1 July 1964 (1964 Hague Formation Convention) and the Convention relating to a Uniform Law on the International Sale of Goods done at The Hague on 1 July 1964 (1964 Hague Sales Convention) shall at the same time denounce, as the case may be, either or both the 1964 Hague Sales Convention and the 1964 Hague Formation Convention by notifying the Government of the Netherlands to that effect.

(4) A State party to the 1964 Hague Sales Convention which ratifies, accepts, approves or accedes to the present Convention and declares or has declared under article 52 that it will not be bound by Part II of this Convention shall at the time of ratification, acceptance, approval or accession denounce the 1964 Hague Sales Convention by notifying the Government of the Netherlands to that effect.

(5) A State party to the 1964 Hague Formation Convention which ratifies, accepts, approves or accedes to the present Convention and declares or has declared under article 92 that it will not be bound by Part III of this Convention shall at the time of ratification, acceptance, approval or accession denounce the 1964 Hague Formation Convention by notifying the Government of the Netherlands to that effect.

(6) For the purpose of this article, ratifications, acceptances, approvals and accessions in respect of this Convention by States parties to the 1964 Hague Formation Convention or to the 1964 Hague Sales Convention shall not be effective until such denunciations as may be required on the part of those States in respect of the latter two Conventions have themselves become effective. The de-

positary of this Convention shall consult with the Government of the Netherlands, as the depositary of the 1964 Conventions, so as to ensure necessary coordination in this respect.

● Article 100

(1) This Convention applies to the formation of a contract only when the proposal for concluding the contract is made on or after the date when the Convention enters into force in respect of the Contracting States referred to in subparagraph (1)(a) or the Contracting State referred to in subparagraph (1)(b) of article 1.

(2) This Convention applies only to contracts concluded on or after the date when the Convention enters into force in respect of the Contracting States referred to in subparagraph (1)(a) or the Contracting State referred to in subparagraph (1)(b) of article 1.

● Article 101

(1) A Contracting State may denounce this Convention, or Part II or Part III of the Convention, by a formal notification in writing addressed to the depositary.

(2) The denunciation takes effect on the first day of the month following the expiration of twelve months after the notification is received by the depositary. Where a longer period for the denunciation to take effect is specified in the notification, the denunciation takes effect upon the expiration of such longer period after the notification is received by the depositary.

Done at Vienna, this day of eleventh day of April, one thousand nine hundred and eighty, in a single original, of which the Arabic, Chinese,
English, French, Russian and Spanish texts are equally authentic.

In Witness Whereof the undersigned plenipotentiaries, being duly authorized by their respective Governments, have signed this Convention.

APPENDIX II

Contract Law of the People's Republic of China

General Provisions

Chapter 1 General Provisions

● Article 1

This Law is formulated with a view to protecting the lawful rights and interests of the parties to contracts, maintaining the social economic order and promoting the progress of the socialist modernization drive.

● Article 2

A contract in this Law refers to an agreement establishing, modifying and terminating the civil rights and obligations between subjects of equal footing, that is, between natural persons, legal persons or other organizations.

Agreements involving personal status relationship such as on matrimony, adoption, guardianship, etc. Shall apply the provisions of other Laws.

● Article 3

The parties to contract shall have equal legal status. No party may impose its will on the other party.

● Article 4

The parties shall have the rights to be voluntary to enter into a contract in accordance with the law. No unit or individual may illegally interfere.

● Article 5

The parties shall abide by the principle of fairness in defining the rights and obligations of each party.

● Article 6

The parties must act in accordance with the principle of good faith, no matter in exercising rights or in performing obligations.

● Article 7

In concluding and performing a contract, the parties shall abide by the laws and administrative regulations, observe social ethics. Neither party may disrupt the socio-economic order or damage the public interests.

● Article 8

As soon as a contract is established in accordance with the law, it shall be legally binding on the parties. The parties shall perform their respective obligations in accordance with the terms of the contract. Neither party may unilaterally modify or rescind the contract.

The contract established according to law shall be under the protection of law.

Chapter 2 Conclusion of Contracts

● Article 9

In concluding a contract, the parties shall have appropriate civil capacity of right and civil capacity of conduct.

The parties may conclude a contract through an agent in accordance with the law.

● Article 10

The parties may conclude a contract in written, oral or other forms.

Where the laws or administrative regulations require a contract to be concluded in written form, the contract shall be in written form. If the parties agree to do so, the contract shall be concluded in written form.

● Article 11

The written forms mean the forms which can show the described contents visibly, such as a written contractual agreement, letters, and data-telex (including telegram, telex, fax, EDI and E-mails).

● Article 12

The contents of a contract shall be agreed upon by the parties, and shall contain the following clauses in general:

(1) title or name and domicile of the parties;

(2) contract object;

(3) quantity;

(4) quality;

(5) price or remuneration;

(6) time limit, place and method of performance;

(7) liability for breach of contract; and

(8) methods to settle disputes.

The parties may conclude a contract by reference to the model text of each kind of contract.

● Article 13

The parties shall conclude a contract in the form of an offer and acceptance.

● Article 14

An offer is a proposal hoping to enter into a contract with other parties. The proposal shall comply with the following stipulations:

(1) Its contents shall be detailed and definite;

(2) It indicates the proposal of the offeror to be bound in case of acceptance.

● Article 15

An invitation for offer is a proposal for requesting other parties to make offers to the principal. Price forms mailed, public notices of auction and tender, prospectuses and commercial advertisements, etc. Are invitations for offer.

Where the contents of a commercial advertisement comply with the terms of the offer, it may be regarded as an offer.

● Article 16

An offer becomes effective when it reaches the offeree.

If a contract is concluded by means of data-telex, and recipient appoints a specific system to receive the data-telex, the time when the data-telex enters the system shall be the time of arrival; if no specific system is appointed, the time when the data-telex first enters any of the recipient's systems shall be regarded as the time of arrival.

● Article 17

An offer may be withdrawn, if the withdrawal notice reaches the offeree before or at the same time when the offer arrives.

● Article 18

An offer may be revoked, if the revocation reaches the offeree before it has dispatched an acceptance.

● Article 19

An offer may not be revoked, if

(1) the offeror indicates a fixed time for acceptance or otherwise explicitly states that the offer is irrevocable; or

(2) he offeree has reasons to rely on the offer as being irrevocable and has

made preparation for performing the contract.

● Article 20

An offer shall be null and void under any of the following circumstances:

(1) The notice of rejection reaches the offeror;

(2) The offeror revokes its offer in accordance with the law;

(3) The offeree fails to make an acceptance at the time when the time limit for acceptance expires;

(4) The offeree substantially alters the contents of the offer.

● Article 21

An acceptance is a statement made by the offeree indicating assent to an offer.

● Article 22

Except that it is based on transaction practices or that the offer indicates an acceptance may be made by performing an act, the acceptance shall be made by means of notice.

● Article 23

An acceptance shall reach the offeror within the time limit fixed in the offer.

Where no time is fixed in the offer, the acceptance shall arrive in accordance with the following provisions:

(1) If the offer is made in dialogues, the acceptance shall be made immediately except as otherwise agreed upon by the parties;

(2) If the offer is made in forms other than a dialogue, the acceptance shall arrive within a reasonable period of time.

● Article 24

Where the offer is made in a letter or a telegram, the time limit for acceptance commences from the date shown in the letter or from the moment the telegram is handed in for dispatch. If no such date is shown in the letter, it commences from the date shown on the envelope. Where an offer is made by means of instantaneous communication, such as telephone or facsimile, the time limit for acceptance commences from the moment that the offer reaches the offeree.

● Article 25

A contract is established when the acceptance becomes effective.

● Article 26

An acceptance becomes effective when its notice reaches the offeror. If an acceptance needn't be notified, it becomes effective when an act of acceptance is performed in accordance with transaction practices or as required in the offer. Where a contract is concluded in the form of data-telex, the time when an acceptance arrives shall apply the provisions of Paragraph 2, Article 16 of this law.

● Article 27

An acceptance may be withdrawn, but a notice of withdrawal shall reach the offeror before the notice of acceptance reaches the offeror or at the same time when the acceptance reaches the offeror.

● Article 28

Where an offeree makes an acceptance beyond the time limit for acceptance, the acceptance shall be a new offer except that the offeror informs the offeree of the effectiveness of the said acceptance promptly.

● Article 29

If the offeree dispatches the acceptance within the time limit for acceptance which can reach the offeror in due time under normal circumstances, but the acceptance reaches the offeror beyond the time limit because of other reasons, the acceptance shall be effective, except that, the offeror informs the offeree promptly that it does not accept the acceptance because it exceeds the time limit for acceptance.

● Article 30

The contents of an acceptance shall comply with those of the offer. If the offeree substantially modifies the contents of the offer, it shall constitute a new offer. The modification relating to the contract object, quality, quantity, price or remuneration, time or place or method of performance, liabilities for breach of contract and the settlement of disputes, etc., shall constitute the substantial modification of an offer.

● Article 31

If the acceptance does not substantially modifies the contents of the offer, it shall be effective, and the contents of the contract shall be subject to those of the acceptance, except as rejected promptly by the offeror or indicted in the offer that an acceptance may not modify the offer at all.

● Article 32

Where the parties conclude a contract in written form, the contract is established when both parties sign or affix a seal on it.

Article 33

Where the parties conclude the contract in the form of a letter or data-telex, etc., one party may request to sign a letter of confirmation before the conclusion of the contract. The contract shall be established at the time when the letter of confirmation is signed.

Article 34

The place of effectiveness of an acceptance shall be the place of the establishment of the contract.

If the contract is concluded in the form of data-telex, the main business place of the recipient shall be the place of establishment. If no main business place, its habitual residence shall be considered to be the place of establishment. Where the parties agree otherwise, the place of establishment shall be subject to that agreement.

Article 35

Where the parties conclude a contract in written form, the place where both parties sign or affix a seal shall be the place where the contract is established.

Article 36

A contract, which shall be concluded in written form as provided for by the laws and administrative regulations or as agreed upon by the parties, shall be established, as the parties do not use the written form, but one party has performed the principal obligation and the other party has received it.

Article 37

A contract, which is concluded in written form, shall be established, if one party has performed its principal obligation and the other party has received it before signiture or affixing with a seal.

Article 38

In case the State issues a mandatory plan or a State purchasing order task based on necessity, the relevant legal persons or other organizations shall conclude contracts between them in accordance with the rights and obligations as stipulated by the relevant laws and administrative regulations.

Article 39

Where standard terms are adopted in concluding a contract, the party which supplies the standard terms shall define the rights and obligations between the parties abiding by the principle of faimess, request the other party to note the exclusion or restriction of its liabilities in reasonable ways, and explain the standard terms according to the requirement of the other party.

Standard terms are clauses which are prepared in advance for general and repeated use by one party and which are not negotiated with the other party in concluding a contract.

● Article 40

When standard terms are under the circumstances stipulated in Article 52 and Article 53 of this Law, or the party which supplies the standard terms exempts itself from its liabilities, weights the liabilities of the other party, and excludes the rights of the other party, the terms shall be null and void.

● Article 41

If a dispute over the understanding of the standard terms occurs, it shall be interpreted according to general understanding. Where there are two or more kinds of interpretation, an interpretation unfavourable to the party supplying the standard terms shall be preferred. Where the standard terms are inconsistent with non-standard terms, the latter shall be adopted.

● Article 42

The party shall be liable for damages if it is under one of the following circumstances in concluding a contract and thus causing losses to the other party:

(1) disguising and pretending to conclude a contract, and negotiating in bad faith;

(2) concealing deliberately the important facts relating to the conclusion of the contract or providing deliberately false information;

(3) performing other acts which violate the principle of good faith.

● Article 43

A business secret the parties learn in concluding a contract shall not be disclosed or unfairly used, not matter the contract is established or not. The party who causes the other party to suffer from losses due to disclosing or unfairly using the business secret shall be liable for damages.

Chapter 3 Effectiveness of Contracts

● Article 44

The contract established according to law becomes effective when it is established.

With regard to contracts which are subject to approval or registration as provide for by the laws or administrative regulations, the provisions thereof shall be followed.

● Article 45

The parties may agree on some collateral conditions relating to the effectiveness of a contract. The contract with entry-into-force conditions shall be effective when such conditions are accomplished. The contract with dissolving conditions shall be null and void when such conditions are accomplished.

To unfairly prevent the conditions from being accomplished by one party for its own interests shall be regarded as those conditions have been accomplished. To unfairly promoting the accomplishment of such conditions by one party shall be regarded as non-accomplishment.

● Article 46

The parties may agree on a conditional time period as to the effectiveness of the contract. A contract subject to an effective time period shall come into force when the period expires. A contract with termination time period shall become invalid when the period expires.

● Article 47

A contract concluded by a person with limited civil capacity of conduct shall be effective after being ratified afterwards by the person's statutory agent, but a pure profit-making contract or a contract concluded which is appropriate to the person's age, intelligence or mental health conditions need not be ratified by the person's statutory agent.

The counterpart may urge the statutory agent to ratify the contract within one month. It shall be regarded as a refusal of ratification that the statutory agent does not make any expression. A bona fide counterpart has the right withdraw it before the contract is ratified. The withdrawal shall be made by means of notice.

● Article 48

A contract concluded by an actor who has no power of agency, who oversteps the power of agency, or whose power of agency has expired and yet concludes it on behalf of the principal, shall have no legally binding force on the principal without ratification by the principal, and the actor shall be held liable.

The counterpart may urge the principal to ratify it within one month. It shall be regarded as a refusal of ratification that the principal does not make any expression. A bona fide counterpart has the right withdraw it before the contract is ratified. The withdrawal shall be made by means of notice.

● Article 49

If an actor has no power of agency, oversteps the power of agency, or the power of agency has expired and yet concludes a contract in the principal's name, and the counterpart has reasons to trust that the actor has the power of agency, the act of agency shall be effective.

● Article 50

Where a atatutory representative or a responsible person of a legal person or other organization oversteps his/her power and concludes a contract, the representative act shall be effective except that the counterpart knows or ought to know that he/she is overstepping his/her powers.

● Article 51

Where a person having no right to disposal of property disposes of other persons' properties, and the principal ratifies the act afterwards or the person without power of disposal has obtained the power after concluding a contract, the contract shall be valid.

● Article 52

A contract shall be null and void under any of the following circumstances:

(1) A contract is concluded through the use of fraud or coercion by one party to damage the interests of the State;

(2) Malicious collusion is conducted to damage the interests of the State. A collective or a third party;

(3) An illegitimate purpose is concealed under the guise of legitimate acts;

(4) Damaging the public intersts;

(5) Violating the compulsory provisions of the laws and administrative regulations.

● Article 53

The following immunity clauses in a contract shall be null and void:

(1) those that cause personal injury to the other party;

(2) those that cause property damages to the other party as a result of deliberate intent or gross fault.

● Article 54

A party shall have the right to request the people's court or an arbitration institution to modify or revoke the following contracts:

(1) those concluded as a result of serious misunderstanding;

(2) those that are obviously unfair at the time when concluding the contract.

If a contract is concluded by one party against the other party's true intentions through the use of fraud, coercion or exploitation of the other party's unfavorable position. The injured party shall have the right to request the people's court or an arbitration institution to modify or revoke it.

Where a party requests for modification, the people's court or the arbitration institution may not revoke the contract.

● Article 55

The right to revoke a contract sahll extinguish under any of the following circumstances:

(1) A party having the right to revoke the contract fails to exercise the right within one year from the day that it knows or ought to know the revoking causes;

(2) A party having the right to revoke the contract explicitly expresses or conducts an act to waive the right after it know the revoking causes.

● Article 56

A contract that is null and void or revoked shall have no legally binding force ever from the very beginning. If part of a contract is null and void without affecting the validity of the other parts, the other parts shall still be valid.

● Article 57

If a contract is null and void, revoked or terminated, it shall not affect the validity of the dispute settlement clause which is independently existing in the contract.

● Article 58

The property acquired as a result of a contract shall be returned after the contract is confirmed to be null and void or has been revoked. Where the property can not be returned or the return is unnecessary, it shall be reimbursed at its estimated price. The party at fault shall compensate the other party for losses incurred as a result therefrom. If both parties are at fault, each party shall respectively be liable.

● Article 59

If the parties have maliciously conducted collusion to damage the interests of the State, a collective or a third party, the property thus acpuired shall be turned over to the State or returned to the collective or the third party.

Chapter 4 Performance of Contracts

● Article 60

The parties shall perform their obligations thoroughly according to the terms of the contract.

The parties shall abide by the principle of good faith and perform the obligations of notice, assistance and maintaining confidentiality, etc. Based on the character and purpose of the contract or the transaction practices.

● Article 61

Where, after the contract becomes effective, there is no agreement in the contract between the parties on the terms regarding quality, price or remuneration and place of performance, etc. Or such agreement is unclear, the parties may agree upon supplementary terms through consultation. In case of a failure in doing so, the terms shall be determined from the context of relevant clauses of the contract or by transaction practices.

● Article 62

If the relevant terms of a contract are unclear, nor can it be determined according to the provisions of Article 61 of this Law, the provisions below shall be applied:

(1) If quality requirements are unclear, the State standards or trade standards shall be applied; if there are no State standards or trade standards, generally held standards or specific standards in conformity with the purpose of the contract shall be applied.

(2) If the price or remuneration is unclear, the market price of the place of performance at the time concluding the contract shall be applied; if the government-fixed price or government-directed price shall be followed in accordance with the law, the provisions of the law shall be applied.

(3) If the place of performance is unclear, and the payment is currency, the performance shall be effected at the place of location of the party receiving the payment; if real estate is to be delivered, the performance shall be effected at the place of location of the real estate; in case of other contract objects, the performance shall be effected at the place of location of the party fulfilling the obligations.

(4) If the time limit for performance is unclear, the obligor may at any time fulfill the obligations towards the obligee; the obligee may also demand at any time that the obligor performs the obligations, but a time period for necessary prepa-

ration shall be given to the obligor.

(5) If the method of performance is unclear, the method which is advantageous to realize the purpose of the contract shall be adopted.

(6) if the burden of the expenses of performance is unclear the cost shall be assumed by the obligor.

● Article 63

In cases where the government-fixed price or government-directed price is followed in a contract, if the said price is readjusted within the time limit for delivery as stipulated in the contract, the payment shall be calculated according to the price at the time of delivery. If the delivery of the object is delayed and the price has risen, the original price shall be adopted; while the price has dropped, the new price shall be adopted. In the event of delay in taking delivery of the object or late payment, if the price has risen, the new price shall be adopted; while the price has dropped, the original price shall be adopted.

● Article 64

Where the parties agree that the obligor performs the obligations to a third party, and the obligor fails to perform the obligations to the third party or the performance does not meet the terms of the contract, the obligor shall be liable to the obligee for the breach of contract.

● Article 65

Where the parties agree that a third party performs the obligations to the obligee, and the third party fails to perform the obligations or the performance does not meet the terms of the contract, the obligor shall be liable to the obligee for the breach of contract.

● Article 66

If both parties have obligations toward each other and there is no order of priority in respect of the performance of obligation, the parties shall perform the obligations simultaneously. One party has the right reject the other party's request for performance if the other party's performance. One party has the right to reject the other party's corresponding request for performance if the other party's performance does not meet the perms of the contract.

● Article 67

Where both parties have obligations towards each other and there has been an order of priority in respect of the performance, and the party which shall render its performance first has not rendered the performance, the party which may render its performance lately has the right to reject the other party's request for performance. Where the party which shall render its performance first violates the terms of a contract while fulfilling the obligations, the party which may render its performance lately has the right to reject the other party's corresponding request for performance.

● Article 68

One party, which shall render its performance first, may suspend its performance, if it has conclusive evidence that the other party is under any of the following circumstances:

(1) Its business conditions are seriously deteriorating;

(2) It moves away its property and takes out its capital secretly to evade debt;

(3) It loses its commercial credibility;

(4) Other circumstances showing that it loses or is possible to lose the capacity of credit.

Where a party suspends performance of a contract without conclusive evidence, it shall be liable for the breach of contract.

● Article 69

One party to a contract which suspends its performance of the contract in accordance with the provisions of Article 68 of this Law, shall promptly inform the other party of such suspension. It shall resume its performance of the contract when the other party provides a sure guarantee. After the suspension of the performance, if the other party does not reinstate its capacity of performance and does not provide with a sure guarantee, the party suspending performance of the contract may rescind the contract.

● Article 70

If the obligee does not notify the obligor its separation, merger or a change of its domicile so as to make it difficult for the obligor to perform the obligations, the obligor may suspend the performance of the contract or have the object deposited.

● Article 71

The obligee may reject an advance performance of the contract by the obligor, except that the advance performance does not damage the interests of the obligee.

Additional expenses caused to the obligee by advance performance shall be borne by the obligor.

●Article 72

The obligee may reject the partial performance of the contract by the obligor, except that the partial performance does not damage the interests of the obligee. Additional expenses caused to the obligee by partial performance shall be borne by the obligor.

●Article 73

If the obligor is indolent in exercising its due creditor's right, thus damaging the interests of the obligee, the obligee may request the people's court for subrogation in its own name, except that the creditor's right exclusively belongs to the obligor.

The subrogation shall be exercised within the scope of the creditor's right of the obligee. The necessary expenses caused to the obligee by exercising subrogation shall be borne by the obligor.

●Article 74

If the obligor renounces its due creditor's right or transfers its property gratis, thus damaging the interests of the obligee, the obligee may request the people's courts to revoke the obligor's act. If the obligor transfers its property at an obviously unreasonable low price, thus damaging the interests of the obligee, and the transferee knows such situation, the obligee may request the people's court to revoke the obligor's act.

The right of revocation shall be exercised within the scope of the creditor's right of the obligee. The necessary expenses caused to the obligee by exercising the right of revocation shall be borne by the obligor.

●Article 75

The time limit for exercising the right of revocation shall be one year, commencing from the day when the obligee is aware or ought to be aware of the causes of revocation. If the right of revocation has not been exercised within five years from the day when the act of the obligor takes place, the right of revocation shall be extinguished.

●Article 76

After a contract becomes effective, the parties may not reject to perform the obligations of the contract because of modification of the title or name of the parties, or change of the statutory representative, the responsible person or the executive person of the parties.

Chapter 5 Modification and Assignment of Contracts

● Article 77
A contract may be modified if the parties reach a consensus through consultation.

If the laws or administrative regulations stipulate that a contract shall be modified through the procedures of approval or registration, such provisions shall be followed.

● Article 78
If the contents of the modified contract agreed by the parties are unclear, it shall be presumed that the contract is not modified.

● Article 79
The obligee may assign, wholly or in part, its rights under the contract to a third party, except for the following circumstances:

(1) The rights under the contract may not be assigned according to the character of the contract;

(2) The rights under the contract may not be assigned according to the agreement between the parties;

(3) The rights under the contract may not be assigned according to the provisions of the laws.

● Article 80
An obligee assigning its rights shall notify the obligor. Without notifying the obligor, the assignment shall not become effective to the obligor.

The notice of assignment of rights may not be revoked, unless the assignee agrees thereupon.

● Article 81
If the obligee assigns is rights, the assignee shall acquire the collateral rights relating to the principal right, except that the collateral rights exclusively belong to the obligee.

● Article 82
After the obligor receives the notice of assignment of the creditor's right, it may claim its demur in respect of the assignor to the assignee.

● Article 83
When the obligor receives the notice of assignment of the creditor's rights, and

the obligor has due creditor's rights to the assign or, and the creditor's rights of the obligor are due in priority to the assigned creditor's rights or due at the same time, the obligor may claim to offset each other to the assignee.

● Article 84

If the obligor assigns its obligations, wholly or in part, to a third party, it shall obtain consent from the obligee first.

● Article 85

If the obligor assigns its obligations to a third party, the new obligor may claim the demur belonging to the original obligor in respect of the obligee.

● Article 86

If the obligor assigns its obligations to a third party, the new obligor shall assume the collateral obligations relating to the principal obligations, except that the obligations exclusively belong to the original obligor.

● Article 87

Where the laws or administrative regulations stipulate that the as signment of rights or transfer of obligations shall go through approval or registration procedures, such provisions shall be followed.

● Article 88

One party to a contract may assign its rights and obligations under the contract together to a third party with the consent of the other party.

● Article 89

If one party to a contract assigns its rights and obligations under the contract together to a third party, the provisions of Article 79, Article 81 to 83, and Article 85 to 87 of this Law shall be applied.

● Article 90

If one party to a contract is merged after the contract has been concluded, the legal person or other organization established after the merger shall exercise the contract rights and perform the contract obligations. If one party is separated after the contract has been concluded, the legal persons or other organizations thus established after the separation shall exercise the contract rights or assume the contract obligations jointly and severally.

Chapter 6 Termination of the Rights and Obligations of Contracts

● Article 91

The rights and obligations of contracts shall be terminated under any of the following circumstances:

(1) The debt obligations have been performed in accordance with the terms of the contract;

(2) The contract has been rescinded;

(3) The debts have been offset against each other;

(4) The obligor has deposited the object according to law;

(5) The debt obligations have been exempted by the obligee;

(6) The creditor's rights and debt obligations are assumed by the same person; or

(7) Other circumstances for termination as stipulated by the laws or agreed upon by the parties in the contract.

● Article 92

When the rights and obligations of contracts are terminated, the parties to a contract shall, abiding by the principle of good faith, perform such obligations as making a notice, providing assistance and maintaining confidentiality according to transaction practices.

● Article 93

A contract may be rescinded if the parties to the contract reach a consensus through consultation.

The parties to a contract may agree upon the conditions to rescind the contract by one party. When such conditions are accompanished, the party entitled to rescind the contract may rescind it.

● Article 94

The parties to a contract may rescind the contract under any of the following circumstances:

(1) The purpose of the contract is not able to be realized because of force majeure;

(2) One party to the contract expresses explicitly or indicates through its acts, before the expiry of the performance period, that it will not perform the principal debt obligations;

(3) One party to the contract delays in performing the principal debt obligations

and fails, after being urged, to perform them within a reasonable time period;

(4) One party to the contract delays in performing the debt obligations or commits other acts in breach of the contract so that the purpose of the contract is not able to be realized; or

(5) Other circumstances as stipulated by law.

● Article 95

Where the laws stipulate or the parties agree the time limit to exercise the right to rescind the contract, and no party exercises it when the time limit expires, the said right shall be extinguished.

Where the law does not stipulate or the parties make no agreement upon the time limit to exercise the right to rescind the contract, and no party exercises it within a reasonable time period after being urged, the said right shall be extinguished.

● Article 96

One party to a contract shall make a notice to the other party if it advances to rescind the contract according to the provisions of Paragraph 2, Article 93 and Article 94 of the Law. The contract shall be rescinded upon the arrival of the notice at the other party. The party may, if the other party disagrees therewith, request the people's court or an arbitration institution to confirm the effectiveness of rescinding the contract.

Where the laws or administrative regulations stipulate that the rescinding of a contract shall go through the formalities of approval and registration, the provisions thereof shall be followed.

● Article 97

If a contract has not yet been performed, its performance shall be terminated after the rescission. If it has been performed, a party to the contract may, in light of the performance and the character of the contract, request that the original status be restored or other remedial measures be taken.

● Article 98

The termination of the rights and obligations of a contract may not affect the force of the settlement and clearance clauses in the contract.

● Article 99

Where the parties to a contract have debts due mutually and the category and character of the debts are the same, any party may offset his debt against the other's one, except that the debts may not be offset according to the provisions of the laws or to the character of the contract.

Any party advancing to offset the debts shall make a notice to the other party. Such notice shall be effective upon the arrival at the other party. The offset may not be accompanied by any conditions or time limit.

● Article 100

Where the parties to a contract have debts due mutually and the category and character of the debts are different, the debts may be offset against each other if both parties have reached a consensus through consultation.

● Article 101

The obligor may deposit the object if the debt obligations are difficult to be performed under any of the following circumstances:

(1) The obligor refuses to accept them without justified reasons;

(2) The obligee is missing;

(3) The obligee is deceased and the heir is not yet determined, or the obligee has lost his conduct capacity and the guardian is not yet determined; or

(4) Other circumstances as stipulated by law.

If the object is not fit to be deposited or the deposit expenses are excessively high, the obligor may, according to law, auction or sell the object and deposit the money obtained therefrom.

● Article 102

After the object is deposited, the obligor shall, except that the obligee is missing, make a notice promptly to the obligee or the obligee's heir or guardian.

● Article 103

The risk of damage to and missing of the object after being deposited shall be borne by the obligee. During the period of depositing, the fruits generated by the object shall belong to the obligee. The deposit expenses shall be borne by the obligee.

● Article 104

The obligee may claim the deposited object at any time. However, if the obligee is under a debt due to the obligor the deposit authorities shall refuse him to claim the deposited object at the request of the obligor, before the obligee has performed his debt obligations or provides a guaranty.

The right to claim the deposited object by the obligee shall be extinguished if it has not been exercised within 5 years as of the date of deposit. The deposited

object shall be owned by the State with deduction of the deposit expenses.
● Article 105

If the obligee exempts the obligor from the debt obligations wholly or in part, the whole or part of the rights and obligations of a contract shall be terminated.

● Article 106

If the creditor's rights and debt obligation are assumed by the same person, the rights and obligations of a contract shall be terminated, except for those involving the interests of a third party.

Chapter 7 Liability for Breach of Contracts

● Article 107

Where one party to a contract fails to perform the contract obligations or its performance fails to satisfy the terms of the continue to perform its obligations, to take remedial measures, or to compensate for losses.

● Article 108

Where one party to a contract expresses explicitly or indicates through its acts that it will not perform the contract, the other party may demand it to bear the liability for the breach of contract before the expiry of the performance period.

● Article 109

If one party to a contract fails to pay the price or remuneration, the other may request it to make the payment.

● Article 110

Where one party to a contract fails to perform the non-monetary debt or its performance of non-monetary debt fails to satisfy the terms of the contract, the other party may request it to perform it except under any of the following circumstances:

(1) It is unable to be performed in law or in fact;

(2) The object of the debt is unfit for compulsory performance or the performance expenses are excessively high; or

(3) The creditor fails to request for the performance within a reasonable time period.

● Article 111

If the quality fails to satisfy the terms of the contract, the breach of contract damages shall be borne according to the terms of the contract agreed upon by the parties. If there is no agreement in the contract on the liability for breach of contract or such agreement is unclear, nor can it be determined in accordance with the provisions of Article 61 of this Law, the damaged party may, in light of the character of the object and the degree of losses, reasonably choose to request the other party to bear the liabilities for the breach of contract such as repairing, substituting the goods, or reducing the price or remuneration.

● Article 112

Where one party to a contract fails to perform the contract obligations or its performance fails to satisfy the terms of the contract, the party shall, after performing its obligations or taking remedial measures, compensate for the losses, if the other party suffers from other losses.

● Article 113

Where one party to a contract fails to perform the contract obligations or its performance fails to satisfy the terms of the contract and causes losses to the other party, the amount of compensation for losses shall be equal to the losses caused by the breach of contract, including the interests receivable after performance of the contract, provided not exceeding the probable losses caused by the breach of contract which has been foreseen or ought to be foreseen when the party in breach concludes the contract.

The business operator who commits default activities in providing to the consumer any goods or service shall be liable for paying compensation for damages in accordance with the Law of the People's Republic of China on the Protection of Consumer Rights and Interests.

● Article 114

The parties to a contract may agree that one party shall, when violating the contract, pay breach of contract damages of certain amount in light of the breach, or may agree upon the calculating method of compensation for losses resulting from the breach of contract.

If the agreed breach of contract damages are lower than the losses caused, any party may request the people's court or an arbitration institution to increase it; if it is excessively higher than the losses caused, any party may request the people's court or an arbitration institution to make an appropriate reduction.

If the parties to a contract agree upon breach of contract damages in respect to the delay in performance, the party in breach shall perform the debt obligations after paying the breach of contract damages.

● Article 115

The parties to a contract may, according to the Guaranty Law of the People's Republic of China, agree that one party pays a deposit to the other party as the guaranty for the creditor's rights. After the debt obligations are performed by the obligor, the deposit shall be returned or offset against the price. If the party that pays the deposit fails the perform the agreed debt obligations, it shall have no right to reclaim the deposit. If the party that receives the deposit fails to perform the agreed debt obligations, it shall return twice the amount of the deposit.

● Article 116

Where the parties to a contract agree on both breach of contract damages and a deposit, when one party violates the contract, the other party may choose to apply the breach of contract damages clause or the deposit clause.

● Article 117

In case that a contract is not able to be performed because of force majeure, the liabilities shall be exempted in part or wholly in light of the effects of force majeure, except as otherwise stipulated by law. If the force majeure occurs after one party has delayed in performance, the liability may not be exempted.

Force majeure as referred to in this Law means the objective circumstances that are unforeseeable, unavoidable and insurmountable.

● Article 118

One party to a contact that is not able to perform the contract because of force majeure shall make a notice to the other party promptly so as to reduce the probable losses to the other party and provide evidence within a reasonable time limit.

● Article 119

After one party violates a contract, the other party shall take proper measures to prevent from the enlargement of losses; if the other party fails to take proper measures so that the losses are enlarged, it may not claim any compensation as to the enlarged losses.

The reasonable expenses paid by the party to prevent from the enlargement of losses shall be borne by the party in breach.

● Article 120

In case that both parties violate a contract, they shall bear the liabilities respectively.

● Article 121

One party that violates the contract because of a third party shall be liable for the breach of contract to the other party. The disputes between the said party and the third party shall be settled according to law or their agreement.

● Article 122

In case that the breach of contract by one party infringes upon the other party's personal or property rights, the aggrieved party shall be entitled to choose to claim the assumption by the violating and infringing party of liabilities for breach of contract according to this Law, or to claim the assumption by the violating and infringing party of liabilities for infringement according to other laws.

Chapter 8 Miscellaneous Provisions

● Article 123

If there are provisions as otherwise stipulated in respect to contracts in other laws, such provisions shall be followed.

● Article 124

Any contract which is not addressed explicitly in the Specific Provisions of this Law or in other laws shall apply the provisions of the General Provisions of this Law or in other laws may be applied mutatis mutandis.

● Article 125

With regard to disputes between the parties to a contract arising from the understanding of any clause of the contract, the true intention of such clause shall be determined according to the terms and expressions used in the contract, the contents of the relevant clauses of the contract, the purpose for concluding the contract, the transaction practices and the principle of good faith.

Where two or more languages are adopted in the text of a contract and it is agreed that both texts are equally authentic, it shall be presumed that the terms and expressions in various versions have the same meaning. In case that the terms and expressions in different versions are inconsistent, they shall be interpreted according to the purpose of the contract.

● Article 126

The parties to a contract involving foreign interests may choose the law applicable to the settlement of their contract disputes, except as otherwise stipulated by law. If the parties to a contract involving foreign interests have not made a choice, the law of the country to which the contract is most closely connected shall be applied.

The contracts for Chinese-foreign equity joint ventures, for Chinese-foreign contractual joint ventures and for Chinese-foreign cooperative exploration and development of natural resources to be performed within the territory of the People's Republic of China shall apply the laws of the People's Republic of China shall apply the laws of the People's Republic of China shall apply the laws of the People's Republic of China.

● Article 127

The departments of administration for industry and commerce and other competent departments shall, within the scope of their respective competence and functions, be responsible for supervision over and dealing with illegal acts in taking advantage of contracts to endanger and harm the State interests and public interests. In case that a crime is constituted, criminal responsibility shall be investigated.

● Article 128

The parties may settle their disputes relevant to the contract through conciliation or mediation.

The parties may, if unwilling to settle their disputes through conciliation or mediation or failing in the conciliation or mediation, apply to an arbitration institution for arbitration according to their arbitration agreement. The parties to a contract involving foreign interests may, according to their arbitration agreement, apply for arbitration to a Chinese arbitration institution or other arbitration institutions. If there is no arbitration agreement between the parties or the arbitration agreement is null and void, they may bring a lawsuit before the people's court. The parties shall perform the court judgments, arbitration awards or mediation documents with legal effectiveness. In case any refusal in respect to the performance, the other party may request the people's court for execution.

● Article 129

The time limit for action before the people's court or for arbitration before an arbitration institution regarding disputes relating to contracts for international sales of goods and contracts for technology import and export shall be four years, calculating from the date on which the party knows or ought to know the infringement on its rights. The time limits for action before the people's court or for arbitration before an arbitration institution regarding other contracts disputes shall be in accordance with the provisions of the relevant laws.

中华人民共和国合同法(总则)

第一章 一般规定

第一条 为了保护合同当事人的合法权益,维护社会经济秩序,促进社会主义现代化建设,制定本法。

第二条 本法所称合同是平等主体的自然人、法人、其他组织之间设立、变更、终止民事权利义务关系的协议。

婚姻、收养、监护等有关身份关系的协议,适用其他法律的规定。

第三条 合同当事人的法律地位平等,一方不得将自己的意志强加给另一方。

第四条 当事人依法享有自愿订立合同的权利,任何单位和个人不得非法干预。

第五条 当事人应当遵循公平原则确定各方的权利和义务。

第六条 当事人行使权利、履行义务应当遵循诚实信用原则。

第七条 当事人订立、履行合同,应当遵守法律、行政法规,尊重社会公德,不得扰乱社会经济秩序,损害社会公共利益。

第八条 依法成立的合同,对当事人具有法律约束力。当事人应当按照约定履行自己的义务,不得擅自变更或者解除合同。

依法成立的合同,受法律保护。

第二章 合同的订立

第九条 当事人订立合同,应当具有相应的民事权利能力和民事行为能力。

当事人依法可以委托代理人订立合同。

第十条 当事人订立合同,有书面形式、口头形式和其他形式。

法律、行政法规规定采用书面形式的,应当采用书面形式。当事人约定采用书面形式的,应当采用书面形式。

第十一条 书面形式是指合同书、信件和数据电文(包括电报、电传、传真、电子数据交换和电子邮件)等可以有形地表现所载内容的形式。

第十二条 合同的内容由当事人约定,一般包括以下条款:

(一)当事人的名称或者姓名和住所;

（二）标的；

（三）数量；

（四）质量；

（五）价款或者报酬；

（六）履行期限、地点和方式；

（七）违约责任；

（八）解决争议的方法。

当事人可以参照各类合同的示范文本订立合同。

第十三条 当事人订立合同，采取要约、承诺方式。

第十四条 要约是希望和他人订立合同的意思表示，该意思表示应当符合下列规定：

（一）内容具体确定；

（二）表明经受要约人承诺，要约人即受该意思表示约束。

第十五条 要约邀请是希望他人向自己发出要约的意思表示。寄送的价目表、拍卖公告、招标公告、招股说明书、商业广告等为要约邀请。

商业广告的内容符合要约规定的，视为要约。

第十六条 要约到达受要约人时生效。

采用数据电文形式订立合同，收件人指定特定系统接收数据电文的，该数据电文进入该特定系统的时间，视为到达时间；未指定特定系统的，该数据电文进入收件人的任何系统的首次时间，视为到达时间。

第十七条 要约可以撤回。撤回要约的通知应当在要约到达受要约人之前或者与要约同时到达受要约人。

第十八条 要约可以撤销。撤销要约的通知应当在受要约人发出承诺通知之前到达受要约人。

第十九条 有下列情形之一的，要约不得撤销：

（一）要约人确定了承诺期限或者以其他形式明示要约不可撤销；

（二）受要约人有理由认为要约是不可撤销的，并已经为履行合同作了准备工作。

第二十条 有下列情形之一的，要约失效：

（一）拒绝要约的通知到达要约人；

（二）要约人依法撤销要约；

（三）承诺期限届满，受要约人未作出承诺；

（四）受要约人对要约的内容作出实质性变更。

第二十一条　承诺是受要约人同意要约的意思表示。

第二十二条　承诺应当以通知的方式作出,但根据交易习惯或者要约表明可以通过行为作出承诺的除外。

第二十三条　承诺应当在要约确定的期限内到达要约人。

要约没有确定承诺期限的,承诺应当依照下列规定到达:

(一)要约以对话方式作出的,应当即时作出承诺,但当事人另有约定的除外;

(二)要约以非对话方式作出的,承诺应当在合理期限内到达。

第二十四条　要约以信件或者电报作出的,承诺期限自信件载明的日期或者电报交发之日开始计算。信件未载明日期的,自投寄该信件的邮戳日期开始计算。要约以电话、传真等快速通讯方式作出的,承诺期限自要约到达受要约人时开始计算。

第二十五条　承诺生效时合同成立。

第二十六条　承诺通知到达要约人时生效。承诺不需要通知的,根据交易习惯或者要约的要求作出承诺的行为时生效。

采用数据电文形式订立合同的,承诺到达的时间适用本法第十六条第二款的规定。

第二十七条　承诺可以撤回。撤回承诺的通知应当在承诺通知到达要约人之前或者与承诺通知同时到达要约人。

第二十八条　受要约人超过承诺期限发出承诺的,除要约人及时通知受要约人该承诺有效的以外,为新要约。

第二十九条　受要约人在承诺期限内发出承诺,按照通常情形能够及时到达要约人,但因其他原因承诺到达要约人时超过承诺期限的,除要约人及时通知受要约人因承诺超过期限不接受该承诺的以外,该承诺有效。

第三十条　承诺的内容应当与要约的内容一致。受要约人对要约的内容作出实质性变更的,为新要约。有关合同标的、数量、质量、价款或者报酬、履行期限、履行地点和方式、违约责任和解决争议方法等的变更,是对要约内容的实质性变更。

第三十一条　承诺对要约的内容作出非实质性变更的,除要约人及时表示反对或者要约表明承诺不得对要约的内容作出任何变更的以外,该承诺有效,合同的内容以承诺的内容为准。

第三十二条　当事人采用合同书形式订立合同的,自双方当事人签字或者盖章时合同成立。

第三十三条 当事人采用信件、数据电文等形式订立合同的,可以在合同成立之前要求签订确认书。签订确认书时合同成立。

第三十四条 承诺生效的地点为合同成立的地点。

采用数据电文形式订立合同的,收件人的主营业地为合同成立的地点;没有主营业地的,其经常居住地为合同成立的地点。当事人另有约定的,按照其约定。

第三十五条 当事人采用合同书形式订立合同的,双方当事人签字或者盖章的地点为合同成立的地点。

第三十六条 法律、行政法规规定或者当事人约定采用书面形式订立合同,当事人未采用书面形式但一方已经履行主要义务,对方接受的,该合同成立。

第三十七条 采用合同书形式订立合同,在签字或者盖章之前,当事人一方已经履行主要义务,对方接受的,该合同成立。

第三十八条 国家根据需要下达指令性任务或者国家订货任务的,有关法人、其他组织之间应当依照有关法律、行政法规规定的权利和义务订立合同。

第三十九条 采用格式条款订立合同的,提供格式条款的一方应当遵循公平原则确定当事人之间的权利和义务,并采取合理的方式提请对方注意免除或者限制其责任的条款,按照对方的要求,对该条款予以说明。

格式条款是当事人为了重复使用而预先拟定,并在订立合同时未与对方协商的条款。

第四十条 格式条款具有本法第五十二条和第五十三条规定情形的,或者提供格式条款一方免除其责任、加重对方责任、排除对方主要权利的,该条款无效。

第四十一条 对格式条款的理解发生争议的,应当按照通常理解予以解释。对格式条款有两种以上解释的,应当作出不利于提供格式条款一方的解释。格式条款和非格式条款不一致的,应当采用非格式条款。

第四十二条 当事人在订立合同过程中有下列情形之一,给对方造成损失的,应当承担损害赔偿责任:

(一)假借订立合同,恶意进行磋商;

(二)故意隐瞒与订立合同有关的重要事实或者提供虚假情况;

(三)有其他违背诚实信用原则的行为。

第四十三条 当事人在订立合同过程中知悉的商业秘密,无论合同是否成立,不得泄露或者不正当地使用。泄露或者不正当地使用该商业秘密给对方造成损失的,应当承担损害赔偿责任。

第三章 合同的效力

第四十四条 依法成立的合同,自成立时生效。

法律、行政法规规定应当办理批准、登记等手续生效的,依照其规定。

第四十五条 当事人对合同的效力可以约定附条件。附生效条件的合同,自条件成就时生效。附解除条件的合同,自条件成就时失效。

当事人为自己的利益不正当地阻止条件成就的,视为条件已成就;不正当地促成条件成就的,视为条件不成就。

第四十六条 当事人对合同的效力可以约定附期限。附生效期限的合同,自期限届至时生效。附终止期限的合同,自期限届满时失效。

第四十七条 限制民事行为能力人订立的合同,经法定代理人追认后,该合同有效,但纯获利益的合同或者与其年龄、智力、精神健康状况相适应而订立的合同,不必经法定代理人追认。

相对人可以催告法定代理人在一个月内予以追认。法定代理人未作表示的,视为拒绝追认。合同被追认之前,善意相对人有撤销的权利。撤销应当以通知的方式作出。

第四十八条 行为人没有代理权、超越代理权或者代理权终止后以被代理人名义订立的合同,未经被代理人追认,对被代理人不发生效力,由行为人承担责任。

相对人可以催告被代理人在一个月内予以追认。被代理人未作表示的,视为拒绝追认。合同被追认之前,善意相对人有撤销的权利。撤销应当以通知的方式作出。

第四十九条 行为人没有代理权、超越代理权或者代理权终止后以被代理人名义订立合同,相对人有理由相信行为人有代理权的,该代理行为有效。

第五十条 法人或者其他组织的法定代表人、负责人超越权限订立的合同,除相对人知道或者应当知道其超越权限的以外,该代表行为有效。

第五十一条 无处分权的人处分他人财产,经权利人追认或者无处分权的人订立合同后取得处分权的,该合同有效。

第五十二条 有下列情形之一的,合同无效:

(一)一方以欺诈、胁迫的手段订立合同,损害国家利益;

(二)恶意串通,损害国家、集体或者第三人利益;

(三)以合法形式掩盖非法目的;

(四)损害社会公共利益;

(五)违反法律、行政法规的强制性规定。

第五十三条 合同中的下列免责条款无效:

(一)造成对方人身伤害的;

(二)因故意或者重大过失造成对方财产损失的。

第五十四条 下列合同,当事人一方有权请求人民法院或者仲裁机构变更或者撤销:

(一)因重大误解订立的;

(二)在订立合同时显失公平的。

一方以欺诈、胁迫的手段或者乘人之危,使对方在违背真实意思的情况下订立的合同,受损害方有权请求人民法院或者仲裁机构变更或者撤销。

当事人请求变更的,人民法院或者仲裁机构不得撤销。

第五十五条 有下列情形之一的,撤销权消灭:

(一)具有撤销权的当事人自知道或者应当知道撤销事由之日起一年内没有行使撤销权;

(二)具有撤销权的当事人知道撤销事由后明确表示或者以自己的行为放弃撤销权。

第五十六条 无效的合同或者被撤销的合同自始没有法律约束力。合同部分无效,不影响其他部分效力的,其他部分仍然有效。

第五十七条 合同无效、被撤销或者终止的,不影响合同中独立存在的有关解决争议方法的条款的效力。

第五十八条 合同无效或者被撤销后,因该合同取得的财产,应当予以返还;不能返还或者没有必要返还的,应当折价补偿。有过错的一方应当赔偿对方因此所受到的损失,双方都有过错的,应当各自承担相应的责任。

第五十九条 当事人恶意串通,损害国家、集体或者第三人利益的,因此取得的财产收归国家所有或者返还集体、第三人。

第四章 合同的履行

第六十条 当事人应当按照约定全面履行自己的义务。

当事人应当遵循诚实信用原则,根据合同的性质、目的和交易习惯履行通知、协助、保密等义务。

第六十一条 合同生效后,当事人就质量、价款或者报酬、履行地点等内容没有约定或者约定不明确的,可以协议补充;不能达成补充协议的,按照合同有关条款或者交易习惯确定。

第六十二条 当事人就有关合同内容约定不明确，依照本法第六十一条的规定仍不能确定的,适用下列规定：

(一)质量要求不明确的,按照国家标准、行业标准履行；没有国家标准、行业标准的,按照通常标准或者符合合同目的的特定标准履行。

(二)价款或者报酬不明确的,按照订立合同时履行地的市场价格履行；依法应当执行政府定价或者政府指导价的,按照规定履行。

(三)履行地点不明确,给付货币的,在接受货币一方所在地履行；交付不动产的,在不动产所在地履行；其他标的,在履行义务一方所在地履行。

(四)履行期限不明确的,债务人可以随时履行,债权人也可以随时要求履行,但应当给对方必要的准备时间。

(五)履行方式不明确的,按照有利于实现合同目的的方式履行。

(六)履行费用的负担不明确的,由履行义务一方负担。

第六十三条 执行政府定价或者政府指导价的,在合同约定的交付期限内政府价格调整时,按照交付时的价格计价。逾期交付标的物的,遇价格上涨时,按照原价格执行；价格下降时,按照新价格执行。逾期提取标的物或者逾期付款的,遇价格上涨时,按照新价格执行；价格下降时,按照原价格执行。

第六十四条 当事人约定由债务人向第三人履行债务的，债务人未向第三人履行债务或者履行债务不符合约定,应当向债权人承担违约责任。

第六十五条 当事人约定由第三人向债权人履行债务的，第三人不履行债务或者履行债务不符合约定,债务人应当向债权人承担违约责任。

第六十六条 当事人互负债务,没有先后履行顺序的,应当同时履行。一方在对方履行之前有权拒绝其履行要求。一方在对方履行债务不符合约定时,有权拒绝其相应的履行要求。

第六十七条 当事人互负债务,有先后履行顺序,先履行一方未履行的,后履行一方有权拒绝其履行要求。先履行一方履行债务不符合约定的,后履行一方有权拒绝其相应的履行要求。

第六十八条 应当先履行债务的当事人,有确切证据证明对方有下列情形之一的,可以中止履行：

(一)经营状况严重恶化；

(二)转移财产、抽逃资金,以逃避债务；

(三)丧失商业信誉；

(四)有丧失或者可能丧失履行债务能力的其他情形。

当事人没有确切证据中止履行的,应当承担违约责任。

第六十九条 当事人依照本法第六十八条的规定中止履行的,应当及时通知对方。对方提供适当担保时,应当恢复履行。中止履行后,对方在合理期限内未恢复履行能力并且未提供适当担保的,中止履行的一方可以解除合同。

第七十条 债权人分立、合并或者变更住所没有通知债务人,致使履行债务发生困难的,债务人可以中止履行或者将标的物提存。

第七十一条 债权人可以拒绝债务人提前履行债务,但提前履行不损害债权人利益的除外。

债务人提前履行债务给债权人增加的费用,由债务人负担。

第七十二条 债权人可以拒绝债务人部分履行债务,但部分履行不损害债权人利益的除外。

债务人部分履行债务给债权人增加的费用,由债务人负担。

第七十三条 因债务人怠于行使其到期债权,对债权人造成损害的,债权人可以向人民法院请求以自己的名义代位行使债务人的债权,但该债权专属于债务人自身的除外。

代位权的行使范围以债权人的债权为限。债权人行使代位权的必要费用,由债务人负担。

第七十四条 因债务人放弃其到期债权或者无偿转让财产,对债权人造成损害的,债权人可以请求人民法院撤销债务人的行为。债务人以明显不合理的低价转让财产,对债权人造成损害,并且受让人知道该情形的,债权人也可以请求人民法院撤销债务人的行为。

撤销权的行使范围以债权人的债权为限。债权人行使撤销权的必要费用,由债务人负担。

第七十五条 撤销权自债权人知道或者应当知道撤销事由之日起一年内行使。自债务人的行为发生之日起五年内没有行使撤销权的,该撤销权消灭。

第七十六条 合同生效后,当事人不得因姓名、名称的变更或者法定代表人、负责人、承办人的变动而不履行合同义务。

第五章 合同的变更和转让

第七十七条 当事人协商一致,可以变更合同。

法律、行政法规规定变更合同应当办理批准、登记等手续的,依照其规定。

第七十八条 当事人对合同变更的内容约定不明确的,推定为未变更。

第七十九条 债权人可以将合同的权利全部或者部分转让给第三人,但有下列情形之一的除外:

(一)根据合同性质不得转让;

(二)按照当事人约定不得转让;

(三)依照法律规定不得转让。

第八十条 债权人转让权利的,应当通知债务人。未经通知,该转让对债务人不发生效力。

债权人转让权利的通知不得撤销,但经受让人同意的除外。

第八十一条 债权人转让权利的,受让人取得与债权有关的从权利,但该从权利专属于债权人自身的除外。

第八十二条 债务人接到债权转让通知后,债务人对让与人的抗辩,可以向受让人主张。

第八十三条 债务人接到债权转让通知时,债务人对让与人享有债权,并且债务人的债权先于转让的债权到期或者同时到期的,债务人可以向受让人主张抵销。

第八十四条 债务人将合同的义务全部或者部分转移给第三人的,应当经债权人同意。

第八十五条 债务人转移义务的,新债务人可以主张原债务人对债权人的抗辩。

第八十六条 债务人转移义务的,新债务人应当承担与主债务有关的从债务,但该从债务专属于原债务人自身的除外。

第八十七条 法律、行政法规规定转让权利或者转移义务应当办理批准、登记等手续的,依照其规定。

第八十八条 当事人一方经对方同意,可以将自己在合同中的权利和义务一并转让给第三人。

第八十九条 权利和义务一并转让的,适用本法第七十九条,第八十一条至第八十三条、第八十五条至第八十七条的规定。

第九十条 当事人订立合同后合并的,由合并后的法人或者其他组织行使合同权利,履行合同义务。当事人订立合同后分立的,除债权人和债务人另有约定的以外,由分立的法人或者其他组织对合同的权利和义务享有连带债权,承担连带债务。

第六章 合同的权利义务终止

第九十一条 有下列情形之一的,合同的权利义务终止:

(一)债务已经按照约定履行;

(二)合同解除;

(三)债务相互抵销;

(四)债务人依法将标的物提存;

(五)债权人免除债务;

(六)债权债务同归于一人;

(七)法律规定或者当事人约定终止的其他情形。

第九十二条 合同的权利义务终止后,当事人应当遵循诚实信用原则,根据交易习惯履行通知、协助、保密等义务。

第九十三条 当事人协商一致,可以解除合同。

当事人可以约定一方解除合同的条件。解除合同的条件成就时,解除权人可以解除合同。

第九十四条 有下列情形之一的,当事人可以解除合同:

(一)因不可抗力致使不能实现合同目的;

(二)在履行期限届满之前,当事人一方明确表示或者以自己的行为表明不履行主要债务;

(三)当事人一方迟延履行主要债务,经催告后在合理期限内仍未履行;

(四)当事人一方迟延履行债务或者有其他违约行为致使不能实现合同目的;

(五)法律规定的其他情形。

第九十五条 法律规定或者当事人约定解除权行使期限,期限届满当事人不行使的,该权利消灭。

法律没有规定或者当事人没有约定解除权行使期限,经对方催告后在合理期限内不行使的,该权利消灭。

第九十六条 当事人一方依照本法第九十三条第二款、第九十四条的规定主张解除合同的,应当通知对方。合同自通知到达对方时解除。对方有异议的,可以请求人民法院或者仲裁机构确认解除合同的效力。

法律、行政法规规定解除合同应当办理批准、登记等手续的,依照其规定。

第九十七条 合同解除后,尚未履行的,终止履行;已经履行的,根据履行情况和合同性质,当事人可以要求恢复原状、采取其他补救措施,并有权要求赔偿损失。

第九十八条 合同的权利义务终止，不影响合同中结算和清理条款的效力。

第九十九条 当事人互负到期债务，该债务的标的物种类、品质相同的,任何一方可以将自己的债务与对方的债务抵销，但依照法律规定或者按照合同性质不得抵销的除外。

当事人主张抵销的,应当通知对方。通知自到达对方时生效。抵销不得附条件或者附期限。

第一百条 当事人互负债务,标的物种类、品质不相同的,经双方协商一致,也可以抵销。

第一百零一条 有下列情形之一,难以履行债务的,债务人可以将标的物提存：

(一)债权人无正当理由拒绝受领；

(二)债权人下落不明；

(三)债权人死亡未确定继承人或者丧失民事行为能力未确定监护人；

(四)法律规定的其他情形。

标的物不适于提存或者提存费用过高的,债务人依法可以拍卖或者变卖标的物,提存所得的价款。

第一百零二条 标的物提存后,除债权人下落不明的以外,债务人应当及时通知债权人或者债权人的继承人、监护人。

第一百零三条 标的物提存后,毁损、灭失的风险由债权人承担。提存期间,标的物的孳息归债权人所有。提存费用由债权人负担。

第一百零四条 债权人可以随时领取提存物,但债权人对债务人负有到期债务的,在债权人未履行债务或者提供担保之前,提存部门根据债务人的要求应当拒绝其领取提存物。

债权人领取提存物的权利,自提存之日起五年内不行使而消灭,提存物扣除提存费用后归国家所有。

第一百零五条 债权人免除债务人部分或者全部债务的,合同的权利义务部分或者全部终止。

第一百零六条 债权和债务同归于一人的,合同的权利义务终止,但涉及第三人利益的除外。

第七章 违约责任

第一百零七条 当事人一方不履行合同义务或者履行合同义务不符合约定的,应当承担继续履行、采取补救措施或者赔偿损失等违约责任。

第一百零八条 当事人一方明确表示或者以自己的行为表明不履行合同义务的,对方可以在履行期限届满之前要求其承担违约责任。

第一百零九条 当事人一方未支付价款或者报酬的,对方可以要求其支付价款或者报酬。

第一百一十条 当事人一方不履行非金钱债务或者履行非金钱债务不符合约定的,对方可以要求履行,但有下列情形之一的除外:

(一)法律上或者事实上不能履行;

(二)债务的标的不适于强制履行或者履行费用过高;

(三)债权人在合理期限内未要求履行。

第一百一十一条 质量不符合约定的,应当按照当事人的约定承担违约责任。对违约责任没有约定或者约定不明确,依照本法第六十一条的规定仍不能确定的,受损害方根据标的的性质以及损失的大小,可以合理选择要求对方承担修理、更换、重作、退货、减少价款或者报酬等违约责任。

第一百一十二条 当事人一方不履行合同义务或者履行合同义务不符合约定的,在履行义务或者采取补救措施后,对方还有其他损失的,应当赔偿损失。

第一百一十三条 当事人一方不履行合同义务或者履行合同义务不符合约定,给对方造成损失的,损失赔偿额应当相当于因违约所造成的损失,包括合同履行后可以获得的利益,但不得超过违反合同一方订立合同时预见到或者应当预见到的因违反合同可能造成的损失。

经营者对消费者提供商品或者服务有欺诈行为的,依照《中华人民共和国消费者权益保护法》的规定承担损害赔偿责任。

第一百一十四条 当事人可以约定一方违约时应当根据违约情况向对方支付一定数额的违约金,也可以约定因违约产生的损失赔偿额的计算方法。

约定的违约金低于造成的损失的,当事人可以请求人民法院或者仲裁机构予以增加;约定的违约金过分高于造成的损失的,当事人可以请求人民法院或者仲裁机构予以适当减少。

当事人就迟延履行约定违约金的,违约方支付违约金后,还应当履行债务。

第一百一十五条 当事人可以依照《中华人民共和国担保法》约定一方向对方给付定金作为债权的担保。债务人履行债务后,定金应当抵作价款或者收回。给付定金的一方不履行约定的债务的,无权要求返还定金;收受定金的一方不履行约定的债务的,应当双倍返还定金。

第一百一十六条　当事人既约定违约金,又约定定金的,一方违约时,对方可以选择适用违约金或者定金条款。

第一百一十七条　因不可抗力不能履行合同的,根据不可抗力的影响,部分或者全部免除责任,但法律另有规定的除外。当事人迟延履行后发生不可抗力的,不能免除责任。

本法所称不可抗力,是指不能预见、不能避免并不能克服的客观情况。

第一百一十八条　当事人一方因不可抗力不能履行合同的,应当及时通知对方,以减轻可能给对方造成的损失,并应当在合理期限内提供证明。

第一百一十九条　当事人一方违约后,对方应当采取适当措施防止损失的扩大;没有采取适当措施致使损失扩大的,不得就扩大的损失要求赔偿。

当事人因防止损失扩大而支出的合理费用,由违约方承担。

第一百二十条　当事人双方部违反合同的,应当各自承担相应的责任。

第一百二十一条　当事人一方因第三人的原因造成违约的,应当向对方承担违约责任。当事人一方和第三人之间的纠纷,依照法律规定或者按照约定解决。

第一百二十二条　因当事人一方的违约行为,侵害对方人身、财产权益的,受损害方有权选择依照本法要求其承担违约责任或者依照其他法律要求其承担侵权责任。

第八章　其他规定

第一百二十三条　其他法律对合同另有规定的,依照其规定。

第一百二十四条　本法分则或者其他法律没有明文规定的合同,适用本法总则的规定,并可以参照本法分则或者其他法律最相类似的规定。

第一百二十五条　当事人对合同条款的理解有争议的,应当按照合同所使用的词句、合同的有关条款、合同的目的、交易习惯以及诚实信用原则,确定该条款的真实意思。

合同文本采用两种以上文字订立并约定具有同等效力的,对各文本使用的同句推定具有相同含义。各文本使用的词句不一致的,应当根据合同的目的予以解释。

第一百二十六条　涉外合同的当事人可以选择处理合同争议所适用的法律,但法律另有规定的除外。涉外合同的当事人没有选择的,适用与合同有最密切联系的国家的法律。

在中华人民共和国境内履行的中外合资经营企业合同、中外合作经营企业合同、中外合作勘探开发自然资源合同,适用中华人民共和国法律。

第一百二十六条 工商行政管理部门和其他有关行政主管部门在各自的职权范围内,依照法律、行政法规的规定,对利用合同危害国家利益、社会公共利益的违法行为,负责监督处理;构成犯罪的,依法追究刑事责任。

第一百二十八条 当事人可以通过和解或者调解解决合同争议。

当事人不愿和解、调解或者和解、调解不成的,可以根据仲裁协议向仲裁机构申请仲裁。涉外合同的当事人可以根据仲裁协议向中国仲裁机构或者其他仲裁机构申请仲裁。当事人没有订立仲裁协议或者仲裁协议无效的,可以向人民法院起诉。当事人应当履行发生法律效力的判决、仲裁裁决、调解书;拒不履行的,对方可以请求人民法院执行。

第一百二十九条 因国际货物买卖合同和技术进出口合同争议提起诉讼或者申请仲裁的期限为四年,自当事人知道或者应当知道其权利受到侵害之日起计算。因其他合同争议提起诉讼或者申请仲裁的期限,依照有关法律的规定。

附录三

APPENDIX III

UNIDROIT PRINCIPLES OF INTERNATIONAL COMMERCIAL CONTRACTS 2004
国际商事合同通则

PREAMBLE

(*Purpose of the Principles*)

These Principles set forth general rules for international commercial contracts.

They shall be applied when the parties have agreed that their contract be governed by them.

They may be applied when the parties have agreed that their contract be governed by general principles of law, the lex mercatoria or the like.

They may be applied when the parties have not chosen any law to govern their contract.

They may be used to interpret or supplement international uniform law instruments.

They may be used to interpret or supplement domestic law.

They may serve as a model for national and international legislators.

CHAPTER 1 — GENERAL PROVISIONS

ARTICLE 1.1 (*Freedom of contract*)

The parties are free to enter into a contract and to determine its content.

ARTICLE 1.2 (*No form required*)

Nothing in these Principles requires a contract, statement or any other act to be made in or evidenced by a particular form. It may be proved by any means, including witnesses.

ARTICLE 1.3 (*Binding character of contract*)

A contract validly entered into is binding upon the parties. It can only be modified or terminated in accordance with its terms or by agreement or as otherwise provided in these Principles.

ARTICLE 1.4 (*Mandatory rules*)

Nothing in these Principles shall restrict the application of mandatory rules, whether of national, international or supranational origin, which are applicable in accordance with the relevant rules of private international law.

ARTICLE 1.5 (*Exclusion or modification by the parties*)

The parties may exclude the application of these Principles or derogate from or vary the effect of any of their provisions, except as otherwise provided in the Principles.

ARTICLE 1.6 (*Interpretation and supplementation of the Principles*)

(1) In the interpretation of these Principles, regard is to be had to their international character and to their purposes including the need to promote uniformity in their application.

(2) Issues within the scope of these Principles but not expressly settled by them are as far as possible to be settled in accordance with their underlying general principles.

ARTICLE 1.7 (*Good faith and fair dealing*)

(1) Each party must act in accordance with good faith and fair dealing in international trade.

(2) The parties may not exclude or limit this duty.

ARTICLE 1.8 (*Inconsistent Behaviour*)

A party cannot act inconsistently with an understanding it has caused the other party to have and upon which that other party reasonably has acted in reliance to its detriment.

ARTICLE 1.9 (*Usages and practices*)

(1) The parties are bound by any usage to which they have agreed and by any practices which they have established between themselves.

(2) The parties are bound by a usage that is widely known to and regularly observed in international trade by parties in the particular trade concerned except where the application of such a usage would be unreasonable.

ARTICLE 1.10 (*Notice*)

(1) Where notice is required it may be given by any means appropriate to the circumstances.

(2) A notice is effective when it reaches the person to whom it is given.

(3) For the purpose of paragraph (2) a notice "reaches" a person when given to that person orally or delivered at that person's place of business or mailing

address.

(4) For the purpose of this article "notice" includes a declaration, demand, request or any other communication of intention.

ARTICLE 1.11 (*Definitions*)

In these Principles

"court" includes an arbitral tribunal;

where a party has more than one place of business the relevant "place of business" is that which has the closest relationship to the contract and its performance, having regard to the circumstances known to or contemplated by the parties at any time before or at the conclusion of the contract;

"obligor" refers to the party who is to perform an obligation and "obligee" refers to the party who is entitled to performance of that obligation.

"writing" means any mode of communication that preserves a record of the information contained therein and is capable of being reproduced in tangible form.

ARTICLE 1.12 (*Computation of time set by parties*)

(1) Official holidays or non-business days occurring during a period set by parties for an act to be performed are included in calculating the period.

(2) However, if the last day of the period is an official holiday or a non-business day at the place of business of the party to perform the act, the period is extended until the first business day which follows, unless the circumstances indicate otherwise.

(3) The relevant time zone is that of the place of business of the party setting the time, unless the circumstances indicate otherwise.

CHAPTER 2 — FORMATION AND AUTHORITY OF AGENTS

SECTION 1: FORMATION

ARTICLE 2.1.1 (*Manner of formation*)

A contract may be concluded either by the acceptance of an offer or by conduct of the parties that is sufficient to show agreement.

ARTICLE 2.1.2 (*Definition of offer*)

A proposal for concluding a contract constitutes an offer if it is sufficiently definite and indicates the intention of the offeror to be bound in case of acceptance.

ARTICLE 2.1.3 (*Withdrawal of offer*)

(1) An offer becomes effective when it reaches the offeree.

(2) An offer, even if it is irrevocable, may be withdrawn if the withdrawal reaches the offeree before or at the same time as the offer.

ARTICLE 2.1.4 (*Revocation of offer*)

(1) Until a contract is concluded an offer may be revoked if the revocation reaches the offeree before it has dispatched an acceptance.

(2) However, an offer cannot be revoked

(a) if it indicates, whether by stating a fixed time for acceptance or otherwise, that it is irrevocable; or

(b) if it was reasonable for the offeree to rely on the offer as being irrevocable and the offeree has acted in reliance on the offer.

ARTICLE 2.1.5 (*Rejection of offer*)

An offer is terminated when a rejection reaches the offeror.

ARTICLE 2.1.6 (*Mode of acceptance*)

(1) A statement made by or other conduct of the offeree indicating assent to an offer is an acceptance. Silence or inactivity does not in itself amount to acceptance.

(2) An acceptance of an offer becomes effective when the indication of assent reaches the offeror.

(3) However, if, by virtue of the offer or as a result of practices which the parties have established between themselves or of usage, the offeree may indicate assent by performing an act without notice to the offeror, the acceptance is effective when the act is performed.

ARTICLE 2.1.7 (*Time of acceptance*)

An offer must be accepted within the time the offeror has fixed or, if no time is fixed, within a reasonable time having regard to the circumstances, including the rapidity of the means of communication employed by the offeror. An oral offer must be accepted immediately unless the circumstances indicate otherwise.

ARTICLE 2.1.8 (*Acceptance within a fixed period of time*)

A period of acceptance fixed by the offeror begins to run from the time that the offer is dispatched. A time indicated in the offer is deemed to be the time of dispatch unless the circumstances indicate otherwise.

ARTICLE 2.1.9 (*Late acceptance. Delay in transmission*)

(1) A late acceptance is nevertheless effective as an acceptance if without un-

due delay the offeror so informs the offeree or gives notice to that effect.

(2) If a communication containing a late acceptance shows that it has been sent in such circumstances that if its transmission had been normal it would have reached the offeror in due time, the late acceptance is effective as an acceptance unless, without undue delay, the offeror informs the offeree that it considers the offer as having lapsed.

ARTICLE 2.1.10 (*Withdrawal of acceptance*)

An acceptance may be withdrawn if the withdrawal reaches the offeror before or at the same time as the acceptance would have become effective.

ARTICLE 2.1.11 (*Modified acceptance*)

(1) A reply to an offer which purports to be an acceptance but contains additions, limitations or other modifications is a rejection of the offer and constitutes a counter-offer.

(2) However, a reply to an offer which purports to be an acceptance but contains additional or different terms which do not materially alter the terms of the offer constitutes an acceptance, unless the offeror, without undue delay, objects to the discrepancy. If the offeror does not object, the terms of the contract are the terms of the offer with the modifications contained in the acceptance.

ARTICLE 2.1.12 (*Writings in confirmation*)

If a writing which is sent within a reasonable time after the conclusion of the contract and which purports to be a confirmation of the contract contains additional or different terms, such terms become part of the contract, unless they materially alter the contract or the recipient, without undue delay, objects to the discrepancy.

ARTICLE 2.1.13 (*Conclusion of contract dependent on agreement on specific matters or in a particular form*)

Where in the course of negotiations one of the parties insists that the contract is not concluded until there is agreement on specific matters or in a particular form, no contract is concluded before agreement is reached on those matters or in that form.

ARTICLE 2.1.14 (*Contract with terms deliberately left open*)

(1) If the parties intend to conclude a contract, the fact that they intentionally leave a term to be agreed upon in further negotiations or to be determined by a third person does not prevent a contract from coming into existence.

(2) The existence of the contract is not affected by the fact that subsequently

(a) the parties reach no agreement on the term; or

(b) the third person does not determine the term, provided that there is an alternative means of rendering the term definite that is reasonable in the circumstances, having regard to the intention of the parties.

ARTICLE 2.1.15 (*Negotiations in bad faith*)

(1) A party is free to negotiate and is not liable for failure to reach an agreement.

(2) However, a party who negotiates or breaks off negotiations in bad faith is liable for the losses caused to the other party.

(3) It is bad faith, in particular, for a party to enter into or continue negotiations when intending not to reach an agreement with the other party.

ARTICLE 2.1.16 (*Duty of confidentiality*)

Where information is given as confidential by one party in the course of negotiations, the other party is under a duty not to disclose that information or to use it improperly for its own purposes, whether or not a contract is subsequently concluded.

Where appropriate, the remedy for breach of that duty may include compensation based on the benefit received by the other party.

ARTICLE 2.1.17 (*Merger clauses*)

A contract in writing which contains a clause indicating that the writing completely embodies the terms on which the parties have agreed cannot be contradicted or supplemented by evidence of prior statements or agreements. However, such statements or agreements may be used to interpret the writing.

ARTICLE 2.1.18 (*Modification in a particular form*)

A contract in writing which contains a clause requiring any modification or termination by agreement to be in a particular form may not be otherwise modified or terminated. However, a party may be precluded by its conduct from asserting such a clause to the extent that the other party has reasonably acted in reliance on that conduct.

ARTICLE 2.1.19 (*Contracting under standard terms*)

(1) Where one party or both parties use standard terms in concluding a contract, the general rules on formation apply, subject to Articles 2.1.20 – 2.1.22.

(2) Standard terms are provisions which are prepared in advance for general and repeated use by one party and which are actually used without negotiation with the other party.

ARTICLE 2.1.20 (*Surprising terms*)

(1) No term contained in standard terms which is of such a character that the other party could not reasonably have expected it, is effective unless it has been expressly accepted by that party.

(2) In determining whether a term is of such a character regard shall be had to its content, language and presentation.

ARTICLE 2.1.21 (*Conflict between standard terms and non-standard terms*)

In case of conflict between a standard term and a term which is not a standard term the latter prevails.

ARTICLE 2.1.22 (*Battle of forms*)

Where both parties use standard terms and reach agreement except on those terms, a contract is concluded on the basis of the agreed terms and of any standard terms which are common in substance unless one party clearly indicates in advance, or later and without undue delay informs the other party, that it does not intend to be bound by such a contract.

SECTION 2: AUTHORITY OF AGENTS

ARTICLE 2.2.1 (*Scope of the Section*)

(1) This Section governs the authority of a person ("the agent"), to affect the legal relations of another person ("the principal"), by or with respect to a contract with a third party, whether the agent acts in its own name or in that of the principal.

(2) It governs only the relations between the principal or the agent on the one hand, and the third party on the other.

(3) It does not govern an agent's authority conferred by law or the authority of an agent appointed by a public or judicial authority.

ARTICLE 2.2.2 (*Establishment and scope of the authority of the agent*)

(1) The principal's grant of authority to an agent may be express or implied.

(2) The agent has authority to perform all acts necessary in the circumstances to achieve the purposes for which the authority was granted.

ARTICLE 2.2.3 (*Agency disclosed*)

(1) Where an agent acts within the scope of its authority and the third party knew

or ought to have known that the agent was acting as an agent, the acts of the agent shall directly affect the legal relations between the principal and the third party and no legal relation is created between the agent and the third party.

(2) However, the acts of the agent shall affect only the relations between the agent and the third party, where the agent with the consent of the principal undertakes to become the party to the contract.

ARTICLE 2.2.4 (*Agency undisclosed*)

(1) Where an agent acts within the scope of its authority and the third party neither knew nor ought to have known that the agent was acting as an agent, the acts of the agent shall affect only the relations between the agent and the third party.

(2) However, where such an agent, when contracting with the third party on behalf of a business, represents itself to be the owner of that business, the third party, upon discovery of the real owner of the business, may exercise also against the latter the rights it has against the agent.

ARTICLE 2.2.5 (*Agent acting without or exceeding its authority*)

(1) Where an agent acts without authority or exceeds its authority, its acts do not affect the legal relations between the principal and the third party.

(2) However, where the principal causes the third party reasonably to believe that the agent has authority to act on behalf of the principal and that the agent is acting within the scope of that authority, the principal may not invoke against the third party the lack of authority of the agent.

ARTICLE 2.2.6 (*Liability of agent acting without or exceeding its authority*)

(1) An agent that acts without authority or exceeds its authority is, failing ratification by the principal, liable for damages that will place the third party in the same position as if the agent had acted with authority and not exceeded its authority.

(2) However, the agent is not liable if the third party knew or ought to have known that the agent had no authority or was exceeding its authority.

ARTICLE 2.2.7 (*Conflict of interests*)

(1) If a contract concluded by an agent involves the agent in a conflict of interests with the principal of which the third party knew or ought to have known, the principal may avoid the contract. The right to avoid is subject to Articles 3.12 and 3.14 to 3.17.

(2) However, the principal may not avoid the contract

(a) if the principal had consented to, or knew or ought to have known of, the agent's involvement in the conflict of interests; or

(b) if the agent had disclosed the conflict of interests to the principal and the latter had not objected within a reasonable time.

ARTICLE 2.2.8 (*Sub-agency*)

An agent has implied authority to appoint a sub-agent to perform acts which it is not reasonable to expect the agent to perform itself. The rules of this Section apply to the sub-agency.

ARTICLE 2.2.9 (*Ratification*)

(1) An act by an agent that acts without authority or exceeds its authority may be ratified by the principal. On ratification the act produces the same effects as if it had initially been carried out with authority.

(2) The third party may by notice to the principal specify a reasonable period of time for ratification. If the principal does not ratify within that period of time it can no longer do so.

(3) If, at the time of the agent's act, the third party neither knew nor ought to have known of the lack of authority, it may, at any time before ratification, by notice to the principal indicate its refusal to become bound by a ratification.

ARTICLE 2.2.10 (*Termination of authority*)

(1) Termination of authority is not effective in relation to the third party unless the third party knew or ought to have known of it.

(2) Notwithstanding the termination of its authority, an agent remains authorized to perform the acts that are necessary to prevent harm to the principal's interests.

CHAPTER 3 — VALIDITY

ARTICLE 3.1 (*Matters not covered*)

These Principles do not deal with invalidity arising from (a) lack of capacity; (b) immorality or illegality.

ARTICLE 3.2 (*Validity of mere agreement*)

A contract is concluded, modified or terminated by the mere agreement of the parties, without any further requirement.

ARTICLE 3.3 (*Initial impossibility*)

(1) The mere fact that at the time of the conclusion of the contract the performance of the obligation assumed was impossible does not affect the validity of the contract.

(2) The mere fact that at the time of the conclusion of the contract a party was

not entitled to dispose of the assets to which the contract relates does not affect the validity of the contract.

ARTICLE 3.4 (*Definition of mistake*)

Mistake is an erroneous assumption relating to facts or to law existing when the contract was concluded.

ARTICLE 3.5 (*Relevant mistake*)

(1) A party may only avoid the contract for mistake if, when the contract was concluded, the mistake was of such importance that a reasonable person in the same situation as the party in error would only have concluded the contract on materially different terms or would not have concluded it at all if the true state of affairs had been known, and

(a) the other party made the same mistake, or caused the mistake, or knew or ought to have known of the mistake and it was contrary to reasonable commercial standards of fair dealing to leave the mistaken party in error; or

(b) the other party had not at the time of avoidance reasonably acted in reliance on the contract.

(2) However, a party may not avoid the contract if

(a) it was grossly negligent in committing the mistake; or

(b) the mistake relates to a matter in regard to which the risk of mistake was assumed or, having regard to the circumstances, should be borne by the mistaken party.

ARTICLE 3.6 (*Error in expression or transmission*)

An error occurring in the expression or transmission of a declaration is considered to be a mistake of the person from whom the declaration emanated.

ARTICLE 3.7 (*Remedies for non-performance*)

A party is not entitled to avoid the contract on the ground of mistake if the circumstances on which that party relies afford, or could have afforded, a remedy for non-performance.

ARTICLE 3.8 (*Fraud*)

A party may avoid the contract when it has been led to conclude the contract by the other party's fraudulent representation, including language or practices, or fraudulent non-disclosure of circumstances which, according to reasonable commercial standards of fair dealing, the latter party should have disclosed.

ARTICLE 3.9 (*Threat*)

A party may avoid the contract when it has been led to conclude the contract by the other party's unjustified threat which, having regard to the circumstances, is so imminent and serious as to leave the first party no reasonable alternative. In particular, a threat is unjustified if the act or omission with which a party has been threatened is wrongful in itself, or it is wrongful to use it as a means to obtain the conclusion of the contract.

ARTICLE 3.10 (*Gross disparity*)

(1) A party may avoid the contract or an individual term of it if, at the time of the conclusion of the contract, the contract or term unjustifiably gave the other party an excessive advantage. Regard is to be had, among other factors, to

(a) the fact that the other party has taken unfair advantage of the first party's dependence, economic distress or urgent needs, or of its improvidence, ignorance, inexperience or lack of bargaining skill, and

(b) the nature and purpose of the contract.

(2) Upon the request of the party entitled to avoidance, a court may adapt the contract or term in order to make it accord with reasonable commercial standards of fair dealing.

(3) A court may also adapt the contract or term upon the request of the party receiving notice of avoidance, provided that that party informs the other party of its request promptly after receiving such notice and before the other party has reasonably acted in reliance on it. The provisions of Article 3.13 (2) apply accordingly.

ARTICLE 3.11 (*Third persons*)

(1) Where fraud, threat, gross disparity or a party's mistake is imputable to, or is known or ought to be known by, a third person for whose acts the other party is responsible, the contract may be avoided under the same conditions as if the behaviour or knowledge had been that of the party itself.

(2) Where fraud, threat or gross disparity is imputable to a third person for whose acts the other party is not responsible, the contract may be avoided if that party knew or ought to have known of the fraud, threat or disparity, or has not at the time of avoidance reasonably acted in reliance on the contract.

ARTICLE 3.12 (*Confirmation*)

If the party entitled to avoid the contract expressly or impliedly confirms the contract after the period of time for giving notice of avoidance has begun to run, avoidance of the contract is excluded.

ARTICLE 3.13 (*Loss of right to avoid*)

(1) If a party is entitled to avoid the contract for mistake but the other party declares itself willing to perform or performs the contract as it was understood by the party entitled to avoidance, the contract is considered to have been concluded as the latter party understood it. The other party must make such a declaration or render such performance promptly after having been informed of the manner in which the party entitled to avoidance had understood the contract and before that party has reasonably acted in reliance on a notice of avoidance.

(2) After such a declaration or performance the right to avoidance is lost and any earlier notice of avoidance is ineffective.

ARTICLE 3.14 (*Notice of avoidance*)

The right of a party to avoid the contract is exercised by notice to the other party.

ARTICLE 3.15 (*Time limits*)

(1) Notice of avoidance shall be given within a reasonable time, having regard to the circumstances, after the avoiding party knew or could not have been unaware of the relevant facts or became capable of acting freely.

(2) Where an individual term of the contract may be avoided by a party under Article 3.10, the period of time for giving notice of avoidance begins to run when that term is asserted by the other party.

ARTICLE 3.16 (*Partial avoidance*)

Where a ground of avoidance affects only individual terms of the contract, the effect of avoidance is limited to those terms unless, having regard to the circumstances, it is unreasonable to uphold the remaining contract.

ARTICLE 3.17 (*Retroactive effect of avoidance*)

(1) Avoidance takes effect retroactively.

(2) On avoidance either party may claim restitution of whatever it has supplied under the contract or the part of it avoided, provided that it concurrently makes restitution of whatever it has received under the contract or the part of it avoided or, if it cannot make restitution in kind, it makes an allowance for what it has received.

ARTICLE 3.18 (*Damages*)

Irrespective of whether or not the contract has been avoided, the party who knew or ought to have known of the ground for avoidance is liable for damages so as to put the other party in the same position in which it would have been if it had not concluded the contract.

ARTICLE 3.19 (*Mandatory character of the provisions*)

The provisions of this Chapter are mandatory, except insofar as they relate to the binding force of mere agreement, initial impossibility or mistake.

ARTICLE 3.20 (*Unilateral declarations*)

The provisions of this Chapter apply with appropriate adaptations to any communication of intention addressed by one party to the other.

CHAPTER 4 — INTERPRETATION

ARTICLE 4.1 (*Intention of the parties*)

(1) A contract shall be interpreted according to the common intention of the parties.

(2) If such an intention cannot be established, the contract shall be interpreted according to the meaning that reasonable persons of the same kind as the parties would give to it in the same circumstances.

ARTICLE 4.2 (*Interpretation of statements and other conduct*)

(1) The statements and other conduct of a party shall be interpreted according to that party's intention if the other party knew or could not have been unaware of that intention.

(2) If the preceding paragraph is not applicable, such statements and other conduct shall be interpreted according to the meaning that a reasonable person of the same kind as the other party would give to it in the same circumstances.

ARTICLE 4.3 (*Relevant circumstances*)

In applying Articles 4.1 and 4.2, regard shall be had to all the circumstances, Including (a) preliminary negotiations between the parties;

(b) practices which the parties have established between themselves;

(c) the conduct of the parties subsequent to the conclusion of the contract;

(d) the nature and purpose of the contract;

(e) the meaning commonly given to terms and expressions in the trade concerned;

(f) usages.

ARTICLE 4.4 (*Reference to contract or statement as a whole*)

Terms and expressions shall be interpreted in the light of the whole contract or statement in which they appear.

ARTICLE 4.5 (*All terms to be given effect*)

Contract terms shall be interpreted so as to give effect to all the terms rather than to deprive some of them of effect.

ARTICLE 4.6 (*Contra proferentem rule*)

If contract terms supplied by one party are unclear, an interpretation against that party is preferred.

ARTICLE 4.7 (*Linguistic discrepancies*)

Where a contract is drawn up in two or more language versions which are equally authoritative there is, in case of discrepancy between the versions, a preference for the interpretation according to a version in which the contract was originally drawn up.

ARTICLE 4.8 (*Supplying an omitted term*)

(1) Where the parties to a contract have not agreed with respect to a term which is important for a determination of their rights and duties, a term which is appropriate in the circumstances shall be supplied.

(2) In determining what is an appropriate term regard shall be had, among other factors, to

(a) the intention of the parties;

(b) the nature and purpose of the contract;

(c) good faith and fair dealing;

(d) reasonableness.

CHAPTER 5 — CONTENT AND THIRD PARTY RIGHTS

SECTION 1: CONTENT

ARTICLE 5.1.1 (*Express and implied obligations*)

The contractual obligations of the parties may be express or implied.

ARTICLE 5.1.2 (*Implied obligations*)

Implied obligations stem from

(a) the nature and purpose of the contract;

(b) practices established between the parties and usages;

(c) good faith and fair dealing;

(d) reasonableness.

ARTICLE 5.1.3 (*Co-operation between the parties*)

Each party shall cooperate with the other party when such co-operation may reasonably be expected for the performance of that party's obligations.

ARTICLE 5.1.4 (*Duty to achieve a specific result. Duty of best efforts*)

(1) To the extent that an obligation of a party involves a duty to achieve a specific result, that party is bound to achieve that result.

(2) To the extent that an obligation of a party involves a duty of best efforts in the performance of an activity, that party is bound to make such efforts as would be made by a reasonable person of the same kind in the same circumstances.

ARTICLE 5.1.5 (*Determination of kind of duty involved*)

In determining the extent to which an obligation of a party involves a duty of best efforts in the performance of an activity or a duty to achieve a specific result, regard shall be had, among other factors, to

(a) the way in which the obligation is expressed in the contract;

(b) the contractual price and other terms of the contract;

(c) the degree of risk normally involved in achieving the expected result;

(d) the ability of the other party to influence the performance of the obligation.

ARTICLE 5.1.6 (*Determination of quality of performance*)

Where the quality of performance is neither fixed by, nor determinable from, the contract a party is bound to render a performance of a quality that is reasonable and not less than average in the circumstances.

ARTICLE 5.1.7 (*Price determination*)

(1) Where a contract does not fix or make provision for determining the price, the parties are considered, in the absence of any indication to the contrary, to have made reference to the price generally charged at the time of the conclusion of the contract for such performance in comparable circumstances in the trade concerned or, if no such price is available, to a reasonable price.

(2) Where the price is to be determined by one party and that determination is manifestly unreasonable, a reasonable price shall be substituted notwithstanding any contract term to the contrary.

(3) Where the price is to be fixed by a third person, and that person cannot or will not do so, the price shall be a reasonable price.

(4) Where the price is to be fixed by reference to factors which do not exist or have ceased to exist or to be accessible, the nearest equivalent factor shall be treated as a substitute.

ARTICLE 5.1.8 (*Contract for an indefinite period*)

A contract for an indefinite period may be ended by either party by giving notice a reasonable time in advance.

ARTICLE 5.1.9 (*Release by agreement*)

(1) An obligee may release its right by agreement with the obligor.

(2) An offer to release a right gratuitously shall be deemed accepted if the obligor does not reject the offer without delay after having become aware of it.

SECTION 2: THIRD PARTY RIGHTS

ARTICLE 5.2.1 (*Contracts in favour of third parties*)

(1) The parties (the "promisor" and the "promisee") may confer by express or implied agreement a right on a third party (the "beneficiary").

(2) The existence and content of the beneficiary's right against the promisor are determined by the agreement of the parties and are subject to any conditions or other limitations under the agreement.

ARTICLE 5.2.2 (*Third party identifiable*)

The beneficiary must be identifiable with adequate certainty by the contract but need not be in existence at the time the contract is made.

ARTICLE 5.2.3 (*Exclusion and limitation clauses*)

The conferment of rights in the beneficiary includes the right to invoke a clause in the contract which excludes or limits the liability of the beneficiary.

ARTICLE 5.2.4 (*Defences*)

The promisor may assert against the beneficiary all defences which the promisor could assert against the promisee.

ARTICLE 5.2.5 (*Revocation*)

The parties may modify or revoke the rights conferred by the contract on the beneficiary until the beneficiary has accepted them or reasonably acted in reliance on them.

ARTICLE 5.2.6 (*Renunciation*)

The beneficiary may renounce a right conferred on it.

CHAPTER 6 — PERFORMANCE

SECTION 1: PERFORMANCE IN GENERAL

ARTICLE 6.1.1 (*Time of performance*)

A party must perform its obligations:

(a) if a time is fixed by or determinable from the contract, at that time;

(b) if a period of time is fixed by or determinable from the contract, at any time within that period unless circumstances indicate that the other party is to choose a time;

(c) in any other case, within a reasonable time after the conclusion of the contract.

ARTICLE 6.1.2 (*Performance at one time or in instalments*)

In cases under Article 6.1.1(b) or (c), a party must perform its obligations at one time if that performance can be rendered at one time and the circumstances do not indicate otherwise.

ARTICLE 6.1.3 (*Partial performance*)

(1) The obligee may reject an offer to perform in part at the time performance is due, whether or not such offer is coupled with an assurance as to the balance of the performance, unless the obligee has no legitimate interest in so doing.

(2) Additional expenses caused to the obligee by partial performance are to be borne by the obligor without prejudice to any other remedy.

ARTICLE 6.1.4 (*Order of performance*)

(1) To the extent that the performances of the parties can be rendered simultaneously, the parties are bound to render them simultaneously unless the circumstances indicate otherwise.

(2) To the extent that the performance of only one party requires a period of time, that party is bound to render its performance first, unless the circum‐ stances indicate otherwise.

ARTICLE 6.1.5 (*Earlier performance*)

(1) The obligee may reject an earlier performance unless it has no legitimate interest in so doing.

(2) Acceptance by a party of an earlier performance does not affect the time for the performance of its own obligations if that time has been fixed irrespective of the performance of the other party's obligations.

(3) Additional expenses caused to the obligee by earlier performance are to be borne by the obligor, without prejudice to any other remedy.

ARTICLE 6.1.6 (*Place of performance*)

(1) If the place of performance is neither fixed by, nor determinable from, the contract, a party is to perform:

(a) a monetary obligation, at the obligee's place of business;

(b) any other obligation, at its own place of business.

(2) A party must bear any increase in the expenses incidental to performance

which is caused by a change in its place of business subsequent to the conclusion of the contract.

ARTICLE 6.1.7 (*Payment by cheque or other instrument*)

(1) Payment may be made in any form used in the ordinary course of business at the place for payment.

(2) However, an obligee who accepts, either by virtue of paragraph (1) or voluntarily, a cheque, any other order to pay or a promise to pay, is presumed to do so only on condition that it will be honoured.

ARTICLE 6.1.8 (*Payment by funds transfer*)

(1) Unless the obligee has indicated a particular account, payment may be made by a transfer to any of the financial institutions in which the obligee has made it known that it has an account.

(2) In case of payment by a transfer the obligation of the obligor is discharged when the transfer to the obligee's financial institution becomes effective.

ARTICLE 6.1.9 (*Currency of payment*)

(1) If a monetary obligation is expressed in a currency other than that of the place for payment, it may be paid by the obligor in the currency of the place for payment unless

(a) that currency is not freely convertible; or

(b) the parties have agreed that payment should be made only in the currency in which the monetary obligation is expressed.

(2) If it is impossible for the obligor to make payment in the currency in which the monetary obligation is expressed, the obligee may require payment in the currency of the place for payment, even in the case referred to in paragraph (1)(b).

(3) Payment in the currency of the place for payment is to be made according to the applicable rate of exchange prevailing there when payment is due.

(4) However, if the obligor has not paid at the time when payment is due, the obligee may require payment according to the applicable rate of exchange prevailing either when payment is due or at the time of actual payment.

ARTICLE 6.1.10 (*Currency not expressed*)

Where a monetary obligation is not expressed in a particular currency, payment must be made in the currency of the place where payment is to be made.

ARTICLE 6.1.11 (Costs of performance)

Each party shall bear the costs of performance of its obligations.

ARTICLE 6.1.12 (*Imputation of payments*)

(1) An obligor owing several monetary obligations to the same obligee may specify at the time of payment the debt to which it intends the payment to be applied. However, the payment discharges first any expenses, then interest due and finally the principal.

(2) If the obligor makes no such specification, the obligee may, within a reasonable time after payment, declare to the obligor the obligation to which it imputes the payment, provided that the obligation is due and undisputed.

(3) In the absence of imputation under paragraphs (1) or (2), payment is imputed to that obligation which satisfies one of the following criteria in the order indicated:

(a) an obligation which is due or which is the first to fall due;

(b) the obligation for which the obligee has least security;

(c) the obligation which is the most burdensome for the obligor;

(d) the obligation which has arisen first.

If none of the preceding criteria applies, payment is imputed to all the obligations proportionally.

ARTICLE 6.1.13 (*Imputation of non-monetary obligations*)

Article 6.1.12 applies with appropriate adaptations to the imputation of performance of non-monetary obligations.

ARTICLE 6.1.14 (*Application for public permission*)

Where the law of a State requires a public permission affecting the validity of the contract or its performance and neither that law nor the circumstances indicate otherwise

(a) if only one party has its place of business in that State, that party shall take the measures necessary to obtain the permission;

(b) in any other case the party whose performance requires permission shall take the necessary measures.

ARTICLE 6.1.15 (*Procedure in applying for permission*)

(1) The party required to take the measures necessary to obtain the permission shall do so without undue delay and shall bear any expenses incurred.

(2) That party shall whenever appropriate give the other party notice of the grant or refusal of such permission without undue delay.

ARTICLE 6.1.16 (*Permission neither granted nor refused*)

(1) If, notwithstanding the fact that the party responsible has taken all measures required, permission is neither granted nor refused within an agreed period or, where no period has been agreed, within a reasonable time from the conclusion of the contract, either party is entitled to terminate the contract.

(2) Where the permission affects some terms only, paragraph (1) does not apply if, having regard to the circumstances, it is reasonable to uphold the remaining contract even if the permission is refused.

ARTICLE 6.1.17 (*Permission refused*)

(1) The refusal of a permission affecting the validity of the contract renders the contract void. If the refusal affects the validity of some terms only, only such terms are void if, having regard to the circumstances, it is reasonable to uphold the remaining contract.

(2) Where the refusal of a permission renders the performance of the contract impossible in whole or in part, the rules on non-performance apply.

SECTION 2: HARDSHIP

ARTICLE 6.2.1 (*Contract to be observed*)

Where the performance of a contract becomes more onerous for one of the parties, that party is nevertheless bound to perform its obligations subject to the following provisions on hardship.

ARTICLE 6.2.2 (*Definition of hardship*)

There is hardship where the occurrence of events fundamentally alters the equilibrium of the contract either because the cost of a party's performance has increased or because the value of the performance a party receives has diminished, and

(a) the events occur or become known to the disadvantaged party after the conclusion of the contract;

(b) the events could not reasonably have been taken into account by the disadvantaged party at the time of the conclusion of the contract;

(c) the events are beyond the control of the disadvantaged party; and

(d) the risk of the events was not assumed by the disadvantaged party.

ARTICLE 6.2.3 (*Effects of hardship*)

(1) In case of hardship the disadvantaged party is entitled to request renegotiations. The request shall be made without undue delay and shall indicate the grounds on which it is based.

(2) The request for renegotiation does not in itself entitle the disadvantaged party to withhold performance.

(3) Upon failure to reach agreement within a reasonable time either party may resort to the court.

(4) If the court finds hardship it may, if reasonable,

(a) terminate the contract at a date and on terms to be fixed, or

(b) adapt the contract with a view to restoring its equilibrium.

CHAPTER 7 — NON-PERFORMANCE

SECTION 1: NON-PERFORMANCE IN GENERAL

ARTICLE 7.1.1 (*Non-performance defined*)

Non-performance is failure by a party to perform any of its obligations under the contract, including defective performance or late performance.

ARTICLE 7.1.2 (*Interference by the other party*)

A party may not rely on the non-performance of the other party to the extent that such non-performance was caused by the first party's act or omission or by another event as to which the first party bears the risk.

ARTICLE 7.1.3 (Withholding performance)

(1) Where the parties are to perform simultaneously, either party may withhold performance until the other party tenders its performance.

(2) Where the parties are to perform consecutively, the party that is to perform later may withhold its performance until the first party has performed.

ARTICLE 7.1.4 (*Cure by non-performing party*)

(1) The non-performing party may, at its own expense, cure any nonperformance, provided that

(a) without undue delay, it gives notice indicating the proposed manner and timing of the cure;

(b) cure is appropriate in the circumstances;

(c) the aggrieved party has no legitimate interest in refusing cure; and

(d) cure is effected promptly.

(2) The right to cure is not precluded by notice of termination.

(3) Upon effective notice of cure, rights of the aggrieved party that are inconsistent with the non-performing party's performance are suspended until the time for cure has expired.

(4) The aggrieved party may withhold performance pending cure.

(5) Notwithstanding cure, the aggrieved party retains the right to claim damages for delay as well as for any harm caused or not prevented by the cure.

ARTICLE 7.1.5 (*Additional period for performance*)

(1) In a case of non-performance the aggrieved party may by notice to the other party allow an additional period of time for performance.

(2) During the additional period the aggrieved party may withhold performance of its own reciprocal obligations and may claim damages but may not resort to any other remedy. If it receives notice from the other party that the latter will not perform within that period, or if upon expiry of that period due performance has not been made, the aggrieved party may resort to any of the remedies that may be available under this Chapter.

(3) Where in a case of delay in performance which is not fundamental the aggrieved party has given notice allowing an additional period of time of reasonable length, it may terminate the contract at the end of that period. If the additional period allowed is not of reasonable length it shall be extended to a reasonable length. The aggrieved party may in its notice provide that if the other party fails to perform within the period allowed by the notice the contract shall automatically terminate.

(4) Paragraph (3) does not apply where the obligation which has not been performed is only a minor part of the contractual obligation of the non-performing party.

ARTICLE 7.1.6 (*Exemption clauses*)

A clause which limits or excludes one party's liability for non-performance or which permits one party to render performance substantially different from what the other party reasonably expected may not be invoked if it would be grossly unfair to do so, having regard to the purpose of the contract.

ARTICLE 7.1.7 (*Force majeure*)

(1) Non-performance by a party is excused if that party proves that the non-performance was due to an impediment beyond its control and that it could not reasonably be expected to have taken the impediment into account at the time of the conclusion of the contract or to have avoided or overcome it or its consequences.

(2) When the impediment is only temporary, the excuse shall have effect for such period as is reasonable having regard to the effect of the impediment on

the performance of the contract.

(3) The party who fails to perform must give notice to the other party of the impediment and its effect on its ability to perform. If the notice is not received by the other party within a reasonable time after the party who fails to perform knew or ought to have known of the impediment, it is liable for damages resulting from such nonreceipt.

(4) Nothing in this article prevents a party from exercising a right to terminate the contract or to withhold performance or request interest on money due.

SECTION 2: RIGHT TO PERFORMANCE

ARTICLE 7.2.1 (*Performance of monetary obligation*)

Where a party who is obliged to pay money does not do so, the other party may require payment.

ARTICLE 7.2.2 (*Performance of non-monetary obligation*)

Where a party who owes an obligation other than one to pay money does not perform, the other party may require performance, unless

(a) performance is impossible in law or in fact;

(b) performance or, where relevant, enforcement is unreasonably burdensome or expensive;

(c) the party entitled to performance may reasonably obtain performance from another source;

(d) performance is of an exclusively personal character; or

(e) the party entitled to performance does not require performance within a reasonable time after it has, or ought to have, become aware of the non-performance.

ARTICLE 7.2.3 (*Repair and replacement of defective performance*)

The right to performance includes in appropriate cases the right to require repair, replacement, or other cure of defective performance. The provisions of Articles 7.2.1 and 7.2.2 apply accordingly.

ARTICLE 7.2.4 (*Judicial penalty*)

(1) Where the court orders a party to perform, it may also direct that this party pay a penalty if it does not comply with the order.

(2) The penalty shall be paid to the aggrieved party unless mandatory provisions of the law of the forum provide otherwise. Payment of the penalty to the aggrieved party does not exclude any claim for damages.

ARTICLE 7.2.5 (*Change of remedy*)

(1) An aggrieved party who has required performance of a non-monetary obligation and who has not received performance within a period fixed or otherwise within a reasonable period of time may invoke any other remedy.

(2) Where the decision of a court for performance of a non-monetary obligation cannot be enforced, the aggrieved party may invoke any other remedy.

SECTION 3: TERMINATION

ARTICLE 7.3.1 (*Right to terminate the contract*)

(1) A party may terminate the contract where the failure of the other party to perform an obligation under the contract amounts to a fundamental non-performance.

(2) In determining whether a failure to perform an obligation amounts to a fundamental non-performance regard shall be had, in particular, to whether

(a) the non-performance substantially deprives the aggrieved party of what it was entitled to expect under the contract unless the other party did not foresee and could not reasonably have foreseen such result;

(b) strict compliance with the obligation which has not been performed is of essence under the contract;

(c) the non-performance is intentional or reckless;

(d) the non-performance gives the aggrieved party reason to believe that it cannot rely on the other party's future performance;

(e) the non-performing party will suffer disproportionate loss as a result of the preparation or performance if the contract is terminated.

(3) In the case of delay the aggrieved party may also terminate the contract if the other party fails to perform before the time allowed it under Article 7.1.5 has expired.

ARTICLE 7.3.2 (*Notice of termination*)

(1) The right of a party to terminate the contract is exercised by notice to the other party.

(2) If performance has been offered late or otherwise does not conform to the contract the aggrieved party will lose its right to terminate the contract unless it gives notice to the other party within a reasonable time after it has or ought to have become aware of the offer or of the non-conforming performance.

ARTICLE 7.3.3 (*Anticipatory non-performance*)

Where prior to the date for performance by one of the parties it is clear that there will be a fundamental non-performance by that party, the other party may terminate the contract.

ARTICLE 7.3.4 (*Adequate assurance of due performance*)

A party who reasonably believes that there will be a fundamental non-performance by the other party may demand adequate assurance of due performance and may meanwhile withhold its own performance. Where this assurance is not provided within a reasonable time the party demanding it may terminate the contract.

ARTICLE 7.3.5 (*Effects of termination in general*)

(1) Termination of the contract releases both parties from their obligation to effect and to receive future performance.

(2) Termination does not preclude a claim for damages for non-performance.

(3) Termination does not affect any provision in the contract for the settlement of disputes or any other term of the contract which is to operate even after termination.

ARTICLE 7.3.6 (*Restitution*)

(1) On termination of the contract either party may claim restitution of whatever it has supplied, provided that such party concurrently makes restitution of whatever it has received. If restitution in kind is not possible or appropriate allowance should be made in money whenever reasonable.

(2) However, if performance of the contract has extended over a period of time and the contract is divisible, such restitution can only be claimed for the period after termination has taken effect.

SECTION 4: DAMAGES

ARTICLE 7.4.1 (*Right to damages*)

Any non-performance gives the aggrieved party a right to damages either exclusively or in conjunction with any other remedies except where the non-performance is excused under these Principles.

ARTICLE 7.4.2 (*Full compensation*)

(1) The aggrieve ed party is entitled to full compensation for harm sustained as a result of the non-performance. Such harm includes both any loss which it suffered and any gain of which it was deprived, taking into account any gain to the aggrieved party resulting from its avoidance of cost or harm.

(2) Such harm may be non-pecuniary and includes, for instance, physical suffering or emotional distress.

ARTICLE 7.4.3 (*Certainty of harm*)

(1) Compensation is due only for harm, including future harm that is established with a reasonable degree of certainty.

(2) Compensation may be due for the loss of a chance in proportion to the probability of its occurrence.

(3) Where the amount of damages cannot be established with a sufficient degree of certainty, the assessment is at the discretion of the court.

ARTICLE 7.4.4 (*Foreseeability of harm*)

The non-performing party is liable only for harm which it foresaw or could reasonably have foreseen at the time of the conclusion of the contract as being likely to result from its non-performance.

ARTICLE 7.4.5 (*Proof of harm in case of replacement transaction*)

Where the aggrieved party has terminated the contract and has made a replacement transaction within a reasonable time and in a reasonable manner it may recover the difference between the contract price and the price of the replacement transaction as well as damages for any further harm.

ARTICLE 7.4.6 (*Proof of harm by current price*)

(1) Where the aggrieved party has terminated the contract and has not made a replacement transaction but there is a current price for the performance contracted for, it may recover the difference between the contract price and the price current at the time the contract is terminated as well as damages for any further harm.

(2) Current price is the price generally charged for goods delivered or services rendered in comparable circumstances at the place where the contract should have been performed or, if there is no current price at that place, the current price at such other place that appears reasonable to take as a reference.

ARTICLE 7.4.7 (*Harm due in part to aggrieved party*)

Where the harm is due in part to an act or omission of the aggrieved party or to another event as to which that party bears the risk, the amount of damages shall be reduced to the extent that these factors have contributed to the harm, having regard to the conduct of each of the parties.

ARTICLE 7.4.8 (*Mitigation of harm*)

(1) The non-performing party is not liable for harm suffered by the aggrieved party to the extent that the harm could have been reduced by the latter party's taking reasonable steps.

(2) The aggrieved party is entitled to recover any expenses reasonably incurred in attempting to reduce the harm.

ARTICLE 7.4.9 (*Interest for failure to pay money*)

(1) If a party does not pay a sum of money when it falls due the aggrieved party is entitled to interest upon that sum from the time when payment is due to the time of payment whether or not the non-payment is excused.

(2) The rate of interest shall be the average bank short-term lending rate to prime borrowers prevailing for the currency of payment at the place for payment, or where no such rate exists at that place, then the same rate in the State of the currency of payment. In the absence of such a rate at either place the rate of interest shall be the appropriate rate fixed by the law of the State of the currency of payment.

(3) The aggrieved party is entitled to additional damages if the non-payment caused it a greater harm.

ARTICLE 7.4.10 (*Interest on damages*)

Unless otherwise agreed, interest on damages for non-performance of non-monetary obligations accrues as from the time of non-performance.

ARTICLE 7.4.11 (*Manner of monetary redress*)

(1) Damages are to be paid in a lump sum. However, they may be payable in instalments where the nature of the harm makes this appropriate.

(2) Damages to be paid in instalments may be indexed.

ARTICLE 7.4.12 (*Currency in which to assess damages*)

Damages are to be assessed either in the currency in which the monetary obligation was expressed or in the currency in which the harm was suffered, whichever is more appropriate.

ARTICLE 7.4.13 (*Agreed payment for non-performance*)

(1) Where the contract provides that a party who does not perform is to pay a specified sum to the aggrieved party for such non-performance, the aggrieved party is entitled to that sum irrespective of its actual harm.

(2) However, notwithstanding any agreement to the contrary the specified sum may be reduced to a reasonable amount where it is grossly excessive in relation to the harm resulting from the non-performance and to the other circumstances.

CHAPTER 8 — SET-OFF

ARTICLE 8.1 (*Conditions of set-off*)

(1) Where two parties owe each other money or other performances of the same kind, either of them ("the first party") may set off its obligation against that of its obligee ("the other party") if at the time of set-off,

(a) the first party is entitled to perform its obligation;

(b) the other party's obligation is ascertained as to its existence and amount and performance is due.

(2) If the obligations of both parties arise from the same contract, the first party may also set off its obligation against an obligation of the other party which is not ascertained as to its existence or to its amount.

ARTICLE 8.2 (*Foreign currency set-off*)

Where the obligations are to pay money in different currencies, the right of set-off may be exercised, provided that both currencies are freely convertible and the parties have not agreed that the first party shall pay only in a specified currency.

ARTICLE 8.3 (*Set-off by notice*)

The right of set-off is exercised by notice to the other party.

ARTICLE 8.4 (*Content of notice*)

(1) The notice must specify the obligations to which it relates.

(2) If the notice does not specify the obligation against which set-off is exercised, the other party may, within a reasonable time, declare to the first party the obligation to which set-off relates. If no such declaration is made, the set-off will relate to all the obligations proportionally.

ARTICLE 8.5 (*Effect of set-off*)

(1) Set-off discharges the obligations.

(2) If obligations differ in amount, set-off discharges the obligations up to the amount of the lesser obligation.

(3) Set-off takes effect as from the time of notice.

CHAPTER 9 — ASSIGNMENT OF RIGHTS, TRANSFER OF OBLIGATIONS, ASSIGNMENT OF CONTRACTS

SECTION 1: ASSIGNMENT OF RIGHTS

ARTICLE 9.1.1 (*Definitions*)

"Assignment of a right" means the transfer by agreement from one person (the "assignor") to another person (the "assignee"), including transfer by way of security, of the assignor's right to payment of a monetary sum or other performance from a third person ("the obligor").

ARTICLE 9.1.2 (*Exclusions*)

This Section does not apply to transfers made under the special rules governing the transfers:

(a) of instruments such as negotiable instruments, documents of title or financial instruments, or

(b) of rights in the course of transferring a business.

ARTICLE 9.1.3 (*Assignability of non-monetary rights*)

A right to non-monetary performance may be assigned only if the assignment does not render the obligation significantly more burdensome.

ARTICLE 9.1.4 (*Partial assignment*)

(1) A right to the payment of a monetary sum may be assigned partially.

(2) A right to other performance may be assigned partially only if it is divisible, and the assignment does not render the obligation significantly more burdensome.

ARTICLE 9.1.5 (*Future rights*)

A future right is deemed to be transferred at the time of the agreement, provided the right, when it comes into existence, can be identified as the right to which the assignment relates.

ARTICLE 9.1.6 (*Rights assigned without individual specification*)

A number of rights may be assigned without individual specification, provided such rights can be identified as rights to which the assignment relates at the time of the assignment or when they come into existence.

ARTICLE 9.1.7 (*Agreement between assignor and assignee sufficient*)

(1) A right is assigned by mere agreement between the assignor and the assignee, without notice to the obligor.

(2) The consent of the obligor is not required unless the obligation in the cir-

cumstances is of an essentially personal character.

ARTICLE 9.1.8 (*Obligor's additional costs*)

The obligor has a right to be compensated by the assignor or the assignee for any additional costs caused by the assignment.

ARTICLE 9.1.9 (*Non-assignment clauses*)

(1) The assignment of a right to the payment of a monetary sum is effective notwithstanding an agreement between the assignor and the obligor limiting or prohibiting such an assignment. However, the assignor may be liable to the obligor for breach of contract.

(2) The assignment of a right to other performance is ineffective if it is contrary to an agreement between the assignor and the obligor limiting or prohibiting the assignment. Nevertheless, the assignment is effective if the assignee, at the time of the assignment, neither knew nor ought to have known of the agreement. The assignor may then be liable to the obligor for breach of contract.

ARTICLE 9.1.10 (*Notice to the obligor*)

(1) Until the obligor receives a notice of the assignment from either the assignor or the assignee, it is discharged by paying the assignor.

(2) After the obligor receives such a notice, it is discharged only by paying the assignee.

ARTICLE 9.1.11 (*Successive assignments*)

If the same right has been assigned by the same assignor to two or more successive assignees, the obligor is discharged by paying according to the order in which the notices were received.

ARTICLE 9.1.12 (*Adequate proof of assignment*)

(1) If notice of the assignment is given by the assignee, the obligor may request the assignee to provide within a reasonable time adequate proof that the assignment has been made.

(2) Until adequate proof is provided, the obligor may withhold payment.

(3) Unless adequate proof is provided, notice is not effective.

(4) Adequate proof includes, but is not limited to, any writing emanating from the assignor and indicating that the assignment has taken place.

ARTICLE 9.1.13 (*Defences and rights of set-off*)

(1) The obligor may assert against the assignee all defences that the obligor could assert against the assignor.

(2) The obligor may exercise against the assignee any right of set-off available to

the obligor against the assignor up to the time notice of assignment was received.

ARTICLE 9.1.14 (*Rights related to the right assigned*)

The assignment of a right transfers to the assignee:

(a) all the assignor's rights to payment or other performance under the contract in respect of the right assigned, and

(b) all rights securing performance of the right assigned.

ARTICLE 9.1.15 (*Undertakings of the assignor*)

The assignor undertakes towards the assignee, except as otherwise disclosed to the assignee, that:

(a) the assigned right exists at the time of the assignment, unless the right is a future right;

(b) the assignor is entitled to assign the right;

(c) the right has not been previously assigned to another assignee, and it is free from any right or claim from a third party;

(d) the obligor does not have any defences;

(e) neither the obligor nor the assignor has given notice of set-off concerning the assigned right and will not give any such notice;

(f) the assignor will reimburse the assignee for any payment received from the obligor before notice of the assignment was given.

SECTION 2: TRANSFER OF OBLIGATIONS

ARTICLE 9.2.1 (*Modes of transfer*)

An obligation to pay money or render other performance may be transferred from one person (the "original obligor") to another person (the "new obligor") either

(a) by an agreement between the original obligor and the new obligor subject to Article 9.2.3, or

(b) by an agreement between the obligee and the new obligor, by which the new obligor assumes the obligation.

ARTICLE 9.2.2 (*Exclusion*)

This Section does not apply to transfers of obligations made under the special rules governing transfers of obligations in the course of transferring a business.

ARTICLE 9.2.3 (*Requirement of obligee's consent to transfer*)

The transfer of an obligation by an agreement between the original obligor and the new obligor requires the consent of the obligee.

ARTICLE 9.2.4 (*Advance consent of obligee*)

(1) The obligee may give its consent in advance.

(2) If the obligee has given its consent in advance, the transfer of the obligation becomes effective when a notice of the transfer is given to the obligee or when the obligee acknowledges it.

ARTICLE 9.2.5 (*Discharge of original obligor*)

(1) The obligee may discharge the original obligor.

(2) The obligee may also retain the original obligor as an obligor in case the new obligor does not perform properly.

(3) Otherwise the original obligor and the new obligor are jointly and severally liable.

ARTICLE 9.2.6 (*Third party performance*)

(1) Without the obligee's consent, the obligor may contract with another person that this person will perform the obligation in place of the obligor, unless the obligation in the circumstances has an essentially personal character.

(2) The obligee retains its claim against the obligor.

ARTICLE 9.2.7 (*Defences and rights of set-off*)

(1) The new obligor may assert against the obligee all defences which the original obligor could assert against the obligee.

(2) The new obligor may not exercise against the obligee any right of set-off available to the original obligor against the obligee.

ARTICLE 9.2.8 (*Rights related to the obligation transferred*)

(1) The obligee may assert against the new obligor all its rights to payment or other performance under the contract in respect of the obligation transferred.

(2) If the original obligor is discharged under Article 9.2.5 (1), a security granted by any person other than the new obligor for the performance of the obligation is discharged, unless that other person agrees that it should continue to be available to the obligee.

(3) Discharge of the original obligor also extends to any security of the original obligor given to the obligee for the performance of the obligation, unless the security is over an asset which is transferred as part of a transaction between the original obligor and the new obligor.

SECTION 3: ASSIGNMENT OF CONTRACTS

ARTICLE 9.3.1 (*Definitions*)

"Assignment of a contract" means the transfer by agreement from one person (the "assignor") to another person (the "assignee") of the assignor's rights and obligations arising out of a contract with another person (the "other party").

ARTICLE 9.3.2 (*Exclusion*)

This Section does not apply to the assignment of contracts made under the special rules governing transfers of contracts in the course of transferring a business.

ARTICLE 9.3.3 (*Requirement of consent of the other party*)

The assignment of a contract requires the consent of the other party.

ARTICLE 9.3.4 (*Advance consent of the other party*)

(1) The other party may give its consent in advance.

(2) If the other party has given its consent in advance, the assignment of the contract becomes effective when a notice of the assignment is given to the other party or when the other party acknowledges it.

ARTICLE 9.3.5 (*Discharge of the assignor*)

(1) The other party may discharge the assignor.

(2) The other party may also retain the assignor as an obligor in case the assignee does not perform properly.

(3) Otherwise the assignor and the assignee are jointly and severally liable.

ARTICLE 9.3.6 (*Defences and rights of set-off*)

(1) To the extent that the assignment of a contract involves an assignment of rights, Article 9.1.13 applies accordingly.

(2) To the extent that the assignment of a contract involves a transfer of obligations, Article 9.2.7 applies accordingly.

ARTICLE 9.3.7 (*Rights transferred with the contract*)

(1) To the extent that the assignment of a contract involves an assignment of rights, Article 9.1.14 applies accordingly.

(2) To the extent that the assignment of a contract involves a transfer of obligations, Article 9.2.8 applies accordingly.

CHAPTER 10 — LIMITATION PERIODS

ARTICLE 10.1 (*Scope of the Chapter*)

(1) The exercise of rights governed by these Principles is barred by the expiration of a period of time, referred to as "limitation period", according to the rules of this Chapter.

(2) This Chapter does not govern the time within which one party is required under these Principles, as a condition for the acquisition or exercise of its right,

to give notice to the other party or to perform any act other than the institution of legal proceedings.

ARTICLE 10.2 (*Limitation periods*)

(1) The general limitation period is three years beginning on the day after the day the obligee knows or ought to know the facts as a result of which the obligee's right can e exercised.

(2) In any event, the maximum limitation period is ten years beginning on the day after the day the right can be exercised.

ARTICLE 10.3 (*Modification of limitation periods by the parties*)

(1) The parties may modify the limitation periods.

(2) However they may not

(a) shorten the general limitation period to less than one year;

(b) shorten the maximum limitation period to less than four years;

(c) extend the maximum limitation period to more than fifteen years.

ARTICLE 10.4 (*New limitation period by acknowledgement*)

(1) Where the obligor before the expiration of the general limitation period acknowledges the right of the obligee, a new general limitation period begins on the day after the day of the acknowledgement.

(2) The maximum limitation period does not begin to run again, but may be exceeded by the beginning of a new general limitation period under Art. 10.2 (1).

ARTICLE 10.5 (*Suspension by judicial proceedings*)

(1) The running of the limitation period is suspended

(a) when the obligee performs any act, by commencing judicial proceedings or in judicial proceedings already instituted, that is recognised by the law of the court as asserting the obligee's right against the obligor;

(b) in the case of the obligor's insolvency when the obligee has asserted its rights in the insolvency proceedings; or

(c) in the case of proceedings for dissolution of the entity which is the obligor when the obligee has asserted its rights in the dissolution proceedings.

(2) Suspension lasts until a final decision has been issued or until the proceedings have been otherwise terminated.

ARTICLE 10.6 (*Suspension by arbitral proceedings*)

(1) The running of the limitation period is suspended when the obligee performs any act, by commencing arbitral proceedings or in arbitral proceedings already

instituted, that is recognised by the law of the arbitral tribunal as asserting the obligee's right against the obligor. In the absence of regulations for arbitral proceedings or provisions determining the exact date of the commencement of arbitral proceedings, the proceedings are deemed to commence on the date on which a request that the right in dispute should be adjudicated reaches the obligor.

(2) Suspension lasts until a binding decision has been issued or until the proceedings have been otherwise terminated.

ARTICLE 10.7 (*Alternative dispute resolution*)

The provisions of Articles 10.5 and 10.6 apply with appropriate modifications to other proceedings whereby the parties request a third person to assist them in their attempt to reach an amicable settlement of their dispute.

ARTICLE 10.8 (*Suspension in case of force majeure, death or incapacity*)

(1) Where the obligee has been prevented by an impediment that is beyond its control and that it could neither avoid nor overcome, from causing a limitation period to cease to run under the preceding articles, the general limitation period is suspended so as not to expire before one year after the relevant impediment has ceased to exist.

(2) Where the impediment consists of the incapacity or death of the obligee or obligor, suspension ceases when a representative for the incapacitated or deceased party or its estate has been appointed or a successor has inherited the respective party's position. The additional one-year period under paragraph (1) applies accordingly.

ARTICLE 10.9 (*The effects of expiration of limitation period*)

(1) The expiration of the limitation period does not extinguish the right.

(2) For the expiration of the limitation period to have effect, the obligor must assert it as a defence.

(3) A right may still be relied on as a defence even though the expiration of the limitation period for that right has been asserted.

ARTICLE 10.10 (*Right of set-off*)

The obligee may exercise the right of set-off until the obligor has asserted the expiration of the limitation period.

ARTICLE 10.11 (*Restitution*)

Where there has been performance in order to discharge an obligation, there is no right of restitution merely because the limitation period has expired.

参考文献
Bibliography

1.Michael H. Whincup. Contract Law and Practice. Kluwer Law International, 2001.

2.Chris Thope, John Bailey. Commercial Contracts. 华夏出版社,2004 版.

3.Kenneth W. Clarkson. West's Business Law. 东北财经大学出版社,1998.

4.Restatement of the Law of Conflict of Laws, Second, American Law Institute.

5. 赖来琨,《当代国际私法学之构造理论》,神州图书出版有限公司,2001.

6.[英] 莫里斯著,李来东等译,《法律冲突法》,中国对外翻译出版公司,1990.

7.[英] 莫里斯著,李双元译,《戴西和莫里斯论冲突法》,中国大百科全书出版社,1998.

8.陈卫佐,《瑞士国际司法法典研究》,法律出版社,1998.

9. 李克兴、张新红,《法律文本与法律翻译》,中国对外翻译出版公司,2006.

10.吴坚、傅殿英,《实用逻辑学》,首都经济贸易大学出版社,2005.

11.shippey, K.C.《国际商务简明教程系列——国际商务合同》,上海外语教育出版社,2000.

12.兰天,《国际商务合同翻译教程》,东北财经大学出版社,2007.

13.廖瑛、莫再树,《国际商务英语语言与翻译研究》,机械工业出版社,2005.

14.胡庚申、王春晖、申云帧,《国际商务合同起草与翻译》,外文出版社,2001.

15.王道庚,《新编英汉法律翻译教程》,浙江大学出版社,2006.

16.戚云方,《合同与合同英语》,浙江大学出版社,2004.

18.秦定,《国际贸易合同实践教程》,清华大学出版社,2006.

19.戴长洪,《公司常用英文法律文书指南》,中国民主法制出版社,2003.

20.王辉,《英文合同解读:语用、条款及文本范例》,法律出版社,2007.

21.吴江水,《完美的合同——合同的基本原理及审查与修改》,中国民主法制出版社,2005.

22.吕立山,《合同与法律咨询文书制作技能》,法律出版社,2007.

23.吕昊、刘显正、罗萍,《商务合同写作及翻译》,武汉大学出版社,2005.

24.龚柏华,《国际商事合同制作原理》,立信会计出版社,2005.

25.肖辉,《财经、商贸汉英互译误译举隅——兼谈其翻译原则》,US-China Foreign Language, Dec. 2006, Volume 4, No.12 (Serial No. 39).

26.皮继伟、李延林,《从语域理论的角度看商务合同的翻译》,《长沙铁道学院学报》,2008年第3期。

27. 郑建祥,《论英语商务合同的语言特征》,《科技情报开发与经济》,2007年第7期。

28. 王春岩,《模糊语在英文商务合同中的语用功能分析及风险规避》,《晋中学院学报》,2007年第10期。

29. 莫再树,《商务合同英语的文体特征》,《湖南大学学报》,2003年第5期。

30.杨芳,《商务合同英语用词特点及翻译的特色标记》,《洛阳师范学院学报》,2004年第1期。

31.莫再树,《商务合同英语的词汇特征》,《山东外语教学》,2003年第6期。

32. 张慧清,《商务英语合同中的名词化结构及其语篇功能》,《长沙大学学报》,2007年第4期。

33.周燕、廖瑛,《英文商务合同长句的语用分析及其翻译》,《中国科技翻译》,2004年第11期。

34. 莫再树,《商务英语词汇的文体色彩》,《长沙电力学院学报(社科版)》,2002年第4期。

35. 季益广,《法律英语的文体特点及英译技巧》,《中国科技翻译》,1999年第4期。

36.李全申,《谈谈商务合同的翻译》,《中国翻译》,1998年第2期。

37.沈娟,《合同当事人意思自治的确定和限制》,http://www.iolaw.org.cn.

38.陈建平,《对外经贸合同翻译失真问题分析》,《中国科技翻译》,2003年第4期。

39.孙志祥,《合同英译理解过程中的"合法"前提和求信标准》,《中国翻译》,2001年第5期。

40.陈明瑶,《WTO文本的词汇特点及其翻译》,《上海科技翻译》,2003年第4期。

编委会

主　编：严　明
副主编：袁　田　佟敏强
主　审：王　妍
编　者：曹　飞　崔常亮　吉绍昱
　　　　　　焦　健　刘晓丹　齐　欣
　　　　　　关　健　朱雪琳　柳春光